The Complete Teacher's Guide to Retirement Wealth

The Complete Teacher's Guide to Retirement Wealth

Featuring the 403(b)—the last million dollar tax shelter around

Vincent D. Tate

ISBN 1-880451-43-3

Rainbow's End Company
354 Golden Grove Road
Baden, PA 15005

Dedication

To my mother and father who, through example,
instilled a strong work ethic in me. Thank
you for all you have done for me
through the years

To my wife Annette, my daughter Mallory,
and my son Adam, for their endless
patience, love, and support

To Bettie, John, Susan, and Wayne at Rainbow's End
whose dedication and hard work made the
publication of this book possible

A special thanks to Bettie Tucker, a blessing from
above, for her kindness, knowing guidance,
and generous heart

Contents

Disclaimer

Introduction

What do you think of when you hear the letters "IRS"? That is what I thought. Me too. We simply do not think of the IRS or the Internal Revenue Code as a force for good. I think it is because our political process assures us that the tax code, at any particular moment, has less to do with sound policy than with which lobbies are currently influencing Congress. The tax code itself is unimaginably complex—all 4,100 pages of it. Not even the top experts can accurately foresee all the ripple effects of any new tax provision. But, even so, out of this mire of code sections, letter rulings, paragraphs and subparagraphs, something brilliantly useful occasionally surfaces that is of genuine benefit to America and her citizens.

One such item is the 403(b) savings plan. As an employee of a non-profit organization, you are in a *most advantageous* position. You have at your fingertips one of the most powerful, supplemental retirement investment opportunities found anywhere in the world—the 403(b). The wealthiest and most successful investors in the world call the 403(b) *the last million dollar tax shelter* around. It is arguably the sturdiest lifeline to a future of financial security. I know that sounds like a pretty bold statement, but it just happens to be true. To employees who approach their 403(b) with the proper blend of discipline, patience, and basic investing know-how, it offers a reliable way to build a nest egg worth hundreds of thousands of dollars—or considerably more. No other investment even comes close. Furthermore, *only* public school, college, university, and non-profit organization employees (such as those employed by hospitals, churches, etc.) can participate in it. It offers an amazing opportunity to accumulate wealth, and it is so easy to do, if you know some basic strategies.

Considering how indispensable 403(b) plans have become for non-profit organizations, it is amazing how they accidentally came into being. Unlike other investment vehicles such as Individual Retirement Accounts (IRAs), etc., which had vocal supporters in Washington, no congressman ever campaigned for the creation of 403(b) plans. No think tank ever dreamed them up. Instead, Internal Revenue Code Section 403(b)—known by the section of the IRS Tax Code that authorizes it—was quietly slipped into the code by the Revenue Act of 1978. A 403(b) is a tax-deferred retirement-savings plan similar to the very popular 401(k) plans which are primarily offered by private industry to their employees. A 403(b) is sometimes known as a deferred tax plan, a tax shelter, a TSA (Tax Shelter Annuity), etc. Call it anything you want, but one fact stands alone—it is the best supplemental retirement opportunity in the world, and *everyone* who qualifies should have one.

Currently, there are over 5 million employees of non-profit organizations who have over $200 billion invested in 403(b) plans. If you are not one of them, you should plan to be. You can have total financial freedom when you retire, and the beauty is that you can have this financial freedom *without* sacrificing your current life-style.

Estimates show that as many as three-quarters of those who are eligible already participate in a 403(b) plan. Many have already racked up impressive savings. The average active employee in the plan has more than $28,000 in his/her account. Nearly 10% of them have more than $50,000.

The projected growth of the plans is equally astonishing. A record number of Americans say a retirement plan, rather than a bank savings account or certificate of deposit, is the best place to save money in the coming year, according to the results of an annual survey released recently. The survey, conducted by *Roper Starch Worldwide*, a public opinion research firm, said 43% of those surveyed say they will be better off putting money in personal or corporate retirement savings vehicles rather than savings accounts or certificates of deposit, a 12% jump from the 1995 survey's 31%.

According to the research firm, it is the first time, since the survey began in 1983, that retirement savings plans like the 403(b) have surpassed traditional savings accounts as the best place for savings. This shift from traditional savings choices to personally directed retirement savings is part of a growing lack of confidence in the Social Security system.

People are leaning toward self-reliance. The number of working people who say they can rely on Social Security in their retirement has declined to 49% from 88% in 1974. People were also asked in 1974 whether they thought they would have enough to live on comfortably in their retirement and 51% said, "yes." That is down to only 39% today.

Almost two in three Americans, 65%, say self-funded retirement savings, such as 403(b)s, offer good or excellent value, which is slightly more than that of home mortgages, at 63%. Among those with self-funded retirement plans, the average monthly contribution is $227. One in three $75,000-plus-a-year households puts away $500 or more monthly, with 63% of the households in that bracket saying they invest in retirement and pension. Within the next 5 years the amount of money invested in 403(b)s is expected to double. Within 10 years the money stored in 403(b)s will be the employees' single largest source of wealth exceeding, not only the value of their other retirement plans, but also the equity in their homes.

Unfortunately, supplemental retirement plans do not come with a set of instructions for maximizing either tax benefits or profits. Realize also that the employer is absolved of any responsibility as to the operation of the plan. It is up to you and you alone to make sure that you have enough money when you retire. Not surprising, statistics plainly show that the vast majority of those who do have a 403(b) plan are most likely *not* benefiting from the full potential of the plan. It is estimated that most participants *lose* 83% of their potential benefits over time. Consequently, they are passing up *literally* tens of thousands of future retirement dollars, simply because they are uninformed of what options are available, and how simply they can be utilized through a well-planned retirement strategy. Simply put, they just do not know how to maximize their investment dollars.

Make no mistake about it, if you do not take the initiative to contribute to the plan, it will do nothing for you at all. Unless you learn to invest it wisely, it will never live up to its potential. These are not small matters. Believe it or not, postponing your first investment from age 25 to age 40 will shrink your returns by more than half. Choosing investments that underperform by as little as one percentage point a year can shrivel your nest egg by more than $150,000 over the course of your career. Accept the fact that decisions you make (or avoid) today regarding your 403(b) have real consequences.

The good news is that making the most of your 403(b) is not as difficult as you may think. Even if you are a complete novice at investing, you can master your 403(b) and take charge of your future. Although some of the investing concepts you will encounter in the manual may be unfamiliar, they certainly are not mysterious. All of the principles behind them obey the laws of common sense. You do not have to be a financial wizard to earn a respectable return from your 403(b). All you need is a firm grasp of the basic investing principles outlined in this manual and the combination of courage and patience to abide by them.

This manual is intended to help you make the right decisions regarding your 403(b) plan at every point in the process. The information is presented in a "storybook" fashion with the hope that each chapter will be looked at as a logical progression from the previous one. Most educational materials on this subject (if you can find them) are often hopelessly superficial and vague. Hopefully, you will find in this manual a solid, rational approach to intelligent 403(b) plan investing. There are no hidden agendas here. As an objective guide unaffiliated with any 403(b) sponsor, this manual's only agenda is to help you make the most of your 403(b) plan. Also, along the way, I have included specific information about retirement planning which is designed to edify and enlighten you in your decision-making process. Before you begin reading through the rest of the manual, test your general retirement knowledge by taking the short quiz below. The answers are provided at the end, but try to avoid the temptation to look at them before you have finished the entire quiz. After all, it is not as though you will be getting a grade.

1. Including Social Security and other sources of income, in general, about what percentage of your final, annual working income do many financial planners suggest you may need to maintain your lifestyle after retirement?

    A. 40% to 60%   **B.** 60% to 80%   **C.** 80% to 100%   **D.** 100% or more

2. According to a recent U.S. census, what percentage of an individual's total retirement income do most people receive from Social Security and pension plans?

    A. less than 20%   **B.** 20% to 40%   **C.** 40% to 60%

3. According to actuarial tables on life expectancy, how many years can the average person retiring today at age 65 expect to spend in retirement?

    A. 8 years for men; 10 years for women   **B.** 11 years for men; 14 years for women
    C. 18 years for men; 22 years for women

4. If you retire before the age of 65, your monthly Social Security benefits may be reduced below what they might otherwise be.

    A. true   **B.** false

5. Under current law, what is the earliest age at which individuals can collect Social Security benefits, assuming they are not disabled?

    A. 59 ½   **B.** 62 ½   **C.** 65

6. Under normal circumstances, at what age can a person begin withdrawing money from a 403(b) without paying a 10% withdrawal tax penalty?

    A. 59 ½   **B.** 62 ½   **C.** 65

7. While everyone can contribute to an IRA, deductibility of IRA contributions is deter-

mined by:

    A. your age   **B.** whether you or your spouse are covered by an employer-sponsored retirement plan **C.** whether or not you decide to file a tax return

8. If you are also self-employed, you can contribute to both a SEP-IRA and a regular 403(b).
    A. true **B.** false

9. The age of eligibility for full Social Security retirement benefits will be raised gradually to age 67 to reflect longer life spans. In what year will the new rules start to take effect?

    A. 2000 **B.** 2005 **C.** 2010

10. Anyone under the age of 70 ½ with earned income is allowed to contribute to an IRA.
    A. true **B.** false

11. As far as the IRS is concerned, you must be 59 ½ before you can withdraw 403(b) funds without a 10% penalty.
    A. true **B.** false

12. Over 80 % of 403(b) investors do not know their allowable maximum yearly contribution.
    A. true **B.** false

13. You may transfer money from a standard savings account into a 403(b) plan.

    A. true **B.** false

14. Asset allocation for your 403(b) is primarily determined by your age.

    A. true **B.** false

15. Most 403(b) investors have no idea what a Maximum Exclusion Allowance is.

    A. true **B.** false

Answers

1. C	6. A	11. B
2. B	7. B	12. A
3. B	8. A	13. B
4. A	9. A	14. B
5. B	10. A	15. A

CHAPTER ONE

Pre-Retirement Considerations

It **is never too early**—During the prime of your life, you do not think much about retirement. After all, it is a long way off. Not to mention that you are having a hard enough time meeting today's obligations, let alone tomorrow's. It is funny how Mother Nature works. She sometimes forces us to make decisions about things that just do not seem important right now. Retirement is one of those things. But if we do *nothing* now, we will not be able to do *anything* later. Time has a funny way of sneaking up on you and, when retirement comes, there will not be anyone there waiting to ensure that your golden years are comfortable. Let's face it, your retirement is primarily up to you.

More and more people are fantasizing of retiring early. Retirement symbolizes one of the deepest of human yearnings—freedom. It represents the eternal vacation. A recent survey of employed Americans found that 83 percent planned to retire before age 65. Traveling to exotic islands or foreign countries, relaxing on the beach in Florida, golfing in sun-parched Arizona, or just plain enjoying yourself at home with family and friends is a fantasy we all have.

The reality for most people, however, is that early retirement will remain just that—a fantasy. In fact, the fantasy can turn into an opiate unless you figure out the way to turn the dream into a well-focused goal. To do that you will have to rearrange some of the furniture in your life. You almost certainly will need to figure out a way to spend less so you can save more. It sounds like a drag, and, undoubtedly, it will be uncomfortable at first. But it is that old unavoidable—*reality.*

You see, many people are not too smart about attaining wealth. They want the good life, naturally enough, but they concentrate on owning *things*—like new cars, boats, bigger TVs—instead of securities in companies that *make* the things they want. So instead of owning wealth-producing assets (stocks, bonds, mutual funds, etc.) that will make them money, eventually allowing them to buy whatever they want, they blow their seed capital on assets that actually *shrink* in value. I just can not believe how many people pass up the chance to partake in the greatest wealth-building device ever designed—participatory capitalism. And all it takes is a phone call to a stockbroker or mutual fund.

Actually, the odds of making money are strongly in your favor. That is because over the years, the stock market goes up about two out of three days. With such friendly odds, you *risk more* by being *out* of the market than being *in* it.

It is a culture thing—You see, we live in a hyperconsumer economy. More than an economy, it is a consumer culture, impossible to escape unless you quit society entirely and live alone in the desert. Our society knows not the face of self-denial. It has forgotten the concept of postponed pleasure upon which middle-class life was built. So you must accept the proposition that you are deeply affected by this culture, that you are really part of it. Then you must realize that when someone says, "I just can't save a cent," that person really believes what he or she is saying.

The problem is that many individuals harbor rosy misconceptions about how much income and/or assets they would need to become financially independent and live a comfortable retirement. According to many recent public attitude studies, most people do not realize how long they will spend in retirement. Fully one-third of those surveyed had not even begun to save for retirement! And although approximately 67% of American workers age 53 and older have saved something for retirement, only 45% of them have ever tried to determine just how much it will take to fund it.

The United States sports one of the lowest savings rates in the world, far lower than that of many poorer countries. The low-savings mind-set starts early, when children become raving consumers as they absorb hour after hour of TV commercials. By the time these consumers are in the workforce themselves, they are beaten down by the widely accepted notion that young people today cannot possibly achieve the wealth their parents amassed. They deny, telling themselves that they will never have the money we say they need to do it correctly anyway, so why bother.

According to the national income and product accounts (NIPA) measure, published by the Department of Commerce, the net national saving rate fell from 7.1 percent during the 1970s, to 3.8 percent during the 1980s, and to 1.8 percent by the end of 1993. But the tides are turning. People are beginning to save more. Retirement saving has risen 28 percent from the end of 1994 through 1998. That is good news because pension and Social Security benefits are not what they once were, financial institutions and insurance companies have become a concern and require close scrutiny, and health care costs seem to be rising out of control. With all of these scenarios continuing to be played out, wise planning and increased investing are essential.

You have to recognize the fact that the whole meaning of retirement has changed. It used to consist of a few years of exhausted old age. Period. Now it is decades of healthy seniority, what has come to be called the new third quarter. Throughout history, life was divided into thirds: youth, middle age, and old age.

But technological advances in medicine have substituted a four-part setup: the first quarter (growing up and being educated); the second quarter (work); the third quarter (continued work or retirement or a combination of both); and the fourth quarter (old age, largely leisure, but some work as well if you can and want to). The third quarter is a historical innovation that no one was prepared for because no one had experienced it before this generation. America's baby-boom generation can anticipate spending nearly one-third of their adult lives in retirement. Yet, because most do not start serious saving until age 40 or beyond, they have less than one-third of their lives to prepare.

As mentioned earlier, we Americans hold high expectations for our retirement. But what is retirement? A kind of prolonged vacation, right? What experience do you have with this kind of life? If you are a teacher you probably have the best kind of experience—your summer vacations, of course. *What could be better—a life with endless summer vacations.* Would you believe that the majority of retirement planners report that roughly six months after their clients stop working, the vacation phase ends and reality sets in? In short, they get tired of being "on vacation" and get bored. To make matters worse, a quarter of these new retirees report that they are unhappy, largely because they have discovered too late that they were not financially prepared to retire in the first place. "That will never be me," you say—do not kid yourself.

A retirement with unlimited free time, expensive gratification and a return to the freedom of childhood may be an unrealistic picture for most. People are living longer and having children later. Retirees face the daunting financial and emotional challenges of rearing their children and caring for their parents simultaneously during their early retirement years. Three or four years ago, many were saying that they planned to retire at 55 and enjoy a laid-back life. Now they realize they have to work a few more years while they direct financial resources to the immediate needs of their families.

But do not despair. The early retirement dream can become a reality, but it requires effort on your part. Early retirement requires an enormous amount of personal planning, a firm grasp on some basic investment strategies, an aggressive savings plan, and discipline. It takes time, and the longer you wait, the harder it becomes to build your minifortune. You have taken the first step by purchasing this manual.

We need to face it, it is never convenient to start saving money. To people in their early twenties, saving sounds punitive. There is not enough money to stretch to buy all the things you need, let alone sock some of it away. But if a comfortable retirement is in the cards for you, then you better resign yourself to the fact that saving is not a luxury, it is a *necessity*. Everyone today must plan for their retirement and have a financial road map to assist them on obtaining their goals.

One of the most valuable things an investor has is time—and compound interest. Both are discussed thoroughly in chapter 6. The sooner you start to accumulate assets and plan for your retirement years, the better, and the *less you will need to set aside each year* in order to achieve the same objective.

Retirement as a three-legged stool—Retirement income often is figured as a *three-legged stool*. Those legs are Social Security, personal savings/investments, and company pensions. Any inequities among them, discussed later in this chapter, can produce instability in the stool and shaky support for retirement. The only one of this trio over which retirees can exercise direct control is their savings/investments. But investing wisely is a formidable task because making the right decisions is compounded by the increasingly complex nature of financial products available to consumers. Almost no lay person knows all the options or what is best for his or her unique circumstances. This year, most of us will spend more time planning for our vacation than for our 30-year retirement. Not a good allocation of our time. Whatever you do, do not put off planning. Your retirement is too important.

One guideline to consider when thinking about your retirement is that you will need at *least* 15 years to amass a nest egg that will provide you with enough income to last at least 40 years in retirement. "But I have a great pension plan," you shout in frustration. That may be true. However, unless it is unusually generous, your pension alone, supplemented only by what *may* be available through Social Security, probably will not be enough to give you the lifestyle you need and deserve at retirement. Approximately 96 percent of pension plans have no automatic cost-of-living adjustments, according to the U.S. Bureau of Labor Statistics. Most pension plans offer a fixed income equal to a percentage of salary. At an inflation rate of 3 percent per year, in just 15 years the value of your pension plan will decrease by almost 40 percent. You begin retirement with an income shortfall which worsens as inflation steadily erodes the purchasing power of your income as shown on page 16.

15

The Buying Power of $100 Over Time

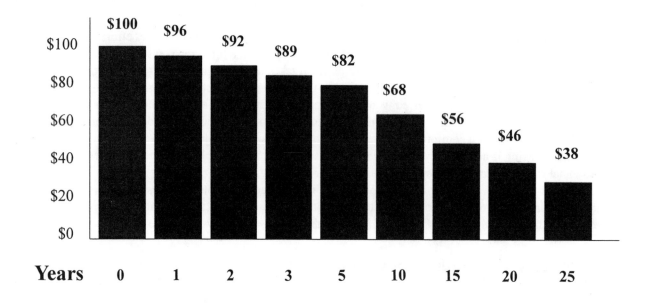

This chart shows the impact of inflation on the value of $100 over time. Each year the buying power of $100 decreases as the price of goods increases with inflation. The chart assumes a 4% average annual inflation rate.

If you want to ensure an adequate income in retirement, there is no question that *you* will have to provide a significant portion of the money. Ask yourself these questions: "How well do I want to live? How much money will I need to live that way?" The younger you are, the more you will need to accumulate for retirement as the cost of living continues to rise. If you are already in mid-career, there is no time to wait. The cost of waiting even one year can be high. If you had 30 years to save for retirement and could save $300 a month at 8 percent interest, you would lose over *$34,000* by delaying your savings program for *only one year*.

Years to Save	Dollars Saved ($200 @8%)
20	$422,565
19	$387,810

Maintaining your lifestyle—To maintain your current lifestyle during retirement, many experts say you will need between 70 and 85 percent of your present income. Upwards of two-thirds of that income will have to come from one's private assets. If you plan to use your retirement to fulfill lifelong dreams (such as traveling), you are going to need a little more than 70 to 85 percent. That probably means continuing—or exceeding—your present income level.

Knowing how much you will need to live on after you retire is only the first step. There are many other factors that you must consider. One such consideration is the fact that you will probably live longer. When Social Security was first established, few people were expected to live past age 62. Times have changed, and they will continue to do so. Today the average man will live into his mid-seventies and the average woman into her late seventies. That is 10 to 15 years past 65. There are 77 million baby boomers who were born between 1946 and 1964. By the time these baby-boomers get to retirement, around 2008, life expectancy will probably have exceeded 80. A full 15 extra years of retirement. Fifteen extra years to live. Fifteen extra years to fund.

To be safe, more and more experts are adding a minimum of 15 years to life expectancy for purposes of computing how much money will be needed by retirees to last them the rest of their lives. Some experts add 20 years, and lately some have simply been assuming that to be super-safe you should plan to live to be 100. I could not agree more. Although this is being very safe, it is also very expensive as you will see if you ever run the numbers. Plan to be very safe. Otherwise, you may run out of money before you run out of time. Suppose you need $48,000 a year to retire on. If you retire at 65 and live to 90, you will need $1,200,000 of income over that 25-year time span. More if you retire earlier than 65, as most teachers do. And let's not forget inflation.

The Impact of Inflation—Inflation has been a part of our national experience for most of this century. During some periods, it has been rampant. For planning purposes, expect inflation to continue be a fact of life. What is inflation? Inflation is a constant, steady erosion of money's value. The amount of erosion varies—in some years the rate of inflation is higher than in others. But the effect of inflation never changes—the cost of living keeps going up, so you need more money just to stay even. It means that your money will not buy as much tomorrow as it does today. Forgive me for stating such an obvious fact, but at times we need to be reminded of those things to which we grow too accustomed. Remember that even a low rate of inflation, like the 3 percent of the past few years, builds up over time. Over 15 years, 3 percent inflation will cut your purchasing power by more than 50 percent. Over the same period, a 4 percent rate will cut it by 60 percent! With a 4 percent per year inflation rate, you will need almost $100,000 in your first year of retirement to buy what $60,000 buys today. Or, let us say you expect to receive a $30,000 per year pension over the course of a 20-year retirement period. If inflation averages just 4 percent, the buying power of that pension will be reduced to $13,700. In other words, if your pension is not independent of inflation (meaning that it increases as inflation does—and most are not), you will need to put away an additional $111,000 and invest it at seven percent merely to maintain the $30,000 buying power you started with. It is kind of depressing!

The two primary U.S. indicators of the inflation rate are the *Consumer Price Index* and the *Producer Price Index.* If you wish to follow them, the rates are announced monthly and track changes in prices paid by consumers and by producers.

Inflation Happens

Though unexpected changes in the world politics, like a war or an oil embargo can cause a sudden leap in prices, inflation is not random or arbitrary. It is cyclical, closely linked to the country's overall economy. When things are booming, inflation is higher. When employment decreases and the economy slows down, inflation drops. And its natrural cycle can be influenced, if not always controlled, by changes in the interest rate.

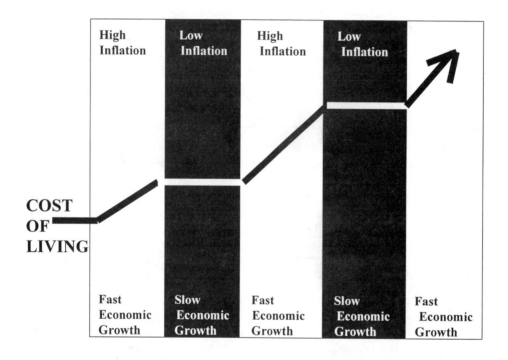

Inflation is bad enough when you are working and receiving pay raises to compensate for it. When you retire on a fixed income, it really starts to bite hard. Of course, a recession could turn us toward deflation for a while, but do not count on it. The way to safely plan is to expect for inflation to continue while trying to add a little inflation protection. Of course you can not stop inflation, but you can protect yourself against it by investing for growth. Generally speaking, that means putting at least some of your money into stocks and/or stock mutual funds. Since 1926, *equity* investments have returned an average of 10 percent a year, while the inflation rate in the same period averaged around 4 percent. That is a *net gain*.

The rule of thumb is that you need to earn more than the current inflation rate on your combined investments to keep ahead of the game. That is because your *real rate of growth* is what remains after subtracting the inflation rate from your rate of return. The higher the real rate of return you are earning on your combined investments, the better your defense against the effects of inflation. For example, if inflation is running at 3 percent, your goal is 4 percent or better: a 4 percent return minus 3 percent inflation equals a 1 percent *real return*. CDs, money market accounts, and other *cash investments* rarely, if ever, pay more than inflation and often pay less. That is why you need to invest your money in other ways. As a rule, if the bulk of your investments is not in stocks or stock mutual funds, you will probably find yourself earning less than the inflation rate. Take a close look at the ever-diminishing buying power of the dollar over the last generation.

LOOK AT THE EVER-DIMINISHING BUYING POWER
OF THE DOLLAR OVER THE LAST GENERATION

1963	1999	1963	1999
A Cup of Coffee		**A Luxury Car**	
$0.10	$0.75	$2,800	$41,000
A Pair of Sneakers		**A Postage Stamp**	
$4.95	$110.00	$0.05	$.033
A Newspaper		**A Quart of Milk**	
$0.40	$1.10	$0.27	$0.90
A Gallon of Gasoline		**A Movie Ticket**	
$0.30	$1.00	$1.00	$7.50
A Can of Soda		**A Candy Bar**	
$0.10	$0.50	$0.05	$0.60

19

If it makes you feel better to know how fast your money is losing its value, you can use *the rule of 72.* Just divide 72 by the current inflation rate to find the number of years it will take prices to double.

$$\frac{72}{\text{(Current inflation rate)}} = \begin{array}{l} \text{Number of years} \\ \text{prices are doubled} \end{array}$$

For example, if the rate of inflation is 3 percent, prices will double in 24 years. The movie ticket that cost $7.50 in 1999 will cost $15.00 in 2023. There is one bright spot, though. You will probably be eligible for a senior citizen discount!

To figure the impact of higher inflation rates on your cost of living, you can use the same rule. If inflation were running at 10 percent, that movie ticket would double in just over 7 years. If the inflation got to 15 percent, it would take less than five years. Inflation erodes what money is worth. If the rate stays a relatively modest 3 percent, the $100.00 you have today will be worth only about $50.00 in 12 years, and absolutely nothing in 24. Since many people are living 25-30 years after they retire, you can see why inflation is a matter for concern. There is no doubt about it, inflation creates serious problems for people living on fixed incomes, such as pensions, annuity payments, or interest on bonds. A fixed income means that the dollar amount of the payment is set from the beginning and does not change. A $10,000 bond paying 7 percent will give you $700.00 a year for as long as you hold it. That means your buying power will decline because as prices rise the value of your money will be less. The flip side of inflation's negative effect is that bonds, CDs, and bank accounts pay slightly higher interest during periods of high inflation, providing a higher return even though the real return will still be too low to produce growth.

Many retired people saw their interest income decline dramatically during the early nineties because interest rates plummeted during a period of minimal inflation. When CDs that were paying 8 percent or more matured, new ones were paying only 3 percent, a huge decline for people depending on interest earning to pay their bills.

Be safe. Think, *It's all up to me.* Believe it, because it probably is. "Life is too short; live for today" does not wash anymore. "I'll save for retirement next year; I've got plenty of time," is a popular attitude. Popular, but foolish. Even if you save more later, you will *never* be able to catch up. If you invest $200 per month for 30 years at an assumed tax-deferred annual yield of 8.5 percent, you will make a total investment of $72,000 and accumulate a total of $309,558. If you wait 10 years and invest *twice* the amount ($400 per month) at the same annual yield for *only* 20 years, you will *contribute a higher* total investment of $96,000, but you will only accumulate $241,123—*a full $68,435 less.* That is a lot of money! For another example, look at the following chart:

It Pays to Start Now

Assumption: Employee earns $25,000 at age 25, receives 5% annual raises and contributes 6% of salary to 403(b) funds that return 8% a year.

You, and only you, have the power to determine what your retirement will be like by planning, saving and investing. The old adage to *give 10 percent of your income and save 10 percent* is a good one. Over 20, 30, or 40 years, that savings will add up to a nice nest egg. The key is to start now and save regularly. Take full advantage of all the tax-deferred methods of saving, such as the 403(b). Put as much money each year into them as possible. Once you have done all you can to save through 403(b)s, you will need to figure out how to save even more. Several options are discussed later on in the manual.

If only I had a million dollars—One million dollars—a big, round, juicy number—is the Holy Grail for most investors. We figure that, if we can only accumulate a million bucks by the time we retire, we can live in comfort, or, at the very least, in a style similar to what we enjoyed while we worked. Unfortunately, for many of us, one million dollars will not be enough—not by a long shot. *Why do I state this?* Because figures do not lie.

For a married couple, both 43-years-old and planning to retire at 65 in the year 2021, a million dollar nest egg—plus Social Security—will provide them with an annual retirement income of only $31,476 *in today's dollars*. After taxes, that could be just under $25,000. Even worse, the income and capital from the $1 million is designed to last only 20 years. Unless you die before then, nothing will be left from the nest egg to pass on. Still worse, if you live to 86 or older, as suggested above, you will have to rely strictly on Social Security (if it still exists).

Understand that I am not scoffing at $31,476 a year. Many people can live very well on that amount, especially if they have paid off their mortgages. But it is hardly the sort of money you would imagine that $1 million would produce. In fact, it is about 20 percent *below* the current U.S. median family income!

The reason that the figure is so shockingly low can be summed up in one word: *inflation*. As discussed earlier, it can chew away on your investment much like rust does to a car. In running the numbers, let us assume that consumer prices will rise at 5.5 percent a year. As a result, the buying power of $1 million becomes significantly diminished over time. Some people would argue that a 5.5 percent inflation estimate is too high, considering the fact that the consumer price index has risen only 3.0 percent in the last 10 years. But when you look at the index over a longer—and perhaps more representative—period, from 1966 to 1996, it rose at 5.7 percent. From 1976 to 1996 it rose at 5.6 percent. Remember, it is the long haul that you should focus on. With that in mind, it would pay to be safe and go with the 5.5 percent estimate.

But even with a moderate 3 percent inflation, $1 million will not leave you rolling in dough. According to the figures, your annual income in retirement will be $65,712. Not bad, but again, certainly lower than one would expect to receive from a cool million. If you would like to consider various inflation rates and how they will affect your retirement income, simply multiply your current income by the following factors to see how much you would need each year to maintain your present standard of living:

Inflation Rate	10 yrs.	20 yrs.	30 yrs.
4%	1.5x	2.2x	3.2x
5%	1.6x	2.7x	4.3x
7%	2.0x	3.9x	7.6x

For example, if you are currently earning $45,000/year, you will need an annual income of $99,000 to maintain your present standard of living, assuming an inflation rate of 4%, with 20 years to go before retirement ($45,000 multiplied by 2.2). But remember, as mentioned above, using a 5.5% inflation rate will probably get us a little closer to reality. So, using 5% for inflation, let us take that same $45,000/year salary and multiply it by 2.7. That gives us a figure of $121,500/year needed to maintain your present standard of living. It jumps to $193,500 if you will not retire for another 30 years.

The above figures are based on a few assumptions. Maybe they do not apply to you specifically. If not, then adjust them slightly. First, as I stated above, the example used is for a married couple, both spouses now 43-years-old and planning to retire at age 65 in the year 2021. As I mentioned earlier, that is toward the long end of things if you are a teacher. With varied retirement incentive plans, most teachers retire before that. Considering that, if you are closer to retirement, then $1 million will go farther, since inflation has less time to ravage the nest egg. However, if you are *closer* to retirement, you will also have *less* time to accumulate the million bucks. It appears to be a double-edged sword.

Next, the assumption was made that the $1 million was split—$750,000 in a tax-deferred retirement account, such as a 403(b), and $250,000 in a taxable account. A tax rate of 28% was used, which is the rate on ordinary income for many Americans. An 8.5 percent rate was used to compute annual return. That seems reasonable when you consider that most investor's portfolios will have a mix of stocks and shorter-term bonds at retirement age. Over the last 70 years, stocks have returned 10 to 11 percent annually and intermediate bonds have returned an average of 5 to 6 percent. With that in mind, 8.5 percent seems like a good estimate.

Factoring in Social Security was a bit trickier (this will be discussed in great detail in the next chapter). For now, the assumption was made that one spouse would receive the maximum benefit and the other would get half the maximum. Banking that Social Security will continue to rise with inflation, I scaled back its annual cost-of-living increases to a flat 3 percent (even in the example in which there was a 5.5 percent annual Consumer Price Index rise.) This makes sense because between 2021 and 2041, the retirement years of our imaginary couple, Social Security could be drastically reduced, or gone entirely. Again, just about every expert on the subject predicts large, additional Social Security benefits cuts in the next few years.

Let us continue by taking a different angle on inflation. To be a bit conservative, let us move on with an intermediate example which assumes 4.5 percent inflation. In the first year of retirement, the $1 million nest egg will produce $64,000 in net income and Social Security will pay a total of $59,000. (Note that Social Security represents fully half of income!) That is a total of $123,000, which sounds like a huge chunk of money. Right? And the total keeps rising, eventually to $284,000 at age 85. Wow! That is a lot of money, by anyone's standards. But we are missing something. The catch is that because of inflation, the $284,000 at age 85 is worth only $42,852 *in today's money*. It is not exactly a gold mine! You may be thinking that $42,842 a year is all that you and your spouse need—even if your combined income today is $125,000. You may be correct, but do not bet on it.

Every family is different, of course, and it pays to sit down and list what you spend today and contemplate the style in which you want to retire. How much does it cost you to live today? That is the important number. You will find several guides later on in the manual to help determine specifics about *what, how much,* and *when.*

I stated earlier that some say a good rule of thumb is that in retirement you will spend about 75 to 80 percent of what you spent while working, maybe only 60% if you have paid off your mortgage and the kid's education. Let us be conservative and go with the 60 percent. But 60% of $125,000 is $75,000. Even with only a 3 percent inflation rate, the couple falls $10,000 short. If we go with 75 percent, they fall $30,000 short.

Take control of your future—If you start when you are 35 and put away $8,000 a year in a tax-deferred account filled with equity mutual funds that return 12 percent, then you will have $2,160,000 by the time you are 65. Not too shabby! If one starts putting money away earlier than 35, then the nest egg grows significantly.

Some universal truths apply to retirement investing, no matter what your age or lifestyle. One of those truths is that regular, systematic investing called *dollar-cost averaging* is a habit that should be established early on and maintained throughout your working years (dollar-cost averaging will be covered in chapter 9). Another is that life is not static; neither is a good investment plan. Plan to "tweak" your investment plan by revisiting your retirement portfolios at least once a year. If you do it the same time every year, you can compare performance and make sure you are on target for whatever choices you need to make.

A good time to do this is when you are already going over financial records—at tax time. Once you have reconciled your taxes, check your year-end statements from your retirement accounts to be sure that your savings and investments are working to achieve your plan, so that you can enjoy a well-earned retirement. Also, ask yourself, "How many hours did I work to earn my money last year? Was it around 2,000 hours? Well then, how many hours am I going to spend to make sure my money is still working maximally for me now?" If the task proves too daunting, then enlist some help. Never just sit on it and hope that things work out. At a minimum you should do the following:

- Update your *personal financial summary* each year, including your *personal balance sheet* and *cash flow statements*. A personal balance sheet provides an accounting picture of what you own and what you owe. In other words, a personal balance sheet is a snapshot of your financial condition on a given day. A cash flow statement, on the other hand, is a comparison of how money flows into and out of your life. It is a comparison of your income and expenses that should help you better understand how much money will be available for retirement planning and investment. A worksheet to help you compute both is provided in chapter 6.

- Evaluate the performance of your investments for the past year.

- Evaluate and balance your investment portfolio, if necessary, to maintain the desired mix of investments.

- Ask the question: "Am I still on track to the retirement I want?"

- Ask "What has changed?" to see if any new developments in your life should prompt you to revise your goals.

Remember that the choices you make for retirement planning should depend on your circumstances, goals, and risk tolerance. Obviously, everyone will have divergent paths to follow, but as you will soon see, some basic guidelines for investing apply to all.

CHAPTER TWO

Social Security?

Inflation is not the only concern for retirees. As mentioned earlier, there is Social Security to consider as well. Let us take a closer look. In 1935, President Franklin Roosevelt signed the Social Security Act creating the Old Age, Survivors and Disability Insurance system (OASDI), better known as Social Security. This allowed individuals to collect retirement benefits for themselves and their families at age 64. They also could have elected to receive reduced benefits as early as age 62 or increased benefits if they waited until after age 65 to begin collecting. Things have changed. The current picture is not a pretty one, and it will most likely continue to get worse. Uncle Sam now sees Social Security as an entitlement, and an entitlement is something that has to be cut when considering the Federal budget. If you are young now, to be safe, write off at least half of what your parents are expecting (or getting) from Social Security. You can become eligible for regular Social Security benefits in one of five ways:

1. With your own benefits, based on your lifetime work record.

2. With spousal benefits, based on your husband's or wife's work record (normally half of the spouse's full benefit).

3. With divorced spouse's benefit (providing you were married at least 10 years, your former spouse is receiving Social Security or is more than 62 years old, you are not remarried, and you have been divorced for at least two years).

4. With widow's or widower's benefits (providing you were married at least nine months and did not remarry before you turned 60).

5. With divorced widow's or widower's benefits (providing you were married to your ex-husband or ex-wife at least 10 years, are 60 or older, and married your present spouse before age 60).

People depend on Social Security to provide a retirement base. Today, Social Security replaces approximately 42 percent of an average retiree's income; however, this level of replacement will be lower in the future. More likely, as shown in the chart below, the Social Security pension will replace less than 25% of your nest egg, and you will have to provide the rest. For those who earned low wages most of their working lives, however, Social Security should provide as much as 60% of their final pay. This year, the average benefit for all retired persons was approximately $602 per month, even though the *maximum* monthly benefit was much higher.

How Much of Your Income
Will Social Security Replace?

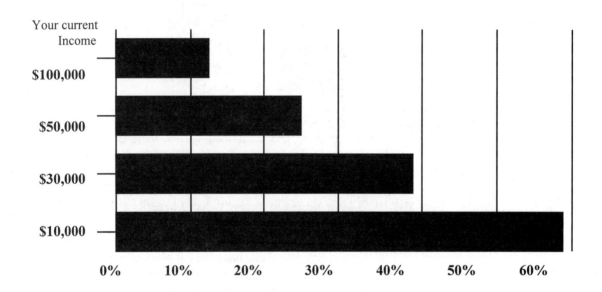

Most Americans are not pleased with what has been going on with Social Security lately. Poll after poll shows that people are extremely worried about Social Security. Over 35 percent of American senior citizens believe they are getting less than they deserve. What will they think in another 5 to 10 years? Currently, people who are single and have $30,000 in total retirement income, or married filing jointly with $35,000 in total income, must pay federal income tax on up to 50% of their Social Security benefit! For single people with $36,000 in income and married couples with $46,000 in income, up to 85% of Social Security is taxable. (For this, the government counts as income half of your Social Security benefits and all your tax-free interest on municipal bonds).

These days, people both inside and outside the government are saying Social Security might not be around when many of the baby-boomers retire. Studies show that more than 83 percent of Americans between 18-34 feel the government has made promises to their generation that it will not be able to keep. One survey revealed that more adults under the age of 34 believe in UFOs than think they will get any Social Security at all. It is practically a given in boomer thinking that by the time they retire, Social Security will not be around to take care of them.

It is no wonder. Despite what skeptics think, Social Security remains part welfare. Even if Social Security does not disappear, it probably will not be as generous in the future as it is today. The average worker who retired in 1995 will collect $182,000 more than he or she paid in. How long can that last?

Under current projections, the first boomers will turn 55 in 2001 and presumably will start their early exodus from the workforce around then. This will decrease revenue flow to the government and cause a tremendous drain on the system. The Social Security trust fund could go bankrupt by the year 2029. As shown in the graphic below, by 2030, when the baby-boom population is fully retired, one-fifth of the population will be older than 65-years-old!

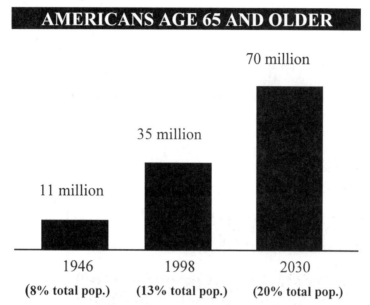

AMERICANS AGE 65 AND OLDER

70 million

35 million

11 million

1946	1998	2030
(8% total pop.)	**(13% total pop.)**	**(20% total pop.)**

There are other factors to consider with regard to Social Security. People are living so much longer that Social Security might have to raise the retirement age for full benefits to age 80. In 1937, when the first Social Security checks were mailed out, there were more than 40 workers paying into the system to support each eligible retiree. Today, there are only three active workers for each retiree collecting benefits. By 2035 there will be two or fewer workers per retiree. The inescapable conclusion is that Social Security benefits will have to be reduced, at least for recipients whose other sources of income make their total retirement income relatively high.

Misconceptions regarding Medicare are just as rampant. Although covered more completely in chapter 4, it is worth noting here that Medicare costs have spiraled upward far faster than inflation, as have costs for the rising number of people receiving disability checks financed by Social Security. Typically, Medicare pays *less than half* of a retiree's *total* medical bills, and you usually cannot start collecting this until age 65. Many do not realize that they have to pay premiums for Medicare, and will most likely need to purchase supplemental health insurance to fill in coverage gaps. As a result of the soaring costs of health care and the aging of America, the future of Medicare is just as uncertain as Social Security. Medicare could very well become insolvent any time between 2002 to 2011, and without reform, by 2040 Social Security's deficit will be over $3 trillion.

Reforming the System—Social Security's problems would not be quite so bad if the current annual Social Security surpluses were saved and invested for the future. But they are not. Washington spends the money on other programs as fast as it comes in. No one knows for sure what the future holds for Social Security, but there are some changes that are likely to occur. Most are "stopgap" solutions at best. The following are the most popular topics today:

- Cutting cost of living adjustments, which lately has been adding 3 percent or so a year to

27

checks.

- Make across-the-board cuts in benefits.

- Mandate savings.

- Remove the cap on wages subject to Social Security taxes.

- Find other revenue sources to feed Social Security growth. For example, taking the budget surplus, which consists entirely of the current excess of Social Security tax receipts over Social Security benefit payments, and buy back a big chunk of outstanding federal debt and put the bonds thus acquired into the Social Security Trust fund. Another proposal involves investing a slice of the budget surplus in the stock market, where it would earn higher returns for the Trust fund than government bond investments would provide. (The backers of the stock market proposal reply that local, state, and even federal government employee pension funds are already major stock market investors, with no apparent social-istic effects).

- **Cut other government programs to feed Social Security growth.**

- **Increase the early retirement penalty for those retiring at age 62**—At present, if you retire at the youngest age, 62, it will cost you 20 percent of what you could have claimed at age 65, which social Security currently considers the full retirement age. In 1995, the maxi-mum annual benefit at age 62 was $11,508 per worker, or $17,256 for a couple with a non-working spouse also age 62.

- **Slowly raising the retirement age to age 70 for full benefits**—Currently, the age is *scheduled* to rise to 67 in the year 2003, which will affect retirees born in 1959. You can be sure, however, that the age of full retirement will continue to rise for people now in their early 50s and younger. At present, if you were born between 1943 and 1954, you will have to wait until you are 66-years-old to get the full benefit.

- **Develop a means or *affluence* test**—This basically involves redistributing from the rich to the poor. It does not exclude the rich because they still will get a portion of Social Security benefits. This solution would be on a graduated rate structure and would only affect those above a certain income level.

- **Institute a two-tiered system**—Part of an individual's FICA tax is invested in a private personal investment account and part is still contributed to the federal government's Social Security program to support retirees. Everyone would have a foundation of benefits, but the private account would supplement the benefits. Surveys show that most young adults would opt to participate in a private system if they were given the option.

Real Reform?—Although some of the above-mentioned strategies are grounded in logic, they are, by themselves, lacking in long-term efficiency. A more comprehensive approach is needed. Most experts agree that, in reality, the real solution would probably be a combination of the above—like two or three.

At present, everybody in Washington has their own idea on how to fix the system with sound, long-term solutions. Potentially good news for investors, most plans involve investing at least part of the pro-ceeds from Social Security payroll taxes in the stock market. Even if this money is put directly into equities rather than through funds, a surge in stock prices would ultimately enrich both funds and their shareholders. Of course, the politicians would have to allow the surpluses, currently almost $100 billion a year, to build, rather than using them to fund current general expenditures, as is now the case.

A plan sponsored by members of the U.S. senate would cut the current payroll tax from its current level of 12.4% to 10.4% until the year 2025, then slowly raise the tax to 13.4% over the next thirty-five years. It would also reduce benefits for future retirees by reducing the cost of living adjustment for Social Security by one percentage point, raising the retirement age to 70 by 2065, and basing benefits on the 38 highest-income years (rather than the current 35). Workers could then (theoretically, at least) invest the extra money in a government-defined individual savings account, or keep it as take-home pay and possibly invest for themselves.

Another plan to keep the system solvent recommends partial privatization of Social Security, but would not cut the payroll tax. Instead, workers would be allowed to take two percentage points from the tax and invest it in one of several government-run funds. After a period of time, the range of investment options would be increased. There is a precedent for this type of option. In 1983, Congress created the Federal Employee Thrift Program, which lowered retiring federal employees' guaranteed benefits and started a 401(k)-type plan. That plan allows employees to invest in three types of government-run funds: an equity index fund, a bond index fund, and a government bond fund.

The debate is far from over; in fact, it has hardly begun. About the only thing agreed upon is that 1999 is the year to begin to restructure Social Security. But even the most optimistic observers say system reform will not happen until next year at the earliest, which leaves plenty of time for groups with other ideas to bend the ears of potential Congressional sponsors. There are two primary reasons for the delay. First, there is no consensus about what exactly should be done. As mentioned there are many suggestions, but each of them is so politically volatile that neither party is willing to formally propose them. Second, time for action this year is running short. The legislative calendar for the balance of 1999 is already established and there is little time to consider such a monumental problem.

President Clinton's plans are for an open forum over the balance of this year culminating in a December-January summit, and negotiations with Congress during the first quarter of 2000. I do not look for any big changes until 2001 (the first year of the next President's term).

Many experts do not think the Social Security system should change much at all. Wendell Primus, Director of Income Security Programs at the Center on Budget and Policy Priorities, a Washington think tank, defends the traditional pay-as-you-go system. Testifying before the Social Security Reform Committee this past March, Primus feels Social Security should remain a universal guaranteed defined-benefit plan. He recommends investing up to half of the trust fund surplus in equities, letting the government take the market risk rather than the individual. He feels that if it is done collectively, one could get most of the benefit from investing in equities without the cost of caring for 160 million different individual accounts.

At the opposite end of the spectrum is the Libertarian Cato Institute. They would like people to be free to choose which system they would like to be in. They favor a private plan, where they could potentially get three to six times their Social Security benefits. The institute dismisses fears of letting people loose in the stock market with their formerly guaranteed retirement money. They feel that no matter how private the plan is, it should be highly regulated. There will probably be restrictions on how risky investments can be and how you have to diversify. They also favor a safety net equal to current Social Security benefit levels, which would be funded from the Federal budget. Given historical returns of stocks, it is implausible that large numbers of people would ever need the net. The months ahead should prove interesting with regard to how Social Security's monumental problems will ultimately be approached.

When Will You be Eligible?—To determine the year you will be eligible for full Social Security benefits (according to today's figures), do the following calculation, using the table below:

	Year	**Month**
1. From the table, based on your year of birth, indicate the age at which you will qualify.	_____	
2. Subtract your current age.	- _____	
3. Answer is number of years until retirement.	= _____	
4. Now, add the current year (i.e., 1999) to the number of years until retirement.	+ _____	
5. The total of the last two gives you the year you will qualify for full benefits.	= =============	

Year of Birth	Normal Retirement Age	Year of Birth	Normal Retirement Age[1]
1937 or earlier	65	1955	66 and 2 months
1938	65 and 2 months	1956	66 and 4 months
1939	65 and 4 months	1957	66 and 6 months
1940	65 and 6 months	1958	66 and 8 months
1941	65 and 8 months	1959	66 and 10 months
1942	65 and 10months	1960 and later	67

Note: *Normal retirement age* is the earliest age at which you can begin receiving unreduced retirement benefits.

As if Social Security were not sick enough, Congress has decided to beat it up even more. In its zeal to lessen the current budget crisis, Congress has quietly broken two long-standing covenants with American taxpayers. Under the new tax law, a growing number of people who receive Social Security benefits will be taxed *twice* on the income they receive—just another reason to hate the new tax bill. If that is not bad enough, the government has mandated *increases* in the amounts that employees must contribute to Social Security today. This will force future returns on those contributions to steadily drop and continue to decline well into the next century. Lawmakers are justifying their new tax tyranny this way: they are only taking away tax benefits from people who do not need them in the first place. So far, nobody seems too worried about these changes. Many taxpayers are likely to shrug their shoulders in indifference, thinking *Isn't Social Security a joke anyway?* The truth is, most people do not understand the numbers, so Congress is assuming that there will not be much of a protest. They are probably correct.

The fact of the matter is that Social Security is no joke to millions of current retirees, who have a pretty good deal going. Consider this: a taxpayer who started working in 1944 and made the maximum contributions to Social Security every year before retiring in 1992 would have put a total of $36,881 into the Social Security system. During those 49 years, the taxpayer's employer would have been matching his contributions dollar for dollar, as required by law, so the worker's real account with Social Security would have amassed a $73,762 stake. Today, our 66-year-old retiree gets monthly checks equaling $14,500 a year, paid out for the rest of his life, after being periodically adjusted for inflation. If that person's spouse was the same age and also entitled to the maximum benefit (a pretty typical case in a two-professional household), the couple would be receiving $29,000 a year, partially tax-free. Not a bad deal. Not a bad deal indeed!

The payout for someone who will retire at age 65 depends on that person's income and present age. To qualify for the highest payment, you will have to earn the highest amount of income subject to Social Security tax, and continue to do so over several years. For example, the top amount subject to the tax in 1991 was $53,400; in 1995 it was $61,200; in 1996 it was $62,700; in 1998 it was $68,400; and in 1999 the figure has risen to $72,600. That is a $19,200 increase in the last 8 years! Remember, there is no wage limit with concern to the Medicare tax, which is currently at 1.45%.

While Social Security is a pretty good deal for *today's* retired population, it is much less of a good deal for *tomorrow's*. Why? To keep Social Security financially afloat, Congress keeps raising the amount that working people have to kick in. From 1937 to 1949, FICA taxes were only 1 percent of the first $3,000 (a $30 maximum). As late as 1965, the maximum paid in taxes was only $174 a year. But since 1973, FICA taxes have been rising annually, sometimes as much as 29.3 percent in one year. That has pushed up the maximum contribution to $4,501.20 in 1999 (excluding the Medicare tax), and the end is nowhere in sight.

As investors we are interested with the *ROI*—the return on investment. So what is the return on our taxpayer's "investment" in Social Security? Assuming that he/she lives to age 80, and that the benefits go up 3 percent a year to keep pace with inflation (which they will not), he/she has made roughly 6.5 percent a year. Not very close to the 10.1 percent that stocks have earned over the same period, but better than the historical return on Treasury bonds. In fact, it is surprisingly comparable to what private insurance companies have offered on retirement annuities in recent years.

All of this means that although the benefits Social Security pays out are guaranteed to keep pace with inflation, the contributions workers pay in have gone up much faster. That means the return on our "investment" is getting lower every year.

Are You Overestimating Your Social Security Benefits?

AGE	% OF FULL BENEFIT	AMOUNT[1]
62	80%	$16,000
63	87%	$17,734
64	93%	$18,666
65	100%	$20,000
66	104%	$20,800
67	108%	$21,600
68	112%	$22,400
69	116%	$23,200
70	120%	$24,000

[1] **Approximate amount you will receive if you begin collecting benefits at the age listed in the column at the far left. The amounts in the chart assume you will retire in the year 2025 or later and will earn an average annual salary of approximately $50,000 over your working life, and are based on current legislation.**

So how much can you look forward to? The previous chart will help you see the picture more clearly in general terms. But for those of you who want the specifics, here are some statistics which give an even clearer picture. If you were born in 1950 and earned $40,000 in 1994, for example, Social Security's computers estimate that your maximum monthly benefit when you eventually retire will be $1,178. If you were born in 1940 and earned $61,200 or more in 1994, your monthly benefit will be an estimated $1,325. Do not forget that those figures are in 1994 dollars. Because actual payments are adjusted each year for inflation, you should view your future benefits in terms of their present buying power.

A taxpayer born in 1946 who retires in 2001—the year he gets full benefits—would have contributed $141,213. Assuming he lives to age 80, his benefits will represent a return of about 1.78 percent a year. This rate is so ridiculously low that no insurance company would dare offer it on the open market. The rate of return goes from bad to worse for people retiring in later years. People retiring in 2023 will not even get all of their own money back!

As mentioned earlier, under the present system, 50 percent of a retiree's benefits is taxed when "provisional" income (that is adjusted gross income plus tax-exempt interest and half of Social Security benefits) exceeds $35,000 on a joint return ($30,000 for a single). Fair enough. But, when provisional income runs over $46,000 on a joint return ($36,000 if you are single), up to 85 percent of the benefit is subject to federal income tax. You should expect that this trend toward taxing more and more of the Social Security benefit will continue. Actually, it would be wise to expect that if retirement income is more than $50,000 or $60,000 a year, you will pay income tax on most, if not all, of the benefit. As a result, upper-income taxpayers will be taxed *twice* on about 10 percent of their Social Security income.

This double taxation will be even worse for future retirees than it is today. That is because employee contributions are increasing much faster than the inflation-indexed benefits that are paid out. Therefore, an increasingly large percentage of the benefits paid to retirees in the future will be their own money returning to them. For example, for people born in 1946 who retire in 2012, 40 percent of their monthly checks will be their own money coming back to them. For those born in 1957, retiring in 2023, it will be more than 50 percent. Under the new tax law, these people will pay double taxes on 25 percent and 35 percent of their "benefits," respectively.

Some people like to work part-time after retirement. Unless you postpone your Social Security pension until age 70, it probably will not pay to work after your Social Security checks start rolling in. If you do, you will be docked for earning more than a minimal amount. These limits increase each year as average wages increase. In 1999, the earnings limits are $9,600 for people under age 65 and $15,500 for people age 65 through 69. Earnings in or after the month you reach age 70 will not affect your Social Security benefits. If you were younger than age 65, the earnings threshold is $9,600, and the penalty for earning more is one dollar in lost Social Security benefits for every two dollars of pay. If you are age 65 through 69, Social Security will deduct one dollar in benefits for each three dollars you earn above $15,500. Though Social Security docks your benefits if you earn more than a certain amount from a job, you can earn *all the investment income you want* and not be docked a dime!

The good news about working beyond age 65 is that the extra income will increase your average earnings once you do retire, so you could wind up ahead in the long run. By staying on the job until age 70, you qualify for benefits as much as 40 percent higher. In addition, people who delay retirement get a special credit. This credit, which is a percentage added to your Social Security benefit, varies depending on your date of birth. For people turning 65 years old in 1995, the rate was 4.5 percent per year. For example, if you delay receiving benefits for 3 years (until age 68) your benefit then increases by 4.5 percent times three, or 13.5 percent. That rate will gradually increase in future years, until it reaches 8 percent per year for people turning 65 in 2008 or later.

Obviously this whole Social Security situation needs a solution. Outside of the Social Security Administration, one of the most talked about involves letting taxpayers put their FICA contributions into an annuity, an IRA, a company-sponsored 401(k), or in a 403(b) plan (whichever is specific to the needs of the investor). They would make a lot more money that way. But for some strange reason, Washington does not appear interested in reducing tax revenues.

The Myths of Social Security

Even though most experts scoff at the idea that Social Security will be a worthy income source, there are some myths concerning Social Security that are worth knowing. Social Security, although currently rife with problems, is one of the most successful U.S. government programs ever designed. It provides close to half of the annual retirement income to average workers and more than 80 percent to low-wage workers. But, as already discussed, the future of Social Security is clouded because of its financing structure and changing demographics.

Over the next few years, Congress will be heavily debating the problems confronting Social Security and possible solutions. This small section will provide background to this debate by addressing four myths often associated with Social Security:

Myth #1

Social Security payments to any retiree consist of his or her contributions plus interest—The connection between the amount someone contributes to Social Security and the size of retirement payments ultimately received is very weak. This connection depends only partly on the number of years worked and the level of wages earned. Other important factors are the year a person reaches retirement age and how long a person lives. For example, if Adam retires today at age 65 after a lifetime of work, he would receive his Social Security contributions through benefit payments in two years or less. Adam is likely to receive a good return on his Social Security contributions unless he dies before age 70. By contrast, if Annette retires after a lifetime of work in 2012 at age 66 (the normal Social Security retirement age at that time), it will take approximately 12 years for her to receive her Social Security contributions. She is not likely to receive a good return on her Social Security contributions unless she lives well into her eighties.

Myth #2

Social Security is financed by a federal trust fund that fully backs all Social Security benefits—At around $370 billion, Social Security is the single largest program in the federal budget. Social Security spending is larger than the combined budgets including agriculture, energy and education. Social Security is not a fully funded system, but a pay-as-you-go system under which Social Security contributions from this year's workers are collected and distributed to this year's beneficiaries. The U.S. government invests any remaining surplus in its own Treasury securities. Over the last decade, these yearly surpluses have built up a reserve to over $500 billion. However, the present value of future Social Security benefits currently exceed the present value of future Social Security contributions by roughly $9 to $11 trillion.

The main reason for this gap (as mentioned above) is that Americans are living longer. The average life expectancy was exactly 61.4 years for those born in 1935, 70.3 years for those born in 1965, and 75.8 years for those born in 1995. Also, American birth rates after

1970 are not as high as those recorded during the port-World War II baby boom. Again, the ratio of workers to retirees will fall from the current level of 3.2 to below 2.0 in the next century. Simply put, there will be fewer workers supporting more retirees.

Myth #3

The financing of Social Security is totally separate from efforts to balance the budget—All the proposals that Congress is seriously considering to balance the federal budget over the next decade utilize the present annual Social Security surplus, despite its temporary nature. Currently, the annual contributions to Social Security exceed its annual benefit payments by $70 billion, and this annual surplus will rise to $100 billion in the initial years of the 21st century. In other words, if Congress tried to balance the budget by 2002 or 2007 without relying on the annual Social Security surpluses, it would have to make larger spending cuts or raise taxes to higher levels.

After the year 2012, annual contributions to Social Security will start to drop below the annual outflows for Social Security benefits, and annual Social Security deficits will expand dramatically. For this reason, as long as Social Security is considered part of a unified federal budget, annual Social Security deficits after 2012 will become a substantial, growing impediment to balancing the federal budget during the 21st century.

Myth #4

If the Social Security trust fund becomes insolvent in 2030, Social Security participants will not receive *any* benefits due—No surprise here. While the annual deficits of the Social Security system after 2012 can initially be run against the reserve built up before 2012, this reserve will be exhausted around 2030. However, many workers will still be making annual Social Security contributions, which are projected to cover approximately 75 percent of the Social Security benefits due that year. This Social Security benefit shortfall would amount to roughly $700 billion in 2030, growing to over $3 trillion by 2040. Thus, in order to provide all Social Security benefits at currently projected levels through the 21st century, Congress would have to finance this shortfall by a significant increase in federal taxes and/or Treasury borrowings.

Just a Reminder—Even though Social Security's future is in question, there are still a few facts that you should keep uppermost in your mind when you begin to approach retirement age. When you reach your 60s, you should be aware that the government will not send you a Social Security check until you notify the local Social Security office that you are ready. So be sure to file an application about six months before you want the first check to arrive. Also, if you are part of a married couple in which only one spouse works for pay, Social Security will send you a monthly check too, amounting to about 1-1/2 times the worker's entitlement.

Remember also that you qualify for Social Security retirement benefits as early as age 62 if you have held a job and paid Social Security taxes for at least 10 years. If you elect to start collecting at age 62 you will spend the rest of your life collecting only 80 percent of what you might have gotten had you just waited three years. But on the other hand, it will take a long time even at a full benefit to make up for the three years of checks you might have been collecting. Perhaps the best way to decide is to look at how you will be financing the early years of your retirement. If giving up those Social Security checks between 62 and 65 means drawing on your investments, then you are probably better off taking the checks right away and leaving your portfolio intact, particularly if it is in growth investments with potential for large returns. If you have other sources of income that make it unnecessary to draw on your investments, then it would be a good idea to put off receiving Social Security checks until age 65.

Also, if you think you will be reentering the job market from time to time, as many early retirees do, it would be wise to put off your Social Security checks. Why? The answer lies in repeating some statistics given earlier—when you are under age 65, you lose $1 of Social Security benefits for every $2 of earned income above $9,600. If you are between 65 and 69, the penalty is reduced slightly to $1 of benefits for every $3 you earn above $15,500.

Get an Estimate—If you are younger and want an official estimate of your future benefits, call toll-free (800) 772-1213, or contact their website at **www.ssa.gov**, and request Form SSA-7004-PC. This form will give you estimates for Social Security retirement, and for disability and survivor benefits as well. Its questions are easy to answer and the form is very complete. You can ask for estimated retirement amounts at various ages, from 62 to 70, the period during which benefits postponed rise handsomely in terms of monthly income.

A few weeks after returning the form, you will receive an 8-page Personal Earnings and Benefit Estimate Statement (PEBES). This statement recaps the amount of Social Security earnings recorded for you each year since you began working. Just remember, *the figures will be in today's dollars*. You will receive an estimate of the amount of Social Security benefits you can expect to receive based on three different retirement ages—ages 62, 65, and 70. The benefit estimate statement not only tells you what you will receive in retirement benefits, but also the monthly amounts that your family would get if you died, or that you and your family would get if you were disabled. It also reports the number of credits you have earned (a credit counts work that earns benefits; you get a credit for each $520 of covered wages, but not more than 4 credits in a year), and tells you how many, if any, additional credits you need to earn benefits.

Remember, your benefits are based on the total amount you have paid in Social Security taxes, as shown on your PEBES, so it is *very important* to immediately correct any errors you may note. With some exceptions, the law only requires the Social Security Administration to correct mistakes discovered within 3 years, 3 months, and 15 days of their occurrence. Notify your local office anyway if you detect any mistakes, since you might still be able to qualify for an adjustment. It is a prudent financial habit to review your Social Security records at least once every 3 years.

If you are presently over 50, your benefits will probably be pretty close to what the government now says it will be. No politician is suicidal enough to impose benefit cuts on people who do not have enough time to prepare for them. The check you will get is based on a mathematical formula that takes into account your average lifetime wages adjusted for inflation and, of course, your age at retirement. The calculation is set up so that the lower your wages, the higher your benefits as a percentage of your income. Thus, the replacement ratio is 42 percent if you have always earned average wages on Social Security's wage scale (about $23,000 today), and 26 percent if you have always earned the highest wage Social Security covers ($72,600 in 1999). So, at best, the government will pay you a little over half of what you will need in retirement if you are an average wage earner (a 42 percent replacement ratio when you need 71 percent). If you are a high wage earner, you will get no more than a third (26 percent when you need 75 percent).

Remember though, this is before the inevitable baby-boom benefit cuts kick in sometime in the next century. Experts' estimates of the cuts that would be necessary to keep the system in the black suggest that if you are in your thirties at present, you should probably expect to see 25 percent *less* than Social Security *now says* it will give you. The bottom line is that if you are not going to retire for another 10 years or more, do not count on getting anything of value out of Social Security, like the estimates shown earlier. Think of it as an inheritance. It will be a pleasant surprise if you get it, but no surprise if you do not.

CHAPTER THREE

Financial Planning

Rethinking Retirement Income—The conventional wisdom on retirement investing used to go something like this: Invest in the stock market for growth during the years leading up to retirement. Shift to bonds in retirement, and live off the income. It is an approach that may have made good sense two generations ago, when the average life expectancy was just shy of 60 years (today it is pushing toward 80). Certainly it was practical when the liquidity of retirement assets was an issue, before the advent of money market and bond funds. It is hard to imagine selling a few shares of IBM each month to pay the bills. So, with few practical alternatives, most retirees met their expenses by clipping bond coupons and withdrawing the interest on their savings accounts. It was a simple decision.

But that was then. Today the realities of retirement have shifted significantly as a new generation of retirees has access to more sophisticated investment tools and must plan for longer life expectancies. An investment strategy that focuses too heavily on bonds and other fixed-income investments will most likely fall perilously short over time. It takes careful planning to provide income that can last for 30 to 35 years.

One must realize that building a sound retirement income plan today is to recognize that your investment strategy and your income strategy are not the same thing. It can be the single biggest misconception about retirement income planning. Why? Due to the fact that fixed-income investments have historically been less volatile than stocks, many investors believe that these are a safer choice. And because fixed income investments pay income, investors feel that they have created a retirement paycheck by buying CDs, bonds, or bond funds.

Although fixed-income investments, especially, short-term fixed-income vehicles, can play an important role in any retirement portfolio, many retirees tend to give too much weight to fixed-income investments in their retirement investing strategy, especially during the early years of retirement. Often they spend too much of the income they earn. The result is that they can lose out to inflation in two different ways:

1. First, with little or no growth potential in their post-retirement portfolios, investors may find themselves with inadequate income in their later retirement years. Where do they turn to make up the shortfall when they are 85. Because inflation has been running less than 3 percent recently, people are tempted to think that it has lost its bite. It has not. Even at a long-term inflation rate of 3.7 percent, $1,000 loses half of its purchasing power in about 20 years.

2. Investors who rely heavily on fixed-income investments in retirement are often tempted to equate the income they collect with the income they can afford to spend. Consequently, they overspend in the early years of retirement. If the value of their portfolio does not continue to increase, inflation will eat into their purchasing power over time. Suddenly, they are in trouble.

So how can you build a retirement income strategy that can stand up to inflation and a longer life span? In chapter 13, which deals with asset allocation, you will see several theories concerning how much you should have and where it should be. Most are related to your feelings about risk. It is important to be comfortable with your decision, and having a firm grasp of the facts is the first step.

The road to financial security is paved with good intentions—By now you should be in agreement that in order to achieve your various financial objectives, you need to have an active savings and investment program because your pension and Social Security will leave you short of the mark. This savings and investment program should be geared not only for your retirement years, but *also* for the large obligations you believe will be coming up in the future such as college funding, weddings, etc. Planning for your financial independence will require some thought and soul-searching analysis to determine what is really important to you since, for most of us, this will mean giving up some objectives in order to achieve others.

One of the first concepts to understand is the distinction between a financial plan and an investment plan. One and the same they are not. A *financial plan* is based on a thorough understanding of where you stand today, what your present financial condition is, and where you will obtain your income and how you spend it. The financial plan will chart a course from the beginning to retirement (and beyond) showing you the tools you need to accomplish your goals. An *investment plan* is comprised of those specific investment tools (types of investments) that you will use to bring your financial plan to fruition.

A two-part financial plan

A financial plan is comprehensive and is composed of two major parts. The first and more fundamental part of a financial plan is the *risk management plan*. Risk management refers to your contingency plans for handling major disasters in your life or the lives of your family. One of the best ways to achieve financial security is by successfully avoiding mistakes. With this in mind, the following *nine common errors* which many people make in the course of their financial lives with concern to risk management are listed below—so that you can detour around them.

1. Neglecting to cover gaps in insurance coverage—The surest way to wipe out years of hard-earned accumulation of capital is to suffer an uninsured loss. Deficiencies in any area of insurance can be financially disastrous. You need to be properly covered for the following: temporary or permanent disability, short and long term medical problems, property and liability and theft losses, survivor needs, loss of job. These areas are generally covered in most comprehensive insurance policies. Most experts agree that it is important to cover yourself with protection against major financial difficulties. In addition, it is wise to carry a three to six month cash reserve for unforeseen crises.

2. Mismanaging credit—Since credit is very easy to obtain, many people lack the self-discipline necessary to manage it effectively. Financial institutions feed off of this consumer flaw. They promote high-limit credit cards, five-year car loans, and large home-equity loans with overly liberal repayment terms. These companies literally do not want you to be financially solvent. The reason is quite simple—the more you owe them, the more money they make on finance charges. Some credit card companies have actually begun to penalize credit cardholders who pay off their balances each month by raising the interest rate used to determine finance charges.

If you have a credit card balance which carries a fairly high interest rate, do yourself a favor and pay off the debt before you invest any savings. You will not find a better investment. Paying off credit cards at an 18 percent interest rate from a bank account earning 4 percent, for example, will yield an immediate 14 percent. If you need quick financing, you can always borrow money from your credit card again. It is a good idea to keep a small amount of cash handy so you can avoid a cash advance fee. Do not worry about building a large cash cushion, though, until you are debt free.

Are you carrying too much credit debt? Use the following worksheet to calculate your debt-to-income ratio, then compare your results to the chart. On the worksheet, the lenders are listed in the first column (do not include rent, utilities, or similar bills). The second column is where you list your total debt to each respective lender. The third column is where you list your monthly payment to each respective lender. To figure your monthly payment on revolving credit cards like Visa and MasterCard, etc., use 4 % of the balance. To calculate your *debt-to-income ratio* simply divide your *total monthly credit payments* by your *gross monthly income* (before tax). The result is your debt-to-income ratio.

Credit Debt		
Lender	**Total Owed**	**Monthly Payment**
Car	_____	_____
Visa	_____	_____
MasterCard	_____	_____
Department Store Credit Card	_____	_____
Equipment Purchased	_____	_____
Other	_____	_____
	TOTAL:	===========
	divided by: Monthly Income (before tax):	_____
	EQUALS: Debt-To-Income Ratio:	===========

How Did You Do?

If your debt-to-income ratio is	Then . . . . .
Under 10	You're in great shape
Approaching 20	Be careful - it's getting too high
Approaching 35	You're in the danger zone
Approaching 50	It's time to consider getting help

3. <u>Failing to save regularly</u>—Regular saving is essential to achieving financial security. As income increases, savings also should increase. Nevertheless, many people do not save regularly. Somehow, they mistakenly think that the equity buildup in their home, an inheritance, or their pensions will provide them with long-term financial security. They are often wrong. More on this when our discussion turns to *Dollar-Cost Averaging* later on in the manual.

4. <u>Making inappropriate investments</u>—Whether it is caused by ignorance or greed, or both, many people make an inappropriate investment at least once in their lifetime. Unfortunately, some people consistently invest their money in the wrong areas by taking either too much—or too little—risk.

5. <u>Using inappropriate planning strategies</u>—There are many complex financial strategies available to anyone who wants to use them, but they often make little or no sense. Generally, basic, straightforward strategies produce the best results. Those presented in this manual should prove effective for the vast majority of 403(b) investors.

6. <u>Failing to take full advantage of tax breaks</u>—Failing to take advantage of available tax deductions as well as other legal tax reduction techniques (such as investing in a 403(b) plan) is another mistake many people make. Reducing taxes is a painless way of reducing expenses so savings levels can be increased. This increase in savings will, of course, make you more money in the long run—much more.

7. <u>Overspending</u>—Many successful people increase their spending in the plenty years to such a high level that when a lean year occurs—when income declines or an unforeseen expense arises—they end up in a financial bind. Living beyond your means always puts your finances in jeopardy. A good financial plan helps to control, if not eliminate, overspending. This, in turn, enables you to handle unforeseen circumstances successfully.

8. <u>Neglecting to prepare a will and other estate planning documents</u>—While not around to witness the havoc, people who do not prepare basic estate planning documents do their heirs a disservice. Inappropriate or nonexistent estate planning can end up costing heirs a great deal in terms of both inconvenience and money. Chapter 19 is devoted in its entirety to estate planning.

9. <u>Not shopping around for the most appropriate financial planning products and services</u>—With the many types of investment, insurance and other financial products available today, choosing one can be bewildering. You can find the right products to meet your needs by taking the time to understand the product and shopping for the best value. However, many people are unwilling to take the time to ensure that they are making the most of each dollar they spend or invest. You have taken a giant step forward by purchasing this manual. Remember, no one can avoid making mistakes in personal financial planning. Some, however, make too many mistakes and, worse yet, repeat them.

<u>**Manage your investments**</u>—Once the above considerations have been addressed, you can move to the second part of your financial plan: the management of your investments. Investment planning includes more than just retirement, children's education, or buying a home. It includes virtually all major purchases, from cars to furniture to art. It even includes your hobbies, some of which you might be able to turn into self-employment business opportunities. A good financial plan works much like a road map; it functions to help you get from where you are now to where you want to be in the future. Because each person's current "financial" location is different and because each person has a different destination, each financial road map has to be individually personalized. There are three key elements in designing your financial plan:

1. Determine your net worth and where your income stream flows.

2. Determine what your goals are and where you want to be.

3. Forecast how much money you will need and how much time you have to accumulate it.

Over 90 percent of Americans do not realize how much they are spending. That makes it that much more difficult to plan for a comfortable retirement. After all, if you are not aware of unnecessary spending how will you be able to locate and budget money that could easily be redirected toward a retirement fund? But do not worry. If you are falling behind, there are ways to make up the shortfall.

In chapter 5 you will be able to evaluate your investment "personality," and in chapter 6 you will be able to calculate your net worth, determine your cash flow, and evaluate your financial goals in life, to see how much they are likely to cost.

<u>The Top Ways to Prepare for Retirement</u>

So, what should you be doing now to ensure you are in good financial shape for the future? Here are some common-sense steps that will set you on the right track:

<u>**Know your retirement needs**</u>—Retirement is expensive. As stated earlier, experts estimate that you'll need about 70 to 80 percent of your pre-retirement income—lower earners, 90 percent or more—to maintain your standard of living when you stop working. The average American will spend 18 - 25 years in retirement. There is never any danger in over-estimating your income needs, but lots of worry if you under-estimate your requirements. Who knows? Maybe you will have more expenses when you retire because you are having a good time! Understand your financial future.

Be realistic—Do not expect a lavish retirement lifestyle that exceeds your ability to obtain. Rather, develop a plan that aims to keep you where you are currently. Accept the fact that if you want to save for the future you can not live a credit-heavy lifestyle today. You have to save as much as possible and you must invest aggressively, especially if retirement is ten or more years away.

Living expenses are certain to rise much more than you expect. You may think you will move into a smaller home, but in thirty years, a home that is half the size of the one you live in today will cost twice as much. Look at the current prices of houses, and you will soon see what I mean. Also, you may still need to make mortgage or rent payments, put children or grand-children through college, care for elderly parents, or cover unforeseen medical bills. All of this can drain your retirement dollars.

Saving money has been a challenge for baby boomers. To beat the odds, determine how much disposable income you have and think of it, not as disposable dollars, but as financial independence dollars. This puts its enormous importance in a clearer light, and it may make you less likely to use these dollars to buy that cappuccino machine you do not really need.

Find out about your Social Security benefits—Social Security was covered adequately in the last chapter. For now, let us suffice in saying that you should call the Social Security Administration for a free Personal Earning and Benefit Estimate Statement (PEBES). It will help you put things into perspective.

Ask your employer to start a plan—If your employer does not offer a 403(b) plan, suggest that he/she start one. These plans can be set up easily with little effort and paperwork. You will find details in chapter 9. By law, you are entitled to contribute to a tax-deferred plan. To receive more information, call the Internal Revenue Service at 1-800-829-3676 and ask for Publication 590.

Study your options—If you start investing your financial independence dollars early enough, you can afford to be aggressive with your investments. Diversification is also an essential element of portfolio success because it spreads the risk. Financial experts have a variety of pie charts that slice investment plans into sectors depending on an individual's age, needs, and goals. Stocks invariable occupy 50 to 80 percent of the total pie, and most long-term plans divide the stock portion of the pie among blue chips, U.S. growth companies, and international stocks. Whether you pick your own stocks or leave that task up to a mutual fund manager, you should have all three stock groups in your investment portfolio. Because they do not necessarily rise and fall in tandem, they will balance your risk. Again, asset allocation will be covered in detail later on in chapter 13.

Contribute to a tax-sheltered savings plan—Only 52 percent of baby boomers participate in a 403(b) plan. Fortunately, the number is steadily rising. The 403(b) provides up-front benefits, such as the tax break bestowed by the federal government, and automatic deductions. Over time, deferral of taxes and compounding of interest make a big difference in the amount of money you will accumulate. As a rule of thumb, each year invest all you can in your retirement plan whether it is a 403(b), an IRA, or a Keogh. There is simply no wiser long-term investment strategy. If you can save as much as you can as soon as you can, then you do not have to feel guilty about spending the rest. In 1995, of those who had 403(b) plans available, a full one-third did not participate. How about you? The specifics of the 403(b) are covered completely in chapter 9.

Do not hoard cash—Despite today's low inflation, cash is a catastrophe as an investment. Certainly, hold some cash in reserve for timing opportunities that will occasionally arise. But do not overdo it.

Take advantage of Dollar-Cost Averaging—Regular monthly contributions are the essence of the 403(b) retirement plan, and its success is hard to beat. Your employer sends an exact amount of money to your investment company each month, regardless of what the market is doing. Dollar-Cost Averaging is discussed in detail in chapter 9.

Do not touch your retirement savings—Do not dip into your retirement savings. You will lose principal and interest, and you may lose tax benefits. If you change jobs, roll over your savings directly into your new employer's plan, or into an IRA

Start now—This is the clincher. Start early. Remember, it is *time*—not timing—that is going to give you the retirement you desire. Even if you can not start early, remember that the sooner you start saving, the more time your money has to grow. Put time on your side. Make retirement saving a high priority. And do not let market swings send you into self-doubt. If you reacted to the alarming warnings of the market bears, you would have missed nearly all of the 1990s' spectacular gains.

Systematically invest (dollar-cost average), and do not falter, for if you waver in your steady investment plan, you can wave goodbye to the best long-term gains. It is the diligent tortoise, not the hare, who will achieve financial independence.

The key element that typifies those who retire wealthy, whether they made a second career out of following the market or simply stashed their savings in a 403(b) plan, is that they invested consistently over a long period of time. Starting early is the real key. For example, take a 21-year-old who annually puts $2,000 away in a 403(b) for 7 years, until age 28, for a total contribution of $14,000. Another investor starts investing at age 28, putting $2,000 per year in a 403(b) for 40 years, for a total contribution of $80,000. Both investors retire at 67. Assuming their money compounds annually at 10 percent—the stock market's historic rate of return, *the investor who began at a younger age and contributed only $14,000 for 7 years will have $930,641 at retirement, while the one who began as a 28-year-old and contributed $66,000 more for 40 years will have $893,704, or $36,937 less.* That is the benefit of compounding and starting early.

If you are past your twenties and you think it is too late to do anything meaningful for your retirement, think again. Here is an example of someone starting to invest at age 35. The table on page 44 shows the benefit of making contributions early on, even at the age of 35. As you can see, the investor who makes ten $5,000 annual contributions will always outperform one who waits ten years and then tries to play catch-up by contributing $7,500 ($2,500 more) every year for the next several dozen years (all results are based on a 12% annual growth of capital).

Early Contributor   ## The Procrastinator

Age	Investment	Value	Investment	Value
35	$5,000	$5,600	0	0
36	5,000	11,872	0	0
37	5,000	18,896	0	0
38	5,000	26,764	0	0
39	5,000	35,576	0	0
40	5,000	45,445	0	0
41	5,000	56,498	0	0
42	5,000	68,878	0	0
43	5,000	82,743	0	0
44	5,000	98,273	0	0
45	0	110,066	$7,500	$8,400
46	0	123,273	7,500	17,808
47	0	138,066	7,500	28,345
48	0	154,634	7,500	40,146
49	0	173,190	7,500	53,364
50	0	193,973	7,500	68,167
51	0	217,250	7,500	84,747
52	0	243,320	7,500	103,317
53	0	272,519	7,500	124,115
54	0	305,222	7,500	147,409
55	0	341,848	7,500	173,498
56	0	382,870	7,500	202,718
57	0	428,814	7,500	235,444
58	0	480,272	7,500	272,098
59	0	537,905	7,500	313,149
60	0	602,453	7,500	359,127
61	0	674,748	7,500	410,623
62	0	755,717	7,500	468,297
63	0	846,403	7,500	532,893
64	0	947,972	7,500	605,240
65	0	1,061,728	7,500	686,269

When it comes to retirement investing, the earlier, the better. But whatever your age—
start saving now.

Set goals and stick to them—Set goals for yourself. Devise a plan and stick to it. Remember, it is never too late to start. You can not actually know how much you will need when you retire, or what the state of the economy will be then. You can get a sense if you can project your salary increases, the rate of inflation, and how much you will be paying in local taxes 10, 20, or 30 years in the future. But there is a strong element of guesswork in any projection. The only thing you can tell for certain is that if you do not invest, you will not have what you need.

In many ways, investing for retirement is just like investing for any other reason. You use your principal, or the money you have, to earn more money, which you can use to pay your bills, buy something you want, or make a new investment. But when you are investing for long-term financial security, there is no fixed moment when you need the money. Instead, it is a continuous process. That means you always have to think about doing three things:

1. Making your investment grow.

2. Producing income.

3. Preserving your principal.

We will take a brief look at each of these now, then concentrate more on each of them when we get to the chapter on Asset Allocation.

The Growth Stage

Growth is the first order of business, and investments grow in many ways:

1. You can beef up your principal on a regular basis by contributing a percentage of your income to your investment pool. Putting $200.00 a month into a 403(b) every month is an example.

2. You can reinvest your investment earnings rather than spend them, either by using an official plan offered by a mutual fund or stock reinvestment program, or by putting all your interest and dividend payments into a special investment account. (When contributing to a 403(b) account, you do not have a choice concerning what to do with dividends and short and long-term capital gains. They are automatically re-invested).

3. You can invest your money in places where it is most likely to grow in value, typically in *equity* products like stock mutual funds.

4. You can *diversify*, or put you money into a variety of investments, to take advantage of ups and downs in the stock market and the interest rate.

The Income Stage—Income-producing investments are especially important when you need the money to live on, typically after you retire. For example, the interest on a bond or the dividends from a stock help cover day-to-day expenses. Since those payments are made regularly, usually quarterly or semi-annually, you can plan on them. You can also time certain investments, like certificates of deposit or certain bonds, to mature on a specific schedule, to replenish your cash reserve or meet anticipated expenses. Income from your investments also produces a regular source of new investment money. Or, you can plan to spend a certain amount and reinvest the rest.

The Preservation Stage—If you will be living on the income your investments provide, you have got a vested interest in making sure they do not shrink in value or, worse yet, disappear altogether. Curiously, the best preservation technique is to concentrate on growth—slower, safer growth than you were looking for when you first began to build your nest egg, but growth nonetheless. Money buried in the backyard, or earning minimal interest in a savings account, does not keep its value. In fact, because of inflation, it shrinks. That is one of the biggest threats to your financial security.

CHAPTER FOUR

Protecting Your Assets

L ong before you can spend a dime of your retirement assets, you have to take action to make sure that they are going to be there when you want/need them. A number of things—namely death, injury, disability, or extended private care, can threaten the security of what you have worked your whole life to build.

In this chapter we will take a look at the most common ways of protecting your present assets and those assets that you will be acquiring between now and retirement. My sole intent is to provide a broad overview of the topics presented, to create an awareness, as it were, so the reader can be more knowledge-able in exploring options, and better prepared to meet with insurance professionals. To cover each topic in strict detail is beyond the scope and purpose of this manual.

<u>Life Insurance</u>

Obviously, the most important asset in your retirement plan is you. If your demise would result in economic hardship for your spouse or other loved ones, you are a candidate for life insurance. But what kind of life insurance should you purchase, and how can you get that needed insurance without diverting any more than is absolutely necessary from your retirement savings?

The American Council of Life Insurance reports that the average insured household owns about $100,000 worth of insurance coverage. Is that enough? Probably not. The payoff from life insurance, invested at a reasonable rate, should be enough for your family to carry on without you, after accounting for amounts available from Social Security and other assets you managed to accumulate. It should be enough to cover all of your family's financial needs, such as income replacement, mortgage payoff, child care, college tuition, as well as your funeral expenses. In other words, it depends on how much you make, how much you owe, and how much you have at present.

A simple questionnaire, which can be obtained from almost any insurance company or its website, can help you estimate the amount of coverage you may need, but there are standards you can use for compari-son. Many experts will tell you to purchase six to eight times your annual salary, but I prefer a more calculated method for determining life insurance needs. As a rule of thumb, you need about $100,000 in life insurance for every $500 of monthly income required. Let us say your household needs $4,000 a month to cover all your expenses. Your worst-case scenario is that the people who survive you have no employ-ment or other income, so they will need the full $4,000. You would divide this by $500 and get 8, so your insurance policy should be in the amount of 8 x $100,000, or $800,000. The following table shows you the simple calculation. You can plug in your own numbers in the blanks at the right.

	Example	**Your Numbers**
Your projected monthly income need is A	A = $4,000	A _____
Divide A by $500 to get B	B = 8	B _____
Multiply B by $100,000 to get C	C = $800,000	C _____

The death benefit in your policy should be the amount in C.

Although there are many life insurance companies, each with a staggering array of products, there are really only two basic choices:

1. **Term Life**—Life insurance, pure and simple, without any complicated investment or tax-deferred savings features.

2. **Cash Value or Whole Life**—Cash value or whole life insurance is a form of life insur-ance policy that offers protection in case the insured dies, and it also doubles as a retirement savings vehicle with the advantage of tax-deferred money growth over the long term. Also, a cash surrender value builds up at a guaranteed rate that can be borrowed against.

You may already have trouble finding enough money to fund your 403(b) or IRA to the maximum each year. If this is the case, buy term. You should not shell out big money for cash value coverage laden with high up-front costs. It also makes little sense to shell out big money for an uncertain investment return, and a large early surrender penalty if you try to cash in the policy before 10 years or so. On the other hand, if you have an existing whole-life policy that already has a built-up cash value, you would probably be wise to keep it. By now, that policy may be providing coverage at a very reasonable cost compared with what you would pay for a newly issued term policy. Besides, you could borrow money from the policy to put in an investment vehicle that gives a much greater return (see the strategy in chapter 7).

Term Life Insurance—If visions of a life insurance agent smiling at you across your kitchen table have kept you from dealing with that part of your financial plan, take heart. A major evolution in the industry now puts you in control of buying life insurance, and makes insurance less costly than ever.

It is called *buying direct*—a process which allows you to purchase the coverage you need directly from the company that actually writes the policies. With the middle man (the insurance agent) out of the sales process, insurers can save on commissions and pass the savings on to you. Buying direct, along with improved actuarial standards and evaluation procedures, has led to a dramatic decrease in rates over the part 10 years.

Without an agent, you can shop for term insurance via phone, mail, Web, and in some cases, walk-in service centers. Term life is the simplest, cheapest form of life insurance around, and with term life insur-ance rates falling nearly 50% since 1991, more Americans are looking to protect their families with this type of coverage. It offers the most coverage for the lowest cost. Simply stated, term life coverage is a specified amount of coverage that is paid to beneficiaries when the policyholder dies. If you die while you own the policy, your beneficiaries receive the money. You select the level of coverage you want—$50,000, $100,000, $500,000, or any amount—and pay an annual premium.

The length of the term insurance you choose should be determined by the period that you want to cover. If you have just had a baby, you may want to consider a long-term policy (20 years or more) that would cover the child's long-term needs in your absence. In order to cover the costs of an older child's college education, a shorter, five-year term may be more suitable. The premium you pay is based on the amount of coverage, your general health, your age when you buy the policy, and, of course, the type of term insurance you purchase. There are two types of term insurance to choose from: *annual-renewable term (ART)* and *level-premium term.*

    1. Annual-Renewable Term—ART premiums start low and increase each year. For example, a 40-year-old's premium might be $400 for five years, $600 for the next five years, $800 for the next five years, and so on. A 40-year-old, nonsmoker in good health can buy a $250,000 one-year policy for approximately $300 - $400 per year to start. At 50-years-old, the same policy would cost about $850 per year. ART policies can be renewed automatically each year without having to reestablish your good health, and should be considered if you need coverage for less than five years.

    2. Level-premium term—Locks in the annual premium for a period of time you select. When considering level-premium term, make sure to ask if the policy is renewable and to what age. If it is renewable, you can choose to restart that policy without going through another health review, but at a higher cost. Also, check that your premium is guaranteed to remain level *for the entire term* of the policy you select. Some policies offer a limited guarantee, which means premiums could increase after five years.

When choosing your term insurance, be careful of those so-called *best-rate* premium quotes. Often that rate is sold only to the healthiest of the healthy. Since you will not know if you qualify for the quoted rate until after the company gets your health history, ask what percentage of applicants are approved at that rate. If it is low, and your health is not perfect, your actual premium will probably be substantially higher.

Cash Value Insurance—Term life insurance is an important component of most retirement plans. But cash value (whole life) insurance coverage can be a sound addition *only* if the following applies to you and your unique situation:

    1. You need lots of insurance—more than $750,000, for example.

    2. You are already contributing the maximum to your 403(b), an IRA for you and your spouse, or to any other tax-sheltered retirement savings plan available to you.

    3. You can afford it—which is to say that you are probably earning more than $150,000 per year.

    4. You plan to keep the insurance coverage for many years (15 or more).

If you meet these criteria, then and only then would cash value coverage probably be your best life insurance choice. The main reason is that cash value life insurance doubles as a tax shelter for retirement savings. The shelter aspect works much the same as a 403(b) or an IRA: cash inside the policy is granted the advantage of *tax-deferred* growth. (Tax-deferred growth is fully explained in chapter 9). It is similar to a tax-favored savings plan with life insurance attached. A portion of what you pay in premiums each year (which is substantial) goes to pay for the life insurance coverage, but the bulk of the money is devoted to the savings and investment features. If you use cash value insurance as a tax shelter for retirement savings, there are two basic ways you can get your money out:

1. **Borrowing**—You can borrow against the policy's cash value while keeping the insurance in force. Because it is a loan, the money is not taxed. Any loan outstanding when you die is automatically deducted from the proceeds of the policy.

2. **Surrendering**—You can collect the entire cash value by surrendering the policy and terminating your insurance coverage. The payment is tax-free, up to the amount you paid in premiums over the years. Any excess is taxable.

Because commissions and fees take such a large bite out of your cash value during the first few years, you need to keep funding a policy for at least 10 years in order for your investment to pay off. If you surrender the policy early, usually before 10 years, you will pay substantial early surrender penalties.

One last thought considering life insurance. I know you want to pay a low price for your coverage, but do not base your decision on price alone. The reputation of the company is important also. You can look at the ratings from *A.M. Best (908-439-2200), Moody's (212-553-0377), Standard & Poor's (212-208-8000), or Duff and Phelps (312-263-2610)* to determine the quality of the insurance company. Also, look for a company with a wide array of plan choices so you can fit the plan to your needs instead of the other way around.

Health Insurance

As mentioned in chapter 2, we need to look at a potentially dangerous pitfall to prudent retirement planning—health care, which is currently in a state of disaster. If it is in the cards for you to be retired fairly young, it is also in the cards that you will be paying more out of your own pocket for your health care insurance than you ever dreamed possible. The simple fact is that health care costs are so badly out of control that something has to be done to rein them in within the next few years. Medicare costs have skyrocketed upward far faster than inflation. And universal coverage, following the crash and burn of the Clinton reform plan, seems dead for the foreseeable future. So it is inevitable that affluent older people are going to have to pay more, maybe a lot more. This you can count on—and should plan for.

The consumer has been largely shielded from the spiraling costs for health care. The government and your employer have been paying, and bleeding cash as a result. If current U.S. trends continue, over the next decade total medical spending will spike to more than $2.5 trillion annually, more than double the current figure. Without reform, Social Security's deficit will be well over $3 trillion by the year 2040. In part that is because of federal medical entitlements—the cost of Medicare, which covers about 80% of medical costs for 96% of the nation's 32 million seniors, is now $160 billion and rising by 8% to 9% annually—more than double the inflation rate.

In the private sector, the situation is far less severe. To rein in rising costs, companies have pushed their employees from traditional fee-for-service medicine, in which you choose your own doctors, into managed-care networks. As a result, private employers have been spending less on health care than they used to, a staggering accomplishment when compared to the public sector, where costs are out of control. But even private-sector costs are so huge that efforts to trim will continue, with particular emphasis on retirees, whose doctor and hospital bills far overshadow those of young employees.

To make matters worse, most retirees have no experience with managed care. But employers, government officials, and others who are trying to limit health care costs are coaxing seniors into managed-care networks. Within the next few years the coaxing may get more demanding, and retirees may be forced into such networks as part of a solution to the wild cost spiral of Medicare. But here is the rub: managed-care operations, such HMOs (health maintenance organizations), succeed by saving money, and they save money by limiting care. While this is working out among younger people, it has not tested so well among older folks, who need far more—and more costly—attention.

So what does all this mean for future retirees who plan to be financially well off? The experts foresee easier access to health insurance as Congress and state legislatures pass enabling laws. They also predict ever-improving medical care as technology continues to make further breakthroughs. But it will cost more, and there is no guarantee you will be covered if you are not able to pay. As it stands now, Medicare pays less than half of a retiree's *total* medical bills. This is covered in more detail later on in this chapter in the section on Long-Term health care.

Between now and the end of the century, major changes will have to be made in the overall system of health care in general, and in Medicare in particular if it is to survive. No one can accurately predict what the landscape will look like as a result, but anyone contemplating retirement needs to address the following issues. And the earlier you plan to call it quits, the more seriously you will need to take them.

Make sure you are covered for the years before you turn 65—Understandably, few of the optimists who plan early retirements think much at all about this point, but it becomes more important every year. That is because employers are gradually whittling away at benefits for retirees. A growing minority of employers, in fact, have either eliminated all health coverage for future retirees or are considering doing so. And many more are cutting way back in coverage or raising premiums.

If you are contemplating early retirement, then you will need to build this cost into your budget. First you might want to get an idea from your employer of just how much your health care coverage would be affected by retirement. At present, as a negotiated benefit, many employers allow the retiree to continue coverage by paying their own premiums at the employer's group rate—a discount if you will. If it turns out you will be on you own, you will need to figure on paying between $6,300 and $10,500 a year for a couple for medical coverage, depending on the amount of insurance you decide on and on where you live.

At the very least, your employer is required under COBRA (Consolidated Omnibus Budget Reconciliation Act of 1986) to allow you to stay in its group health plan for 18 months after you leave the employer. You have to pay whatever the company's cost is plus a 2% fee. (The average annual cost to employers for providing medical coverage to retirees runs just under $4,500 for a single and around $8,000 for a couple.)

After the 18 months of COBRA coverage are over, you can usually convert from the employer's group plan to an individual plan. These are generally very limited in coverage but do not require a medical exam. You might also shop group plans offered by professional associations you belong to (NEA), or to such groups as the American Association of Retired Persons.

Beyond that, it makes sense to become as sharp a consumer of health care services as you can. For instance, if your employer offers a choice between traditional indemnity coverage and managed care, it pays to at least try the new way. Managed care can save you $500 or more a year in out-of-pocket costs, and if you decide that you like it well enough, you will be better positioned for the future, when managed care will probably be the standard for almost everybody.

Another way to become a good consumer is to get into the habit of shopping for medical services, something Americans have never before been encouraged to do. You will feel more comfortable about it knowing that studies show that doctors' bills can vary by as much as 250% in the same geographic area! You can call your local medical society or consumer-action group, both of which are listed in the Yellow

Pages, to find out what price surveys are published in your city or town.

Make a separate assessment of the after 65 years—When you are eligible for Social Security benefits, you automatically become eligible for Medicare—earlier if you meet specific disability requirements. Medicare comes in two pieces. Medicare's Part A covers 100 days of your annual hospital bills and pays for skilled nursing care—but not for custodial care such as assistance with activities of daily living (ADLs)—bathing, dressing, eating meals, etc. Medicare's Part B covers doctors' bills, out-patient surgery, emergency room treatment, X-rays, laboratory tests and some medical supplies.

Medicare pays for 80% of *what it deems to be* reasonable charges above an annual deductible; there is a list of reasonable charges for every procedure. A doctor who accepts assignment charges no more than the Medicare maximum. Even if your doctor does not accept assignment, under current federal law, he or she cannot charge a Medicare beneficiary more than 115% of Medicare's approved fee for most procedures—less, if you live in a state that has additional fee limits of its own. Medicare coverage is also limited to appropriate, medically necessary treatment—you can be denied coverage if Medicare does not believe your treatment was appropriate or necessary. If you disagree, you can appeal the decision; Medicare's claim denial decisions frequently are appealed, often successfully. Instructions for how to appeal are enclosed with the form that denies your claim.

Everyone eligible for Medicare automatically receives Part A coverage. But Part B coverage is optional; you have to pay extra for it and can only sign up for it during specific enrollment periods. You should sign up for Medicare during the three months before you reach 65 to avoid any waiting period for Part B coverage.

A major part of your retirement planning should include cost projections for health care expenses after you reach age 65. You will need to build these projections into your budget. However, these may be the toughest cost projections you will ever have to make in planning your retirement, for two reasons:

1. The Medicare program that brings health care insurance to everyone when they reach the age of 65, as previously noted, is headed for bankruptcy, and its fate is presently in the hands of politicians. Therefore, one can not project exactly how things will turn out. But the best estimates available indicate that the better off you are, the more you will have to pay. Deductibles would most likely be raised for those with incomes above, say, $70,000 a year, and so would premiums and co-payments.

2. Employers almost always retain the right to modify or cancel medical benefits for retirees. They can and do make adjustments—almost always in their favor—all the time. For example, most large employers either have changed their retiree medical plans in recent years or plan to do so very soon, according to a major benefits survey.

You will be able to deal with some, but not all, of these concerns through Medigap insurance. Medigap insurance is private insurers' answer to bridging the gap between what the U.S. government's Medicare insurance system is willing to pay and what medical care actually costs. Usually you pay a premium, over and above Medicare, to a private insurance company for Medigap coverage. Accordingly, federal law currently provides that insurance companies can offer up to 10 standard Medigap policies, ranging from one that pays only the basic deductibles to one that covers everything from preventive drugs to skilled nursing care. Premiums cover a wide spectrum, too, depending on your age as well as your coverage. Expect to pay anywhere from $450 to more than $1,800 a year. According to the experts, you should sign up for Medigap at age 65 when Medicare kicks in. Be sure to check how much it pays per day for hospital room and board, and the maximum it will pay for each illness or injury.

There are a couple of ways to lower your Medicare-Medigap bill, but you have to give up some flexibility in the bargain: One is Medicare Select, a program that is available in more than a dozen states and will probably be expanded. Under Medicare Select, you buy a supplemental policy that is less expensive than ordinary Medigap policies. But in exchange for the price break, you have to agree to use only those doctors and hospitals that are members of the plan's formal network. If you visit a doctor or hospital outside the network, you are responsible for paying any deductibles or co-payments under Medicare.

The other option is to join an HMO that has agreed to take Medicare patients. You may have to pay a premium in addition to your regular Medicare Part B premium. In some cases, joining the HMO brings you a wider range of services plus an emphasis on prevention. But you also have to pay in full for any services you use that are outside the HMO. You will not even get the usual 80% payment from Medicare, because Medicare pays HMO for taking you in. If you do not like the HMO, you have the option of dropping out with a month's notice.

On a lighter note, some employers provide their retirees with continued coverage even after Medicare starts, in effect giving you very inexpensive Medigap coverage. Those who are so generous often hold out this benefit for you and your spouse, even allowing the spouse to keep the coverage after you death on the understanding that it would be very expensive for him or her to switch to a standard Medigap policy at that late date. If you work for a large employer, find out if you will get this coverage; if so, you can omit provision for full Medigap premiums later on. If you do not have this coverage, you might take the opportunity to bargain with your employer to get it.

Private Disability Insurance

Disability income insurance is important protection for nearly all working people. Although long-term care protection (discussed next in this chapter) is invaluable, in my opinion, disability insurance is the single most important piece of protection an individual can have. Unfortunately, most people do not realize just how vital it is. Ask yourself, what would happen if you were no longer able to provide for yourself or your family? What would you do? How would you pay your bills? Although many uninformed people consider disability insurance a waste of money, they quickly change their minds when tragedy strikes and they are left alone to pick up the pieces.

While most Americans insure their lives and material assets like their homes, cars, etc., many overlook the need to protect their most valuable asset—*their ability to earn an income.* While your house, car, stocks, business, and other possessions may seem more important, it is your ability to earn an income that makes your lifestyle possible. Whether you are single or married, you need to protect your income. For single parents supporting a child, this need is especially important. Regardless of your situation, it's important to consider the consequences should you suffer an injury or illness and become unable to work.

Insurance claims studies indicate that the probability of becoming disabled for 90 days or longer are much greater than dying during one's work years. Because of modern medicine, the diseases which used to kill people now disable us. For the most part, if a person is disabled for six months, the probability is that the person will be disabled for 4-5 years or longer. However, statistics show that fewer than 20% of all working people have a personally-owned disability income policy, insuring their incomes against the threat of an unexpected accident or illness.

Sources of protection—Generally, there are five sources of disability insurance: the State, Workman's Compensation, the Federal Government, your Employer, and Individually Purchased Insurance. All states generally offer Workman's Compensation benefits that will provide some level of benefits for injuries sustained on the job. But unfortunately, most disabilities occur outside the workplace.

At present, only four states and one territory cover their employees with disability benefits for injuries and illnesses occurring outside the workplace—California, New York, Hawaii, New Jersey, Rhode Island, and Puerto Rico. Maximum weekly benefit amounts, total amount of benefits available, and waiting periods vary from state to state.

The federal government through the Social Security Administration provides long-term disability benefits. The benefits usually max out at approximately $1,300 a month ($2,000 if you have two or more children), have long elimination periods (5 months), and stringent criteria for eligibility (e.g. Social Security requires that you be unable to perform the duties of *any* occupation).

Some employers do offer some form of disability insurance for their employees. However, you should check the type of coverage from your employer very carefully. The employer's policy may not be just what you need. In this case, you will probably want to supplement the employer's policy with an individual policy of your own.

If a policy is not offered to you at your place of employment, and most are not, then you need to look into getting your own private disability policy to cover you sufficiently. By *sufficiently* I mean a policy that covers your monthly living expenses (including savings for retirement). Generally, there is a period of time (elimination period) you must be disabled before you can begin collecting disability payments from the insurance company. This period may vary. I recommend an elimination period of 60 days from the inception of the disability.

Working the odds—As I stated earlier, the odds of a person having a disabling injury or illness before the age of 65 is significantly higher than the odds of dying (see table below). However most people don't insure themselves against a disabling occurrence beyond what their employer, state government and federal government do.

The odds of having at least one disability lasting 90 days or more prior to age 65

Age	Ratio	Percentage
20	4 out of 5	80%
25	3 out of 4	75%
30	7 out of 10	70%
35	2 out of 3	67%
40	2 out of 3	67%
45	1 out of 2	50%
50	1 out of 2	50%
55	1 out of 3	33%
60	1 out of 5	20%

If you have assets—or future income—to protect, you can not afford to overlook disability insurance. Having it can give you peace of mind and relieve stress.

The premiums for a disability policy are based on age, sex, occupation, and income. Insurance companies will allow an individual to take out a policy covering anywhere from about 50% to 70% of the lost monthly income. And keep this in mind. If your employer pays your disability insurance, you pay tax on that income. If you pay for the disability insurance yourself, the disability income is tax-free. For this reason, it may be beneficial to ask your employer if you can trade their disability coverage for cash in order to buy your own coverage. If you can, I recommend doing this.

Most of the time, insurance companies either consider you good enough to work or not good enough. You are either disabled or not disabled. However, since most of us do not live in Insurance World, we live on the planet earth, you and I know that many times one can return to work part-time and ease back into the swing of things. The insured can add on what is called a *Residual Rider*. It may add about 20% to the cost of the policy; and therefore, it might not be worth it to you. However, it will allow you to return to work part-time, collect part of your salary, and receive a partial disability payment.

Many policies will allow the insured to increase to monthly coverage annually for the first two to four years for up to 10% without getting a new physical. The cost of the premium will increase. But you will only be paying extra for the added coverage. Not for a whole new policy. After this period of time, the insurance company will also allow you to increase the amount of the new coverage, but you may have to take another physical examination. However, if your policy is a *guaranteed future insurability*, you will be able to increase the policy every time you get a raise. But be prepared to pay extra every time the policy limits are increased. Many policies have a COLA (cost of living) rider. With cost of living increases, you can increase the coverage with no additional physicals.

Always get a policy which is guaranteed renewable. Otherwise, the insurance company can cancel the policy. If it is guaranteed renewable, the only reason for cancellation is non payment of the premium. Also, try to get a policy which is noncancelable. This means that the premium rate stated on the policy can never change.

Tips for purchasing disability insurance—Many insurance companies either have stopped offering disability insurance altogether, only offering coverage in selected states (the incidence of fraud and insurance losses are dramatically higher in some states), or have increased the premiums dramatically. You should shop for a private disability policy as carefully as you would look for a new car. Research thoroughly all policies you consider. As I have already stated, premiums are based on the amount of monthly benefit and a variety of other factors, including how soon benefit payments start after you become disabled, how long benefits will continue, and how disability is defined by the policy. When purchasing disability insurance keep the following in mind:

- **Benefit Period**—Disability policies are generally offered in two forms, one that covers short-term disabilities (five years or less), and one that covers long-term disabilities (age 65 or lifetime). Obviously the longer time period you choose for your benefit period the higher the cost of the premium.

- **Waiting Period**—You can reduce the cost of your policy by increasing the length of the waiting period, also called the elimination period. The waiting period is how long you must be disabled before you start collecting your disability benefits.

- **Residual Benefit**—A great way to protect yourself against partial disabilities, and disincentives to work. A residual benefit will pay you the difference between your pre-disability income and post-disability income after you have experienced disability. It is also less expensive than an own-occupation disability policy.

- **Own-Occupation**—An own-occupation disability policy pays benefits if you are unable to work at the occupation you presently have. It is the most expensive type of disability policy.

- **Taxation**—If you pay the premiums on your disability policy your benefits are tax-free.

- **Group Disability**—If you have the option of obtaining disability insurance through your employer, do so. It is usually 20%-30% less expensive than trying to purchase a policy on your own.

Questions and Answers

1. **If I cannot afford to buy both life insurance and disability insurance, which coverage should I buy?**—Both life and disability insurance are important and vital to the financial security of most individuals. In some instances, however, financial resources are inadequate to purchase the needed amounts of both types of insurance. Generally speaking, throughout the typical working lifetime (e.g. ages 20-65), the probability of an individual suffering a major disability (e.g. a disability lasting 3 months or longer) is considerably greater that the likelihood of dying. The probability of a young worker suffering a major disability is as much as 6 (or more) times the probability of dying; the multiple is still 2 or more even at the higher working ages. These relative probabilities would suggest that the purchase of disability income insurance is a more important purchase than is the purchase of life insurance. Another factor supporting this view is that, in the case of disability, total expenses of the family unit will also be higher due to the costs of caring for the disabled worker.

2. **How much disability insurance should I own?**—The recommended amount of disability income insurance generally ranges from 60-70 percent of pretax income. The applicable percentage for higher-income persons is usually somewhat lower than the percentage recommended for lower-income individuals, due primarily to differences in income taxes. Amounts considerably less than full replacement of earnings are recommended due to a reduction in income taxes and decreases in commuting and other work-related costs that are likely to occur in the event of disability.

On the other hand, medical, rehabilitation and certain other expenses are often higher for disabled individuals creating a need for larger amounts of replacement income. In determining how much disability income insurance to buy, any benefits payable under Workers' Compensation, Social Security, and employer-provided disability benefits under pension or group insurance plans should also be considered. Whether the disability benefits themselves are subject to income taxation should also be factored into this determination. Normally, the assistance of an insurance professional should be sought in making this determination.

3. **What type of disability income insurance is best—insurance covering short-term disabilities only or policies that cover long-term disabilities?**—Assuming that only one of these types of disability insurance products will be purchased, sound risk management principles would suggest the purchase of long-term disability (LTD) insurance. LTD insurance protects the insured against disabilities that may last many years, or even a lifetime, and thus provides protection against large losses of a potentially catastrophic magnitude. Although long-term disabilities occur less frequently than disabilities of a relatively short duration (e.g. several weeks or even a few months), the loss of income for a short duration can be more easily absorbed by the family unit than can an income loss that lasts for several years or longer.

4.   What are the primary differences between short-term disability (STD) and long-term disability (LTD) insurance policies?—These two types of insurance coverage differ most importantly in terms of the length of the elimination (waiting) period, the length of the maximum benefit period, coordination of the benefits payable under the policy with benefits payable under social insurance programs (e.g. Social Security and Workers' Compensation), and the "definition of disability" incorporated into the contract language.

5.   What is an elimination, or waiting, period and how does its definition differ between STD and LTD insurance policies?—The elimination, or waiting, period in disability insurance refers to the length of time between the onset of a qualifying disability and the point in time when benefits under the disability insurance policy first become payable. In STD plans, waiting periods may range from 0 days to 3, 7, 10 or 14 days, depending on the specific insurance policy and the cause of disability. Disabilities resulting from accidents often are subject to shorter elimination periods (e.g., 3 or 7 days) than are disabilities caused by sickness. In LTD plans, elimination periods generally range from 3 to 6 months, or longer, for disabilities arising from both accidents and illnesses.

6.   What is a maximum benefit period and how does its definition differ between STD and LTD insurance policies?—The maximum benefit period in disability income insurance refers to the maximum length of time during which benefits will be payable to an insured with an ongoing, qualifying disability. By definition, STD insurance policies are those policies whose maximum benefit period does not exceed two years (24 months) in length. Typically, however, STD insurance provides coverage for benefit periods lasting a maximum of 13 or 26 weeks. In contrast, LTD insurance policies typically provide benefits (contingent on continued disability, of course) for as long as 5 years, to age 65 or 70, or even lifetime.

7.   What types of *definitions of disability* are commonly included in STD and LTD insurance policies?—Some disability income insurance contracts provide coverage only for total and permanent disabilities. Others provide coverage for total and permanent disabilities, partial disabilities, and temporary disabilities. Some policies providing partial disability coverage require that the partial disability be proceeded by a period of total disability. Since these terms are often confusing, with their definitions differing somewhat from one policy to the next, it is recommended that those insured discuss this issue at length with their insurance professional.

8.   In addition to coverage of partial or total disabilities and temporary or permanent disabilities, what other aspects of a definition of disability are important to consider when purchasing disability income insurance?—The way in which a disability is defined, especially as it relates to the inability of the insured to perform a particular occupation, is exceedingly important. Several insurers market policies that define total disability in terms of the inability of the insured to perform the usual and customary duties of his or her "own occupation"—the job the insured was doing at the time of the injury or onset of sickness. Other policies define total disability in terms of the inability to perform the regular duties of "any occupation." This is often defined as a job for which the insured has the necessary skills and training and, possibly, at a salary commensurate with the one in which the insured was employed at the time of the incident. The "own occupation" definition is more liberal to the insured and is frequently recommended over an "any occupation" definition. Sometimes a "split definition" is used which incorporates an "own occupation" definition for an initial period (e.g. 2 years), followed by an "any occupation" definition thereafter.

9.   Are disability insurance policies available that do not express the eligibility for disability

benefits in terms of an occupational definition?—Some insurers market disability insurance policies that define disability not in terms of a particular occupation, but rather simply in terms of the amount of income actually lost. Under these contracts, if an insurable event occurs such as an accident or illness, then disability benefits are payable to the extent that the insured suffers a loss of income that exceeds a threshold amount, e.g. a loss of 20 percent or more of the individual's earnings prior to the happening of the insured event. When the threshold amount is exceeded, the policy pays a benefit that is based on the percentage of total prior earnings lost due to the disability.

10. Do all disability insurance policies cover losses arising from both accident and sickness?— No. Some policies cover only disabilities arising from an accidental injury, providing no coverage for disabilities caused by sickness. A careful reading of the contract is recommended to determine the extent of coverage provided under the disability insurance policy that you are considering purchasing. Sound risk management suggests the purchase of a policy that covers disabilities arising from either an accident or an illness.

11. What specific causes of disability, if any, are generally excluded from coverage in disability insurance contracts?—Generally, injuries that are intentionally self-inflicted or caused by war or an act of war are excluded. Disability policies may also include a preexisting conditions exclusion whose purpose is to exclude from coverage, during an initial period (e.g. the first one or two policy years), a disability arising from an undisclosed health condition that was both present within a prescribed time period prior to policy issuance and required medical treatment or otherwise caused symptoms that normally would require medical care. Through the military suspension provision, coverage under a disability insurance policy is suspended during any period that the insured is on active duty in the military.

12. The terms *noncancelable* and *guaranteed renewable* are often used when referring to disability income insurance policies. What do these terms imply, and how do they differ?—*Noncancelable* policies provide those insured with the right to renew their policies each year, typically to age 65, by the timely payment of the required premium. A guaranteed premium is stipulated in the contract and may not be changed by the insurer. During the noncancelable period, the insurer is precluded from canceling the contract or otherwise making any unilateral change in the policy benefits. Guaranteed renewable contracts also provide those insured with the right to renew their policies to age 65 (typically) through the timely payment of the premium. However, under guaranteed renewable policies, the insurer retains the right to change premiums if it does so for all those insured in the same rating class. The insurer is not permitted to cancel the policy or unilaterally amend the policy benefits during the period that the policy is guaranteed renewable. Further, under both types of contracts, the insurer is not permitted to increase the premiums, on a selective basis, only for those insured whose health status has deteriorated. Because of the premium guarantee feature, noncancelable policies may be somewhat more expensive than guaranteed renewable policies. In general, disability policies containing a guaranteed renewable or a noncancelable feature provide better protection to an insured, albeit possibly at a higher cost, than do conditionally renewable or other similar types of disability insurance policies that give the insurer a right to refuse to renew coverage for reasons stated in the policy (and typically also give the insurer the right to increase premiums and change benefits so long as these changes apply to all those insured in the same class).

13. What factors affect the premium cost for disability income insurance?—A number of contract features and options affect the premium cost for disability income insurance. Several of the more important factors are:

- The amount of weekly or monthly benefit purchased.

- The length of the elimination (waiting) period.

- The length of the maximum benefit period.

- Whether or not the disability insurance benefits are coordinated with social insurance benefits.

- The occupational class of the insured.

- the definition of disability.

- Whether the policy is noncancelable or guaranteed renewable.

14. How do the lengths of the waiting (elimination) period and the maximum benefit period affect the premium cost of disability insurance?—The elimination (waiting) period in disability income insurance serves the same purpose as a deductible in medical expense, automobile and other types of insurance. It eliminates initial, or *first-dollar*, benefits from coverage under the insurance policy. As such, longer waiting periods result in lower premiums. There is a similar, but opposite, relationship between varying maximum benefit periods and the premium cost for disability income insurance. As the length of the maximum benefit period increases, total premium cost also increases. When limited dollars are available to purchase disability income insurance, it is generally recommended that longer waiting periods be selected so that longer maximum benefit periods can be afforded. Of course, the amount of cash reserves available to the insured as a safety net should also be factored into the determination of the length of the waiting period that is selected.

15. Why is it frequently true that group long term disability (LTD) insurance purchased at work is less expensive than individually purchased LTD insurance?—There are a number of reasons why group LTD may be purchased by employees at a lower premium cost than what these same individuals can purchase on their own, away from their place of employment:

- An employer often contributes toward the premium cost of group LTD coverage, thereby reducing the out-of-pocket cost to employees.

- Group LTD plans almost always coordinate their benefits (i.e. plan benefits are reduced) with any disability benefits payable under Workers' Compensation or Social Security. In contrast, individual disability income insurance typically pays benefits in addition to any benefits payable under social insurance programs.

- Individual policies often contain a longer maximum benefit period, a noncancelable feature, a "cost-of-living" benefit rider, and an option to purchase additional insurance—expensive features not always found in group LTD policies

- Marketing and sales, administrative, underwriting and other expenses are usually lower for employer-provided group insurance than for insurance purchased individually from an agent.

16. What is the federal income tax treatment surrounding benefits received from a disability

insurance policy?—The answer to this question depends on who paid the insurance premiums. If the insured paid the premiums with after-tax dollars, then the disability benefits should be received income tax-free. In contrast, if an employer paid part or all of the premiums then an equivalent portion of the benefits are generally taxable to the insured (in this instance, however, an income tax credit may be available to the insured). In any event, your tax professional should be consulted with respect to the probable income tax treatment of any disability income coverage that you currently have or are contemplating purchasing.

Long-Term Care

Before we begin our discussion on long-term care (LTC), I would like you to take a close look at a few statistics.

- For a couple turning 65, there is a 70% chance that one of them will need long-term care.

- Over 50% of all people entering a care situation are penniless within one year.

- 97% of people over age 85 require assistance in the last year of life.

- 60% of people over 75 need long-term care—many stay in facilities for about 3 years.

- The average cost of LTC in a nursing home today is approximately $4,000 a month.

- The average cost of LTC in a nursing home thirty years from now is projected to be $13,000 a month.

- Singles are at risk because they are usually not with someone who can properly care for them. The same is true for wives, who tend to outlast their husbands by a seven-year average.

As you can see, most of us are going to need LTC in one form or another before we leave this precious eaarth. The growing population of elderly, particularly those over the age of 85, and the concomitant increase in chronic conditions has created a rising demand for LTC services in the United States. Combined with a health insurance industry which offers little financial protection for the costs of LTC and a health care reimbursement system that has fueled the demand for LTC, there remains a significant imbalance between the supply and demand for LTC insurance and care management programs. Now, more than ever, we must take a long hard look at the way the future health needs of our nation's elderly will be financed. Accordingly, it behooves us all to have a basic understanding of what LTC is and how it works.

What is LTC?—LTC refers to the bundle of non-medical services associated with caring for people who need assistance with daily living. These services can be performed either at an institution such as a nursing home, a care center, an assisted-living community, or in the residence of the person receiving the care. These services include skilled nursing care, interned nursing care, home health care, adult day care, assisted living and respite care.

More than 5 million Americans have significant physical limitations due to illness or disability. Approximately two-thirds of these individuals are older Americans. Millions of adults and a growing number of children need living assistance because of a health condition from birth or a chronic illness developed later in life. Since the number of Americans age 65 and older is projected to double by 2030, the number of people needing living assistance is expected to increase dramatically.

Since the mid-1980s, private insurers and the government have made various attempts either to create programs to ease the burden of LTC or to provide some form of insurance to relieve families of the high cost of such care. The average annual cost of nursing home care is about $4,000 a month, or $50,000 a year, and fewer than 20% of those that need LTC are able to cover the cost for just one spouse, let alone both. The reality is that most people just can not save enough to cover LTC expenses.

A demographic transition and demand for LTC—Currently, there are 31 million people in the United States who are over 65-years-old, with over three million of these individuals over 85 years of age. It is this latter group who are most in need of LTC services due to their higher incidence of chronic conditions. By 2020, the U.S. population over the age of 65 is projected to grow to 55 million while the population over the age of 85 is projected to increase by four times to over 13 million. As age increases, the need for LTC also increases. While approximately 3% of persons aged 65-69 will need LTC, approximately 5% of those aged 70-79 and 17% of those aged 80-84 will require LTC. For those aged 85 and older, more than one-third will require LTC. In aggregate, 42% of all individuals over the age of 65 will enter a nursing home in their lifetime.

Although most elderly persons are healthy, 7.3 million of them currently require LTC, with 1.5 million of these individuals already in nursing homes. The need for assistance with *activities of daily living (ADLs)*— an effective predictor of LTC utilization—also increases dramatically with age. For instance, nearly 13% of elderly aged 65-74 need assistance with ADLs, compared with 46% of elderly over the age of 85. Moreover, 10% of those over age 85 had severe limitations (requiring assistance with five or more ADLs), compared to 2% of those aged 65-74.

The fear and perceptions of aging are as real as the actual need for LTC services. Numerous studies of people over 50 have shown that the greatest single fear among the elderly is being sent to a nursing home. Older persons share an intense desire to retain independence, remain in their homes, and above all to avoid ending up as indigent, LTC residents of a nursing home. This is compounded by the fear of leaving a surviving spouse without adequate financial means of support, and of having to spend nearly all assets in order to qualify for public assistance for nursing home coverage.

The dismal thought of parents and in-laws growing old and becoming impoverished to pay for LTC places a tremendous burden on younger relatives who are functioning as working employees. To keep elders from losing their independence, their respect and their dignity, younger relatives will provide services to keep their elders in their own homes or in community-based residential facilities. Nearly 2 million working adults provide significant levels of unpaid care to elderly relatives who need help at home. In fact, over 80% of all LTC patients are individuals simply in need of assistance with everyday activities, rather than medical care.

Health care reimbursement—The restructuring of the U.S. health care system has added to the imbalance of the supply and demand for LTC insurance and management programs. Increased competition and the growth of managed acute-care companies has created continuous pressure for cost savings. This pressure, along with changes in technology, has created incentives to shorten hospital stays and to substitute hospital stays with less expensive providers of care. The effects of this substitution has been an increase in the demand for LTC services and a shift in costs to patients and their families, since costs for these services are often not reimbursable by Medicare or other health care benefit plans.

The absence of organized care management systems to assist patients and families needing chronic and LTC services leaves patients and their families with a greater emotional and physical burden. Since these individuals often end up having to make complex decisions about the most appropriate type of care and, because of the high costs, many end up providing much of the care themselves.

The cost of insurance for LTC—In 1997, LTC costs in the U.S. exceeded $121 billion. These costs are projected to grow to $225 billion by the year 2000. Currently, the government pays the majority of these costs, equaling $78 billion or 64% of the total, with Medicaid accounting for nearly 65% of all public dollars. Private sources paid the rest, about $43 billion, mostly as out-of-pocket spending by individuals and families. Private LTC insurance contributed only 0.2% of the total.

A lot of people think that they can rely completely on government programs like Medicaid and Medicare for help. Unfortunately, they can not. These programs can be hard to qualify for and they only provide limited coverage for LTC costs. For example, Medicare only pays for up to 100 days of nursing home care—and you have to be hospitalized before you can qualify for the benefits. The average length of a covered stay in 1997 was 27 days. Also, the facility must be a Medicare-approved skilled nursing home where registered nurses are on hand twenty-four hours a day, seven days a week. Only 1% of all the people in nursing homes today are in skilled nursing homes. The other 99% need custodial care, not skilled nursing care. Remember also that Medicare pays the full amount for only the first 20 days, after which you pay the first $81.50 a day. So, basically, Medicare does *not* cover any LTC, just short-term rehabilitation.

Medicare does cover some limited convalescent skilled nursing care and some limited home health care under restrictive, short-term conditions, but not for LTC. As I said, this short-term care is limited to 100 days, and to get it the following three conditions must be met:

1. You must have been in a hospital for at least three days immediately prior to entering the nursing facility. This eliminates most Alzheimer's and Parkinson's cases.

2. You must go into the facility for the same condition for which you were previously hospitalized, and it must be within thirty days of discharge.

3. You must be getting better each day. If you level off, Medicare stops paying.

In any case, Medicare, covers only Skilled Nursing care and does not cover Intermediate or Custodial care at all! The cold hard fact is that if you ever need long-term care, it will not be covered by Medicare. Period. You need LTC insurance. Medicare, HMO's and Medigap insurance do not pay for nursing home care for long-term stays.

With concern to Medicaid, only after an individual has spent down his or her life savings does Medicaid step in and help pay their LTC bill. Medicaid pays for nearly half of all nursing home care, but to receive this assistance you must meet federal poverty guidelines for income and assets. Simply put—it is welfare. As you can see, LTC can have a distressing effect on families—wiping out a lifetime of savings before a individual, spouse, parent or grandparent becomes eligible for Medicaid. For elderly married couples in particular, it can leave the well spouse without financial resources for their living expenses. And believe me, incidences like these are typical, not isolated, and they are on the rise. Between 2010 and 2030, over 77 million more Americans will turn 65 and become eligible for Medicare, and millions more will be forced to resort to Medicaid for their nursing home care. So what are your options for solving the LTC problem? Basically there are three:

1. Those who are wealthy can self-insure. I am referring to individuals with more than $1,000,000 to $1,500,000 in liquid assets, outside of real estate.

2. For those who are poor (broke with less than $2,500 in assets and very sick) Medicaid or medical welfare will cover the cost of LTC.

3. For those caught in the middle, Mr. and Mrs. Average America, private LTC insurance is the most viable option. LTC insurance is used more than any other kind of insurance, yet it is the kind of policy that way too few of us have. We will focus our remaining discussion here.

Purchasing LTC Insurance—LTC insurance covers a person *in conjunction* with Medicare or private health insurance. Generally speaking, anyone in reasonably good health up to age 99 can qualify. There are many conditions and maladies which can cause a person to become uninsurable at any age, so the best time to consider LTC coverage is when you are *healthy*. If you wait until you become ill, you not only risk being uninsurable, but you also will probably pay higher premiums.

Think of LTC insurance as another form of disability insurance. But, instead of covering the loss of income from a disability, it protects against the costs associated with disabilities. The biggest of those costs is nursing home care. And do not think that health insurance will help you out. There is not one health insurance policy in existence that covers LTC.

Under an LTC policy, you receive a daily benefit to cover the cost of a nursing home stay or skilled or custodial care in your home. Companies use one or more benefit triggers to determine eligibility for payment, and these may vary from policy to policy. Generally, your benefits are paid when you are unable to handle two or more activities of daily living such as bathing, continence, dressing, eating, toileting and transferring. A second trigger is *cognitive impairment*, or mental incapacity. You can usually receive benefits if you suffer a cognitive impairment such as Alzheimers disease.

Basically, there are two types of LTC insurance: comprehensive plans (those that cover care at all levels) and non-comprehensive plans (those that cover only home-health care or nursing-home care). Home-health care only plans cover care from nurses and therapists, as well as personal care from health aides and housekeepers provided in your own home. Nursing-home only plans provides a daily benefit to cover the cost of a stay in a skilled nursing facility. Comprehensive plans cover both Home-Health and Nursing-Home care as well as care in a community-based setting (Assisted Living).

The LTC benefit payments you receive depend on the plan you select. Of course, the cost of your coverage varies depending on the plan you choose. When you buy LTC insurance, you'll want to consider the following:

1. **Choose the best agent**—Realistically, you can not get all the answers you want until you eventually sit down with a licensed LTC insurance specialist. Sooner or later, you want a personal guide to help you through the LTC insurance maze. LTC insurance is complicated, and there are features which can be easily misunderstood. A knowledgeable, experienced specialist can be your greatest ally to help you gain a firm grasp and make informed choices. If an agent only works with *one* company, it is called *captive agent status*. This limits your choices, as no one company can fulfill every person's needs. Your agent should be an independent broker/consultant who can pick and choose from the best offerings available in the marketplace. In addition, your agent should be working directly with home office underwriters, so that you can be represented in the best possible light. This can save you up to 15% on your premiums. Also, your agent must be experienced in handling paperwork at claims time. This is when experience counts.

2. **Choose the best company that your health allows**—-There are well over 100 companies in the LTC insurance market. You want to be with the company that gives you the most coverage for an affordable price. An experienced broker can help you narrow the field down to the most appropriate choices. This ability is what makes your broker so valuable to you, and this is why you want to interview with a seasoned broker.

3. **Choose coverage that is custom-tailored to fit your situation**—LTC insurance coverage is based on a handful of choices you make regarding what you actually want. You may be able to get away with less than full coverage due to your asset base and income stream. The appropriate coverage for you will surface during the broker interview. Everyone's needs are different, and there are over 3,000 different prices that any one person could pay

for LTC insurance protection, depending on their coverage choices. Here are some common questions that inevitably arise when discussing LTC coverage:

- **How much does LTC insurance cost?**—Most people want to know the answer to that question right away. Unfortunately, no one can answer accurately because for every single person there can be over 3000 different premium levels, depending on how much and what kind of coverage you want. Premiums are based on three factors:

  - Age
  - Current Health
  - What features you design into the plan

LTC insurance plans have level premiums and are guaranteed renewable. That means your rate is the same for the life of the plan.

- **When is the best time to take out my coverage?**—After running the numbers, my opinion is that the best age to purchase LTC insurance is around age 54 or 55. Other advisors might tell you the best time to purchase coverage is right now. Why? The insurance is always cheaper the sooner you buy it. The amounts are set at a higher rate for each additional year of age at application. The rule of thumb is: the longer you wait, the more it will cost. When you apply, your lifetime annual payment amount is locked in—frozen—for the life of the policy. The payments remain the same until you enter a care center—then they cease altogether. From that point on the care is free. You save a bundle over the long term by getting a lower rate locked in at a younger age. The following chart illustrates this point:

Entry Age	Minimal Coverage[1]	Generous Coverage[2]
40	$ 75 / year	$ 1,400 / year
45	$ 95 / year	$ 1,500 / year
50	$ 100 / year	$ 1,600 / year
55	$ 125 / year	$ 1,800 / year
60	$ 170 / year	$ 2,700 / year
65	$ 240 / year	$ 3,500 / year
70	$ 375 / year	$ 5,100 / year
80	$ 625 / year	$ 8,000 / year
85	$1,085 / year	$12,100 / year

These figures are hypothetical, generalized, and do not reflect any one particular company.

[1] **Minimal Coverage**—Facility Only; $50/day Maximum Daily Benefit; 2-year Benefit Period; 90-day Elimination Period; No Inflation Protection Rider

[2] **Generous Coverage**—Includes Integrated Home Care @ 100%; $140 per day Maximum Daily Benefit; Lifetime Unlimited Benefit Period; 90-day Elimination Period; Inflation Protection Rider

Definitions

Options for the Setting of Care

- **Facility Only**—Covers you for care received in a licensed Assisted-Living or Skilled Nursing Facility, but not for care received in a non-licensed setting such as your home.

- **Integrated Home Care @100%**—Covers you for care received in a licensed Assisted-Living or Skilled Nursing Facility. In addition, covers you for care received in a non-licensed setting such as your home.

Benefit Payment Options

- **The Maximum Daily Benefit**—This is how much you want the policy to pay out each day.

- **The Elimination Period**—Sometimes called a deductible or waiting period, it is the period of time you choose to wait before you start receiving benefits. This is the number of days you are willing to pay for care out of your own pocket. For instance, benefits can begin 20, 30, 60, 90, or 100 days after you become eligible. Lower elimination periods usually increase the policy cost. Longer elimination periods means a lower premium to you.

- **The Benefit Period**—This is the length of time that you will receive benefits. How long do you want the company to pay out for your care—2, 3, 4, 5, or unlimited years?

- **Inflation Protection Rider**—This rider automatically increases your daily benefit amount each year to help keep up with increasing medical costs.

> 1. **How much benefit amount per day should I buy?**—LTC insurance coverage is bought in dollars-per-day payout amounts, in ten dollar increments. You can purchase from, say, $40/day to as much as, say, $250/day. That means when you are disabled, the company will reimburse you for the actual cost of care up to the benefit amount that you purchase. Any higher daily care charges must be born by you. But, if your cost of care is, say, $180/day, that does not exactly mean that you must insure for the entire $180/day amount—here is why: Hopefully, you will have a dependable lifetime income from your pension, your social security benefit, your 403(b), your IRA, and any other investments that will stream in whether you are sick or well. That income stream will most likely support your entire retirement lifestyle (living expenses, travel, entertainment, hobbies, etc.). But when you are incapacitated, you will no longer have to use your income to support the lifestyle extras, so you will be able to redirect that part of it to help co-pay for needed care costs. For example:

> | | |
> |---|---|
> | $65,700 | Annual cost of care ($180/day) |
> | -24,000 | Income (extras money) |
> | $41,700 | Amount to insure for (approximately $115/day) |

> So, if you are following the above example, you would only need to purchase approximately $115/day of LTC coverage, not $180.

2. How many benefit years are best for me?—The average stay in a skilled nursing facility is 2.8 years (8.0 years if you have Alzheimer's). But, that does not include any previous care received in-home or in an assisted-living facility. Policies will cover three years of care, five years of care, or Unlimited Lifetime of care. Lifetime costs the most, and 3 years costs the least. Your best bets are Unlimited Lifetime or 5 years. You do not want to take the chance of running out of payments midway.

3. Can I save money with deductibles?—Deductibles, called *elimination periods* or *waiting periods* come not in dollars, but in days. The company will lower your cost if you elect to foot your own bill for a period of time: 30, 60, 180, or 365 days. Of course, the choice is yours. You can pay part of it yourself, or have the company pick up the tab from day one.

4. Is in-home care cheaper than facility care?—No. 24-hour care can be prohibitively expensive. Just one 2-hour skilled nursing visit can cost $165. So, staying in-home can be done, but you must prepare to meet these costs through your insurance. The general consensus is—if you need more than five hours of care in your home each day, you should be located in a care center setting where your needs can be properly met.

5. What if I die and never use the LTC insurance I purchased?—It depends. Contingent upon your initial choices, a couple of things could happen:

- **Standard Option**—Just like auto, home, or accident insurance, if you do nott use it, you do not get any money back. Remember, you are paying to protect yourself against the worst-case situation. With this type of insurance you hope you never need it, but are glad to have it if you do.

- **Return of Premium Upon Death Option**—You can get your money back through a return-of-premium rider which pays back your heirs any premiums that were not paid out for your care. This option can raise the cost of the premium some 35%.

- **Survivorship Option**—A *survivorship* rider will free your spouse from further payments upon your death on a joint policy. With this option the survivor's coverage is automatically paid up upon the first death.

6. What does it take to qualify for benefits?—In order for you to qualify for your benefits, and have your insurance company start paying your LTC bills, you are going to have to prove to the company that you really need LTC. Any one of the three benefit triggers that follow must be present:

- The simplest qualification is *medical necessity*. This is where your doctor says you need LTC. Just make sure that your policy reads that it is your doctor who gets to decide if you need LTC and not someone you have never seen before who probably works for the insurance company.

• When you are not able to carry out certain *activities of daily living (ADLs)*. Generally, your benefits are paid when you are unable to handle two or more ADLs. These ADLs are: being able to bathe yourself, walk, use the toilet, dress yourself, feed yourself, be continent, and transfer yourself (get in and out of bed, chairs, etc. without help).

• A third trigger is *cognitive impairment*, or mental incapacity. You can usually receive benefits if you suffer a cognitive impairment such as Alzheimers' disease, where you can not think or act clearly on your own and therefore can not care for yourself. Again, doctors make the decision, so make sure it is your doctor who decides, not the insurance company's doctor.

7. **Can a good agent get me a better deal?**—Most definitely. An experienced specialist in the area of LTC coverage can help you make the right decisions for getting you the best coverage for the money. Plus, you can avoid any unnecessary over-insurance. The right advisor can help make this a painless planning decision that brings peace of mind for all concerned.

A Long-Term Care insurance Policy Checklist

When shopping for LTC insurance, there are many things to consider. Here are a few to ask about:

1. **Premium Costs**—Make a comparison.

2. **How long has the company been writing this insurance?**—Make sure the answer is 10 year, minimum. If the answer is 1, 2, or 3, forget them, they are still experimenting.

3. **In how many states are they currently selling LTC insurance?**—The only acceptable answer is: every state.

4. **What are your ratings from *AM Best, Moody's, Standard & Poor's*, and/or *Duff and Phelps*?**—Make sure as least two of the companies have awarded ratings that are AA or better.

5. **What is their history on payouts?**

6. **If there is a company history of premium increases for policyholders?**—Only accept a company with two times or fewer.

7. **What are the settings for covered care?**—Nursing home? Assisted-Living Facility?

8. **When can benefits start?**—Day 1, day 30, day 90, etc.? How does this fit with your current health insurance coverage?

9. **How do they treat pre-existing conditions?**

10. **What are their choices of daily maximum?**—Is it indexed for inflation? How is the indexing calculated?

11. **Under what conditions are premiums waived?**

12. **What benefits do they cover, besides basic nursing home costs?**

13. **What are the choices for how many days must you wait before coverage starts ?** (referred to as an elimination period or deductible)?

14. **What are their choices for payout/benefit years?**

15. **What other optional benefits are available? At what cost?**

A Problem That Needs All Our Attention

We Americans are not dealing with the LTC problem adequately. Despite rising costs and the probability of needing LTC, only 4% of Americans have purchased LTC insurance policies, with an annual growth rate of 36% between 1988 and the mid-1990s. This is not a result of a lack of purchasing power. One study estimates that by 2005, about 93% of all married couples and 60% of all single persons aged 65 and older would be able to buy LTC insurance with less than 5% of their cash income!

Do yourself and your loved ones a favor. See a LTC specialist and make arrangements to have you and your spouse protected. LTC insurance is a way for you to insure that you maintain control of your money, your independence, and your freedom to choose. You deserve to preserve your lifestyle as long as appropriate. You deserve to avoid being a burden on your children and/or spouse by relieving them of future caregiving hardships. Obtaining LTC insurance is the most responsible gesture you can make to those you love.

The first step is to look at available resources and get a basic understanding of the terms used by insurance companies and agents. One such resource is a free publication, *A Shopper's Guide to Long-Term Care Insurance*. It can be obtained by writing the Texas Department of Insurance, Distribution/MC 9999, P.O. Box 149104, Austin, TX 78714-9104. Also, for expert information over the Internet, you should visit the Mr. Long-Term Care's website at **www.mr-longtermcare.com/ltc/index.html.** There you will find a world of information pertaining to LTC that is informative, thorough, and up-to-date. As a matter of fact, at that website you will also find a personal endorsement by none other than the First Lady herself, Hillary Clinton. The site is definitely worth your time.

Finally, although I tried to present this material on protecting your assets in a matter-of-fact fashion, it is difficult for me to be dispassionate. With regard to LTC, I have seen, first hand, not only how financially draining a lack of LTC protection can be on the loved ones left to foot the bill, but also how guilt-ridden the patient can become thinking that he/she is responsible for the loss of finances. A lack of LTC protection is definitely a no-win situation for all family members involved. It usually leaves patients and their families with even greater emotional and physical burdens to bear.

CHAPTER FIVE

Profile of a Pre-Retiree

Most people wonder how they stack up financially with the rest of society. They want to know if they are on track with their savings or playing catch-up. This chapter will give you an insight into those very issues. But before I bombard you with statistics, I want to present you with a few important ideas to keep in mind.

Many people think that money is everything when it comes to retirement planning. Nothing could be further from the truth. While money is important, it is the lifestyle decisions and personality makeups that are really the most important concerns for your retirement years. Money is important in that it is needed in order to finance the lifestyle decisions you make, and for this reason it is important to plan as early as possible for funding the lifestyle you would like to lead.

Where you live, how and where you will vacation, what you will do with your spare time, and a realization of your participation in other interests all become extremely important issues during your retirement years. You may even decide to start a second business, enter a different career, or possibly make one of your hobbies or interests your remaining life's work. The whole point here is that a comfortable and successful retirement is about fulfillment of objectives and not just an accumulation of money. It is about enjoying your life to the fullest, which is based on your definition of happiness. Money is a tool to help you achieve these ends, but it is not the end itself.

As you think about retirement, ask yourself whether or not you are basing your own financial independence upon any pre-conceived notions that you may have picked up from the marketing sector of corporate America. If so, it is time to take an introspective look at yourself to see if you have what it takes to get on track, so that your retirement years can be lived to their fullest in the manner you wish, and not be constrained by the mistake(s) you made in previous years. Many people want to go in a certain direction, yet lack the intestinal fortitude to proceed. If that sounds like you, do not be ashamed. First and foremost, you must be comfortable with your financial plan. Spending sleepless nights worrying about your money only ends in disaster, both for you and your loved ones.

<u>Who are America's Pre-Retirees?</u>—In the financial world a favorite catchphrase of the media today is the pre-retirement generation. But who are America's pre-retirees? They are aged 45 to 59 and generally at the height of their achievement in work and family life. Three-quarters work: some in their own businesses (15 percent), most full-time for someone else (52 percent), and some part-time for someone else (10 percent). Some (6 percent) are in the labor force but currently unemployed. Only 7 percent have retired already, and 4 percent are not working because of a disability. 10 percent (20 percent of the women) are homemakers.

Three-quarters of the pre-retirees are either married (73 percent) or living as married (3 percent). Fourteen percent are separated or divorced; 5 percent are widowed; and 5 percent never married. More men than women in this age group are married (80 percent versus 66 percent). More whites and Hispanics (75 percent and 73 percent, respectively) are married than blacks (55 percent).

Most of the people who are married or living as married have a partner who also is in the pre-retirement age group. 15 percent have a partner younger than 45, and 10 percent have a partner aged 60 or older. Among 63 percent of these couples, both partners work. 28 percent of pre-retirees have children under the age of 18, and an additional 61 percent only have children aged 18 or older. Half of this group (52 percent) have grandchildren, while 11 percent have never had children of their own.

Seven in ten (70 percent) have at least one living parent, mother-in-law, or father-in-law, and almost half (45 percent) have attended college. Only 17 percent did not graduate from high school.

Eighty-four percent of the pre-retiree group own their own homes, while 14 percent rent. A fifth (21 percent) have been able to accumulate assets, not including the value of their resident, of at least $100,000. But 12 percent have less than $5,000 saved.

How Pre-Retirees Look at the Future—How does America's pre-retirement generation look at the future?—with much trepidation. Most feel that they are looking down a troubled road. People aged 45 to 59 approach the years ahead with anxiety, and few feel well-prepared financially for the transitions that await them: retiring from a job, putting a child through college, helping to support a parent. Only slightly more feel well-prepared to assume new caregiving responsibilities in the coming years for a grandchild or a sick parent. In fact, some are worried that they will lose their jobs and benefits before retirement and (as discussed before) virtually no one in this age group believes that the government can be relied upon to help with the challenges ahead. These are some of the not-so-surprising beliefs of this age group that were revealed in a recent nationwide survey.

Most of the pre-retirees have started to save for retirement, but few think their current course of saving and investment will lead to a very comfortable lifestyle in their leisure years. About one-third of them expect to depend mainly on Social Security.

Income is the single most important factor shaping this group's feelings about the future and their ability to plan ahead. Affluent people feel ready for retirement and confident they can meet the challenges ahead, but low-income people have been unable to save for retirement and are worried about their future.

A typology of pre-retirement age people classifies two in ten as secure and taking charge of their futures, plus another one in ten secure, despite having trouble planning for the future. At the other extreme, two in ten are insecure, living with few financial resources or worried about a job loss. The remaining half is in the middle, just getting by. Seven in ten people in this group (69 percent) have started to save for retirement. But many (28 percent) still have nothing put away. About nine in ten (88 percent) with incomes of at least $50,000 have saved something for retirement. But fewer than half (42 percent) with incomes below $30,000 have started to save.

Most (64 percent) of the pre-retirees expect retirement to pose either a very (24 percent) or somewhat (40 percent) serious problem. Only 10 percent believe that retirement income will pose no problem. Just over a quarter (27 percent) characterize themselves as well-prepared to face retirement in the next five or ten years.

Those with incomes under $30,000 feel unprepared (52 percent versus 20 percent for those with higher incomes) and worry that they will have a very serious income problem when they retire (44 percent versus 11 percent). People with incomes of at least $100,000 feel well-prepared (50 percent) and anticipate little problem with retirement income (65 percent *not too* or *not at all* serious).

Only 3 percent of the pre-retiree group believe that they can count on government to help solve the problems they anticipate facing as they approach retirement. About one-quarter (26 percent) think they can rely somewhat on government. But most are cynical, believing government can be relied on only a little (37 percent) or not at all (33 percent). About one-quarter (23 percent) of pre-retirement age workers (not including those who are self-employed) worry that they may lose their jobs within the next year or so.

Approximately half (47 percent) of pre-retirees have given financial help to a relative during the past five years. Most of this assistance came out of earnings (86 percent of those who gave some help), but some (37 percent) used savings or investments to provide the support. One-fifth (21 percent) of those who helped a relative did so by borrowing money or co-signing a loan.

About 28 percent of pre-retirement age adults have a child under the age of 18. Parents say they are most concerned about helping their children develop the right values (41 percent) and are somewhat less concerned about providing for their children's financial needs (31 percent) or staying healthy and having enough energy (19 percent). Eight in ten (80 percent) have an adult child aged 18 or older. About 29 percent have an adult child living with them.

Approximately 28 percent of people aged 45 to 59 currently are helping to pay for a child's college education. Most (54 percent) are using their current income, while one-third (32 percent) are drawing on their savings. About 9 percent have taken out a loan to help pay for college.

About 70 percent of pre-retirement age individuals have a parent or in-law still living who may become dependent on them for financial assistance, or need help at some point with the tasks of daily life. Only 18 percent feel well-prepared to give financial support to a parent or other older relative. Many (44 percent) feel they are somewhat prepared to do this, but 38 percent feel unprepared. Approximately one-quarter (27 percent) believe they are well-prepared to help an older relative deal with a major illness or disability. About 45 percent feel somewhat prepared, while 27 percent think they are unprepared to do this.

How Pre-Retirees Slot Their Savings—Recently, 1,300 working Americans of all ages were surveyed concerning their knowledge about retirement savings plans. The results showed that more than 85% do not know that 59 ½ is the age when they can withdraw money from their 401(k) or 403(b) without penalty. One quarter of respondents do not understand the precise meaning of the term "tax-deferred." More than half have never heard of "lump-sum" distributions. One in ten believe they do not have to pay taxes on the money they save in qualified retirement plans.

Another recent study revealed some surprising and useful differences in the way the pre-retirement population saves money both for general savings and as financial preparation for their retirement.

The study examined the kind of savings procedures followed by the pre-retirement population as well as the extent of their asset levels. Other factors weighed were the need this age group expressed toward getting financial planning information to guide their retirement savings, and their confidence that they would be able to achieve adequate retirement income. More than two out of three respondents (69 percent) reported that they had money saved for retirement. These individuals were part of a group with both similar and differing characteristics.

Concerning predictors of retirement savings, one's income level is by far the strongest. This includes the number of household incomes—whether it be one wage-earner or, if married, two incomes. The second greatest predictor was the general health of the wage-earner(s), followed by the level of confidence that one's retirement income would turn out to be adequate. The last predictor was an overall sense that one's present lives were satisfactory. There are, however, fairly distinct differences across income levels among those reporting money saved for retirement:

Upper-Income—(median income above $50,000) level individuals who had pre-retirement savings programs were likely to be older, single, have a higher education, good job stability, lower major expenses, and to be satisfied with their lives.

Middle-income—(median income between $20,000 and $50,000) level persons generally had an affinity for planning, good life satisfaction, a view that retirement savings is not a problem, and a feeling that they had adequate financial information.

Lower-Income—(median income under $20,000) level, health status and fear of job loss bringing the end of health insurance were the key factors predicting the presence of a retirement savings program.

The study also determined that there was a strong probability relationship between retirement savings and general savings. A number of general conclusions can be drawn from the survey:

- Income and health are more important influences on saving than not understanding the situation or having overconfidence in pensions and entitlements.

- There are distinct differences in savings attitudes between income groups.

- Married households with two wage-earners are more likely to have retirement savings plans.

- The need for more financial information is felt most acutely within the middle-income and mid-level education subgroups.

- Homeowners are more likely to have savings than renters, contrary to the notion that homeowners use equity build-up in lieu of savings.

- Participation in a contributory retirement plan is a major source of retirement income confidence.

- Among lower-income groups, individuals without retirement savings are likely to plan to retire later or even plan not to retire at all.

Life-Cycle Investing—No two investors are alike either in terms of personality or in their own financial situations. So why should their investment plans be similar? In fact, they should not be. Instead, an individual's investment plan should be tailored to his/her own personal investment profile. There are four basic aspects that compose an investor's personal investment profile:

- Your personal tolerance for risk.

- Return needs and whether current income or future growth needs to be emphasized.

- Time horizon.

- Tax exposure.

Risk—The amount of risk you are willing to take on is an extremely important factor to consider before making an investment because of the severe consequences of taking on too much risk. Risk is uncertainty—the possibility that the investment will not perform as expected. Properly assessing risk tolerance is designed to prevent an investor from making panic decisions and abandoning an investment plan mid-stream at the worst possible time. How can tolerance be measured? The best approach is to simply examine the worst-case scenario—a loss over a one-year period—and ask yourself whether you could stick with your investment plan in the face of such a loss.

Investors with a low tolerance for risk generally can sustain losses of no more than 5% over a one-year period. Investors with a moderate tolerance for risk can generally withstand losses of between 6% to 15% over a one-year period. Investors with a high tolerance for risk can generally withstand losses of 16% to 25% over one year. Where do you fall? More on that at the end of this chapter. Later on in this chapter you will have the opportunity to gauge your risk tolerance by taking a risk tolerance quiz.

Return Needs—Determining your return needs is important because you can not have all of everything—there is no investment that offers a high certain payout each year, protects your principal, and offers a high potential for growth at the same time. There are a number of trade-offs, based on the risk/return trade-off. First, the price for principal protection is lower returns, usually in the form of lower annual income. There is also a trade-off between income and growth: The more certain the annual payment, the less risky the investment, and therefore, the lower the potential return in the form of growth.

Time Horizon—The length of time you will or can be investing is important because it can directly affect your ability to reduce risk. Time diversification is most critical for volatile investments such as stocks, where prices fluctuate greatly over the short term, but are considerably smoothed over longer time periods.

If your time horizon is short, you can not effectively be diversified across different market environments. Longer time horizons allow you to take on greater risks—with a greater return potential—because some of that risk can be reduced through time diversification. How should time horizon be measured? Your time horizon starts with whenever your investment portfolio is implemented, and ends when you will need to take the money out of your investment portfolio.

If you are investing to save for a specific event, such as tuition payments or the purchase of a house, your time horizon is fairly easily measured—it ends when you need the cash. If you are investing to accumulate a sum for periodic withdrawals, such as during retirement, your time horizon is more difficult to quantify as you approach the time that withdrawals will begin.

What constitutes short, intermediate, and long-term time horizons? To diversify over various economic cycles, you must be invested through one complete economic cycle *at the very least*. In general, the economic cycle lasts about five years, which can be considered a long-term horizon. Conversely, if you need money within a year or two, you have a short-term horizon. A somewhat longer-term outlook—two to five years—constitutes an intermediate-term horizon.

Taxes—The bottom line to all investors is what is left after taxes. Investors who are in higher income tax brackets need to be concerned with the tax implications of their investments. Investors who are in lower income tax brackets need to worry less about the tax implications, but they also need to avoid securities that benefit high-tax-exposure investors, such as municipal bonds.

With the tax laws changing regularly, it is difficult to quantify what constitutes higher and lower tax exposure (perhaps the terms should be changed to *high* and *even higher*). However, if your annual income level puts you within the top federal income tax categories, you fall within the higher category.

The Taxpayer Relief Act of 1997 introduces significant new opportunities for individual investors across America, including significant tax cuts, and a number of targeted new tax incentives.

Clearly, different investors have different profiles. But the same individual will also have different profiles at different stages in life. For instance, your tolerance for risk may change as you get older, as you acquire more assets, and as you become more financially secure. When you approach retirement, your time horizon may shift and become a blend of long-term and medium-or short-term needs. The table below shows how an investor's profile may change. Of course, your own profile may be very different than this one; it may even fit one of those listed here, such as early retirement, even though you are in a different stage, such as early career.

Life Cycle Investing: An Example of a Changing Profile

	Early Career	Middle Career	Late Career	Early Retirement	Late Retirement
Risk Tolerance	High	High	Moderate	Moderate	Low
Return Needs	Growth	Growth	Growth	Growth/Income	Income
Time Horizons	Long	Long	Long	Short/Long	Short/Long
Tax Exposure	Lower	Higher	Higher	Lower	Lower

An effective investment plan is based on a balance between the risks you are willing to take on and the returns you need to achieve your goals. An understanding of your investment profile will help you achieve that balance.

The Personality Factor—Some of us are better than others when it comes to saving for retirement. Here is why—and what you can do if you think you are falling behind in your quest for future security. We Americans have been bombarded by messages urging us to take a closer look at whether we are saving enough for retirement, and many of us have risen to the challenge. But an extensive one-year study conducted in 1995 by the Public Agenda Foundation, a nonprofit, nonpartisan research and education group in New York City, concludes that an alarming number of people still underestimate their retirement needs. As a result, they are doing far less than they should to prepare for it, even though 60% of those surveyed agree that they themselves, not government or business, should be responsible for meeting their goals.

The study surveyed 1,100 nonretired Americans and 450 American leaders in such fields as government, media, and business. According to the results, 70% of those leaders say that future retirees will be worse off financially than those currently retired. These leaders worry that the proportion of elderly Americans in poverty will rise because of inadequate retirement savings and problems with the Social Security system. And further findings support that concern. Of those surveyed, about one-third have saved little or nothing for their retirement. For example, about two-thirds, or 68% say they could eat out less often and put the money they save toward retirement—but only 18% of them say they are likely to make that small sacrifice. In fact, lower-income people are more than twice as likely as higher-income people to cut back on vacation or travel to save for retirement.

Why are more Americans not acting on their concerns about retirement? After conducting focus groups with workers from various age ranges and income brackets, researchers have concluded that personality, or your personal savings profile, may be one barrier to saving for a comfortable retirement. The survey identified four savings profiles: *strugglers, planners, impulsives, and deniers.* Where you fit in these categories may influence your approach to retirement saving and ultimately determine your future financial security. The four savings profiles are described below, along with a savings suggestion for each of them:

Strugglers

Profile—According to the survey, strugglers are burdened with unpredictable financial expenses. They would like to save for retirement but believe they simply do not make enough money. And the survey found that those who feel that way are not necessarily lower-income individuals. In fact, many of those interviewed complained that they are overwhelmed by the financial demands of the moment—no matter what their savings profile or income bracket. "We're trying to save. But between day care, the mortgage, and car payment," said one man, "we're really just taking care of today."

Savings Suggestion—Often, strugglers fail to save anything for retirement. If you are in this category, perhaps the thought of how much you might need for retirement overwhelms you. Such thoughts, indeed, can be paralyzing. Let us face it, you will never have $200,000 to set aside all at once. You have to take it one small step at a time. You might begin, for example, by saving a mere 2% of your take-home pay by contributing to a 403(b). As your income rises, you can boost that percentage. If you receive, say, a $2,000 raise, you can direct a hefty percentage of it to savings without cutting into your current living standard.

Planners

Profile—According to the survey, planners have control of their finances. They are most likely to know where they spend their money and to have the discipline to save regularly for retirement. Such traits also allow planners to worry less than the other three groups about their futures and to feel more comfortable with the amount they are saving. In addition, planners tend to educate themselves on the rules of prudent investing. Nevertheless, only 26% of these planners are likely to choose investments that bring higher risk along with greater potential reward, so many may find their savings ultimately being eroded by inflation.

Savings Suggestion—The planners surveyed are not alone in their cautious approach to retirement investing. Indeed, according to a 1996 study by the Employee Benefits Research Institute, participants in such savings plans as 403(b)s and 401(k)s invest on average almost half (47%) of their contributions in Guaranteed Investment Contracts (GICs). But GICs, certificates of deposit, and other insured investments expose you to another risk—the chance that over time, your retirement savings will be unable to outpace the inevitable increases in the cost of living. Playing it safe is understandable, but you have to know which investments are truly prudent, given your goals. Many investors who put their retirement money in such supposedly low-risk investments as money market accounts do not realize that inflation can threaten their future security.

The solution for investors with goals that are ten years or more down the road may be to put a significant portion of retirement savings in such growth investments as stocks, or stock mutual funds. Over long periods, stocks or stock mutual funds tend to outpace inflation and other investments, such as bonds, by a significant margin—despite periodic stock-market slumps.

So in a retirement portfolio that is designed to support you in at least a decade from now, you probably can afford to ride out stock-market dips in pursuit of long-term gains. If you are leery of stocks and other growth investments, consider investing just a small portion of your holdings in stocks, or stock mutual funds, for now. You can increase the percentage once you become more comfortable with the investment.

Impulsives

Profile—Impulsives, notes the survey, are free spenders who admit they waste money on things they do not really need; they would rather enjoy today than worry about saving for tomorrow. Certainly some Americans who have trouble saving for retirement have limited means. But impulsives have trouble because they tend to be capricious and have difficulty controlling their spending. Our generation has made it so easy to buy. The technology in marketing has changed so much that you literally do not even have to leave your house anymore.

Savings suggestion—Scaling back spending can be tough once you have established spending patterns. To make it easier, earmark a portion of your salary for automatic-savings programs. That way, if the money does not appear in your paycheck, you are unlikely to spend it. For example, you may be able to have your employer automatically invest a percentage of your salary in a savings plan such as a 403(b). Or you can set up an automatic-investing program with a mutual-fund company that deducts money from your paycheck or bank account and deposits it in the investment of you choice. Remember, though, that periodic investment plans do not assure a profit or protect against a loss.

Budgeting also helps—although admittedly many in this category may find such an exercise contrary to their natures. But simply tracking your spending might help you begin to make informed decisions about future spending.

Deniers

Profile—Deniers refuse to worry about retirement, let alone take steps to plan for it. They want to believe that the future will take care of itself. Deniers are also more likely than those with other savings profiles to believe that money for retirement will come from sources other than themselves. Deniers may, in fact, be overestimating the amount they will get from Social Security and their standard retirement plans, and underestimating their future income needs. Social Security and pension benefits make up only 20% to 40% of the total yearly income for today's average retired American. For teachers, that figure averages closer to 60%. The rest comes from personal savings. Remember, as discussed earlier, to maintain current standards of living, many financial planners suggest that workers will need 69% to 80% of their current income—a sum that Social Security alone could never provide.

Savings suggestion—If you are currently in denial, perhaps the key to getting started is to contemplate the consequences of deferring saving for retirement indefinitely. I have illustrated several examples earlier in the manual as to how a nominal sum of money can turn into a significant sum, but one more example might drive that point home even further. Consider a person who invests $2,000 annually in a 403(b) for *only eight years,* beginning at age 21. If that money remains untouched, and grows at a 10% annual rate, it will amount to approximately $800,000 by the time the saver reaches age 65. Imagine, a $16,000 investment turning into almost $800,000!!! By contrast, if that same person waits until age 29 to begin saving $2,000 a year and continued making contributions until age 65 (a total contribution of $72,000), only approximately $680,000 will accumulate—a difference of more than $120,000, or two to three years' worth of income for a middle-class household. Still, by a denier's standards, even the hypothetical 29-year old late bloomer will be accumulating a comparatively comfortable nest egg, given those hypothetical returns.

Many people do not focus on retirement because they have no sense of immediacy. When you realize the cost of waiting 10, 20, or 30 years, perhaps you will be able to see the importance of starting as early as possible. Changing behavior based on ingrained personality traits may seem like a tall order—but it is by no means impossible. The best way for individuals to alter their approach to financial issues is by making incremental changes. For example, rent an economy car rather than a luxury model on your next vacation. For more examples, see the suggestions that are offered in the chapter entitled *Sources of Additional Funding*. Once you have made such adjustments a few times, you will realize how the money you can save will affect your future. Eventually, you can significantly change your lifestyle.

A slow but steady approach to creating better savings and investment habits can be the key to successful retirement planning, which does not mean the task is easy. As stated several times earlier, the future of Social Security is uncertain, at best. Although most teachers will have a pension that will guarantee them a predictable income for life, it will still fall far short of the mark. Still, retirement planning is not as complicated as some think. Often, the hardest part is getting started. Begin with small steps, and the goal will seem less formidable.

Can You Take the Heat?—I mentioned above that we would be taking a closer look at risk. How you allocate your assets will be greatly affected by how much risk you are willing to take. Once again, your personality factor comes into play here. As stated earlier, at the end of this chapter is a risk tolerance test to see how well you might handle it. But first, some additional information to consider.

You know you can not avoid risk. But you can understand it and look for ways to manage it to your advantage. That is what you will need to do, to be able to *comfortably* take appropriate risks in order to increase your odds of achieving your objectives. Sometimes it will be more difficult to stay the course—especially during intemperate markets. But the markets have never been dead calm, and likely never will be. The result is that you need to assess investment risks in relation to their potential rewards, and in terms of your overall portfolio. That is the best way to avoid the losses that uncertainty can yield, and to maintain your prime directive: to invest in a better future for yourself.

Managing risk is only partially possible—no matter what some experts would like you to believe—but it is still worth trying to do. Many experts state that investing is a game of nerves. The following will help ensure that you have covered some of the risk-related bases that can arise unexpectedly, leaving one or more of your investments vulnerable to an unwanted degree of new risk, or threatening your conviction in an investment even though that risk has not fundamentally changed:

- **Knowing past performance**—Even if you do not have the resources to find or calculate a *beta* or *alpha,* chances are you can locate a security's or fund's past performance and get a relative sense of how it has performed over time—in good and bad markets, economic environments, and industry cycles. Doing so will help you avoid investments which have performed poorly on a consistent basis (a risk not worth taking) and, hopefully, find some better performers which, over time, have provided a market-beating return.

- **Understanding how the performance was derived**—Some securities may have a spectacular record for a few months, one year, maybe even a bit longer. But, unless they have consistently done so over 3 or more years, chances are they took substantially more risk than their peers to deliver the wide margin of performance-related difference.

- **Finding out any significant changes in the economy**—Market, industry and the company (if it is a fund, such a change could be a new manager). While subsequent chapters will help you discern these qualities, it is worth keeping in mind that changes in any of the above categories will necessitate a review of the individual risks that may be increased (or decreased) as a result.

- **Reviewing your objectives**—If your objectives change, and your time frame for achieving them changes, then you have injected a degree of risk into your overall investment plan that did not exist when you put your portfolio together. Chances are you will need to review your portfolio in light of the changes and the risks they bring to your portfolio.

- **Reviewing your portfolio's risk**—Each security or fund in your portfolio has a degree of risk which, when combined with the other securities or funds in the portfolio, creates an average risk of your overall mix. You want to be sure that this risk remains in line with your level of tolerance and ability to manage it.

- **Determining volatility**—What is volatility? It is simply the uncertainty of an investment's return. Remember standard deviation? By convention, volatility is usually expressed as the standard deviation of the investment's past 36 months of monthly total returns.

Relative volatility is simply the fund's standard deviation divided by the standard deviation of the S&P 500 index (the most common index of larger-cap US stock market performance) for the same period. So the S&P 500 has a relative volatility of 1.00, and aggressive stock funds have relative volatilities of somewhat greater than 1.00.

The more commonly used statistic called *beta* is a number always the same as or less than the relative volatility, since beta is a narrower measure reflecting only that part of an investment's risk due to movements in the broader stock market. For most diversified US stock funds, beta is close to relative volatility and is thus a fairly meaningful and useful measure of risk, but for specialized areas (e.g., gold funds) where returns are largely independent of the rest of the US stock market, beta may be quite low whereas total risk (and relative volatility) are still quite high.

Relative volatility and beta sound pretty complex, but they are really pretty easy to understand. For example, a stock fund with a relative volatility of 1.45 is 45% more volatile than the market benchmark (the S&P 500), and a fund with a relative volatility of 0.85 is 15% less volatile.

Calculating a fund's standard deviation or beta takes some doing (you need 36 months of returns for the fund and for the *S&P 500 index*, and a good spreadsheet program), but why bother? There are several sources which provide such information for stock funds and/or stocks. For example, almost all monthly investment newsletter subscriptions provide this information. Also, companies like *Morningstar* and *Value Line* provide the same information, plus a lot more. The better deal is to log on to one of the hundreds of financial websites on the Internet which provide the information you need for free.

The bottom line when it comes to taking on risk is that risk for risk's sake alone is seldom worth your while. But risk in relation to a return that is reasonable (relative to your objectives) is always worth pursuing. If you are going to remain in control of your investments, you will have to learn to handle the risks involved in investing. While this may sound trite, the truth is that too many savers are either swayed by their risk-aversion to avoid investing altogether (which leaves their money prone to the damage inflation can do), or perhaps more commonly, too many investors are enticed by recent sky-high returns on a fund, or the limitless heights promised by the arrival of a brand-new stock or stock fund.

Sure, there is the middle ground of investors who have made the transition from saving into investing, who have not over-committed themselves to extremely risky types of investments. Chances are, that is where you will find yourself. But the majority of investors who are new to the market have not experienced a full market cycle—from good, to bad, to good again. More than any other factor, an investor's risk tolerance is put to the test by a protracted down market. In a down market, almost all securities are affected, although some are certainly more affected than others. That is why investors who want to build a relatively risk-average portfolio select defensive stocks, or funds that invest in them. For most investors, however, your best defense is a solid offense of growth-oriented stocks. Why? Time is on your side—time enough, that is to weather a market downturn and ride the following upswing.

Not all tests are severe. You might find yourself being tested by one or a handful of investments that you thought were sure things only a matter of months or weeks ago. What made you change your mind? Chances are it had something to do with a drop in the stock's or fund's performance. What made you select the investment to begin with? Chances are, if it was a fund, past performance played a decisive role in your decision-making. The unexpected drop in performance simply serves to underline the way risk adheres to performance.

In fact, risk is simply a measure of how consistent and predictable a stock's or fund's returns are. Does a stock fund deliver similar returns from month to month, or do they fluctuate wildly? Of course, as long as the up periods last longer and/or are substantially stronger than the down-ticks, a risky investment like a small company stock fund can prove to be more rewarding than a less volatile large-cap growth fund (of course, the reverse can be true, also), and either one is very likely to outperform a safe bond or money market in the long run.

So why is everyone not investing in small-caps? For one thing, small company stocks are most appropriate (in large doses) for younger investors precisely because of their volatility. The older you get, the more defensive of your principal you will become; but for now, you want to focus on investments that build your principal. For another thing, the intemperate nature of small company stocks increases the risk that an investor in them will sell in a down market (the worst time to get out—unless something has fundamentally changed with the fund itself). If you have done your homework, then chances are the reasons you bought the stock or fund in the first place remain valid enough for you to hold onto it. Do not panic. Do not sell during a steep down-draft. Learn to tolerate risk—by testing your risk tolerance and matching investments to your understanding of the risks involved.

What is your level of risk tolerance? OK, it is not exactly a scientific experiment, but the following risk quiz is designed to help you gauge your risk tolerance, as well as your ability to take the right kinds of risks—in life and when it comes to investing. What does one have to do with the other? Chances are you are already somewhat familiar with your risk-taking skills and desires when it comes to such things as driving a car—speeding or not, lane changing or not, driving on fumes, or never letting the gauge drop below half a tank. Answer the following 23 questions as honestly as possible, then score yourself with the answers that follow.

1. Would you ever consider attempting a sport like bungee-jumping or parachuting?

    A. yes   **B.** no   **C.** maybe

2. Have you ever decided to do something major without knowing the potential consequences?

    A. yes   **B.** no   **C.** almost

79

3. Have you traveled abroad?

    A. yes   **B.** no

4. Would you go to an urban ATM machine at night?

    A. yes   **B.** no   **C.** maybe

5. Without looking at the top ten companies one of your funds invests in, can you name:

    A. all 10   **B.** more than 5   **C.** any   **D.** zero

6. How often do you check the air pressure in your tires?

    A. regularly   **B.** sometimes   **C.** never

7. If the pilot light in a gas stove is not working, do you:

    A. light it   **B.** stand by while someone lights it for you   **C.** leave the house

8. If you had to rank your current investments from most to least risky, your grade would be a(an):

    A. A+   **B.** B   **C.** C   **D.** F

9. Does the probability of losing 10% or more of your total invested savings make you:

    A. not want to invest   **B.** invest a modest amount   **C.** ignore short-term dips

10. If you inherited a lump sum of money, say $25,000, would you:

    A. invest it all at once   **B.** gradually invest it   **C.** put it in a CD

11. Do you feel more comfortable when:

    A. you are in total control   **B.** sharing decisions   **C.** being told what to do

12. Would you risk everything for a potentially huge return?

    A. yes   **B.** no   **C.** maybe

13. Which strategy suits you best?

    A. taking your time to get to trust someone   **B.** trusting someone before you
                    C. trusting no one   know them

14. Are you easily influenced by others when it comes to making decisions about your well-being?

    A. yes   **B.** no   **C.** sometimes

15. How often do you pretend to know something—but really do not?

               A. frequently   **B.** occasionally   **C.** almost never

16. You would rather:

    A. impress your friends   **B.** impress yourself   **C.** impress your best friend or spouse

17. When you were applying for your latest job did you:

    A. tell everyone you thought you would get it   **B.** tell only a handful of people
          C. keep it to yourself, until you actually got it

18. If you had to rate the riskiest thing you have ever done, compared to the greatest risk incurred by most people, on a scale from 10 (being the most risky) to 1 (being the least risky) would you rate yourself a:

             A. 10   **B.** 7   **C.** 5   **D.** 3   **E.** 1

19. If you were not federally guaranteed to get all your money out of the bank account it is now in, would you be less inclined to keep it in that bank account?

    A. yes   **B.** no   **C.** keep only the amount you were guaranteed to get back

20. In general you think that compared to the stock market, banks are:

    A. safer places to keep your money   **B.** better places to keep your money
          C. safer and better   **D.** safer, but not necessarily better

21. When you hear about the stock market you think it is:

          A. too risky to invest in   **B.** too risky and too expensive
          C. not too risky, but too expensive   **D.** worth the risks

22. When taking a trip by plane, you check to ensure you have your ticket:

          A. once   **B.** twice   **C.** three times   **D.** more

23. When it comes to long-term commitments you would say that you are:

    A. unshakable   **B.** mostly committed   **C.** susceptible to change

SCORECARD

	A	B	C	D	E			A	B	C	D	E			A	B	C	D	E
1.	2	0	1				9.	0	1	2				17.	0	1	2		
2.	2	0	1				10.	2	1	0				18.	2	2	1	0	0
3.	2	0					11.	2	1	0				19.	1	0	2		
4.	2	0	1				12.	2	0	1				20.	2	0	0	3	
5.	4	2	1	0			13.	2	0	0				21.	0	1	2	3	
6.	0	1	2				14.	0	2	1				22.	2	2	1	0	
7.	2	1	0				15.	0	1	2				23.	1	2	1		
8.	3	2	1	0			16.	1	3	2									

40-plus—You are a well-rehearsed risk-taker who knows how to set reasonable limits in accordance with realizable goals. Not unwilling to try to take on a new challenge, you are also against leaps of faith for faith's sake. Chances are you could be a successful entrepreneur, which, by the way, is the same profile it would take to be a successful investor. You are willing to take charge of a new situation in an informed, objective way while, at the same time, able to recognize the potential pitfalls and calculate the consequences. You are also generally able to spot trouble before you are in it. To be a successful investor, you need to be able to tolerate and accomplish all of the above without being overwhelmed by second doubts. You are on you way.

40 to 20—Depending on where your score falls, you are more or less likely to take risks with a greater or lesser degree of probability that there will be a reward waiting for you on the other side. You have tended to either take too much risk with too little thought about the possible consequences, or too little risk without understanding the potential downside in terms of paltry gains. As an investor, you will need to learn more about the potential risks and rewards in order to ensure that you flourish, rather than founder, when it comes to new investments which are better suited to your age and objectives. You will need to learn more before you can take on more risks which, in turn, will help you increase your long-term chances of successfully achieving your investment objectives. When studying potential investments, pay particular attention to the sections on each investment category's particular risks and potential rewards.

20 or less—You are either much too willing to take risks without knowing and understanding the consequences, or too unwilling to take on necessary risks in order to achieve reasonable objectives. As a younger investor, you will need to come to terms with the fact that some risks are not worth taking—while others decidedly are. Familiarizing yourself with appropriate risks and rewards for each type of investment vehicle within each investment category will help you overcome your timidity and/or tame your overconfidence when it comes to taking risks.

CHAPTER SIX

Getting There—Saving for Retirement

Have you ever turned on *Wall Street Week* or *CNBC* and heard a guest talk about drawing up a budget, buying disability insurance, or writing a will? Probably not. Investing is the glamorous side of personal finance. If we just manage to pick the right investment, it seems, everything else will fall neatly into place. It does not work that way, though. The real money horror stories are not about people who forgot to invest, but about those who failed to set aside *enough* money for their needs or forgot to protect their assets.

Of course, smart investing is critical if you are to achieve the life you want. That is a given. But before you can invest, you have got to build a base—and you have got to protect what you have. To do that, you need to work out a budget. You need to know what items can go. See where you can shave or juggle to help you save for a comfortable retirement. Two invaluable tools to help you properly prepare a budget are the *cash flow statement* and the *personal balance sheet*. Both are discussed in detail later on in this chapter.

Financial security is not so much dependent on how much you earn as it is on how much you spend. Many rich people spend more than they earn; many people of very modest means spend a lot less than they earn. There are people out there who have the same income as you, the same number of mouths to feed, and the same rent or mortgage to pay, but they are probably spending a lot less than you are.

Successful budgeting is the engine of growth for your personal financial machine. Unless you have a handle on what comes in and where it goes, you will never be able to move on to building your net worth with maximum efficiency. And successful budgeting almost always requires one to spend less. But why do we find it so very difficult to cut down on our spending? We all know how important it is to spend less so that we can save more, but far too few of us do a good job at it. Statistics show Americans to be abysmal savers. Statistics show that 54% of Americans feel they save way too little. Why? Our society worships the good life. We can not let our neighbors, friends, or co-workers beat us in the game of acquiring *things*. Advertisers tell us how important it is to have things; if we do not have them, we are made to feel that we have failed somehow. To give you an idea of how acquisitive we have become, many bankruptcy attorneys are reporting the absolute unwillingness of near-bankrupt people to take action to avoid bankruptcy—to give up their second homes, their boats, their late-model cars, and other trappings of the wealth they do not really possess. As precarious as their financial situation is, they feel entitled to them. This is how bad it has become.

For many Americans, budgeting is tedium. They see it as both chore and punishment. And budgeting should involve more than just listing your utility and grocery bills and thinking about where you can cut back. "Cut back," I hear you say in frustration. "Who can afford to cut back?" *Almost everyone* can cut back. Ask any expert on credit or financial planning and you will be told that the bottom-line reality is that unless you are truly poor, there is always some give in your budget, something that can be cut far short of the bone. One image that comes to mind is the young people who consume several $3 caffe lattes each day while complaining that they will never be able to afford to buy a home of their own. Should they deny themselves the pleasure of good coffee? Not necessarily. The point is that today's superconsumers have holes in their designer jeans they do not even know are there. What they have surely never done is figure out how much those holes are costing them, how much a home would cost them, comparing the two sides of the ledger, and then making an informed decision about what really matters to them most.

A successful retirement takes careful planning. Sounds easy, but apparently it is not. Do you know that over 70% of Americans over the age of 65 have a retirement income of $15,000 a year or less? Careful planning can help you have the retirement you want. And careful planning requires careful saving.

If retiring young and rich appeals to you, or even if you are more motivated by not retiring old and poor, you will have to save regularly. There is no way around it. The amount you will have to save will probably be a lot more than you now save or think you can manage. For the time being, let us follow the consensus advice of financial experts who say that from your thirties on—that is, once you get settled in your career with expectations of regular raises as well as increasing expenses—you should be aiming to save at least 10% of your pretax income. I advise 15% to 20%, if possible. I feel that you should start saving that amount as soon as you obtain employment. You make $55,000 a year? If you are not saving at least $5,500 of that, you are falling behind. And you know what that means: If you start saving in earnest sometime later on, you may have to hike that percentage to 20% or more to make up, not only for the savings you did not stash, but for the investment returns you did not get along the way.

A *bare minimum* plan for saving is to begin saving for retirement (at age 25 or earlier) by investing 5% of your pretax income. Then increase that amount by one percentage point a year. After you reach the 10% level, take stock of your financial position and determine if you could put more away, say 15% or 20%. Believe me, you can not save too much!

Time and Money—When dealing with time and money, it is essential to understand the interplay among *three* important concepts in order to budget and save properly. They are:

    1. The power of compounding—Albert Einstein once called it *the eighth wonder of the world.* There is no greater mathematical force working for investors than compounding. When money is invested, it produces earnings that can then be reinvested, so that you receive earnings on your earnings in addition to the earnings on your original investment. This mushrooming effect is an added boost to the power of compounding, and the longer the money is invested, the more explosive are its effects. Compounding an initial investment at 10% a year for 15 years increases capital by four fold. Not bad. But compounding at 10% for 50 years boosts each initial dollar *117 times!!!* That is quite a bonus for the 35 additional years.

    Time is the determining factor as to how much money you will have at retirement. But it does not happen overnight. Here is how it works. If you save $2,000 a year and earn 10%, your investment earns $200. Nothing to get excited about. But once you have built your stash up to, say, $12,500, the interest on your savings will add more each year to your 403(b)

84

plan than your own contributions. By 15 years from the starting point, your annual investment earnings will more than double your annual contributions, and by 20 years out, they will more than triple them. In effect, your money will be working three times as hard as you. The higher your returns, the more powerful the effect of compounding. If you earn 10% on your investments, for example, the annual interest you earn will overtake your annual contributions within 7 years and double them within 12. Look at the chart that follows.

How Long It Takes Before
Annual Investment Earnings Surpass
Annual Savings

Rate of Return	6%	7%	8%	9%	10%
Years until Annual Return Overtakes Annual Contributions	12	10	9	8	7

Over long periods of time—20 - 40 years—the effects of compounding over *different* time periods can be substantial, also. Remember the example given in chapter 3? If you invest $2,000 in a tax-deferred retirement account each year between the ages of 21 and 28 (only 7 seven years), and *never* invest another cent, you will have more money when you reach age 65 than if you wait until you are 28 and invest *$2,000 every year for the next 40 years.* Ah, the magic of compounding. Investing a lump sum of $10,000 today would give you $132,676 at the end of 30 years if it earned 9%. Actually, the stock market (mutual funds included) has averaged about 10% since its inception.

Here is another example: If, at age twenty-five, you start putting $100 a month into an account that averages a 10% return, you will have approximately $555,035 by age sixty-five. If you start ten years later, at thirty-five, your $100 a month will grow to $206,284 by age sixty-five. If you are forty-five, and start saving $100 a month, you will have only $71,826 by age sixty-five. Time accounts for the difference. For every year that you wait to take the first step, it costs you an average of about $25,000 a year of future growth. That is a lot of money, my friend. By waiting twenty years, from age twenty-five to age forty-five, to start saving just $100 a month, you pass up almost $484,000!!! If you bump up the monthly contribution to $200, you pass up almost *$1 million* by waiting twenty years to start saving. One million dollars!!!

To make the most of this compounding, always arrange to have your interest and dividends reinvested so that they, too, can compound. Here is something else to keep in mind. You can see the advantages of earning higher returns over long time periods. But you must be very careful when making retirement plans that involve extremely long time periods—small differences in return assumptions can turn into large differences in accumulation. Be conservative in your estimates.

2. The Rule of 72—Remember it from chapter 1 when we discussed inflation? This time, however, we will take a look at it with respect to making money. The rule of 72 can show you how long it will take to *double* your money, depending on the rate of return. When money doubles over a certain time, the product of the number of years and the rate of return per year equals roughly 72. So if you pick an annual rate of return and divide it into 72, the answer tells you how many years it will take for your money to double. At 7 percent, for example, your money doubles in roughly 10 years (72 divided by 7). At 9 percent, it takes about eight years (72 divided by 9) to double.

How many years will it take to quadruple your money? Take the years required to double your dollars and multiply that times two. At 8 percent, for example, your money will double in nine years—and quadruple in 18 (9 times 2).

The Rule of 72 works the other way as well, telling you what interest rate you will need to double your money in a specific amount of time. Pick the number of years in which you want your money to double and divide that number into 72. The answer will be your required rate of return. If six years is your target to double your money, then you will need an annual rate of return of about 12 percent (6 divided into 72).

3. The value of a dollar today versus tomorrow—In the first chapter we discussed the eroding power of inflation. No need to put too fine a point on it here. Suffice it to say that over time, inflation lessens the worth of money, so that a given amount buys less in the future than it can today. The other side to this coin deals with *time value*. Time value refers to the fact that a dollar received today is worth more than a dollar received at some point in the future. Why? Today's dollar can be invested in the meantime and earn a return. For example, a dollar in your pocket today will be worth $1.23 three years from now, assuming a 7 percent annual investment return and no taxes. (Ultimately though, inflation would have to be considered in order to get a truly accurate picture as to the worth of that dollar).

That brings me to a point worth remembering. When you are planning for the future, you are examining dollars over numerous time periods. To compare them, you need to put them on an equal purchasing-power footing, so that they are all in equivalent dollar terms.

Liquidity—Before we begin charting a plan to help with saving money to be used strictly for investment purposes, we should address a topic that many investors who are eager to make money on their investments overlook—liquidity. One should always be concerned with adequate liquidity. By liquidity, of course, we mean cash on hand or that is easily accessible—such as money invested in money market funds, passbook savings, etc. A quick rule of thumb is that you should have anywhere from three to six months' take-home pay as a liquid emergency fund. Having six months' take-home pay is safer, and more prudent. A more accurate—and a more time-consuming approach is to match possible emergency needs with readily available resources. The difference between these two is your liquidity need.

What are possible emergency needs? Most of these needs arise to offset a loss. These losses fall into two categories: a loss of income due to loss of work or disability and losses due to unforeseen emergencies—such as the loss of an asset or the creation of a new expense incurred due to damage to an asset or an individual.

Let us begin with the liquidity need for replacing income. In order to obtain this number, you will need to know what income is coming into the household and what amounts of expenses are going out. To determine this, keep a worksheet of income and expenses on a monthly basis. A sample worksheet is provided toward the end of this chapter. Logging the various income and expense numbers will give you a feel for your cash flow on a month-to-month basis. Hopefully, this cash flow number will be positive, with the excess allocated to savings or investment for future use.

For determining income replacement liquidity needs, it is best to assume a worst-case scenario. For instance, assume that all earned income sources are discontinued—in other words, jobs are lost by both the husband and wife.

On a month-to-month basis, the total expenses can now be subtracted from the remaining income, which will divulge any shortcomings in monthly cash flow. Assuming that you are properly insured, disability insurance should eventually cover most of the shortfall, if the loss of income is due to a disability.

In this case, your primary liquidity need will be during the waiting period when there are no disability benefits. Of course, this will depend on your own disability insurance. You may want to adjust this waiting period if you are uncomfortable with the length of time without income, but this will result in higher insurance premiums, which should be included on your monthly expense worksheet. The shorter the waiting period, the less the need for liquidity under the disability income loss circumstance.

What happens if the loss of income is not due to a disability, but rather a job loss due to a firing, a cutback in employees because of budget issues, etc.? Loss of income due to unemployment of this type may or may not be covered by Unemployment Compensation, depending upon the cause of unemployment. If it is covered, you can determine approximately what your unemployment benefit would be by contacting the district office of the Department of Labor. You would then take this amount, add it to income and net expenses against remaining income to find out your liquidity need.

You now have monthly income shortfalls under unemployment and disability scenarios. When planning conservatively, you will want to take the higher of the two as your need for each month. This gives you the monthly amount of liquidity needed under a worst-case scenario in the event of either the disability or unemployment causes for loss of income and cash flow.

You will now need to determine how long these monthly shortfalls will last. Under the disability scenario this will be fairly simple, since it will last normally for the time of the waiting period on your disability coverage. However, if your disability coverage is inadequate, it could last longer. The length of the unemployment shortfall is a much more difficult time period to determine. A best estimate is made by the individual by determining other job opportunities based on area of discipline. For most of us, covering this need for a one-year period should be sufficient.

Totaling all of these monthly shortfalls will now give you a liquidity number that equates to a lump sum that you should have available to cover your income shortfalls and maintain your current standard of living under disability or unemployment loss of income scenarios. Of course, your monthly shortfalls will vary. If you are seeking liquidity for a time horizon of less than a year, you may want to use the months of greatest shortfall to be conservative. To this figure you should also add an amount to cover unforeseen emergencies. In essence, the liquidity need for unforeseen emergencies is the amount that must be covered out of current assets because a loss is not or cannot be currently insured.

A good example of this would be in the hospitalization and major medical insurance area. If you have this coverage, your liquidity need may extend only to the payment of deductibles and possibly coinsurance costs. However, if you do not have this coverage, or you do and you lose it, you risk loss of all current assets if a major medical catastrophe were to occur. Thus, someone not carrying insurance has a much higher liquidity need than someone who is covered with insurance.

This analysis should provide you with a more definitive answer than the rule of thumb, but the question still depends considerably on personal preferences for risk. In addition, everyone defines liquidity differently. For the most conservative of investors liquidity means having assets available that can be turned into cash immediately, and whose conversion to cash will not create any additional liability or potential loss. Under this definition, stocks, bonds, CDs, and many other investments that can be turned into cash quickly would not be considered liquid vehicles, since there would be the potential for a loss. I personally don't share this hard line opinion. I'll cover this in more detail in chapter 16. But if you want to cover your liquidity needs under this most conservative definition, you should stick to bank instruments and money market accounts to provide for this need.

However, if you are uncomfortable with large accumulations in a money market account, and are willing to risk the potential loss upon sale of an investment due to market value fluctuation, you may want to use other investments to cover your needs. (See chapter 16 for more information on liquidity and for a listing of after-tax investments.) No matter what your calculations show, personal preference is the major factor when determining your bottom-line liquidity needs.

How Much is Enough?—Although your objective and its time horizon dictate the most suitable type of investments, there is one other, trickier factor: estimating how much money you must save to meet your objectives. Or, whether what you are saving will amount to enough to meet your objectives. A *Retirement Savings Worksheet* is provided at the end of the chapter to help you specifically zero in on how much you must save each year to meet your retirement goals. In the meantime the following chart suggests general guidelines for gauging your retirement savings rate. It gives you an idea as to how many years of salary you should have saved by the time you reach a certain age.

Are You On Target?

Age	Years of Salary Saved
35	0.5 to 1.0
40	1.0 to 1.5
45	1.5 to 2.0
50	2.0 to 3.0
55	3.0 to 4.0
60	4.0 to 5.0
65	5.0 to 6.0

As you can see, the figures on the right give you a lot of latitude. With that in mind, let me state that if you are nowhere near the suggested figures, having enough for a comfortable retirement might be a goal that will be difficult to reach.

Predicting the Future—Determining how some investments will turn out is easy. You buy a Treasury Bill for $9,400; you know it will be worth $10,000 when it matures in a year. For others it is much more difficult. You need to make assumptions about likely returns. For example, if your stock-invested portfolio grows by 7.2% per year in real (inflation-adjusted) terms, it will double every 10 years. How do I know this? Because of the rule of 72.

With a long series of additions to your savings, followed by a long series of withdrawals, as is likely to be the case with your retirement savings, you may need a spreadsheet program like Excel to calculate your exact situation. But if that is not your cup of tea, then the following table should prove helpful.

What portion of our income do we have to save in order to retire on 60% of our real current income (not counting Social Security and other pensions)? If we are 40 years from retirement, we need only save

3.7% of income. If 35 years, 5.7%, and so on:

Are You Saving Enough?

Years from Retirement	Percent of Salary to Save
40	3.7%
35	5.7%
30	8.7%
25	13.6%
20	22.0%
15	37.4%
10	54.6%

Assumptions—I have assumed an average 8% real (after inflation) return before retirement, and 7% real return after retirement (when you will be somewhat more conservatively invested). Such returns are reasonably conservative but cannot be guaranteed. These figures also assume that your income is growing at the inflation rate. (If it grows faster, then you will get somewhat more than 60% of your current real income to retire on).

Most importantly, I have assumed you can live as a retiree on 60% of your current real (inflation-adjusted) income. If, for example, you want to do a lot of world traveling, you may actually want to spend *more* after retirement than you are making now. The above figures can simply be ramped up proportionately (e.g., if you want to retire on 120% of your current real income, just double the above savings percentage figures).

As you can plainly see, an early start makes retirement savings much less painful. But again, I recommend that even if you do or did start early, you put *at least* 10% of your income into your 403(b) account, 15% to 20% if possible. You will probably never regret having too much tax-advantaged savings, or getting the head start that may allow you to either retire early or to skip a few years while you are putting your children through college.

What are you worth now?—Before you decide where you want to go with your saving, you might want to find out where you are currently. That means you have to make an assessment of your resources. As mentioned in chapter 1, the best way to assess your current resources is to prepare a *personal financial summary*, which should have two parts: a *cash flow statement* and a *personal balance sheet*. "But I'm not good at accounting," you are saying with enough angst to keep you awake for a week. Not to worry!

- **A cash flow statement**—This is simply a comparison of how money flows into and out of your life. It is a comparison of your income and expenses that should help you better understand how much money will be available for retirement planning. The cash flow statement measures your cash inflow (income) and your cash outflow (expenses) over a period of time, usually a year. The difference between your income and your expenses represents your savings—the amount you will have to parley into the savings needed to finance your eventual retirement—*after* saving for emergency needs.

- **A personal balance sheet (also referred to as a net worth statement)**—Provides an accounting picture of what you own and what you owe. In other words, a personal balance sheet is a snapshot of your financial condition on a given day.

Although it may take hours to organize your financial records and to tabulate a personal cash flow statement and a balance sheet to see how you currently use your financial resources, it is well worth the time. Just do it. You will be amazed at how much money you are wasting. Remember, wasting as little as $30.00 dollars a month now will mean $50,000 to $70,000, 30 years from now. I realize that seems hard to believe, but it is true nonetheless.

Take a Saturday afternoon and sit down with your checkbook and a record of your credit-card charges for the past 12 months. Segregate all your bills by category for the last 12 months. Then total up each category. At the end you will see how many dollars you spent over the past year on housing, utilities, eating out, travel, clothing, and so on. Unless you are an unusually astute bookkeeper, the results should surprise you—some of the results, that is. You will begin to get a sense of just where you have been overspending and, thereby, just where you will be able to cut back in order to beef up your savings. To help you zero in on the culprit categories, here is a general estimate of the ideal percentage ranges for each. There are two sets here—one for young singles in their twenties and one for couples in their forties with two incomes and two children.

Category	Singles	Couples with Two Kids
Housing	20 - 25%	30%
Loan payments	13 - 15%	13 - 15%
Food	10 - 15%	10 - 15%
Child care	0%	8 - 10%
Entertainment	7 - 14%	3 - 7%
Vacations	3 - 7%	3 - 7%
Pocket Money	8 - 12%	5 - 8%
Transportation	7 - 10%	7 - 10%
Clothing, personal care	4 - 8%	4 - 10%
Education	5 - 7%	5 - 7%
Utilities	4 - 7%	4 - 7%
Contributions	2 - 7%	2 - 5%
Savings	5 - 10%	10%
Insurance	1 - 3%	3 - 5%

The next step is to compare these guidelines with the actual figures you record on your cash flow statement and personal balance sheet. You need to be as complete and as accurate as possible to really make this work for you. Pull together as much financial information as you can, including last year's tax return; bank, brokerage and credit union statements; credit card statements; mutual fund and stock reinvestment plan statements; retirement account records; mortgage information; loan repayment schedules, and life insurance policies.

Here is the personal finance summary sheet I promised. It contains both a cash flow statement and a net worth statement for your convenience. Fill in the blanks on both sides of the worksheet and you have it—your preliminary net worth. Now go back at the value you have attached to your business (if you have one), collectibles, and personal property. Most people give these items much more credit than they are worth. I have also provided an additional personal finance summary sheet for you in the bonus gift "Personal Finance Sheet and Retirement Savings Worksheet.".

What Are You Worth?

Cash Flow Statement

Income:
Salary and wages _____
Dividends and interest _____
Capital gains and losses _____
Other income_____

Total Annual Income ========

Expenses:
Federal income tax _____
State and local income tax _____
Other taxes _____
Mortgage or rent _____
Utilities _____
Insurance premiums:
Homeowners _____
Property _____
Life _____
Health _____
Disability
Long-term care

Net Worth Statement

Monetary Assets:
Cash:
Checking and
money market accounts _____
Savings accounts _____
Investments:
Retirement plans _____
Brokerage accounts _____
Cash value of life insurance _____

Fixed Assets:
Market value of home _____
Other real estate _____
Other investments _____
(gold coins, stamps, etc.) _____
Automobiles _____
Value of business _____
Personal property _____
(Jewelry, furniture, etc.) _____

Total Assets ========

91

Personal Finance Sheet (continued)

Medical bills not covered by insurance	_____	**Liabilities:**	
Food	_____	**Short-term liabilities:**	
Clothing	_____	Fed., state, and local taxes	_____
Transportation:		Insurance premiums	_____
Car payments	_____	Rent or mortgage	_____
Auto insurance	_____	Credit card payments	_____
Gasoline	_____	Other	_____
Maintenance and repairs	_____		
Child-related expenses:		**Total S-T Liabilities**	========
College/school tuition	_____		
Alimony/child support	_____	**Long-term liabilities:**	
Child care costs	_____	Bank loans	_____
Entertainment	_____	Home, other mortgage	_____
Recreation	_____	Auto loans	_____
Vacations	_____	Other loans	_____
Retirement savings	_____		
		Total L-T Liabilities	========
Total Annual Expenses	========	**Total Liabilities**	========
Total Annual Income *(Less Total Annual Expenses)*	========	**Net Worth (Total Assets** *Less Total Liabilities)*	========

Not happy with the result? Look at your cash flow to see where you can make changes. Write down every cent you spend for a week. When you see it all in writing, decide what you can cut. The results will help you budget properly for efficient retirement saving. Remember also to build your dreams into your budget. When you set up your budget, do not forget to include anticipated expenses for college, a special vacation, a new home, a home renovation plan—whatever you dream about—under the appropriate expense heading, such as child-related expenses, recreation, etc.

Think hard about your definition of necessities. Necessities have a way of expanding to meet—or exceed—your income. You have to get used to the idea of living beneath your means to achieve retirement goals. That means that when you think about where to cut back, look beyond your discretionary spending (meals out, travel, etc.) to what you consider absolute necessities. That includes groceries, clothing, transportation, insurance, haircuts, dry cleaning, household extras, furniture, etc.

Retirement Savings Worksheet—Here is the Retirement Savings Worksheet I promised. This worksheet will eliminate some of the guess work in deciding how much you must save each year to meet your retirement goals. It is based on some important assumptions. First, it assumes that your investments will yield 8% prior to retirement and 7% during retirement—I feel that both of these assumptions are on the conservative side—better to be safe, than sorry. Second, it assumes that inflation will average 4% per year and that you will want your spending money to increase every year to keep pace. Third, it also assumes that you will live to age 90, longer than your statistical life expectancy, and that the primary objective of these savings is to provide retirement income, not to build an estate. Since all amounts are in today's dollars, you should actually increase your savings each year by the rate of inflation, to assure adequate savings by the date of your retirement. In this hypothetical example, I use a 37-year-old who plans to retire at age 62.

RETIREMENT SAVINGS WORKSHEET

How Will I Meet My Yearly Retirement Needs?

	Example	Yourself
In today's dollars, enter your anticipated annual retirement expenses(use 60-80% of current income).	$ 50,000	_____
B. Subtract the total amount you expect to receive each year in retirement from your retirement plans (company pensions and Social Security).	$ 30,000	_____
C. Amount you will need annually in retirement from your personal savings (line A minus line B).	$ 20,000	_____

What Is My Retirement Savings Goal?

D. What is your target retirement age? Select the age and enter the factor from the table below.   **18.8**   _____

Retirement Age	55	60	62	65	67	70
Factor	21.5	19.6	18.8	17.4	16.4	14.9

E. Amount you may need to have saved by your desired retirement age (line C times line D). $376,000   _____

F. If your target retirement age is younger than age 65, select the age and enter the factor from the table below.   **2.8**   _____

Early Retirement Age	55	60	62
Factor	8.5	4.6	2.8

G. Additional amount you may need to have saved to provide additional retirement income until Social Security and pensions begin or to offset reduction in those benefits due to early retirement (line B times line F). $ 84,000   _____

H. Estimate total savings needed by your desired retirement age (line E plus line G). $460,000   _____

Retirement Savings Worksheet (Continued)

What Will My Current Savings Be Worth?   Example   Yourself

I. Amount you've saved already, including 403(b)s, IRAs, and other savings/ investments. $ 50,000   _____

J. How many years do you have until you retire? Enter the factor from the table below.   2.7   _____

Years Until Retirement	5	10	15	20	25	30
Years Factor	1.2	1.5	1.8	2.2	2.7	3.2

K. Estimated value of your current savings at the time you retire (line I times line J). $135,000   _____

How Do I Achieve My Retirement Savings Goal?

L. The amount you still need in addition to your current savings (line H minus line K). $325,000   _____

M. Enter the factor from the table below for the number of years until you retire.   .024   _____

Years Until Retirement	5	10	15	20	25	30
Years Factor	.184	.083	.050	.034	.024	.018

N. Amount you may need to save each year to reach your goal (line L times line M). $ 7,800   _____

In the next chapter you will be given specific ways to save for retirement. Look at them carefully and choose as many as you can to help you save the maximum towards retirement.

CHAPTER SEVEN

Sources of Funding for Your Retirement

I hope by now I have impressed upon you the need, not only to start saving early for your retirement, but also to save as much as is humanly possible. If you still need a little nudge to get you into that saving frame of mind, look at this example very closely. Danny saved $330 a month for 35 years. Don saved $300 a month for 35 years. They both got a 10% *tax-deferred* return on their money. At the end of 35 years, Danny had $1,121,601, while Don had only $1,019,637—almost *$101,964 less,* despite the fact that Danny saved *only $1.00 a day* more than Don. That is right, *only $1.00 a day more!* The axiom *a little bit goes a long way* could not be more true in saving for retirement..

Just How Thrifty Are You?—Although most of us do not consider ourselves wild spenders, probing our finances shows plenty of holes where money leaks out. Hopefully, you found many of these leaks when you completed your Personal Balance Sheet and Cash Flow Statement from the previous chapter. Plugging those leaks and keeping them plugged will help you to protect yourself from the barrage of marketing exhortations designed to make you spend your money on things that, in many cases, you do not even need. Exercising that new-found spending discipline will help you develop a conscientious saving habit—a habit that could help make you wealthy.

The purpose of this chapter is to concentrate on sources of funding for your retirement. But before we begin, let us see what kind of spender you are. The following statements pertain to spending techniques. Select from the five responses indicating the degree of your likeness to each statement, and mark the number of your response next to the question in the space provided. Should a statement not apply to your situation, skip it and adjust your score accordingly.

Is The Statement

(1) Totally like me **(2)** A lot like me **(3)** Equally like and unlike me

(4) Only a little like me **(5)** Not like me at all

_____ Each income period, I do not keep cash from my paycheck.

_____ Each income period, I deposit my paycheck into an account.

_____ I save each paycheck stub indicating earnings, deductions, taxes, savings, etc.

_____ Each income period, I set aside a portion to cover fixed expenses.

_____ Each income period, I set aside 10% for savings and investments.

_____ All grocery spending is planned in advance and done with a list, and purchases are primarily just from the list.

_____ There is rarely more than one trip a week made to the grocery store.

_____ Grocery and other coupons are utilized whenever possible.

_____ Comparison shopping for quality, value, price, etc., is something I/we do for practically every purchase, large or small.

_____ We do not have any credit cards with a balance owing.

_____ We do not have any loans (excluding first mortgage) with a balance owing.

_____ I have comparison-shopped motor vehicle insurance within the last year—for features and especially premiums (omit if no motor vehicle).

_____ I do not dine out (breakfast, lunch, or dinner) more than once a week.

_____ I have received and reviewed estimated benefit statement from pension and/or Social Security.

_____ At the end of the day, I can account for all cash spent.

_____ I balance my checking/share draft account with each statement.

_____ I have looked into, joined, or am a member of a credit union.

Scoring

17 - 24 **Very Perceptive**—Time to teach others how to do it.

25 - 37 **Pretty Good**—Concentrate on improving a few weaker areas.

38 - 52 **Average**—Need to spend an hour a week on improving spending. This could produce some significant savings.

53 - 67   **Lousy**—Immediate change is required to avoid financial disaster.

67+   **Terrible**—Send a self addressed stamped envelope to: National Center for Financial Education, P.O. Box 34070, San Diego, CA 92163-4070. Request pamphlets on: *Spending by Choice, How to Get Out of Debt, Dealing with Creditors, How to Develop a Spending Plan.*

Even the people who score well may need to do better if they are going to achieve financial security. Retiring comfortably is becoming more difficult with each passing year because of a variety of trends, including longer life-expectancies, higher inflation, earlier retirement, and a shift in the burden of funding retirement income needs away from the employer to the employee. These trends make it all the more important to cut down on spending—and the sooner the better.

Cost-Cutting/Saving Strategies—OK, you have completed a cash flow statement and a personal balance sheet showing income and outgo. You know you want to cut back. You want to develop a spending and savings plan of attack. Now it is time for the nuts and bolts of making changes that will help you save for that wonderful retirement you have been dreaming about. The following list is quite lengthy, but worth your time, so review each one carefully. Some cost-cutting strategies will apply equally to everyone, while some will only apply to a few. Some will seem silly, while others will ring with practicality. Ultimately, only you can decide which ones will fit your lifestyle, investment goals, and financial situation. Remember, saving *only $1.00 extra a day* will make a huge difference in the long run.

- **Stop trying to keep up with others' spending habits**—Even though this is not a specific strategy, I feel it is important to mention because of the deleterious effect a *keeping up with the Joneses* attitude can have on your financial situation. When you adopt this kind of attitude, everything else goes right out the window. Everyone has neighbors or friends who live beyond their means and love to brag about it. They are experts at making us feel like poor slobs. You might even envy them a little—we all would like to have more—but take heart. Free spending and conspicuous consumption are no-no's for wise investors. Trying to keep up with the Joneses is one of the surest ways to bankrupt yourself.

- **Pay yourself first**—Use the 10% solution. Always take at least 10% right off the top of your paycheck and put it into your investment account, before you pay any of your bills. Of course, if you have a 403(b) it will be deducted automatically (more on that later). Do the same with every paycheck for the rest of your life. It is one of those things you can not improve on. If you pay your bills first and save what is left, you will always be broke, because there is never anything left. Always pay yourself first, and you will have that retirement you dream of.

- **Get someone else to save for you**—You will never find a better savings machine than contributing to a 403(b) through your employer's payroll deduction plan. A fixed amount of money is taken out of every paycheck, so the cash never hits your checking account. What you do not see, you do not miss—and you do not spend. We will cover the 403(b) plan in detail in chapter 9.

- **Add one allowance to your W-4 form for every $600 in refunds you got last year**—If your tax bracket is 28%, for every $600 in refund you got last year, add one allowance to

97

your W-4 form and you will automatically add $60 a month or $720 per year to your take-home pay. Why let Uncle Sam hold your money? The money is tax free since taxes have already been deducted, whether the money is withheld or paid to you. This extra money, when invested monthly into your 403(b), will increase the value of your retirement account tremendously over the long haul.

- **Do not spend your next raise**—"Who are you kidding?" You are screaming in frustration. I know. I do not expect you to do this with every raise. But if you do it with one or two at the beginning of your employment life, you will be adding hundreds of thousands of dollars to your *return on investment* in the long run. Remember, toward late middle-age, you should be saving at least 15 to 20 percent of your income. The more money you earn— the more of it you should set aside.

- **Review your mortgage situation**—Are you shortening your mortgage life while passing up profitable investment opportunities? We have all heard that you can save substantial money on your mortgage by shortening its life by making double payments, every-other-week payments, etc. While that is undeniably true, you must also consider the other side of the coin. Many people pass up an investment opportunity that yields 15-20% per year to save money on a mortgage that carries an interest rate of only 6-8%. They pass up an *extra* $200,000 in investment return to save $15,000 on their mortgage interest expense (see below). Remember the power of compounding. Allow it to work for you by making your regular mortgage payment and investing the extra payment money in your retirement account.

- **When buying a house request a lengthier mortgage repayment period**—This strategy is very closely related to the previous one. Circumstances have to be favorable for it to work—a fairly low mortgage rate combined with a decent investment rate of return. The following example brings to light how lengthening your mortgage repayment period can help make you wealthy. The numbers are chosen arbitrarily. Here is how it works: let us say that when you first began working you started investing $200 a month in a 403(b), and continued to contribute to that account for the next 2 years. The market has been returning an average of 12% per year. You decide to buy a house, and can afford an $800/month mortgage payment. You obtain a $90,000 loan with a fairly low mortgage rate of 7%. You have to decide on the length of the loan. Your parents, grandparents, and friends tell you to keep it as short as you can to save on interest expense. *Remember, if you take out a shorter-term loan, you will be obligated to make that higher payment each and every month for the duration of the loan.*

On a 15-year loan (Plan A) your monthly mortgage payment would be $808.95—just what you can afford. But wait! Let us compare it to the same loan extended to 30 years. With a 30-year loan (Plan B) your monthly mortgage payment would be $598.77, a difference of $210.18. Remember, with the longer-term loan, you can always put as much extra money on the principal as you wish, which reduces your payback time. You can make higher payments *without* having to be obligated to do so. This comes in handy if you ever need extra money for a quick investment—you simply make the standard payment, which is much lower, and invest the difference.

With Plan B you can get ahead by budgeting the $808.95 payment, make only the $598.77 payment, then invest the difference ($210.00), each and every month for three years, into

98

your 403(b) account. After that 3-year period you would bump up your monthly mortgage payment to the original 15-year loan payment of $808.95, and at the same time, scale back your 403(b) contribution to $200 a month. So, in essence you are only making the lower payment ($598.77) and the higher 403(b) contribution ($400.00) for 3 years only. But, by allowing the magic of compounding to work for you early in your life, you would be increasing your investment return by *literally hundreds of thousands of dollars,* even if you *never* increased your monthly 403(b) contribution again! Of course, you must also consider the fact that you have extended your mortgage payment period slightly (from 15 years to 17 years), and will incur added interest expense. Do not be concerned, though. When you balance it out, you still come out hundreds of thousands of dollars ahead. The actual numbers look like this:

> Total interest expense on the straight 15-year loan (Plan A) is $55,609.70. The interest expense on the self-structured variable 30-year loan (Plan B) is $69,028.64, a difference of $13,418.94 *more* in interest expense.

But that is only half of the story. You now have to factor in the extra money you will make on your retirement investment. If you contributed a straight $200/month for 35 years at an average of 12%, you would have a total of $1,091,806.30—nice money, to be sure. But, by starting out with a $200/month contribution for 2 years; then bumping it up to $400/month for 3 years; then scaling it back to $200/month for the remaining 30 years (a grand total of only $7,200 more), you will have a total of $1,347,510.52 in your retirement account—even if you never increased your monthly contribution again! *A difference of $255,704.22 more!!!* Would you sacrifice $255,704 in investment income to save $13,418 in interest expense? Believe it or not, most people do because they are uninformed. Do not let it happen to you—be a shrewd investor. Again, the numbers used above were chosen arbitrarily. Of course, every different set of numbers will give you a different result, but the dynamics are still the same. Work out several scenarios and choose one that works the best for you.

- **Refinance your existing mortgage**—If mortgage interest rates drop 1 ½ percent or more below the current rate on your mortgage, figure out how much money you could save by refinancing, keep your budget the same, and invest the extra.

- **Appeal your property tax assessment**—Surprisingly, a large percentage of people who appeal their property tax assessments end up with a lower bill. Don't forget, property values have dropped in many areas of the country and will drop in many more as the recession continues.

- **Save all dividends and interest**—If you have mutual funds, arrange for all dividends to be automatically reinvested. This is done automatically when contributing to a 403(b).

- **Hold on to that car**—The family car is another good place to economize. People who hold on to their cars for ten years can save $400,000 to $450,000 over 40 years, even counting an older car's higher maintenance costs. That is enough money to enable most people to retire 5-7 years earlier than those who trade in cars every three years. Since it is already budgeted, just keep paying the monthly car payment, but put it in your retirement account.

- **Buy new cars at the end of the model year**—If you are determined to have a new car, keep your old one for just a year or two longer. Purchase a new car every 5 years instead of every 2 or 3 years. Again, keep paying the monthly car payment after the 2- or 3-year loan is paid off, but invest the money into your retirement account. This alone could give you an extra $3,600 to $4,800 to invest in each of the extra years without interfering with your budget. When you buy that new car, make sure to buy it at the end of the model year, when cars are cheaper. Dealers need to clear out their inventories and the manufacturers provide additional financial incentives to the dealers to move the remaining inventory. You might even want to wait until the beginning of the next model year, because most dealers will have some of last year's models sitting on the lot, and the only thing they are attracting is dust. Whatever time of the year you buy, however, make sure you are well informed about dealer costs and incentives, and negotiate to the best of your ability.

- **Buy an *almost* new car**—For the more prudent, buy a good used car rather than an expensive new car. Because so many people are obsessed with frequently trading in their cars, there are many excellent used cars that go begging.

- **Rent an economy car**—Rent an economy car instead of the luxury model on your next vacation.

- **Refinance your personal, auto, or other high-interest loans at a lower interest deductible rate**—Consider taking out a home-equity loan, where the interest is, under most circumstances, deductible. Most other loan interest is now considered nondeductible personal interest. Invest the money you are saving, or use it to pay off the loan principal.

- **Save all gifts you get in cash, even small ones**—Nothing is too small to save. Adopt that attitude and you are on your way to successful saving.

- **Quit buying books**—Get a library card, instead.

- **Pay cash for everything**—You will spend less, because it is harder to part with cash than to plunk down a credit card.

- **Take from yourself**—Take $5.00 out of your wallet every day and put it in a coffee can. That is $1,825 a year, almost enough to fund an IRA in full.

- **Work part-time**—Social Security statistics show that earnings provide 24% of income for a typical person 65 or older, with an income of $20,000 or more. Although not appealing to everyone, you could take a part-time job and invest all of the income into a retirement account. Turn a hobby or interest into a second source of income. If this additional income comes from self-employment, it may qualify for the tax-deferred advantages of a self-employed pension or profit-sharing plan, commonly called a Keogh or SEP-IRA. Some experts feel that this strategy might be more beneficial to those who are still young. Why? Because the sooner you put some money away, the longer it has to fatten on compound interest. Saving money *young* is a painless way of saving *more*.

- **Pay off your credit cards**—Pay off your credit cards, then save the money you are no longer spending on interest charges.

- **Put yourself on an allowance**—One of the best ways to get your spending under control is to monitor and limit the amount of cash you spend on incidental day-to-day items. Figure out how you spend your day-to-day cash, look at purchases that can be avoided or reduced, and then put yourself on an allowance. Start each week with a set amount of money that should last you for the week. If you run out of money, of course you will take out more, but you will also force yourself to think about spending less.

- **Sell personal property**—Sell everything that you no longer have a need for and invest the proceeds in your retirement account. Many homeowners have discovered a few thousand dollars by having a garage or yard sale. Remember, *$1,000 invested early in your investment life will turn into as much as $50,000 in the end.*

- **Review your insurance needs**—Review all insurance coverage for duplication. Raise the deductibles on your automobile and homeowner's or renter's insurance policies. You can save hundreds of dollars a year by raising the deductibles.

- **Cut back on your insurance**—The important issue here is that your greatest need for life insurance may have passed, yet you may be paying high premiums that are being at least partly wasted. Ask yourself a few questions. Are your children grown and out of the home? If you were to die, would your spouse and other dependents be financially secure without the proceeds of your insurance? If so, then you are overinsured. Cut the insurance and invest the savings. You may still want to carry some coverage, but it probably will not have to be as much as when you were still building your wealth and your family was in a vulnerable financial state. Periodically review your life insurance needs, and if they are shrinking, consider reducing your coverage.

- **Purchase term life insurance**—If you are concerned about providing the most insurance coverage for the lowest cost now, buy term instead of cash-value life insurance. Although there is an ongoing controversy over which is better, I can say without fear of contradiction that term life insurance is cheaper in the short run. Invest the difference in premiums, which will be substantial, in your retirement account. In the long run, you will come out way ahead.

- **Buy direct when buying life insurance**—Several large insurance companies are now offering both term and cash-value life insurance directly—no agent involved. These so-called low-load life insurance policies are generally far cheaper.

- **Borrow on your life insurance policy**—If you already have cash-value life insurance (i.e. whole life, universal life, variable life, adjustable life), you can borrow on the cash value of your policy. It can be one of the best deals around. You pay a reasonable interest rate, and you can still earn interest on the money borrowed. *Invest the borrowed money in your retirement account for additional growth.* It is cheap money. For example, if the interest rate you are paying on money borrowed from a life insurance policy is 8%, the money you have borrowed may still be earning interest with the insurance company with a rate of, say, 6% interest, so you have a 2% net cost of borrowing. You can pay the loan off

101

by having the payment added to your premiums. If you do not repay the loan, it will simply be deducted from the death benefit. If you let the policy surrender, it would be considered forgiveness of debt and would be a taxable event.

- **<u>Use some of your bank savings</u>**—Studies show that most people have way more money in savings than they need, making only 2% to 3% a year. Once again, *coming up with a one-time extra $1,000 early in your investment life will make you as much as $50,000 in the long run.*

- **<u>Go out to dinner less</u>**—Some families eat out 4 to 6 times a month. Just cutting out one or two meals could save you up to $50 to $100 dollars a month.

- **<u>*Separate shopping trips from spending trips*</u>**—Separate shopping trips (when comparing prices, value, services, etc.) from spending trips (when actually making the purchase). Avoid carrying credit cards, much cash, or a checkbook on the shopping trips.

- **<u>Buy clothes at off-season sales</u>**—If you do not mind comparison shopping, you could save a substantial amount of money—over 50% off the regular price, by buying suits, overcoats, etc., off-season. The last thing a clothing retailer wants is to carry winter clothes into the Spring buying season. You can help take that winter inventory off his/her hands by purchasing those clothes in April—at a huge discount from what other customers paid only a couple of months earlier.

- **<u>Put the savings in the bank</u>**—If you really want to prove that you actually save money when buying something on sale, put the amount of money you saved in your savings or investment account. It will add up quickly.

- **<u>Buy less expensive brands at the grocery store</u>**—Taste tests show that most people can not tell much of a difference among brands, anyway. Unless you absolutely must have a special brand, buy the one that costs less.

- **<u>Shop at food warehouses</u>**—Some grocery stores are cheaper than others, and food warehouses are often the cheapest of all.

- **<u>Anticipate your needs</u>**—Anticipate your needs, then buy in bulk when items are on sale. Although it is more expensive up front to buy in bulk, it is a great way to save on staples and dry goods. But remember, it is not a bargain if you do not really need something.

- **<u>Collect receipts</u>**—Begin collecting receipts and making notes on cash purchases. It will help keep your spending under control.

- **<u>Take advantage of second-hand, rebuilt, and used items when practical</u>**—Lately, many manufacturers offer refurbished products in their catalogs at greatly reduced prices. Most of these products even carry great limited warranties.

- **<u>Take care of what you own</u>**—Change the oil in you car regularly. Clean your hair dryer or vacuum cleaner. Dust your refrigerator coils. You get the picture. Take care of your things and your things will take care of you.

• **<u>Quit playing the lottery</u>**—It is a complete waste of money. Remember the only $1.00 extra a day example at the beginning of the chapter? Quit playing the lottery and you will have at least that. Most of the time, the people who play the lottery are the ones who can afford it the least. I know—someone has to win—but the odds are it will not be you. Bet on a sure thing—put that $1.00 extra a day in your retirement account and let it increase your retirement money by up to $100,000 - $150,000.

• **<u>Do not overpay your estimated taxes</u>**—Many people pay too much in estimated taxes simply because they do not quite understand the rules. In general, estimated-tax payments—plus salary withholding—must equal 90 percent of your tax liability for the current tax year *or* 100 percent of your tax liability for the previous year, whichever is less. Therefore, if you expect to have a larger tax bill in the current year than you did in the one preceding, your estimated tax payment need total only what you paid in the previous year.

Utilize these strategies, and allow the magic of compounding work for you.

CHAPTER EIGHT

Summary of Investment Plans

Time and time again clients ask me about different investment plans they have heard of, but do not quite understand. It is easy to understand their confusion. Lately, we have been bombarded with a plethora of investment terminology, most of which is difficult to understand unless you have a degree in finance. So, before we get into the specific advantages of the 403(b) in the next chapter, let us use this chapter to acquaint you with some of the various investment plans available to investors.

Although the range of retirement plan alternatives is broad, most plans fall into one of two major categories—*defined-benefit plans* and *defined-contribution plans*. One major difference between defined-benefit and defined-contribution plans is who takes responsibility for how well the retirement fund performs. In defined-benefit plans, the employee has no say at all over investment decisions. In fact, the individual probably has no idea where the money is invested. But in defined-contribution plans, making decisions about pension fund investments is mostly the employee's responsibility. The choices made determine the return when it is time to collect.

1. **Defined-benefit plans**—Are pension plans other than individual account plans. Most corporate pensions started before the 1970s are defined-benefit plans. Most plans are covered by the Pension Benefit Guaranty Corporation, or PBGC, a federal agency that protects employer-sponsored defined-benefit plans. Payments from these plans are insured by the PBGC up to a monthly maximum of $2,559.

Depending on the company's pension plan rules, an employee may be eligible for a pension after a period of service (either 5 or 7 years) known as the vesting period. However, not all workers or all jobs may be included.

With defined-benefit plans, retirement benefits are definitely set. Generally, plan benefits are paid out in the form of an *annuity*—a fixed monthly payment for the rest of one's life. They guarantee a specified benefit (usually a percentage of pre-retirement income based on salary and years experience) after the participant reaches a certain age. For example, a plan that entitles you to a monthly pension for life equal to X percent of your monthly or yearly compensation is a defined-benefit plan. One of the most notable characteristics of some defined-benefit plans is that they often encourage early retirement because pensions are reduced only slightly or not at all for workers leaving as early as 55. Other plan formulas weigh years of service more heavily, and the loyal company man/woman is rewarded for longevity, while the job-hopper who moves from job to job and from plan to plan (or no plan at all) suffers.

Usually with a defined-benefit plan, the risk of meeting plan goals falls on the employer. Employers will contribute to the plan each year and invest assets to meet the plan's goals. Employees, meanwhile, will accrue and vest the right to contributions made on their behalf based on the length of participation in the plan. Most *regular* retirement plans, supported by the employer, are defined-benefit plans. But where teachers are concerned, in most cases, the teacher makes substantial contributions to the plan as well—usually in the range of 4% - 6% of salary. In some states this amount is set—it depends on where you live and work.

If you expect a substantial portion of your retirement income to come from your pension, you should find out whether it has a cost of living adjustment (COLA). With a COLA, your annual benefit is increased to keep up with inflation. If your pension does not have a COLA—and most do not—then your pension benefit will be worth far less in the future. Use the table below to help determine an equivalent inflation-adjusted pension that reflects the average value of your benefit based on the impact of inflation. Simply find the factor below the number of years you expect to be in retirement. Multiply that factor by the full annual pension benefit you expect to receive in retirement. The result is what your pension will be worth. For example, if you will receive a pension of $40,000 at retirement. That initial $40,000 will be worth only $25,200 a distant 30 years from now ($40,000 x 0.63).

Factor For Pension Without COLA

Years In Retirement	15	20	25	30	35	40
Inflation Rate of 4%	0.76	0.71	0.67	0.63	0.60	0.58

2. **Defined-contribution plans**—Provide an individual account, which receives monthly or annual contributions, for each participant. The benefits are based solely upon the amount contributed to the participant's account. The employer has no obligation to provide a fixed amount when you retire, as is the case with the defined-benefit plan. Contributions may be based upon the employer's profits, the employee's salary, or a combination of factors such as length of service and salary. The amount available to the employee for future distribution depends upon the performance of the plan investments. If the economy is healthy and your pension account does well, you will be in good shape. But if your account's performance lagged, you could end up with less. There is no way to predict what

you will get until the day you actually retire.

More and more employers, both private and public, are offering defined-contribution plans. In 1980, 70% of all pension plans fit into this category. By 1994, the figure was 84%. At present, it is closer to 88%. Some employers offer them as supplemental savings plans in addition to defined-benefit plans—which is most often the case in the teaching profession. Others have completely replaced their conventional plans with these more flexible ones. Most employers setting up plans for the first time choose to make a defined-contribution rather than provide a defined-benefit. It is easy to see why. Defined-contribution plans are easier to administer and less subject to government regulation, and they can provide employees with investment choices.

One of the major attractions of the defined-contribution plans is its portability, along with quicker, or even instant, vesting rights. When an employee switches jobs, they can often move the accumulated assets to the new employer's plan. That way, they are not starting at pension zero each time they move. If they can not move it, they can often leave the account with the former employer so that it goes on growing until they are ready to retire.

Many times defined-contribution plans remove early retirement thoughts employees might have since workers can only collect whatever is in the pot. So, anyone who is worried about the future because their retirement pot is not large enough can save more by working longer. Consider a worker with $100,000 in a 401(k), earning 8% a year. Delaying retirement for three years raises the amount in the plan to $125,970, even if no extra funds are added. If $2,000 a year is added, the total reaches $132,464. It is easy to understand why corporate America favors the defined-contribution plan. Both the employer and employee win.

Pre-Tax Plans—Pre-tax investment plans offer tremendous benefits to those investors who qualify. They are truly beyond compare. Although explained thoroughly in the next chapter, here is briefly how a pre-tax retirement plan works. An investment company, chosen by an employer or employee for the benefit of the employees, contracts with the employer to provide the appropriate plan covered under the proper Internal Revenue Code Section—(403(b); 403(b)7; 457; 457(f); 401(k); etc.). Your employer deducts an amount that you designate from your paycheck (pre-tax), and deposits it with the chosen investment company. Employees may have a choice of companies if the employer has elected for more than one investment company (in most school districts it is a negotiable contract issue). Each employee also chooses the type of investment into which they wish to invest. The reportable salary to the IRS (W-2 form) is reduced by the amount contributed. For example, if an employee earns $45,000 (gross) and contributes $5,800 to a chosen plan, the employee's W-2 form for that year would show only $39,200 in taxable wages.

	Pre-Tax Plan	After-Tax Plan
Salary	$45,000	$45,000
Contribution	- 5,800	0
Taxable Salary	$39,200	$45,000

The $5,800 contribution (and all other money that has been contributed or has accumulated in the account through the years) grows tax-deferred, which means that the paying of taxes is postponed until the employee starts to withdraw the savings. Then, at that time, it is taxed as ordinary income at the prevailing tax rate. So basically, the more money you put in, the lower your taxable income, the less tax you pay, and the faster your investment grows. These tax-deferred savings enjoy the benefit of tax-deferred compounding. The employee is, in effect, setting up their own retirement plan and saving hundreds to thousands of tax dollars each year. Please note that these tax-deferred savings plans have no affect on Social Security benefits or other retirement plans set up by the employer.

As an employee of a non-profit organization, you have the opportunity to participate in one of the greatest tax-deferred investment opportunities in the world—the 403(b). This plan will be covered in detail in the next chapter, along with further discussion on the advantages of pre-tax plans. For now, let us take a brief look at some of the other pre-tax defined-contribution plans that we most often hear about. Some are used in corporate America, while others are only available to employees of educational, healthcare, and city and state government organizations. The following are the most frequently used pre-tax defined-contribution plans. They fall into three general categories:

- Those plans usually funded by employer contributions only (SEP-IRAs, Keoghs).

- Those plans usually funded by employee contributions only (IRAs, 457s, and 403(b)s).

- Those plans usually funded by employee *and* employer contributions (SIMPLE-IRAs and 401(k)s).

The 401(k)

Volumes have been written concerning the 401(k) plan, but our purpose here is to give only a brief overview of one of the most popular investment plans around. It is virtually impossible to pick up any financial publication that does not mention it at least once. It is no wonder. The benefits to this plan are nothing short of amazing. But before you get too interested, let me state that the 401(k) plan is designed primarily for those working in the private sector. But do not worry, as a an employee in a non-profit organization, you have the opportunity to invest in a plan that runs a close second to the 401(k)—the 403(b). Again, it will be covered in detail in the next chapter.

The 401(k) was established by the federal government in 1981 to encourage workers to establish retirement savings plans. The name refers to the relevant section in the Internal Revenue Code. Because of the administrative costs involved in setting up and maintaining this plan, it is most popular in corporations and private companies that have more than 25 employees. All full-time employees over age 21 who have been with a company for one year must be permitted to join its plan during the next available enrollment period.

A 401(k) plan is a *tax-deferred* investment and savings plan that acts as a personal pension fund for employees. Think of it as a kind of three-way bargain involving the federal government, the employer, and the employee. All the employee has to do to establish a 401(k) account is to fill out some basic paperwork designating how much money the employee wants taken out of his/her paycheck every period and put in the 401(k) plan. That is it. The employer will then take care of the rest, including putting in its matching amount, if choosing to do so.

The most prominent player in the 401(k) is the plan's sponsor, which is usually the employer. It is the company's responsibility to set the rules for participating in the plan, to choose the menu of investment options that the plans will offer, and to decide whether the plan will include optional features. The plan must offer a number of different investment options, which means the employee gets to select investments based on his/her own time horizon, risk aversion, and financial risk tolerance. In most cases the company chooses mutual funds as the primary investment, and they usually cover the investment spectrum, from highly volatile aggressive growth funds to guaranteed T-bills. The employee controls where the money is invested among the choices the firm's plan offers. The employee does not have his/her money pooled with everyone else in the company and then invested by majority rule. 401(k) plans are also portable. When one changes jobs, he/she does not have to leave the 401(k) behind. It can be rolled over into another employer's 401(k) plan or into an IRA.

The company takes care of the paperwork. The employee gets a monthly or quarterly statement showing how much the employee contributed, how much the company contributed, what the value of the account is, and any activity such as a buy or a sell of securities in the account, or dividends and interest received. Because of the substantial paper work to report all the activity in each participant's account, companies tend to offer only one or a few family of funds. These families tend to be the larger fund families, having a wide variety of funds from which to choose.

A 401(k) plan allows employees to voluntarily contribute up to 25% of their salary (called salary reduction contributions), or $10,000 (1999's maximum), whichever is less. The cap is periodically adjusted upward for inflation. The company takes the designated *pre-tax* dollars from the employee's paycheck—dollars that are not subject to federal income taxes now—and puts those dollars right into the employee's 401(k) account. Recently, 401(k) assets topped *1 trillion dollars*. Only the employee will use those dollars in the future. The employee also receives all the dividends, interest income, and capital gains tax-free in this account *until* the money is withdrawn, at which time they are taxed as ordinary income. 401(k)s must meet stringent guidelines in order to qualify for the tax breaks. Once the employee's money is in the plan, the employee can not touch the funds without substantial tax penalties until he/she reaches the age of 59 ½. You might note that once the employee starts withdrawing funds (not borrowing) from a plan, he/she can not add funds later.

Unlike a *SIMPLE IRA*, a 401(k) does not require employer contributions. If the employer is inclined, however, the company can contribute money into the employee's account. This is a company match. A combined employer/employee plan allows contributions of up to 25% of compensation, up to a maximum of $30,000.

Vesting requirements for the company matches vary from plan to plan. By law, however, employees must be fully vested after five years of service, or a company can elect a 20% graded schedule beginning after three years, with full vesting after seven years of service. Though not usually matched 100% with the employee's contributions, this money is also invested tax-free. More than 80% of companies with 401(k)s match employees' savings. About one-in-four kick in a relatively miserly 25 cents for every dollar the employee invests. Even though that sounds low, it is the same as getting an instant 25% return on your money, which is not peanuts. Another 18% of employers match the employee dollar for dollar, and about 2% pitch in more than the employee does. Although the employee's investment grows tax-deferred, the employer can still deduct the contributions it makes. Now, not every plan matches every dollar the employee puts in; often the match applies only to the first 3% or 6% they contribute. Also, the company may choose to make its contribution only in the form of company stock. Regardless as to how the employer matches the employee's savings, it amounts to a gift from the employer. It should never be passed up.

Let us look more closely at this idea of matching contributions from the employer. This is *free* money!! Even though it sounds too good to be true, it is not. Here is how it works. Say the employer has agreed to put ½ of the percentage of the employee's contribution into the plan. If the employee makes $40,000 a year and put $3,200 (8%) of his/her salary in a 401(k) plan, then the employer would contribute another $1,600 (1/2 of 8%) to the plan.

That means the employee put in $3,200—the company another $1,600. All of it tax free! The employee has actually made 50% on his/her money before any other investment growth is realized. Phenomenal!!! In addition, all future interest and dividends those contributions earn are also tax-free.

Why do companies make matching contributions? For the same reason they pay their employees: they want to attract and hold the most talented workers they can. They also want to help those workers go on to a prosperous retirement—not only because that is the responsible thing to do, but also because happy retirees make for good public relations. There is also a more cynical explanation. Because of the anti-discrimination rules, employers are required to file a special tax form each year (Form 5500)—as well as complete annual calculations or tests to make sure the plan is not discriminating in favor of highly compensated employee. So, the highly paid employees (including those responsible for designing the 401(k) plan) have an incentive to attract as many lower-paid employees as possible into the plan. Unless they get enough of their staff into the plan, they can not contribute as much as they would like. Generous matches are among the most reliable ways to get the attention of lower-paid employees.

Most 401(k) plans also have loan privileges. Participants can borrow up to one-half of their own account value up to $50,000. The generally must be repaid within five years. Repayment takes place through automatic payroll deduction. In addition to repayment of loan principal, the employee must also repay a reasonable fixed rate of interest to the account. In essence, the employee is borrowing from and repaying himself/herself. If the employee leaves the company before he/she pays off the amount borrowed, the amount borrowed is considered a distribution, and the employee has to pay taxes and a penalty of 10% to the Federal government and a smaller percent to the State government.

Employees who quit their jobs have three options as to what to do with their 401(k)s. If the employee likes the way the company has been handling his/her funds, and has a vested balance of over $3,500, it can be left at the company until age 70½ or retirement, whichever is later, even if he/she does not work there anymore. Or, he/she can roll the money into an IRA account, or another 401(k) plan if taking a new job. (This is discussed in more detail later on in the manual). Thirdly, the employee can take a lump-sum distribution (full or partial). If he/she decides to take a distribution before age 59½, the financial costs can be steep. In addition to a 10% premature withdrawal penalty, the plan sponsor is required to set aside 20% for federal withholding tax on the amount that is not rolled over directly. This is only an estimate of the tax owed on the withdrawal—the actual amount would be determined when taxes are filed. Distributions can be taken without incurring a 10% penalty when a certain trigger event occurs, such as when the employee:

- Reaches age 59 ½.

- Dies (regardless of age) and proceeds go to a beneficiary or an estate.

- Becomes disabled (as determined by the IRS).

- Terminates employment and arranges for a series of substantially equal periodic payments over his/her life expectancy.

- Elects to retire at age 55.

- Incurs medical expenses that exceed a certain level.

- Uses the withdrawal for a first-time home purchase

The 403(b)

As mentioned earlier, the entire next chapter is devoted to the 403(b), a near mirror-image of the 401(k), but with a few very important differences. Therefore, I will not elaborate on it here. Suffice to say that the 403(b) is a non-profit employee's best friend when it comes to retirement investing. It is called *the last million dollar tax shelter in America,* and for good reason. The advantages of having a 403(b) plan are enormous and should be considered by every person who has the opportunity to invest in one.

The 457

Under Section 457 Of the Internal Revenue Code, employees of state or local governments, their agencies, and tax-exempt employers can set aside money for retirement on a pre-tax basis through a plan sponsored by their employer. 457s do not follow the same rules as 401(k) or 403(b) plans, though some similarities exist. Assets of a 457 plan are owned solely by the employer, and are therefore subject to claims from the employer's general creditors.

The maximum annual contribution to a Section 457 plan from all sources is the lesser of $8,000 or 25% of includible compensation (maximums are indexed to inflation as they are for the other four plans, and generally rise year to year). Employees due to retire in three years may make catch-up contributions in excess of this amount within certain limitations. *Includible compensation* is compensation paid by the employer for service performed which is currently included in taxable income (usually same as the W-2 income). Since the deferred compensation itself in not includible, the calculation is more easily understood if expressed as 25% of otherwise taxable pre-deferral compensation. Coordination with other deferral plans—403(b), 401(k), Section 125 Cafeteria Plans is required. Monies may be distributed at age 70 ½, upon termination of employment, at death, or for an unforeseeable emergency, such as illness, accident, or loss of property due to casualty.

Under current law, a 457 plan can be rolled over only to another 457 plan—not to an IRA or any other type of plan. Distribution options are more limited, too. For example, you cannot receive the favorable five-year averaging treatment for tax purposes that is available to other plans.

The 457(f) plan

Under Section 457(f) of the Internal Revenue Code, an employer can set aside money to supplement retirement income for a select group of employees in his/her organization. Since these programs are designed to attract and retain *key* employees and do not provide a benefit for all employees, these programs do not qualify for all of the tax advantages that are made available for the 457 plan.

IRAs

An IRA, or Individual Retirement Account, is a tax-deferred investment and savings account that acts as a personal retirement fund for people with employment income. In an IRA, your contributions can be deductible or non-deductible, and the earnings can grow tax-deferred until withdrawal (assumed to be retirement), at which time they are taxed as ordinary income.

The new Taxpayer Relief Act of 1997 represents the most sweeping change in the tax rules since 1986. The Act has brought about some significant changes to IRAs that make them more attractive than ever. These changes became effective on January 1, 1998. IRAs can be established for a tax year from January 1 of that year until April 15 of the next year, and contributions can be made at any point along the

111

way. That gives you the opportunity to get your money working for you right away, or allows you to fund it throughout that period. Alternately, it gives you a full 15½ months to make a decision about whether an IRA is right for you. There are three types of IRAs:

- The Traditional IRA.

- The Roth IRA.

- The Education IRA.

Since we are discussing pre-tax plans, we will only address the Traditional IRA here. There are two primary types of traditional IRAs: Regular and Spousal. Regular IRAs are designed for individuals with earned income, while Spousal IRAs are designed for married couples in which only one of the spouses has earned income. Anyone who earns compensation and is under age 70 ½ can open a Regular IRA. According to the IRS, you are eligible to contribute to a Spousal IRA if you meet *all* of the following conditions:

- You must be married at the end of the tax year.

- Your spouse must be under age 70½ at the end of the tax year.

- You must file a joint return for the tax year.

- You must have taxable compensation for the year.

- Your spouse must either have no compensation or choose to be treated as having no compensation for the tax year.

The maximum contribution per year is the lesser of $2,000 or 100% of earned income. This maximum includes both deductible and non-deductible contributions. Married couples may contribute up to $2,000 to each of two separate IRAs (one Regular, one Spousal), provided that the total amount (up to a maximum of $4,000) does not exceed 100% of the working spouse's income. Though almost anyone can *contribute* to an IRA, the rules to date have been very strict on who can *deduct* the amount of their contributions from their income tax returns. The new legislation relaxes the restrictions, meaning that more people will soon qualify for tax-deductible IRAs, making them a much more appealing investment option.

- Your contribution is *fully deductible* if neither you nor your spouse participated in a company-sponsored retirement plan; or you contributed to a company-sponsored retirement plan but are single and earn less than $35,000, *or* are married and have a joint income of less than $50,000. Beginning next year, for active participants in an employer-sponsored retirement plan, the income limit that determines whether your IRA contributions are tax-deductible begins to rise, leveling off in the year 2007. The increased deductible limits provide renewed incentive to invest through an IRA.

- Your contribution is *partially deductible* if you contributed to a company-sponsored retirement plan but are single and earn $30,000 - $40,000, *or* are married and have a joint income of $50,000 - $60,000. (Check with the IRS or see chapter 14 for more information on partially deductible contributions).

112

- Your contribution is *not deductible* if you contributed to a company-sponsored retirement plan and are single and earn more than $35,000 *or* are married and have a joint income of more than $50,000.

If you qualify for a traditional deductible IRA, you will probably be better off making a deductible contribution rather than participating in the new Roth IRA. That is because you get immediate tax savings with a deductible IRA. Contributions to a Roth IRA are not tax-deductible. Most IRAs offer a large number of investment options, including mutual funds and stocks, far more than the average 401(k) or 403(b). Additionally, if you want to move an IRA from one financial institution to another, it is as simple as filling out a form. The same distribution and withdrawal rules that apply to 401(k)s, 403(b)s, etc. also apply to an IRA plan. Further explanations and complete IRA comparisons are made in chapter 14.

SEP-IRAs

The SEP acronym stands for *Simplified Employee Pension*. You will also see it as SEPP *Simplified Employee Pension Plan*. The SEP-IRA is a tax-deferred retirement plan provided by sole proprietors, partnerships, a business owner of either an unincorporated or incorporated business; or an individual who earns any self-employed income by providing a service, either full-time or part-time, even if already covered by a retirement plan at his/her full-time job. SEP-IRAs allow employers to make tax-deductible contributions to employee's accounts. The employer's contributions are included in the employee's income, but the employee can deduct the contribution when they file their federal income tax return. These are ideal plans for self-employed individuals and small companies.

Only employers can contribute to SEP-IRAs (there are no employee contributions). Small business owners with fewer than 26 employees, are allowed to contribute nothing in one year or up to a maximum of 15% of each employee's total compensation, with a maximum contribution of $24,000. The employer must contribute the same percentage of each eligible employee's compensation (W-2 wages) as he/she contributes to himself/herself, and the vesting of contributions is immediate.

SEP-IRA contributions do not reduce the employees salary. Contributions and the investment earnings grow tax-deferred until withdrawal, at which time they are taxed as ordinary income. With the exception of the higher contribution limits, they are subject to the same rules as a regular IRA. Also, an employee is still allowed to contribute to an IRA on top of receiving contributions to a SEP-IRA. The IRA contribution is limited to $2,000 or 100% of compensation. If one is self-employed, the maximum annual contribution he/she can make to his/her SEP-IRA is the lesser of $30,000 or 13.04% of the net self-employment earnings, determined after the deduction allowed for one-half of the self-employment taxes.

If you are employed full-time but have a part-time money-making business, you can establish a SEP-IRA from money you make from your sideline effort. For an example, if you are working as a consultant away from you main job, or any form of self-employment away from a full-time job, you can still have a SEP-IRA even if you are covered by another retirement program at your full-time firm.

The funds in a SEP-IRA are tax-deductible since the contributions are treated as a business expense, and you simply deduct them from your federal income tax, just as you would the equipment you buy for your business.

As with all retirement plans, these funds are allowed to grow without being taxed. The income and capital gains are not taxed on an annual basis. However, when you start to withdraw the money as a distribution, something that must be done when retirement starts, the distributions will be taxed as ordinary income at the then prevailing income tax rate.

One big advantage of the SEP-IRA program is the ease with which it can be set up. This is the easiest, least government interfering retirement plan you can find if you are self-employed, or employed full-time with part-time self-employment. There is only one one-page form to use, government Form 5305-SEP, when opening an account, an account which can be at a brokerage firm, or a mutual fund company, or a bank, almost any financial institution can help set one up, often without charging a set-up fee. There are no annual reportings due to the government. Furthermore, one can make a contribution to the plan as late as April 15 of the following year for the previous year. And you are allowed to continue to contribute to the plan if you are self-employed and over 70 ½-years-old, unlike the IRA program which requires you to start withdrawing funds at that time.

Also, it allows for a large contribution, which is tax deductible, and you have the choice of where you want to invest. There is great flexibility: one year you may contribute the maximum, the next you may contribute nothing, then the following year, put in a little, followed by a year with a maximum amount once again. There are no administrative expenses because each person opens his or her own account and manages it independently. There are, however, some drawbacks to the SEP-IRA program:

- You can not borrow from the account the way you can from a 401(k).

- As an employer, your contributions to an employee's plan are immediately vested; you have no control over the funds.

- A SEP-IRA must cover all employees, including part-time employees, over the age of 21 who have worked for the employer during any three of the past five years.

- SEP-IRA monies do not receive the special five-year averaging taxation that applies to certain lump-sum distributions from qualified pension and profit-sharing plans. Of course, if you take your distribution over your retirement years instead of a one-time distribution, this does not apply to you.

SIMPLE-IRAs

The SIMPLE-IRA, or *S*avings *I*ncentive *M*atch *P*lan for *E*mployees-IRA, replaced the SARSEP-IRA for new plans established on or after January 1, 1997. Designed specifically for companies with 100 or fewer employees, the SIMPLE-IRA is a tax-deferred retirement plan provided by sole-proprietors or small businesses who do not maintain any other qualified retirement plan (including a SEP-IRA) to which contributions are made, or benefits are accrued for service in the calendar year for which the SIMPLE-IRA plan is maintained. They are generally most attractive to small-business owners who want employees to share the responsibility of saving for their own retirement through salary reduction contributions; contribute something toward their employees' retirement; and, want to avoid complex administrative requirements.

Employees are provided the opportunity to share in the responsibility for funding their own retirement. Contributions are made by *both* the employee and the employer, and are immediately 100% vested. In a SIMPLE-IRA, the employee's contributions are taken pre-tax, reducing their taxable salary, and the contributions and the investment earnings can grow tax-deferred until withdrawal (assumed to be retirement), at which time they are taxed as ordinary income. Depending on the company's rules, one may be eligible to contribute to a SIMPLE-IRA in any year where one was a regular employee and earned at least $5,000 in the preceding year.

There are actually two kinds of SIMPLE plans—a SIMPLE-IRA and a SIMPLE 401(k). These plans have most of the same features. The key differences between the two plans are covered in the chart below. For now, we will focus on the SIMPLE-IRA.

114

Eligible employees can elect to contribute up to 100% of their compensation per year up to a maximum of $6,000, by deferring a portion of their salary to the SIMPLE-IRA. (The employees' salary reduction contributions must be expressed as a percentage of compensation). Since these contributions are made on a pre-tax basis, they reduce each participant's current taxable income. While the employer is required to make contributions to the SIMPLE-IRAs of his/her eligible employees, he/she can choose between two different contribution methods. They are:

- The employer can match each participant's contributions on a dollar-for-dollar basis—up to 3% of the participant's compensation (maximum $6,000, as indexed for cost of living adjustments). The employer even has the flexibility of matching as little as 1% of each participant's compensation for any two years in a five-year period provided certain requirements are met.

- The employer can make annual non-elective contributions equal to 2% of each eligible employee's compensation (maximum $3,200)—regardless of whether the employee contributes to the plan or not.

Any contributions the employer makes on behalf of his/her employees are tax-deductible as a business expense, thereby reducing the company's taxable income.

In an established SIMPLE-IRA plan, the employees can take withdrawals from the plan at anytime. However, if an employee is under age 59 1/2, these withdrawals generally would be subject to a 25% early withdrawal penalty if taken within a two-year period beginning on the date the employee first participated in the plan, and a possible 10% early withdrawal penalty if taken after that time period.

The SIMPLE-IRA plan does not require the employer to complete any annual tax filings or special IRS tests. The employer, however, does need to make sure the employee's contributions are automatically deducted from their pay and sent within the required time limits, to the financial institution where the employee established his/her SIMPLE-IRA.

Employees with SIMPLE-IRAs can also invest in regular IRAs, giving them another opportunity to save for retirement. With the exception of the higher contribution limits, SIMPLE-IRAs are subject to the same rules as a regular IRA.

How does a SIMPLE 401(k) differ from a SIMPLE-IRA?

In the area of	The SIMPLE 401(k)
Employer Contributions	Does not allow employer to reduce matching contributions below 3%
Access to Assets	May allow employees to take loans against their plan and take withdrawals in certain hardship situations.
Administrative Responsibilities	Generally requires employer to file a special IRS tax form each year (Form 5500)

Keoghs—A Keogh plan is a tax-deferred retirement plan designed to help self-employed workers or partners, including sole-proprietors who file Schedule C or a partnership whose members file Schedule E, establish a retirement savings program. Keogh plans may be especially appropriate for people who have higher, more stable incomes, and want to contribute a greater amount to their plan than the SEP-IRA allows. Keogh plans generally require more administration than a SEP-IRA, such as filing an IRS Form 5500 annually for certain plans. There are three different types of Keogh plans—the Profit Sharing Keogh, the Money Purchase Keogh, and a Paired Keogh (which combines a Profit Sharing and Money Purchase Keogh).

One of the most attractive features of the Keogh is the high maximum contribution. The contributions are taken pre-tax, reducing your taxable salary, and both the contributions and earnings can grow tax-deferred until they are withdrawn. In addition to the high maximums, you retain the opportunity to invest in regular IRAs. As is the case with IRAs, contributions to a Keogh can be made for the tax year from January 1 of that year until April 15 of the next year. However, with the Keogh, the account must be opened by December 31 of the tax year for which the deduction is to be claimed. Maximum contributions vary among the three types of Keoghs:

1. **The Profit Sharing Keogh**—Offers the most flexibility, contributions can range from 0% to 15% of self-employment income, up to $30,000 per year. The contribution percentage can be adjusted yearly, or skipped entirely for a year. This plan limits you to the lowest annual contribution percentage of all Keogh options.

2. **The Money Purchase Keogh**—Allows you to set aside the highest percentage of compensation each year, thus offering you the potential for the largest tax deductions. With this plan you can contribute from 0% to 25% of compensation, up to a maximum of $30,000 per year. The contribution percentage, however, can not change from year to year, whether you have profits or not. You must make a contribution each year based on the fixed annual contribution percentage you specify when you set up the plan.

3. **The Paired Plan Keogh**—combines the benefits of both a Profit Sharing Keogh and a Money Purchase Keogh. A Paired Keogh may be the ideal choice if you want the maximum annual tax deduction when you can afford to make the maximum annual contribution. A Paired Keogh allows you to contribute 0% to 25% of compensation, up to $30,000 per year, per participant, *and* contribute a fixed annual contribution percentage to your Money Purchase Keogh and vary contributions to your Profit Sharing Keogh.

For any of these Keogh plans, you will need to contribute the same percentage of each eligible employee's compensation (W-2 wages) as you contribute for yourself. Participants can not take distributions from Keogh plans until a trigger event occurs, such as those mentioned above in the 401(k) section.

Beware of the 403(b) - Keogh pitfall—For self-employed workers, Keoghs offer the ability to set aside the largest amount of money in a retirement plan, without question. But those doctors, professors, researchers, etc., who contribute to a 403(b) retirement plan at a non-profit hospital, school, or other organization and then contribute to a separate retirement plan of their own, like a Keogh plan for the self-employed, may collide with some unexpected obstacles. That is because the contribution limits on the two plans can overlap. For a professional who has a 403(b) plan, the retirement vehicle used by non-profit groups, the rules are quite strict. A big contribution to another plan can preclude any participation in the 403(b) plan. The 403(b) is the only retirement plan that is offset by contributions to all other retirement plans.

The annual limit on a 403(b) plan contribution in 1998 and 1999 is $10,000, although other factors may raise or lower it for an individual. (This is explained more fully in the next chapter.) The annual limit for Keogh accounts is $30,000. That $30,000 limit supersedes the 403(b) limit. So a professor who has

116

self-employment income from, say, consulting and contributes $30,000 to a Keogh plan *cannot contribute at all* to a 403(b) plan. To contribute $10,000 to the 403(b) plan he/she would have to limit his/her Keogh contribution to $20,000. This applies to those who control more than 50% of their own company. The situation is quite different for an executive at a corporation, however. There the executive can contribute fully to a 401(k) plan or any other pension plan offered by the employer. And if the executive reports self-employment income for consulting, for example, the executive can contribute a portion of that money to a Keogh self-retirement plan as well.

The problem lies in the fact that most people affected are unaware of the rules. For example, highly-paid medical doctors who are on the staff of a hospital and have contributed the maximum for many years could have as much as $500,000 to $1,000,000 in a 403(b) plan. If these same people made the maximum Keogh contributions through their own private practice, *all* of their 403(b) money could be deemed immediately taxable by the IRS! And the IRS is checking. In the mid-90s, the IRS began to audit 403(b) plans because the agency found a disturbing level of noncompliance in those plans. At about the same time, the IRS began looking at returns of individuals who took a Keogh deduction on their 1040 Form to see whether they complied with all the regulations.

The bottom line is that a doctor who works at a non-profit hospital with a 403(b) plan and who contributes $30,000 to a Keogh plan from private practice cannot contribute anything to the 403(b) plan. But, if the doctor works at a for-profit hospital, he/she could put money in the company 401(k) plan up to its limit while continuing the $30,000 Keogh contribution.

Other Plans—There are other types of defined-contribution plans that do not carry pre-tax advantages. Some employers offer only one type of these defined-contribution plans that is funded by the employer, with the year's contribution tied to how well the company did.

Profit-Sharing Plans—A profit-sharing plan allows plan contributions to be paid out of the profits of the business. Some employers contribute a percentage of profits based on total profits, while some use a sliding scale. The employer may determine the contribution amounts each year so long as they are substantial and recurring. They can also be arranged so that the employer contribution matches an employee's percentage. These plans allow employees to withdraw funds that have been in the plan for two years, and to withdraw all funds if the participant has been in the plan for at least five years. Most profit-sharing plans offer loan privileges. The loan must carry a reasonable interest rate and must be repaid within a specified time.

Money Purchase Plans—Available to all eligible company employees. Under a money purchase plan, contributions are usually determined by a formula which is based upon a percentage of the employee's salary, as well as the length of time in the plan. Contribution streams in money purchase plans are more consistent than those in profit sharing plans. Most money purchase plans do not have loan privileges.

Employee Stock Ownership Plans (ESOPS)—With an ESOPS the employer contributes company stock or subsidizes the employee purchase of company stock. Any employee of the stock-issuing company is eligible for the plan. This plan does not carry loan privileges.

CHAPTER NINE

The 403(b)—The Last Million Dollar
Tax Shelter Around

It is time to introduce you to the most powerful investment tool you have at your disposal for retirement planning—the 403(b) plan.

Suppose your broker called you and pitched an investment that he claimed would shave thousands off this year's tax bill, earn a return of approximately 12% to 25%, and not generate a penny of future income taxes until you decided to sell. If you were smart, you would consider calling the securities regulators and hang up. After all, those types of deals just do not exist, at least not for the everyday workingman, right? *Wrong!!!*

As an employee in a non-profit institution, you are in a most advantageous position. You have at your fingertips what some of the most successful investors in the world call *the last million dollar tax shelter* around—the 403(b) investment plan.

What is a 403(b) plan?—A 403(b) is a *tax-deferred* investment and savings program for employees of certain tax-exempt employers. Uncle Sam permits anyone who works for a 501(c)(3) non-profit institution such as a public school, a college, a university, a philanthropic institution, a hospital or health care organization, a religious organization, a foundation, a museum, or a scientific and research institute, to save and invest for their own retirement. Currently, over 9 million Americans have a 403(b) plan.

The 403(b) plan, known by the section of the IRS Tax Code that authorizes it, is a tax-deferred retirement savings plan similar to the very popular 401(k) plans which are offered primarily by private industry to their employees. A 403(b) is sometimes known as a *deferred tax plan*, a *tax deferred annuity*, a *tax shelter*, a *TSA* (Tax Shelter Annuity), etc. Call it anything you want, but one fact stands alone—it is the best supplemental retirement opportunity in the world, and everyone who qualifies should have one.

Strictly speaking, a 403(b) is an employee benefit, in that you can participate in one only if you are an eligible employee of an institution that offers the plan. Section 403(b) was added to the Internal Revenue Code in 1958, a full 20 years before section 401(k), to permit employees of nonprofits and government agencies to set aside *pretax* money in an annuity contract offered by an insurance company. Thanks to its roots in the insurance industry, the 403(b) plan is most often referred to as a TDA or tax-deferred annuity.

119

However, in 1974 Congress added paragraph 7 to section 403(b). This newer provision permits employees to set up their retirement plans with mutual fund companies instead of insurance companies. That means that today's participants can choose between annuities and mutual funds. But they cannot choose other options permitted in a 401(k) plan such as guaranteed investment contracts or individual stocks.

The pension simplification rules that were tacked on to the minimum wage bill passed in July 1996 provided that all non-profits and government agencies will now be permitted to set up the more popular 401(k) plans if they choose. But that is not likely to happen. After surveying over 50 benefits consultants to find out if any of their clients planned to switch from 403(b) plans to 401(k)s, it was discovered that not one planned to do so. It is really no surprise. The costs for setting up the 401(k) plan are steep and there is no provision in the new law that allows 403(b) money to be rolled over to a 401(k). That means that an employer who chooses to set up a 401(k) would need to maintain both plans. Of course, those non-profits that do not have plans may choose a 401(k) rather than a 403(b). Those employers most likely to shift to a 401(k) plan are those that have *both* non-profit employees and for-profit employees, such as a gallery or museum that also runs a for-profit gift shop.

What it is not—A 403(b) is different from an organization Pension Plan in several ways:

- **Benefit**—With a 403(b) program, benefits depend on individual contribution levels and portfolio performance. A Pension Plan has predetermined benefits based on final salary, years of service and a fixed percentage rate. This was discussed fully in the last chapter.

- **Transferability**—You can roll a 403(b) account into another 403(b) program or an IRA, but when you leave a company, your pension generally stays there. For more information on "rollovers," see Chapter 18.

- **Investment Allocation Decisions**—Each participant in a 403(b) makes decisions for his/her own portfolio. A Plan Administrator makes decisions for the future pensioners.

- **Employee Contributions**—The employee contributes in a 403(b) program. Company Pensions do not require or allow employee contributions.

403(b) programs are often called *401(k)s for non-profits*. While this is generally true for most features, there are some differences:

- **Employer Involvement**—In a 403(b) program, employer involvement is not mandatory (beyond payroll). However, it is mandatory in a 401(k) plan for setting up, administering, and performing discrimination testing on the plan.

- **Subject to ERISA regulations**—Unlike a 401(k) plan, a 403(b) is only subject to ERISA regulations if there is employer involvement in setting up the program.

- **Vesting Schedule**—In most cases, vesting is automatic for a 403(b) program, while in most 401(k) plans, vesting occurs over a three-to-five year period.

- **Type of Account**—A 403(b) is a Custodial Account, a 401(k) is a Trust.

How does a 403(b) plan work?—If your employer does not sponsor a 403(b) program, request that they start one. If/when your employer sponsors a 403(b) program, you choose whether or not you want to participate. Most 403(b)s allow for immediate enrollment into the plan; there is no one-year waiting period like in other plans. If the employer is involved in setting up the program and choosing a financial services vendor or vendors, the program must offer a number of different investment options, which means you get to select your investments based on your own time horizon, risk aversion, and financial risk tolerance. (This will be covered in its entirety in the chapter on asset allocation).

When you join a 403(b) plan you enter into a *Salary Reduction Agreement* with your employer. You decide how much money you want deducted from your paycheck and invested during *each* pay period, up to the legal maximum. Investing a specific amount of money on a pre-determined basis (weekly, semi-monthly, or monthly) is called *dollar-cost averaging*—one of the best investment strategies around. Dollar-cost averaging is covered in more detail at the end of this chapter.

You and your employer agree that this specified amount will be *automatically* deducted from your salary. The payroll department is authorized by Congress to reduce the participant's (that is you) current reportable gross earnings on the W-2 form by the amount contributed to a 403(b). This reduces current taxable income. Since the money you contribute to your account is deducted from your pay *before income taxes are taken out,* it means that by contributing to a 403(b) you can actually lower the amount you pay each pay period in current taxes. For example, if you earn $2,000 each paycheck, and you contribute, say 10% ($200), you are only taxed on $1,800. You do not owe income taxes on the contributions and their earnings until you withdraw them from the plan, when you could be in a lower tax bracket. But even if you are not in a lower tax bracket, your money will have enjoyed years of tax-free compounding. Compounding makes an enormous difference in how fast your money grows. If the participant is in a 28% federal tax bracket, he or she can save up to 28% more than with an after-tax investment and still not reduce take-home pay. Remember, your contributions and earnings grow *tax-deferred*. Tax-deferred contributions and earnings make up the best one-two punch in investing!

Tax-Deferred Versus Taxable Account
($2,000 Annual Investment)

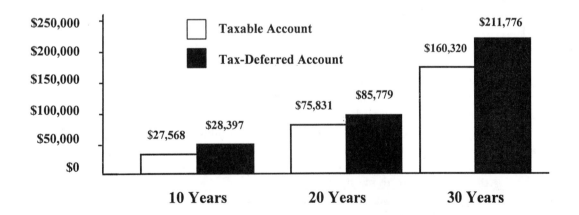

This chart assumes a hypothetical $2,000 annual investment at the beginning of each year, a 9% average annual rate of return and a 36% federal tax bracket. The tax-deferred investments are non-deductible contributions and their earnings grow tax-deferred until withdrawn at the end of the specified period, when the earnings are taxed at the rate of 36%. The taxable investments are invested after-tax and their earnings are taxed every year and the tax liability is deducted from the balance. This hypothetical example is for illustrative purposes only and does not represent the performance of any actual security.

121

What if my employer does not offer a 403(b) plan?—If your employer does not offer a 403(b) plan, suggest that he/she start one. These plans can be set up easily with little effort and paperwork. Keep in mind that by law, you are entitled to contribute to a tax-deferred plan. The greatest task is to choose the investment companies with whom the employer wants to do business. That decision is usually made by the Benefits Office after getting feedback from the employees within the organization. Many times this feedback is obtained through the local union. Once the investment companies have been chosen, it's simply a matter of the employer establishing an account with them. To establish an employer-sponsored retirement savings plan, most investment companies who have been chosen ask the benefits administrator to provide them with the following information:

- The name, address and phone number of a contact person in your Benefits Office.

- The approximate number of eligible employees in your organization.

An Operation Handbook will be mailed, along with the necessary application. After the employer completes and returns the application, the chosen investment companies will be established as investment options for the individual 403(b) accounts. Then, the employees who wish to open their individual 403(b) plan accounts can directly contact the investment companies of their choice to begin investing. It is usually that simple. To receive more information, call the Internal Revenue Service at 1-800-829-3676 and ask for Publication 590.

Contributions—Contributions to a 403(b) plan can come from both employees and employers, although the most popular program offered by employers, by far, is the 403(b) plan in which contributions are made solely by the employee. These *employee only* contributions are called *salary reduction contributions*. As mentioned above, you have your employer deduct a specified amount from your pay and invest that money into your 403(b) account by forwarding the contributions to the chosen investment options. Remember, the investment options are your choice.

These *pre-tax* contributions are automatic. Automatic payroll deduction makes contributing virtually painless, and since your contribution never shows up in your paycheck, you do not miss it. And, since your contribution is untaxed, it is worth more to you in the 403(b) plan than it would be in your paycheck, where it would be reduced by income taxes. When $1.00 goes into your 403(b) account, you have invested all 100 cents of it.

Does this mean that if one saved enough, one could theoretically reduce federal taxable income to nothing? A nice thought, but no. Congress limits the amount that you can contribute to your 403(b) plan to ensure that it still receives revenue from you in the form of federal income tax. Since your contribution is tax-deferred, every dollar that you contribute to your 403(b) plan is a dollar that the government does not immediately receive federal taxes on. It receives the taxes later, when you withdraw your money. By limiting how much income you can protect from current taxes, Congress ensures that it will have a steady revenue flow.

- **Why is the government giving me this tax break?**—Because it wants you to save as much as possible for your retirement. Because of the critical problems with Social Security (see chapter 2), the government has opted to pass up current tax revenue in order to reduce the very real risk that you and millions of other Americans will wind up without enough money to live comfortably in retirement.

- **What kinds of investments can I choose in my 403(b) plan?**—When paragraph 7 was added to Section 403(b) of the Tax Code, it gave 403(b) plan participants the option of choosing between annuities and mutual funds (this topic is discussed more fully in chapter 12).

- **What happens to the money I put into the 403(b) plan?**—It goes into the investments you have chosen from a list of investment options supplied by your employer. Most 403(b) plans offer you a selection of at least three different investments. Many offer five choices or more. Typical investments include stock and mutual bond funds, money market funds, insurance annuities, etc. The chapter on asset allocation contained in this manual will help you decide which investments are right for you.

- **Can I leave my money in the plan indefinitely?**—No. The federal government will allow you to put off paying taxes on this money only for so long. Generally, you must begin to take withdrawals no later than April 1 of the year following the year in which you turn age 70 ½.

- **How do I know how well my investments are doing?**—You will receive financial statements from the investment companies you have selected at least once a year that shows the amounts you have contributed and how all your investments have performed. Most companies report on either a semi-annual, quarterly, or monthly basis.

- **What does the 403(b) plan cost—and who is paying for it?**—Basically, the plan has two kinds of expenses: administrative costs and investment management fees. Administrative costs are slight. The trustee or sponsor (your employer) sees that the contributions are deducted from the employee's paycheck and then transferred to the investment company. Investment management fees are usually charged by the investment company as a percentage of the total assets under management. These fees might range from 0.2% to 2% of the assets, depending on the investment. In general, investment management fees are higher on stock funds than on bond funds, for example.

- **Where do I find the money to invest?**—This is the first question many people ask about a 403(b) plan. Interestingly, this has nothing to do with how much or how little they earn. Surveys consistently show that at every income level the single most frequently cited reason for not participating in a 403(b) plan is that people do not believe they can afford the contributions. If you feel that way, I suggest you re-read chapters 6 and 7. Remember our discussion on saving an extra $1.00 a day? It makes a tremendous difference on your *return on investment*.

The truth is that most people can set aside up to 10% of what they earn and hardly notice the difference, especially if it is automatically deducted from their paychecks. When you do not have it, you do not spend it and you do not miss it. As you know, I suggest that you save *at least* 10% of your income (you really should shoot for 20%). But once again, if 10% sounds like too much to start with, then start smaller, say 5%, and gradually increase your contributions by *at least* 1% a year until you are to the 10% level. If saving that much is a hardship on you, you can always scale it back a little.

- **Can I transfer money from my savings account into my 403(b)?**—No. All contributions must be a salary reduction through your employer.

- **What is the minimum?**—There really is not a *legal* minimum contribution, but most investment companies establish a minimum investment within an account to keep administrative costs down. Allowing people to contribute any dollar amount they wished would add greatly to the costs of the plan, and would eventually have to be absorbed by investors, thereby reducing their investments.

- **What is the maximum?**—Like all tax breaks, this one is strictly limited. Determining the maximum contribution limit for a 403(b) account can get complicated. It is determined by your *Maximum*

Exclusion Allowance—a calculation based on your compensation, years of service, and your previous contributions to your current retirement plan. Under normal circumstances the maximum contribution for tax years 1998 and 1999 is either $10,000 or 25% of compensation, *whichever is less*. The IRS adjusts the contribution amount for inflation in $500 increments. At the current inflation rate, that means an increase every two years. In 1997, the legal limit for pre-tax contributions was $9,500.

Some participants can make *catch-up* elections which allow contributions in excess of the 25% of compensation/$10,000 maximum limit up to a maximum of $13,000 a year for five years. It is contingent on the maximum exclusion allowance. Maximum exclusion allowance and catch-up provisions will be covered completely later.

- **After I have made the maximum pre-tax contribution allowed, can I put additional money into the plan if I want to?**—No. A 403(b) plan allows only pre-tax employee contributions.

- **What happens if I contribute too much to my 403(b)?**—There are specific rules relating to overcontributions and a penalty tax is usually assessed. It is very important to calculate the maximum carefully and not to exceed it. If you do overcontribute, it is a good idea to correct it as quickly as possible.

- **Why can my co-worker contribute more than I can?**—Since the Maximum Exclusion Allowance is based on your personal salary, years of service, amounts contributed in the past, etc., your contributions will tend to be different than your co-worker's.

- **Can I change the amount I contribute?**—Yes. But you may have to wait for a specific date to do it. Every employer has its own rules about how frequently you can change your contribution. Most employers let you do this on a specific date: at the beginning of every calendar quarter, for example, or at the start of every month. Others permit contribution changes at any time.

- **Can I stop contributing to my account if I just can not afford to save the money any longer?**—Yes. There is no legal provision to allow this. You can stop contributing at any time.

- **Can I take my money out of the plan if I stop contributing to it?**—You could, but be careful. The fact that you are no longer contributing to the plan does not mean you can start taking withdrawals. There are only three ways to take money out of your 403(b) account—distributions, early withdrawals, and loans. You can take distributions after age 59 ½; you can take early withdrawals only for reasons specifically approved by the IRS (this is covered completely later on in this chapter); and whether or not you can take a loan depends on your investment company's rules.

- **Can I start contributing again after I have stopped?**—Yes. You may start contributing again. But if you stopped making contributions in conjunction with taking a hardship withdrawal from the plan, you may have to stay out for at least one full year.

- **Can I switch my money from one investment company choice to another that my employer offers?**—Yes. However, it is up to you to open the new account. The employer merely sends your contribution to a different company.

- **Can I invest with more than one company?**—Yes, but make sure your contributions to all companies are within the maximum limits.

- **How often can I switch money among investments?**—That depends on your employer's policy. There is no legal requirement that your employer has to follow when it comes to frequency of transfers between 403(b) investments.

- **If I have more than one investment within an investment company to contribute to, can I change how I allocate my contribution?**—Of course. You simply notify the company with whom you are invested, and tell them what you want to do. Most of the time the change can be made right over the phone. In this case the employer does nothing. Remember, the employer is simply transferring a lump sum of money, which is deducted from your paycheck, to your investment company. It is the investment company who allocates your contributions, based upon your designation.

- **What is the difference between saving money in a 403(b) and putting money into a mutual fund or bank account, etc. on one's own?**—Taxes, taxes, taxes!!! Refer again to the previous chart. An ordinary savings account or mutual fund does not allow you to save on a tax-deferred basis. So, in an ordinary savings account, you are saving money that has already been taxed, and you continue to pay tax on the earnings of that account, too. The money you contribute to a 403(b), however, comes out of your paycheck before taxes are taken out. Thus, you do not pay income tax on the money you contribute to your 403(b) account or on any earnings until you take it out, which is usually at retirement, when you probably will be in a lower tax bracket. The bottom line: more of your money is working for you instead of going toward taxes. Keep in mind, however, that investing in a 403(b) plan is only a *part* of a sound retirement saving plan. As outlined in chapter 6, it is important to have a certain amount of personal savings set aside from your retirement savings in case of an emergency.

- **Should I contribute to a 403(b) plan instead of in an IRA?**—Definitely. Even with the new tax laws, you can still contribute more tax-free dollars to your 403(b)—remember, up to $10,000, depending on your salary. My advice? Use your 403(b) to the max! The only caveat is if the 403(b) investment choices are severely limited. For example, if your employer offers only one plan, and that plan carries heavy load charges, and/or low returns (which is quite common with annuities offered by insurance companies), you might be better off investing in an IRA where you can make the investment choice. But there are other factors to consider. It is easier to save in a 403(b) plan than in an IRA and for a very simple reason: your 403(b) contributions are taken out of your paycheck automatically. Saving in an IRA requires a continuing conscious decision and self-discipline that many people simply do not have. Another important potential advantage 403(b)s have over IRAs is that many 403(b) plans allow loans. You can not ever borrow money from your IRA account.

- **If I contribute to a 403(b), can I also contribute to an IRA?**—Yes. However, depending on your adjusted gross income, those contributions may or may not be fully deductible. Go to chapter 14 for complete details.

- **An IRA seems safer than a 403(b) plan. Can I switch my money from my 403(b) into an IRA?**—First, let us clear up a common misconception. An IRA is no safer than a 403(b) plan. Contrary to what many people assume, IRAs are not government-guaranteed. In most cases, an IRA is not as good a financial deal as a 403(b) plan is. You can contribute a much higher annual maximum to a 403(b) than the $2,000 you can put into an IRA, and your 403(b) contribution reduces your current taxes. Depending on what you earn, an IRA contribution might not do that. Now, the answer to the question. You can not switch your money from a 403(b) into an IRA unless you are getting a 403(b) distribution. Remember, that does not happen unless:

- You are leaving your job.

- You are older than 59 ½.

- You qualify for a hardship withdrawal. If you do qualify for a hardship withdrawal, you will need every dime of this money for a specific emergency—you will not have anything left to roll into an IRA.

26. Can I write a check to add more money to my account?—No. By law, the only way you can contribute money to your 403(b) plan account is by automatic payroll deduction. You can not write a check to add money to your account. If you want to contribute more money to your account, you must fill out a request form asking the payroll department to increase your deduction/contribution. Remember, though, you can not contribute more than the maximum allowed.

27. If I leave my job, is the money I put into the 403(b) plan mine to take with me?—Absolutely. Remember that you own the plan. It is your money. You have three choices as to what to do with the account:

- You can simply leave it where it is. However, you can not contribute additional funds to the plan. The account is placed on a paid-up status and continues to grow tax-deferred until you withdraw the funds once you reach the age of 59 ½ (certain strategies can be used to access the money earlier without penalty, which will be discussed in greater detail later on in the chapter).

- You can roll it over. If you change jobs, you can once again begin contributing to the plan if your new employer has one. To maintain its tax-deferred status and avoid possible early withdrawal penalties, you must roll over your 403(b) account directly into your new employer's 403(b) plan. If they do not have a 403(b) plan, and you do not want to go to the trouble of having them start one, you can roll over your investment into a Rollover (or Conduit) IRA. To ensure a direct rollover, and avoid very stiff penalties, be sure that your former 403(b) plan's custodian makes the check directly payable to your new IRA's custodian. *Do not have the check made payable to you.* Many people make the mistake of having the check made payable to them thinking that they will, in turn, simply write a check and send the withdrawn funds to the new company. Big penalties!!! Big mistake!!! Of course, if this transfer takes place within the same investment company there is nothing to worry about.

- Take a lump sum distribution (full or partial). If you decide to take a distribution before age 59 ½, the financial costs can be steep. In addition to a 10% premature withdrawal penalty, your plan sponsor is required to set aside 20% for federal withholding taxes. This is only an estimate of the tax you will owe on the withdrawal—the actual amount will be determined when you file your taxes.

Whatever you decide to do with the money, be sure to do it the correct way—consult your tax professional. There are hefty taxes to pay if you make a mistake.

- **My spouse and I are both eligible to participate in 403(b) plans. We can not afford to put the maximum contribution into both plans. How do we decide how much of our limited retirement money to put into each plan?**—If you both work for the same organization, there really is not much to think about. But if you work in different organizations, you do have some factors to consider. You will have to compare the two plans carefully. Do not compare a mutual fund that buys bonds with a mutual fund that buys stocks, for example, and when you compare two bond funds, make sure they are the same kind of bond fund. An intermediate-term bond fund buys bonds with an average 5- to 7-year maturity. You should not compare its performance with that of a long-term bond fund, which buys bonds with 15 to 25 year maturities. One plan may feature a greater range of investment choices than the other one, or may include investments that have performed better. Investigate the investment choices thoroughly and choose the best one for your set of circumstances. Finally, consider whether or not you can borrow from the 403(b) accounts. Not all 403(b) plans allow you do to this. If you anticipate that you will need to borrow from your retirement nest egg to cover a major expense—a down payment on a house, for example—a loan feature could be the determining factor in choosing one 403(b) plan over the other.

- **Is there ever a time when I should not contribute to a 403(b) plan?**—Yes! Just because everyone says 403(b)s are the best thing to invest in does not mean that your particular plan is. Not all 403(b) plans are created equal. Some are downright dangerous. For one thing, many 403(b) plans do not provide you with a menu of potential investments that are suited to your particular investment objectives. Or, the investment options available to you may only provide funds in those market areas with poor performance records, or excessive loads or fees. If you think that your plan is too restrictive, do not be afraid to say no.

  A possible solution to the problem would be to drum up support among employees for adding investment options to the existing 403(b) plan. Most employers are willing to make changes once they are convinced that the changes are worth making. (This topic is fully addressed in chapter 12). But if all else fails, and there is not a way to build a portfolio you can live with and prosper by, consider opening an IRA or other retirement account instead.

  Safety—A 403(b) account can grow very quickly into a substantial sum. The bigger it gets, the more likely you are to ask "Is this money safe?" The answer is yes. Your contributions and their earnings can not be breached by your employer, or by its creditors. This is your account. Only you can access it. Investment houses go to great pains to protect your privacy.

- **Does the government guarantee my 403(b) account?**—No. There is no federal agency like the Pension Benefit Guaranty Corporation that guarantees 403(b) benefits. There is no need for one. The PBGC was set up to guarantee pension benefits in case defined-benefit plan assets are not sufficient to pay the promised retirement benefits. Remember, the promised benefits are specific monthly amounts, based on the covered employee's salary and years of service. (see chapter 8). That kind of short-fall is not a risk in a 403(b) plan because your retirement benefit from the plan will never be greater than the assets in your account. In fact, your retirement benefit in a 403(b) is exactly equal to the market value of the assets in your account. How much or how little your accumulated balance will be worth when you reach retirement is determined by the amount of your contributions and the performance of the investments you choose. You could lose money if your investments perform badly. There is no government guarantee to protect you from investment losses.

- **Does the employer guarantee 403(b) accounts?**—No. The employer is simply a *fiduciary* of the 403(b) plan—a sponsor. That means they are only responsible for supervising the transferring of the contributions deducted from your paycheck. The employer in no way offers protection against any investment losses you may suffer.

- **What happens to my account if I am laid off or fired?**—That is no different than if you leave your current employment for another job, or if you resign. The money is still there for you to direct. Just remember, once you get fired or quit your job you can no longer contribute to your 403(b)—not until you resume employment with a new employer that has a 403(b).

- **What happens to my account if I am disabled?**—There are certain trigger events that allow you to tap your 403(b) plan without incurring the standard 10% penalty. Being totally disabled (as defined by the IRS) is one of them, regardless of your age (this topic will be covered in more detail in the section on *withdrawals* later on in the chapter). Be aware, though, that you will owe ordinary income taxes on any money you take out.

- **What happens to my 403(b) account if I die before I retire?**—When you join your 403(b) plan you must designate a beneficiary who will receive the money in your account when you die. (If you do not do this, your estate automatically becomes the beneficiary. That can create huge problems).
  If your beneficiary is your spouse, he or she gets most of the same options with this money that you would have if you were leaving your job: rolling the distribution into an IRA or withdrawing it all and paying income taxes on it, etc. If your survivor elects to withdraw the money and pay taxes on it, the IRS *will not* impose the 10% early withdrawal penalty, regardless of his or her age. Your named beneficiary will receive the total current cash value of your account, or may select a settlement option.
  If your spouse is your beneficiary and wants to delay receipt of the income for tax purposes, he/she can do this up until the date *you* would have reached age 70 ½ and may spread the payments over his or her own life expectancy. A non-spouse beneficiary has fewer options. He or she does not have the option of rolling your 403(b) balance into an IRA, for example. Non-spouse beneficiaries must begin taking distributions no later than December 31 of the year following your death and may take payments over his or her life expectancy. Otherwise, the entire account balance must be depleted in no more than five years.

- **What happens to my 403)b) account if I die after age 70 ½?**—If you die after you attain age 70 ½, your beneficiary must continue to take distribution payments at least as rapidly as the method you selected. The beneficiary may always take a lump sum or a more rapid payment.

- **Can my spouse empty my 403(b) account without my knowledge?**—No. Your spouse can not touch a penny of your retirement account unless you die or get divorced. However, your husband or wife is legally entitled to be the designated beneficiary of your 403(b) account. You do not have a choice in the matter. In fact, the Internal Revenue Code says that on *all* qualified retirement plans (including IRAs), your spouse must be the named beneficiary unless he or she has signed a consent waiver surrendering the right.

- **Can I empty my 403(b) account without my spouse knowing about it?**—Probably not. If your plan follows joint-and-survivor rules, your spouse is legally entitled to the option of receiving a share of your retirement payout in the form of lifetime annuity payments. If that is the case, your plan may require that your spouse approve any loans or hardship withdrawals you take from your account.

- **If I get divorced, is my spouse entitled to a share of my 403(b) account?**—In all probability, yes. Remember, the money that you accumulated in the account during your marriage is considered a marital asset, and marital assets are divided between divorcing spouses. The formula for dividing those asset depends partly on your specific circumstances and partly on the laws of the state in which you live. In community property states, marital assets are generally split 50/50. This does not mean each specific asset is cut in half, but rather that the entire marital estate is divided. The community property states are Arizona,

California, Idaho, Louisiana, Nevada, New Mexico, Texas, Washington, and Wisconsin. In equitable distribution states, marital assets are divided equitably—i.e., fairly, which does not necessarily mean a 50/50 split. Here, inequities can occur. The ultimate decision of what is fair is made by the court. In general, the court determines how much of your pension plan is a marital asset by dividing the number of years you have been married by the number of years you have been a plan participant. For example, if you have been married for two years and a plan participant for three years, two-thirds of your pension would be considered a marital asset. All other things being equal, your spouse would get half of that two-thirds. As you might well imagine, some cases can get quite complicated. Always consult an attorney to protect your rights.

After the court has divided your 403(b) account between you and your former husband or wife, it issues a Qualified Domestic Relations Order (QDRO). The order requires you to split your 403(b) account into two parts. Your former spouse gets all the normal rights of any other plan participant over his or her share, including the right to leave the money invested in the 403(b) plan, unless the court order specifies that it must be paid out immediately. If your ex-spouse opts not to roll his or her share into an IRA, the money will be subject to income tax; but in a divorce situation, the IRS waives the 10% early withdrawal penalty that would normally be levied on any distribution made to a participant under age 59 ½.

- **Can my 403(b) account balance be levied to pay child support?**—Possibly. Under the terms of a Qualified Domestic Relations Order (QDRO), a divorce court can also order that part of your 403(b) balance go directly to your children, or in the form of child support. If that happens, the children can not roll the money into an IRA; taxes will be due on it. The kids do not have to pay the taxes, however. You do.

- **Is my account protected from my creditors if I file for bankruptcy?**—Maybe. What you get to keep when you file for bankruptcy depends on state law. Each state has a different list of assets that are exempt. When you file for bankruptcy, some states give you the choice of selecting either the state's list of exempt assets or the list of exempt assets that is included in the federal bankruptcy law. If you live in a state that gives you that option and you choose the exemptions listed in the federal law, your 403(b) account is protected from creditors if the court finds that considering:

  1. Your age.

  2. The debts you can not avoid even by filing for bankruptcy.

  3. Your other assets.

  4. Your dependents.

  5. Your future employment prospects. This money is reasonably necessary for your support. But most states only permit you to use the exemptions in their own laws which may or may not exempt 403(b) assets.

Some people assume that 403(b) accounts are protected because of a 1992 ruling by the U.S. Supreme Court which said that retirement assets qualifying under ERISA—can not be touched by creditors in a bankruptcy. The Court said a major reason for its ruling is that the debtor has such limited access to those assets. But unfortunately, it is still unresolved whether the Court's ruling does apply to 403(b)s, which give participants much more access to their money—through loans and hardship withdrawals—than a traditional pension does.

Because there are so many variables, it is a mistake to file for bankruptcy without finding out specifically how it might affect your accumulated retirement assets. Even in the same state, interpretation of bankruptcy law can vary from one court to another. If you contemplate filing for bankruptcy, your best course of action is to consult a lawyer in the area where you live to find out how the local courts treat 403(b) assets.

Taxes—The idea of saving money on taxes has already been mentioned, and is worth mentioning again. Why? Because tax savings are about the biggest advantage to joining a 403(b) plan. But these tax savings are strictly regulated. All 403(b) plans are regulated by the Internal Revenue Service, and unless you happen to be a CPA the tax rules governing these plans can seem quite complex. Your best guideline is *never to assume* that you know how the IRS will treat a contribution to a tax-deferred account, a transfer from one tax-deferred account to another, or a withdrawal from a tax-deferred account. Always check with your tax accountant to be sure you understand how the IRS will treat any action you take with your 403(b) money.

41. What is the difference between *pre-tax* and *after-tax* contributions?—There are two types of contributions we refer to when speaking of taxes as related to retirement: *pre-tax* and *after-tax*. *Pre-tax* contributions come out of your pay *before* taxes are calculated. Therefore, pre-tax contributions are taxable when you take them out of the plan because they were not taxed when they went in. *After-tax* contributions are those you make from your net pay, your income *after* taxes. Therefore, after-tax contributions are taxed when they go into the 403(b) plan. Because you have already paid taxes on this money, you will not owe additional taxes on it when you take it out of the plan. But when you withdraw after-tax contributions you made after 1986 you must, at the same time, withdraw a proportionate share of the interest they earned. That interest is subject to income taxes and to an early withdrawal penalty if you are under 59 ½. The following chart shows the significant differences between pre-tax and after-tax contributions:

Pre-tax Contributions Versus After-tax . . . What is the Difference?

Pre-tax contributions		After-tax contributions	
✓	Come out of your pay *before* taxes are calculated	✓	Come out of your pay *after* taxes are calculated
✓	Lower your current taxable income, so you pay less in taxes *now*	✓	Do not lower your current taxable income
✓	Increase your take-home pay *now*	✓	Do not increase your take-home pay
✓	Are taxed as ordinary income when you take money out of the plan	✓	Are not taxed at withdrawal because you've already paid it – but you do have to pay tax on any earnings
✓	Have restrictions on withdrawals before age 59 ½ to encourage you to save for when you'll need it most -- at retirement. If you withdraw **before-tax** contributions before you reach age 59 ½, you pay ordinary income tax and possibly a 10% early withdrawal penalty.	✓	Have fewer restrictions on withdrawals before age 59 ½. If you withdraw from your **after-tax** savings before you're 59 ½, you must also withdraw part of the earnings on that money, which is taxable, and may be subject to the 10% early withdrawal penalty. ***Note: You do not have to withdraw earnings on any money you invested in 1986 or earlier.**

To repeat, the money you contribute to your 403(b) plan is *pre-tax* money. The following advantages to contributing pre-tax money are worth mentioning again:

- You lower your taxable income. For example, if you earn $2,000 each paycheck, and you contribute 10% ($200), you only pay current income tax on $1,800. That means lower income taxes *now*.

- More of your money is working for you. Because you have not paid income tax on that $200, all of it is being invested in your account, instead of going into Uncle Sam's pocket. As I stated earlier in the chapter, when $1.00 goes into your 403(b) account, you have invested all 100 cents of it.

- You do not pay income tax on your contributions until you withdraw them from the plan, which should be at retirement, when you will probably be in a lower tax bracket.

- **Are there are other differences between a pre-tax and an after-tax contribution?**—Not really. The main thing to understand is that eventually, everything is taxable. The big difference between pre-tax and after-tax contributions is *when* the tax falls due. Uncle Sam only gets one slice of the pie. You have to pay taxes sooner or later, but not both sooner *and* later.

- **Do I pay any taxes at all on the money I contribute to the plan?**—Yes. Your contributions are not exempt from Social Security taxes. This has a positive aspect, though. It means your Social Security benefits are unaffected by your participation in the plan. If you put $1,000 into the 403(b) plan, you will pay Social Security tax on the entire amount unless you have already paid the maximum Social Security tax for the year. But 403(b) contributions *are* exempt from federal income tax, and state income tax in all states except Pennsylvania. They are also exempt from local taxes in many municipalities. Check with your employer's business office to see how your municipality treats 403(b) contributions.

- **If I am saving money that I plan to use before I retire, does it make more sense to do it with after-tax 403(b) contributions, or to save it outside the 403(b) plan?**—In general, it makes more sense to do your short-term, after-tax saving outside your 403(b) plan. In doing that you do not have to worry about taxes or penalties on the interest your after-tax contributions earned. For more on that topic, see chapter 15.

- **What happens to the earnings my 403(b) investments make?**—In a 403(b) plan your earnings (dividends and short and long-term capital gains) are automatically re-invested into your account. You do not have a choice in the matter.

- **How are the earnings in my 403(b) account taxed?**—Dividends and capital gains reinvested in your company's retirement plan account will not be taxed until you withdraw them (which ideally will be at retirement, when you could be in a lower tax bracket). They are taxed as ordinary income. If you withdraw them before age 59 ½, you may owe a 10 percent early withdrawal penalty.

Dollar-cost averaging—Dollar-cost averaging is routinely advocated by stock brokers, financial columnists and others as the best way to invest over the long term. It has been mentioned a handful of times in this manual as well. But what is dollar-cost averaging? It is nothing more than making consistent monthly deposits into the same investment category, rather than buying securities in one lump sum. In a 403(b) account, it happens automatically. The contribution that you designate is deducted from your paychecks by your employer and forwarded to your investment company of choice. As mentioned above, it is an inherent part of the 403(b) plan makeup.

A strong case can be made for it: you regularly invest, say, $100, $200, or $300 month after month. If stock and mutual fund prices then go up, you can congratulate yourself for having earned some profits. But what if prices go down? Well, you congratulate yourself on your new opportunity to pick up some bargains. Several months ago, your $300 monthly investment could buy, say, 5 shares; now it can buy 8!

A sound means of practicing dollar-cost averaging is to buy shares of a mutual fund at regular monthly intervals, particularly a no-load fund. It will keep you from getting crushed in the wild up-and-down market swings and help you to avoid two common investor errors: shifting all your money into the stock market at a time when it might be getting ready for a sharp tumble; and selling out at big losses when stocks are deeply depressed.

Again, in a 403(b) plan, dollar-cost averaging happens automatically. That is one of the reasons that the 403(b) plan is a superior investment strategy. (Dollar-cost averaging also can be used to buy individual stocks, although brokerage fees on small transactions can be prohibitive. But if you use a deep-discount broker, dollar-cost averaging is a simple and effective way to reduce market risk). There is even more to say about dollar-cost averaging. It also proves to be an important strategy from a psychological point of view.

Investing is a tough psychological act and many people are afraid they may blow their retirement, college fund for their children, etc. if they make the wrong decision and regret it for the rest of their lives. Dollar-cost averaging has the ability to reduce investor responsibility which is especially helpful for investors who are concerned about their exposure to regret.

Another psychological problem that dollar-cost averaging overcomes is our lack of self-control. We are simply too emotionally involved with our investments to shake off news about the market, whether it is bullish or bearish. Investors who practice dollar-cost averaging are more likely than other investors to continue buying securities after a period of decline in stock prices and less likely to accelerate buying after a period of increases in market prices.

The bottom line? It would be great if humans were like computers when it came to investing. Unfortunately, that is not the case. Most investors, even highly sophisticated money managers, are all too prone to making decisions based on short-term market price movements and psychological fears. Dollar-cost averaging is a way of helping us circumvent some of our humanistic tendencies and build and maintain a profitable nest egg.

MEA—Maximum Exclusion Allowance—Recent IRS audits have found widespread infractions of the 403(b) tax laws. If you are, or will be, one of the millions of employees of tax-exempt organizations who contributes to a 403(b) plan, you may owe a hefty tax bill if you are not careful. A typical problem is that employees put too much money in their plans because they do not understand the formula that limits the amount they are allowed to contribute.

If the IRS finds a problem with your plan, you may be forced to get out your checkbook. If you unknowingly exceeded the contribution limit, you could owe taxes on the savings, plus penalties for up to the past three years. The IRS could even revoke the tax-exempt status of your plan, which would make you liable for taxes on all contributions and earnings!

How can you avoid the problems? By accurately calculating your Maximum Exclusion Allowance. As stated many times, it is extremely important to maximize your contribution to a 403(b) plan in order to fully maximize future returns. Therefore, it is imperative that you know just exactly how much you are legally permitted to contribute each year. This legal maximum is called your Maximum Exclusion Allowance (MEA). The Tax Reform Act of 1986 limits the maximum allowable salary reduction contribution. As stated earlier in the chapter, this year's maximum is $10,000 or 25% of compensation, *whichever is less*.

Your MEA is determined based upon your age, compensation, years of service, previous 403(b) contributions, and other retirement plans in which you may have participated. Remember, your 403(b) contribution may be offset by any additional retirement plans that you have with your current employer. If you are unfamiliar with the retirement plan(s) maintained by your employer, ask your Benefits Office to help you with your questions.

In addition to the standard rules for contributions, you may be eligible for a *Catch-Up* deferral limit. If you have at least 15 full years of service with your current employer, and your total 403(b) contributions are under $75,000, the $10,000 (or 25%) limit may be increased. The increase or catch-up contribution may be as much as $3,000 in a given year. That is the *yearly* maximum. Over your lifetime, the additional catch-up contributions you make may not total more than $15,000. This necessitates a *yearly* calculation of your MEA to make sure that you do not over contribute.

There are a number of factors which determine your catch-up contribution. One factor which must be considered is the total amount of catch-up contributions you make over time, beginning in 1987 and adding each following year. You *must* keep track of your catch-up contributions so that you know when you have reached your lifetime $15,000 limit. If your annual calculations show that you may be eligible for an extra amount of salary reduction, consider the total amount already *caught up* (if any) from previous years, and subtract it from the lifetime $15,000 limit. This will tell you how much catch-up you have left. For example:

Normal Maximum Salary Reduction	**Maximum Salary Reduction Using 402(g) Catch-Up**	**402(g) Catch-Up Used This Year**
$10,000	$13,000	$3,000

Let us use the numbers above and assume you have $12,000 left in your lifetime $15,000 catch-up allowance limit. That means you have already used $3,000 of your lifetime $15,000 catch-up limit. Now you may reduce your salary (contribute) by as much as $13,000 (an extra $3,000), if you wish. If you *do* elect to reduce your salary by the full $13,000, then the additional $3,000 must be subtracted from your lifetime catch-up limit balance ($12,000), which would leave you with a remaining catch-up balance of $9,000 ($12,000 minus $3,000) to be used in subsequent years.

Of course, if you reduce your salary by less than $13,000, say $12,000, then only $2,000 is subtracted from your remaining catch-up balance. If you were to reduce your salary by only $10,000 (the normal maximum), then you would not count any additions to your "catch-up" amount this year, and nothing would be subtracted from your previous catch-up limit balance.

Special Elections for Determining your Maximum Exclusion Allowance—In addition to the MEA amount calculated using "Regular 403(b) Rules", you should be aware of the MEA amounts using various special elections allowed by the Internal Revenue Code. The *Year of Separation From Service Limitation Election* is only available in a year you separate from service and, therefore, is only applicable to you if you plan to retire that year. The *Any Year Limitation Election* and the *Overall Limitation Election* are available in any year.

Once you make any one of the three special elections, you cannot use a different special election during your career (although you may always choose to use the "Regular 403(b) Rules" instead of *your* special election). If you select the *Year of Separation From Service Limitation Election* you may not use any of the special elections in subsequent years. For example: You wish to reduce your salary by more than the maximum calculated using the Regular 403(b) Rules, and the *Any Year Limitation Election* in fact allows a larger salary reduction. If you have never chosen the *Year of Separation From Service Election* or the *Overall Limitation Election* during your career, you may choose to apply the rules of the *Any Year Limitation Election*. Thus, you may have the larger amount of allowable salary reduction for the year. In subsequent years, however, you *must always* choose either the results calculated under the Regular 403(b) Rules, or the *Any Year Limitation Election*, even if either of the other two special elections are more advantageous.

I have deliberately been rather vague with concern to the above-mentioned elections. My intent here is to merely alert you to the alternatives. The full explanation of each should come from a representative of the company with whom you invest. That way you may have quick, complete, expert answers to the questions that will undoubtedly arise during the discussion. Ultimately it is *your* responsibility to decide the amount that will be voluntarily contributed to your 403(b) account each year. To determine the maximum contribution you can make to your 403(b) plan, you can begin by placing a call to your investment company and ask them for a 403(b) MEA calculation request form. The form provides questions which, when answered, will be relied upon by them to help with the computations. Accordingly, the accuracy of their calculations will depend upon the accuracy of the information provided.

After completing and mailing in the form, you will receive a printout explaining your options. You then choose the MEA option you want to use. Should you require further explanation regarding your voluntary maximum exclusion allowance, you should consult your professional tax advisor. If you wish to read more on the subject regarding MEA calculations, you may refer to IRS Publication 571, entitled *Tax-Exempt Annuity Programs for Employees of Public Schools and Certain Tax-Exempt Organizations.*

CHAPTER TEN

Accessing the 403(b)

In this chapter we will take a close look at 3 methods of accessing your 403(b) account: borrowing; early withdrawals from the 403(b); and, regular distributions.

Borrowing From The 403(b)

Some programs allow loans to be taken from your 403(b) account, some do not. A lot of companies (around 55%) even allow participants to have more than one loan at a time. It depends on how your account is set up. Typically, once you reach a minimum balance (determined by the plan), you may be eligible to take a loan from your 403(b) account. According to current statistics, 23% of 403(b) participants have a loan outstanding against their account. Repayment takes place through automatic payroll deduction. In addition to repayment of loan principal, you also repay a fixed rate of interest to your account. In essence, you are borrowing from and repaying yourself.

A word of caution, however. Taking a loan from your 403(b) account can have significant consequences on the growth of the account. You lose out on the earnings growth that would have occurred if the loan amount were still in the plan. Additionally, unlike some loans, the interest payments on 403(b) loans *are not tax deductible*. Also, your money will get taxed twice. You will have to repay the loan, plus interest, with after-tax dollars, but when you withdraw your money, you will pay taxes on all of it. Because these programs are meant for retirement savings, there are usually restrictions, including those on loan frequency and loan amount. Check with your investment company for more details.

- **How do I know if I can borrow from my 403(b)?**—Simply call your investment company and ask. Not all plans allow for loans, that's for sure. It depends on the provisions of your plan.

- **How does a 403(b) loan work?**—When you take a loan from your 403(b) account, you actually take money out of your account, with a promise to repay it. You pay your account back the balance you borrowed, plus interest (a fixed rate determined at the time of the loan), through after-tax payroll deductions. In addition, as long as you repay your loan on time, you will not be subject to withholding taxes or penalties, as you would if you withdraw from your account before retirement.

- **Can I borrow from my 403(b) account instead of making withdrawals?**—Again, it depends on your plan. Legally, loans can be allowed for any reason. But each investment company has its own set of rules and regulations. Call and find out what they are for your company. If a loan is allowed, it is definitely preferable to a withdrawal. Instead of costing you money, a 403(b) loan earns you money because you will pay yourself interest on the amount you borrow. Also, borrowing from a 403(b) is easier than borrowing from a bank because there are no credit standards to meet. As a plan participant, you automatically qualify for a loan if the plan permits them in the first place.

- **How much can I borrow from my 403(b) plan?**—If your plan allows for loans, the most you can borrow is 50% of your vested balance up to $50,000, minus your highest outstanding loan balance over the last 12 months—whichever is less. That is the legal limit. Some plans may have more restrictions and impose a lower ceiling on the total amount you can borrow, so be sure to check.

- **How does taking a loan affect the value of my account?**—First of all, the money you borrow comes out of your own account, so your balance is reduced by the amount of your loan. But taking a loan has another, less visible, effect on your account over the long term. While a loan may be a practical option when you need financial assistance, over time you could miss out on the full potential value of your principal. In other words, the money you take out of your account is no longer working for you, and therefore, loses the potential to grow. Remember the magic of compounding? Your 403(b) is a tax-free compounding engine that you do not want to slow down. Even if you repay a loan to your account and continue to invest in the plan, you still lose earnings potential for the loan amount while you are repaying it.

- **Are there taxes or penalties involved with a loan?**—There are no taxes or penalties when you initially take a loan. Taxes or penalties only come into play if you leave your employer, and/or if you do not repay your loan on time. If you decide to leave your employer, you must repay your loan in full within a certain amount of time. If you are under age 59 ½ and you do not repay your loan within this certain time frame, the loan is then considered a withdrawal and you would have to pay a 10 percent early withdrawal penalty as well as current income taxes.

- **How long does it take to process a loan?**—This depends on your plan. It could take as little as three days, or as long as six weeks to process a loan check. Call your investment company for specifics on your plan.

- **What will a loan cost me?**—The IRS does not let your plan give you a sweetheart deal. It must charge a market rate—in other words, what a bank would charge you on the same loan (currently around 9%). That means you will probably pay one or two percentage points above the prime rate, which is the interest rate that banks charge their best corporate customers. Many plans also charge loan processing and administrative fees. But you are still much better off than you would be if you borrowed from a bank—even if you qualified for its prime rate—because you are paying the interest to yourself. Your loan becomes a fixed-rate investment for your 403(b) account.

- **Are the interest payments on loans tax deductible?**—No.

- **Is the interest I pay on a 403(b) loan tax-deductible if I use the money to buy a house?**—No. Interest on home loans is only tax-deductible when the house is the collateral for the loan. A bank will take a house as collateral for a loan, but a 403(b) plan will not. When you borrow from your 403(b) account, it is your remaining balance that serves as collateral for the loan. As far as the IRS is concerned, your loan is a tax-deferred investment, like everything else your 403(b) account puts money into. Giving you a tax deduction on the interest you are paying yourself would amount to giving you a tax-break on top of a tax break. The IRS is not that generous.

Before borrowing to buy a house, ask potential lenders if they accept 403(b) loans as down payments. Most banks do not like your borrowing down payment money because if you default on your mortgage, they do not want any other creditor coming forward with a claim on the house. But many banks make an exception for 403(b) loans because the loan comes from your own savings.

- **Can I use my 403(b) account as collateral for other types of bank loans?**—I doubt it. The reason is your 403(b) account could be protected from your creditors under federal bankruptcy law. Although your 403(b) balance may improve the impression you make as a would-be borrower because it shows the lender what a hard-working, thrifty, financially responsible person you are, most banks are unlikely to accept collateral that they might be legally barred from collecting if you ever had to file for bankruptcy. As stated before, bankruptcy laws vary from state to state, and sometimes, city to city.

- **Must my spouse agree to the loan?**—Maybe. Some plans follow joint-and-survivor rules, which means that you and your spouse must have the option of receiving your retirement payout in the form of lifetime annuity payments. If your plan follows these rules, your spouse may have to sign off on loans you take from the plan. Once again, checking to see how your plan was set up will more fully answer this question.

- **If my money is divided among several different funds within the plan which one should I borrow from?**—It depends. Some plans tell you which fund you must borrow from. Some plans automatically take a proportionate amount from each investment in your account. Others let you make the choice. From your 403(b) account's perspective, your loan is a fixed-rate investment. To maintain your current mix of investments, you should borrow the money from a fixed-rate fund if you have one.

- **How do I repay my 403(b) plan account?**—You repay the loan to your account through automatic payroll deduction. Interest on the loan is also paid into your plan account so you are, in effect, paying back the interest to yourself. Again, the interest you pay is not tax deductible and is paid with after-tax dollars only. And remember, when you do withdraw your money from your account, you will pay taxes on *all* of it.

- **How soon do I have to repay the loan?**—The loan must be repaid through a series of regular payments which are usually deducted from your paycheck automatically. The entire amount you borrowed must be repaid within five years, with one exception: if you took a loan to buy a principal residence, the law says that it must be repaid in a "reasonable" period of time. In some plans that could mean as long as 25 years. The term of the loan definitely can not extend beyond your normal retirement date, as defined by the plan.

- **What happens if I leave my job while I still have a loan outstanding?**—That could be a big problem for most people. If you leave your job (or are fired) you will have to pay the entire balance immediately or get hit with taxes on the amount outstanding, plus (if you are under 59 ½) a 10% penalty for early withdrawal.

- **Can I take a loan from my IRA?**—No. Loans are not permitted from an IRA in any circumstances. If you absolutely have to take a loan on your investments, be smart about it. If you have the option of deciding which of your investment vehicles to borrow from, choose the one that is returning the least at the time. For example, a bond fund with a 4%-6% return is a much better choice for a loan than a stock fund that is returning 12%-15%.

Early Withdrawals

There is a key fact that you need to keep in mind when determining how much of your salary you want to go to your 403(b) account. That fact is that early withdrawal of funds in your 403(b) is not simply frowned upon by the IRS—it is punished. Uncle Sam has made it clear that in order to get the benefit of tax-deferred growth, you must generally be prepared to put your money away until you turn age 59 ½. As already mentioned, in addition to regular income taxes, there is a 10% penalty for early withdrawal. Basically, that means it will cost you twice: you will owe a hefty tax bill on what you take out, and you will have less when you retire. As a result, you need to be sure that your investing budget does not collide with your living budget.

- **How do I request an early withdrawal?**—That depends on your plan. You usually apply for a withdrawal by calling your investment company direct. Some companies require a written request. Then, as long as your request meets plan guidelines, your investment company sends you a check for the amount you requested.

- **What about the 10 percent penalty for withdrawing early from my retirement plan?**—Retirement plans like 403(b)s are designed to help you save for when you will need it most—at retirement. To discourage you from taking money out before age 59 ½, the IRS may charge you (depending on the circumstances) an early withdrawal penalty, equal to 10 percent of the taxable amount you withdraw. You will also be charged a 10 percent penalty if you are in a *rollover* situation and you do not directly roll over into another employer's plan or into an IRA. Of course, you will also have to pay income tax whenever you withdraw pre-tax money from the plan that is not rolled over.

- **Is there a dollar limit on the amount I can take in a hardship withdrawal?**—In general, you will be limited to the amount of your own pre-tax contributions. Within that limit, you can take out whatever is necessary to satisfy your financial emergency, plus the amount that is needed to cover the taxes you will have to pay. Be sure you do not spend what you need to cover the taxes.

- **Besides the 10% early withdrawal penalty, what else do I have to pay?**—In addition to a 10% early withdrawal penalty, your plan sponsor is required to set aside 20% for federal withholding taxes. This is only an estimate of the tax you will owe on the withdrawal—the actual amount will be determined when you file your taxes. To make sure you have enough to cover the taxes and penalty you will owe the following April, either set the money aside immediately or ask your plan sponsor to withhold more than the customary 20%. If you have spent it all, you will be in a jam.

- **Why is 20 percent in income tax withheld on plan withdrawals?**—The Unemployment Compensation Amendment of 1992 requires that 20 percent of your withdrawal be withheld as a prepayment of your federal taxes. If you withdraw this money and directly roll it over into another retirement plan (like another employer's 403(b) or IRA), this 20 percent withholding will not apply. Remember, too, that you may owe more or less in federal and state income tax when you file your income tax return.

- **Why do I have to pay a penalty for withdrawing my own money?**—Because it is tax-advantaged *retirement* money, not intended to pay for pre-retirement expenses. The tax breaks you get in a 403(b) plan are incentives to encourage you to save for your retirement and to enable you to save as much as possible. The penalty for early withdrawals is an incentive also—designed to help you keep your retirement money where it should be—in your retirement account.

- **How is the 10% penalty on early withdrawals calculated?**—The 10% penalty for early withdrawals is calculated using IRS Form 5329. The penalty applies to the entire untaxed amount that's distributed to you before you reach age 59 ½ if you are still employed. The full amount of the withdrawal is subject to both the 10% penalty *and* income tax (federal, state, and local); no deduction against either tax is allowed. For example: If you take $20,000 from your 403(b) before 59 ½ and do not meet any of the criteria for avoiding the penalty. If your *combined* federal, state and local tax rate is 32%, you will pay:

Penalty	$2,000.00	(10% x $20,000)
Income Tax	+ 6,400.00	(32% x $20,000)
Total	$8,400.00	(42%)

You will end up with only $11,600 of the $20,000 withdrawal. That is why you should consider an early withdrawal from your 403(b) plan only as a last resort. It is terribly expensive money.

- **If I am under the age 59 ½ is there any case in which I can withdraw money from my 403(b) plan without a 10 % early withdrawal penalty?**—Nothing but an emergency should push you into using your 403(b) money. But, if you absolutely, positively have to access the money in your 403(b) plan, there are ways to do so without incurring the 10% penalty. You can take an early withdrawal :

1. If the distribution is attributable to disability, which is defined by the Internal Revenue Code as the inability to engage in any substantial gainful activity and can be expected to result in death or to be of long-continued and indefinite duration.

2. If you are purchasing a first principal residence for yourself, your spouse, a child, or a grandchild. You can withdraw up to $10,000 for this purpose, and you will have to pay regular income tax on the amount you withdraw. The $10,000 maximum is a lifetime limit, so you could, for example, withdraw $5,000 twice to help one child and then another.

3. If you can demonstrate need related to the imminent foreclosure of your principal residence.

4. If the distribution is for the payment of certain uninsured medical expenses as defined by the Internal Revenue Code. These expenses must exceed 7.5% of your adjusted gross income. This exception applies regardless of whether or not the medical expense deductions are itemized.

5. To pay for medical insurance for you and your family, provided you have received unemployment compensation for at least 12 weeks first.

6. If you can demonstrate extreme need for post-secondary tuition, provided it is due within

the next 12 months. The money can be used for yourself, a spouse, or any child or grand-child.

7. If the distribution is a payment to an alternate payee, pursuant to a Qualified Domestic Relations Order (QDRO).

8. If the distribution is made to you after separation from service after attainment of age 55.

9. If money is returned to you to correct a situation of excess deferrals (if you contributed more than the IRS limit to your account).

10. If you are under 59 ½ and you have separated from service, you can withdraw your money in *Substantially Equal Periodic Payments* made at least annually over your life expectancy or joint life-expectancy of you and your designated beneficiary.

Of these various exceptions, the Substantially Equal Periodic Payments exception provides the most interesting planning possibilities. As it turns out, the 10% penalty tax on 403(b) payouts before age 59 ½ is fairly easy to get around. Straightforward and perfectly legal withdrawal patterns tucked away in hard-to-find IRS publications can enable investors to take out more than three times as much each year as allowed under the method the IRS features in its consumer guide.

Substantially Equal Periodic Payments—The first step to using this exception effectively is to understand the mechanics of what actually constitutes substantially equal payments. IRS Notice 89-25 provides a detailed description of the three acceptable methods you can use to calculate the payment stream. Each of the methods base payments on your life expectancy or the joint life expectancies of you and your designated beneficiary.

You should be aware that once a method is selected, it cannot be changed. This means that even if you could have originally selected a higher or lower payout amount, you can not change your mind once your payments begin. However, the good news is that the payments do not need to continue for the rest of your life. Specifically, the payment stream must continue, without modification, for the greater of five years or until you reach age 59 ½. For example, if you start payments when you are age 53, you must continue until you reach age 59 ½. On the other, if you start taking payments at age 57 you must continue until age 62. But beware—if you trip up on any of these rules, the 10% penalty will apply—retroactively. Amended returns for prior years are required and interest penalties will be assessed.

Keeping these parameters in mind, let us take a look at the three acceptable methods outlined by the IRS in Notice 89-25—the *Straight Life Expectancy Method*; the *Amortization Method*; and the *Annuity Factor Method*.

In its generally highly useful taxpayer's guide, *Individual Retirement Arrangements*, the IRS features just one of the approved methods of calculating the annuity exception, the *life expectancy method*. It refers only obliquely to the other two distribution methods. These alternatives, the agency says, "are more complex and generally require professional assistance." What the IRS fails to note, however, is that the two other methods described in IRS Notice 89-25 are *much* more generous to taxpayers than the one it does explain and shows you how to use.

Let us take a close look at how it all works. Suppose you need to pull together some additional dollars to supplement your early retirement. You have evaluated your situation and have determined that you need to tap into your 403(b) account for the needed funds. Your dilemma is that you have not yet reached age 59

½ and you do not want to trigger the 10% early withdrawal penalty. The solution? Structure a payout from your 403(b) according to the substantially equal payment rules. Having made that decision, you now turn your attention to the particular method you should select. Remember, if you select the Straight Life Method, your payout will generally be lower than if you select either the Amortization or Annuity Factor Method. In selecting the method to use, you also need to evaluate whether you will base your payout on your life alone, your life and your spouse's, or your life and some other life. For example, if you are looking for the lowest payout, use the Straight Life Method with a joint life younger than yours. However, you must use the life expectancies that reflect the beneficiary designations on the (403(b) document. The 3 tables which follow will help illustrate how your decision of which method to use can impact your payout in varying degrees.

One—The Straight Life Expectancy

With this method, you simply divide the balance in your account by either your individual life expectancy or the combined life expectancies of you and your beneficiary. This method will give you the lowest annual payment. Look to IRS Publication 939 and/or 590 for life expectancies. The first two tables illustrate the various results assuming the Straight Life Expectancy Method is used:

Table 1—Depicts the range of divisors used at various ages and under different life expectancies. At age 53, the divisors differ by as much as 12 between the Single Life Expectancy and the Joint Life Expectancy with someone 10 years your junior.

Table 2—Quantifies the dollar differences between various ages and life expectancies under the Straight Life Expectancy Method. Remember, this method simply involves taking your account balance and dividing by the appropriate divisor. The table illustrates the bottom line on your pocketbook, assuming a $100,000 403(b) balance. For example, say you are 53-years-old and elect the Single Life Expectancy. Under this scenario, your annual payout amount will be $3,289 ($100,000 divided by 30.4). Contrast this result with the payout amount of $2,358 if you elected to use a Joint Life Expectancy with someone 10 years your junior ($100,000 divided by 42.4). You can check your figures each year by using your 403(b) balance at the close of business on December 31 of the preceding year, and the applicable divisor based upon your life expectancy (or the joint life expectancies of you and your spouse), based on your age at the end of the year in which the withdrawal is made.

TABLE 1

LIFE EXPECTANCY TABLE DIVISORS FROM IRS PUBLICATION 590			
Age	**Single Life Expectancy**	**Joint Life Expectancy (Same Ages)**	**Joint Life Expectancy (Beneficiary 10 Years Younger)**
53	30.4	36.3	42.4
55	28.6	34.4	40.4
57	26.8	32.5	38.5

141

TABLE 2

ANNUAL DISTRIBUTION AMOUNTS UNDER THE STRAIGHT LIFE EXPECTANCY METHOD			
Age	Single Life Expectancy ($)	Joint Life Expectancy (Same Ages) ($)	Joint Life Expectancy (Beneficiary 10 Years Younger) ($)
53	3,289	2,755	2,358
55	3,497	2,907	2,475
57	3,731	3,077	2,597

Two—The Amortization Method

The Amortization Method, which the IRS seems to think is a little too complex for do-it-yourselfers, simply cranks a reasonable rate of interest into the calculation. It assumes, not irrationally, that the balance of your 403(b) assets will continue to appreciate in value even as you are withdrawing part of them each year.

This method allows you to determine your payment by amortizing your account balance over your life expectancy (or the joint life expectancies of you and your spouse) at a reasonable interest rate. There is some leeway allowed in the interest rate you use, as long as it is reasonable at the time you start your payments and you do not change it throughout your required payment period. Generally, you can get larger payments by assuming a higher interest rate. But beware: if you are asked, you will need to be able to justify to the IRS that the rate you used is a reasonable rate.

Exactly what constitutes a reasonable rate of interest for the purpose of the Amortization Method is left ill-defined. Based on figures used in various IRS-supplied examples and market rates at the time the examples were published, it seems that an interest-rate assumption somewhat in excess of the current yield on 30-year Treasury bonds will be viewed as favorable. I suggest you consider the *Applicable Federal Rate* for annuity calculations published monthly by the IRS. This can be found in any research library or on the Internet under *IRS Revenue Rulings*. The IRS has specifically ruled that an interest-rate assumption equal to 120% of the long-term Applicable Federal Rate is reasonable. Recently, the long-term applicable Federal Rate was 6.77%, so 120% of that would be 8.12%. At the same time, the 30-year Treasury bond was yielding a bit over 6½ %. A more aggressive approach is to look at the current yields of high-yield bond funds, which typically pay 1% to 3% more than long-term Treasuries. Taking that approach, an interest rate of 9%, or even 10%, might be assumed to be reasonable. Here again, be careful!

Table 3 illustrates various payout amounts using both 5% and 8% interest rates under the Amortization Method. There are significant differences in the payout amounts depending on the interest rate you select. For example, at all ages and at all life expectancies, there is more than a $2,300 difference in annual withdrawals between these two rates. Even more dramatic is the difference in annual withdrawal amounts between the Straight Life Expectancy Method in Table 2 and the Amortization Method in Table 3. Let us go back to our earlier example at age 53 with a 403(b) account balance of $100,000. Using the 5% interest rate and the Single Life Expectancy, the Amortization Method allows you annual withdrawals of $6,468, which is *almost double* the $3,289 withdrawal using the Straight Life Method. If you increase the interest rate to 8%, your withdrawal amount increases even more significantly to $8,853. Clearly, this method offers you a great deal of flexibility to tailor your payment stream to your needs.

TABLE 3

ANNUAL DISTRIBUTION AMOUNTS UNDER THE AMORTIZATION METHOD, USING 5% & 8% INTEREST RATES						
Current Age	SLE ($)	SLE ($)	JLE (Same Ages) ($)	JLE (Same Ages) ($)	JLE (10 Years Younger) ($)	JLE (10 Years Younger) ($)
	at 5%	at 8%	at 5%	at 8%	at 5%	at 8%
53	6,468	8,853	6,025	8,521	5,723	8,318
55	6,647	8,996	6,148	8,610	5,809	8,374
57	6,854	9,165	6,280	8,714	5,900	8,436

SLE = Single Life Expectancy   **JLE = Joint Life Expectancy**

Three—The Annuity Factor Method

The third method of calculating the annuity exception requires you to use a standard mortality table, which you may obtain from any insurance company. For a 50-year-old, using a reasonable interest rate of 8%, the annuity factor for a $1-per-year-annuity is 11.109. To calculate the penalty-free permissible withdrawal on a $100,000 account, simply divide the $100,000 by 11.109 for an answer of $9,002. A more aggressive assumption about what constitutes a reasonable interest rate can jump the annual withdrawal figure well past $10,000.

Plus, Cost of Living—But the story does not end here. Buried deep in an arcane 1995 "private letter ruling" from the IRS is the conclusion that an annual 3% cost-of-living adjustment to the withdrawal does not violate the basic requirement for "substantially equal payments." Now, 3% a year may not sound like a big difference, but 3% per annum compounded for ten years ultimately permits a 34% increase in the penalty-free annual withdrawals.

A word of caution: When taking early withdrawals from your 403(b), make sure you do not run out of money. The larger withdrawals permitted under the Amortization and Annuity Factor Methods could leave you short if the performance of your 403(b) assets fails to match your interest-rate assumption over a long period of time. In other words, it is fine to be able to justify a 9% or 10%-per-annum interest rate assumption in order to maximize your penalty-free 403(b) withdrawal now. But early-withdrawal maximization also means early depletion of your 403(b) funds.

There is one more very important planning strategy to keep in mind when considering substantially equal periodic payments. If you have multiple accounts (i.e. 403(b), IRA, etc.), these rules apply to each account separately. Therefore, you may further customize the amount you will receive by making sure the account chosen has the appropriate balance in it prior to the first withdrawal. In conclusion, you can avoid the harsh 10% early withdrawal penalty on an amount withdrawn prior to age 59 ½ from your 403(b)

143

account. To do so requires some careful planning, however. In particular, you should have an understanding of the following:

1. The three alternatives presented in IRS Notice 89-25 and how they affect your early withdrawal amount.

2. The impact that a single life versus a joint life calculation has on your early withdrawal amount.

3. The importance of the selection of an interest rate in the amortization and annuity methods.

4. The impact that the "cost-of-living" adjustment has on maximum withdrawal.

5. The importance of keeping a close eye on withdrawals so that the account does not run out of money.

Once you have analyzed these factors, you will have an appreciation of the flexibility of your options under the *Substantially Equal Periodic Payments* exception, and you will be on your way to tailoring a meaningful early withdrawal plan.

Distributions From the 403(b)

Withdrawals from 403(b) plans are often referred to as *distributions*. You probably will not think seriously about distributions from your 403(b) account money until you are within a few years of retirement. When you are nearing retirement, you have several key decisions to make about how to take your plan distributions when you do retire. You have a number of financial options. Take time to weigh the pros and cons of each one before you decide what is best for you. The information that follows will prove useful in understanding how the distribution process works.

• **What happens to my 403(b) account when I retire?**—The topic which contains the answer to this question is covered exclusively in chapter 18, so I will not go into much detail here. There are several important choices to consider and discuss with your spouse, tax accountant, and/or financial advisor. Rules vary from one investment company to another, but your choices usually include one or more of the following:

Take it all in a lump sum—If you do, you will owe income taxes on all of it. But under current tax law, you may get a special break when this lump sum comes from a 403(b) or a

144

rollover IRA—you can often lower the applicable tax rate by using a calculation called five-year averaging (see chapter 18). The government gives you a break on the rate in exchange for collecting tax on the entire amount up front, instead of waiting to collect it a little at a time.

The advantage of taking your money out in a lump sum is that in some cases you get to pay a substantially lower tax on it than you would normally owe. The disadvantage is that after you have taken the lump sum distribution, your money is no longer in a tax-deferred retirement account. That means that the only way to avoid tax on any future earnings is to invest it in tax-exempt instruments.

Get Lifetime Annuity—Some companies give you the option of taking a 403(b) payout in the form of a lifetime annuity. An annuity pays a monthly benefit for your lifetime alone or, if you choose a joint-and-survivor annuity, for your lifetime and your spouse's. If you choose a joint-and-survivor annuity, you will receive a smaller monthly benefit, but it will last for two lifetimes—yours and your spouse's. The advantage of an annuity is that it provides a guaranteed lifetime benefit. The disadvantage is that, because it is a fixed benefit, its purchasing power will be steadily eroded by inflation each year. When you take into consideration the fact that your cost of living could easily double or triple over a 20-year retirement, you might consider investing some of your money in an annuity, and investing the balance for growth. If you are trying to decide which is better for you—a joint-and-survivor annuity or a single life annuity plus a life insurance policy—you owe it to yourself and to your spouse to get a reliable *after-tax* comparison between these two options from a tax professional who has no vested financial interest in your decision.

Leave it where it is—You could leave some, or all, of the money in your 403(b) plan. You must have a minimum balance in your account to do this. This choice makes sense if you like the investments available in the plan and the plan rules permit withdrawals that are frequent enough to meet your needs. Remember, the federal government will allow you to put off paying taxes on this money only for so long.

Take installments—Some companies will pay you a specific monthly amount over a 10 or 15 year period. If you die before collecting all of your money, your heirs receive any balance remaining in your account. There are two inherent risks with this choice: the value of your fixed installment payments will be eroded by inflation; and, you may outlive your money.

Roll it over—You could roll your entire balance into an IRA. Then you can take out money as you need it, paying income taxes only on the amount you withdraw. This gives you more flexibility than any other option. Most of your money will continue to be sheltered in a tax-deferred account. You will have unlimited choice of investments for that account, and you will be able to change investments at will.

- **How does a distribution from my 403(b) account differ from those of other retirement plans?**

Each retirement plan has different withdrawal choices, limits, and tax effects. Here is how some of them stack up:

DISTRIBUTIONS FROM VARIOUS RETIREMENT PLANS		
Type of Plan	**Choices at Retirement**	**Limits & Tax Effects**
Social Security	You get monthly checks for life. But the longer you wait to collect (up to age 70), the bigger your check.	Payment will be taxed if your taxable income tops $32,000 filing jointly, or $25,000 if you're single.
Traditional IRAs	You can take a lump sum or withdraw in installments.	With some exceptions, you cannot make withdrawals until age 59½, and you must start withdrawing by age 70½ to avoid penalties. You pay regular income tax on withdrawals of all earnings and all pretax dollars you contributed.
Roth IRAs	You can take a lump sum or withdraw in installments.	With some exceptions, you cannot make withdrawals until age 59½. You can contribute to a Roth past the cut-off age of 70 ½ without penalty. You pay no income tax on withdrawals because you paid them at the time you contributed.
Qualified Pension or profit-sharing plans, e.g. 403(b), 401(k), etc.	Depending on the plan, you may roll it over into an IRA or take a lump sum. Or, you may get deferred or installment payments. (If you can take a lump sum, it may be eligible for five-or ten-year averaging.	You face generally the same limits and penalties as with IRAs.
KEOGH	Same as above.	You face generally the same limits and penalties as with IRAs.
SEPs (Simplified Employee Pensions)	You get annuity payments for life or take a lump sum	You face generally the same limits and penalties as with IRAs.
Annuities	You can get annuity payments for life, or make withdrawals.	You pay regular income tax on payments. There is a penalty tax if you withdraw before age 59½. The annuity company will also hit you with a penalty (surrender charge) if you withdraw in the early years of the plan.

- **What is an MRD?**—MRD stands for *minimum required distribution.* No tax deferral lasts forever—eventually, Uncle Sam wants his cut. Therefore, you are legally obligated to start taking taxable distributions from your 403(b) plan and other tax-deferred retirement accounts—excluding the Roth IRA for which MRDs are not required after you reach age 70 ½. A rollover from your 403(b) account to an IRA is not a taxable distribution. The government established minimums to ensure that you actually use your 403(b) account balance for *retirement* and not, for instance, to pass onto your heirs. Unless stated otherwise, you must take a distribution from your account at least once a year—this amount is your MRD. The MRD is based on your account balance and your life expectancy. The specifics on this topic are covered in chapter 18.

- **When do I have to start taking money from my 403(b) plan?**—Generally, you must begin to take minimum required distributions from your plan no later than April 1 of the year following the year in which you turn age 70 ½. Subsequent withdrawals must be taken from your account at least once a year, on or before December. However, the IRS has ruled that beginning January 1, 1997, if you are still employed when you turn 70 ½, you are allowed to wait until April 1 of the year following the year in which you retire before beginning distributions from your plan. (Please note that your plan may require you to take distributions earlier than this). For assets in another plan, like an IRA, minimum required distributions must begin no later than April 1 of the year following the year in which you turn age 70 ½, even if you are still an active employee of another organization.

- **What happens if I do not start taking money out of my account at age 70 ½?**—The penalties are severe. The IRS hits you with a 50% excise tax on the difference between what you withdrew from your account and what you should have withdrawn from your account. And you will owe that excise tax annually until you have made the appropriate withdrawal. In other words, if you should have taken $12,000 from your retirement account and you did not, you will owe the IRS $6,000 a year until you take out that $12,000. Of course, when you do take it out, you will owe income taxes on it.

- **How are MRDs calculated?**—An MRD amount is calculated by dividing your account balance (as of December 31 of the calendar year preceding the year in which you are taking the distribution) by your life expectancy or the joint life expectancy of you and your primary beneficiary. The life expectancy numbers are provided by the Internal Revenue Service—IRS Publication 939 and/or 590. Here is an example: You are 70 ½ and retired in 1998. You have no designated beneficiary. Based upon your attained age in 1998 (70 ½), your life expectancy, according to IRS Mortality Tables is 16 years. Your account balance as of December 31, 1998 is $125,000. Your minimum distribution, payable no later than 4/1/99, is $7,812.50 ($125,000 divided by 16). You will be required to take an MRD each calendar year for the next 16 years. This 4/1/99 MRD is for calendar year 1998. You will also be required to take a MRD for calendar year 1999 by December 31, 1999. There are three things to keep in mind:

    1. You must calculate your MRD for each of your retirement accounts (403(b), IRAs, Rollover IRAs, SEP-IRAs, etc.) at all financial institutions. You do not have to withdraw the MRD from each account, however, it is the *total* withdrawal that must meet the MRD requirement. (Remember, Roth IRAs are excluded).

    2. Life expectancy numbers are provided by the IRS in Publication 590 and/or 939. When you turn 70 ½, you can calculate your life expectancy using the publication.

3. You can change beneficiaries as often as you wish. But your first life expectancy number will continue to be the base for all distribution schedule calculations For example, let us say you name your spouse as beneficiary when you start taking distributions. Together, you have a 20-year joint life expectancy. You can change your mind later and name, say, a grandchild as your beneficiary. But the fact that you and the grandchild have a 50-year joint life expectancy will not change your original 20-year joint life expectancy.

- **<u>Can I withdraw my MRD and roll it into another tax-deferred account, like an IRA?</u>**—No. The government wants to be sure that you are using this money for retirement. You can no longer defer paying taxes on it once you have taken your MRD.

- **<u>Does the 20% federal income tax withholding apply to my MRD?</u>**—No. The 20% withholding does not apply to your MRD; however, you are still required to pay income tax on the amount you withdraw through your MRD.

- **<u>Are there any other taxes that I should be aware of?</u>**—Yes. If you are among the fortunate few who will retire wealthy, you should be aware that under current tax law, if distributions from all of your qualified retirement plans are greater than $160,000 in a single calendar year, an excise tax of 15% will be levied on the amount over $160,000. Lump-sum distributions from qualified plans may be subject to the excise tax when they are greater than $800,000. This excise tax has been suspended until January 1, 2000, at which time it will be reinstated.

CHAPTER ELEVEN

Do You Need a Financial Planner?

O K, you are impressed with the wealth-building qualities of the 403(b) plan, and you want to participate in one. In order to move ahead with your retirement planning, however, you must ask yourself a very important question—"Do I need assistance in developing my financial plan?" Investors think of *The Plan*, as it is called, as an obscure tome that financial planners love to extol, a thick binder full of strategies that tell you how to behave from cradle to grave. Forget it. Such plans, even if they did once exist, are artifacts of the 1980s. No client's plan survived the first change in the tax laws. Make no mistake about it, however, you do need a plan outlining your financial objectives, spending limits, fallback positions, and investment strategies. Whether you need someone to construct one for you is another matter, indeed. Hopefully, you purchased this manual because you are, or want to be, a do-it-yourself investor.

Although fearful to go it alone, *98% of the people* are perfectly capable of making a financial plan themselves simply by following suggestions and strategies like those found in this manual. Their investment needs are relatively simple and easy to direct. Only a small minority—those with complicated financial issues—really need outside professional help.

Become a do-it-yourself investor—Most of us do not need professional financial planners. Actually, we do not even need a full-scale plan. Conservative money management isn't hard. You do not have to be a sophisticated investor to become your own financial planner. You simply need a little basic knowledge, like that found in this manual. To be your own planner, you need only a list of objectives, a few simple financial products to choose from to help you meet your objectives, realistic investment expectations, and a time frame that gives your investments time to work out. That is it! In chapter 13, we will cover in detail how to determine your investment objectives, and how to allocate your assets to meet those objectives.

In a recent poll asking everyday people like you and me how effective professional investment advisors were, only 21% found them invaluable for making money in the market. Over 50% of those polled stated that most professional investment advisors can not even beat the market averages! Almost 30% of those polled stated that they would take their chances with *The Wall Street Journal* and a dartboard!!! The truth is, most professional investors do not get the kinds of results worth boasting about. *The Forecaster's*

Hall of Fame is an empty room.

Most people choose not to make their own financial plans do so because they are afraid they will not make the *best* choice in every circumstance. The truth is, however, that rarely is there a *best* choice. Usually, any one of several will work just fine for you. Armed with some basic information and a few sheets of paper, you can develop an action plan within several minutes—right on your dining-room table. It will be far more valuable than the big-hood schemes that planners, banks, and brokers sell, because it is *yours*. Remember, when you take managing your money into your own hands, you end up having *more* money to invest because you do not have to pay a financial planner's fees or commissions, which are usually quite high. And thankfully, a whole industry—*no-load mutual funds*—is prospering on the premise that you *can* take charge of your money.

By now you are probably asking, "But how do I know which mutual funds to buy? What do I look for in a fund. How do I allocate my money?" The answers depend on a number of factors including, but not limited to, your age, your personal tolerance for risk, your time horizon, how long you will live in retirement, and your present financial condition. All of this will be covered in detail in the next two chapters.

When to get help from a financial planner—Occasionally, even the do-it-yourself investor will want an expert opinion—usually to address a narrow question. The following is a handful of circumstances when you would want to arrange a meeting for professional help:

1. You earn good wages but can not manage to save a dime. You need a strong reality lecture. Someone has to show you—in dollars and cents—how little you will have at the end of your life unless you shape up. Most of us shape ourselves up. But if you can not, get help.

2. You face a question that can not be answered without some technical expertise. For example, your employer may have made a general early-retirement offer and you want to examine your alternatives carefully.

3. You are afraid to face financial decisions alone. An advisor can offer reassurance and expertise.

4. You experience a big change in your life—a marriage, a pending divorce, a promotion, the death of a family member, etc.

5. You are ready to retire and you need to develop a retirement savings withdrawal strategy. (Definitely do not do this without professional help).

6. You are following a personal plan but wonder if an expert can improve it. Arrange for a meeting at an hourly fee (minus sales commissions, if you eventually buy any products) and have your plan reviewed. Throughout the conversation, ask yourself whether you are hearing helpful advice. If not, end the meeting and leave.

The meeting will yield one of two results: You will meet with a planner who makes suggestions you are grateful for; or, you will feel more confident than ever that your own decisions have, in fact, been the right ones.

The exact role an advisor plays is up to you. The more hands-on help you want, the more you will end up paying in fees and commissions. If you opt for an advisor who analyzes your financial conditions, strategizes with you on the best route forward, and sends you on your way—in other words, who empowers you to take action on your own—your costs will not be very high.

By now I think you know where I stand on the issue of whether or not to use a financial planner. But I would be remiss in my responsibility towards writing this manual if I did not provide necessary information for those people who feel that they must use a financial planner, or to those who need more information in order to make a prudent decision on the matter. Therefore, the remainder of this chapter is designed to enlighten those who want to know more about obtaining the services of a financial planner. Remember, no one is going to care as much about your money as you do. So, if you must ask for help—ask, but never give up total responsibility.

Who to look for—and look out for when you decide to use a financial planner—Planners should be able to help individuals sort out complicated financial options, meet their financial needs, manage their current assets, plan for future needs and assess the level of risk that is appropriate. They should be familiar with tax law, insurance, securities, trusts and pensions in order to analyze and recommend a sound financial plan. Unfortunately, few have expertise in all these areas and, since the title financial planner has no legal definition, anyone can use it even thought they may have no training, background or expertise in finance. Actually, more than 250,000 men and women call themselves financial planners, including accountants, attorneys, stockbrokers, insurance agents, self-styled money managers, credit counselors and the Internet junkie down the street. But only a small number are registered certified financial planners, a designation that guarantees a person has passed a rigorous set of tests in all parts of personal finance (investing, retirement and estate planning, taxes, insurance and more) as well as has at least three years of experience in the field.

The Consumer Federation of America estimates that consumers lose at least $1 billion a year to fraud, self-dealing (recommending high-risk products that generate large commissions for the planner but may be unsuitable for the client), and incompetence on the part of financial planners. Lack of regulation creates gaps in protection for consumers and leaves some planners outside the jurisdiction of securities regulators.

Consumers are limited in their ability to protect themselves against deceptive or abusive practices because current laws provide only piecemeal protection and information to them. The bottom line? Be very cautious when choosing a financial planner.

Which kind of professional to see—Before you go searching for a financial planner, however, you must be sure that is who you really need to see. Here are some suggestions to help you decide which kind of professional to see:

- See a **Certified Public Accountant**—for tax planning, budget planning, small-business advice, and long-term income and savings projections. Some CPAs have expanded their practice into personal financial planning, too. Enrolled agents, who are licensed to represent you before the IRS, and licensed public accountants also have tax practices.

- See a **Tax Attorney**—for complex wills and estate planning.

- See an **Insurance Agent**—to buy an insurance policy, although some policies you can buy yourself.

- See a **Stockbroker** or a **Discount Broker**—to buy stocks and bonds. Mutual funds you can buy yourself.

- See a **Financial Planner**—to answer narrow general questions about how your finances fit together, and to help in specific circumstances, as outlined previously.

What a financial planner should be able to do for you—As already mentioned, a good financial planner can be hard to find, but there are some guidelines to help you choose the right one. He or she can save you a ton of time, make you substantial money, and help considerably to meet your goals. What can you reasonably expect from a professional planner? A good one should be able to assist you in the following ways:

- Assess your relevant financial history, such as tax returns, investments, retirement and estate planning, wills, and insurance policies.

- Be able to calculate your net worth.

- Help you devise a workable budget.

- Review your net worth statement, examine your debts, and determine if any should be consolidated, paid off from other available funds, or refinanced.

- Help you create a strategy for holding down your taxes.

- Make sure you are properly insured against sickness, disability and death.

- Check that you, your cars and your house are well-protected against damage, injury, and damage suits.

- Help you develop a financial plan, based on your personal and financial goals, history, preferences, and psychological investment risk-level.

- Identify financial areas where you may need help, such as building up a retirement income, improving your investment returns, etc.

- Write down and discuss an individualized financial plan and work plan (timetable) that you both understand and are willing to sign.

- Help you implement your financial plan, including referring you to specialists, such as lawyers or accountants, if necessary.

- Review your will and help you prepare an estate plan for passing along your wealth.

- Develop a retirement savings withdrawal strategy.

- Review your situation and financial plan periodically and suggest changes in your program when needed.

Most planners charge heavily for their services with costs from $500 all the way up to $10,000. These costs depend on three factors: your net worth or income; the planner's reputation; and, whether the planner also collects commissions on any investments you buy from him or her.

How financial planners are paid—Although there are many colorful terms describing how financial planners are paid, there are really only five ways for planners to make a living. They are:

1. Fee Only—Fee-only planners charge only for advice. Their fee structures vary—hourly charges, monthly retainers, fees per job, although hourly or flat fees are most common. They base their charge on analyzing your financial data, recommending a plan of action, and helping you implement it. Standard charges are about $80 to $125 an hour plus an annual fee of 1 to 2 percent of your portfolio. Payment is required even if you don't implement his or her suggested plan (excluding, of course, the annual percentage fee).

Any products they sell are entirely no-load—meaning that no sales commissions are attached. They do not earn income from the financial products they might suggest you buy. You may pay some costs to unaffiliated companies for investment and insurance products, however. Your planner should be able to estimate these costs.

Some fee-only planners (especially certified public accountants) sell no products at all. They give you advice, then turn you loose. In that case, take care to buy no-load products without any further help. Otherwise, you will pay double: once for the plan, and once for the services of a stockbroker or insurance agent, which adds substantially to your plan purchases.

Fees charged for tax and investment advice can be written off on your income-tax return. They are part of that bagful of miscellaneous expenses that are deductible to the extent that they exceed 2 percent of your adjusted gross income. Sales commissions are not similarly deductible up front; they are used to reduce your taxable profits when you sell.

2. Commission Only—These planners do not make a cent unless they sell you something that carries a sales commission, typically about 3 to 5 percent. So do not expect much planning time. Be careful, commission-only planners are sometimes insurance salespeople in disguise. They have to sell, and will probably recommend the highest-commission products going. They are paid their commissions by the marketers of the investment products they sell. For example, if a client buys insurance on the advice of a financial planner, the planner will not charge the client for that advice, but will receive a commission from the insurance company.

If your planner earns a commission, make sure you get a disclosure of the commission you will pay before recommended investments are implemented. Since commissions are often not disclosed, it is difficult to know how much you are paying your advisor and whether, for example, the fee was necessary at all. (Commissions on mutual funds can average about 5 percent. Commissions on insurance can be 50 percent or more of the first year's premium!) Generally, higher risk products offer the highest commissions.

Since most commission-only planners are inclined to direct your financial plan toward the purchase of those products that provides them with the best commissions, you may want to exercise caution in following the advice of someone who works solely on commission, at least until you develop a trusting relationship with a planner who knows your complete financial picture.

As a prerequisite for doing business, make a written agreement to disclose yearly total commissions earned by the planner and the planner's broker/dealer on recommendations made to you.

3. Fee and Commission—This is probably the most common arrangement. The planner charges you a fee for basic advice and earns commissions on any product you buy. The fee is typically equal to 3 to 5 percent of your portfolio annually. Because the planner receives a commission from the company that sells the product you purchase, the fee you are charged by some planners may be less.

Make no mistake about it though: sales commissions are the driving force and produce the same biases you see in commission-only planners. About half the planners disclose their commissions to clients, according to a study by the Securities and Exchange Commission. The rest leave you in the dark unless you press for information. Some certified public accountants are also fee-and-commission salespeople, so always ask.

Watch out for the fee-and-commission planners who press you to start with an overall financial plan that is generated by computer. Asking a computer for advice may make the planner seem more objective; but who writes the programs for the computer? You guessed it, the firms in thrall to financial-product companies and to the planners who do the selling. So biases are programmed in. Do yourself a favor—skip these plans—for the most part they are just selling tools designed to persuade you to spend more of your hard-earned money.

Please remember that I am simply trying to arm you with the facts. So, do not misunderstand my opinion toward fee-and-commission planners. I am not suggesting that you can not get good service and wise advice from them. Not at all. But, I want you to remember that in judging any proposed investment, you should keep in mind that it was chosen with an eye to the planner's need as well as yours. A bias toward high-commission products is easy to spot. More subtle is the bias to sell you *something* in cases where *nothing* would have served just as well.

4. Fee Offset—These planners set a fixed fee for their advice. You might pay by the hour, by the job, or by the month. You might pay a percentage, again about 3 to 5 percent, of the money the planner manages for you. Any sales commissions the planner earns are subtracted from your basic fee (hence the term). So the planner has no strong incentive to urge you to buy risky high-commission products. Either way, you pay the same.

5. Salary and Bonus (or Commission)—This is typical of the financial planners employed by some banks and S&Ls. Generally speaking, they design plans around bank-sold products, such as certificates of deposit, money market deposit accounts, and mutual funds. They may also act as agents for insurance companies, in which case tax-deferred annuities and insurance products rise to the top of their list, as these products make them the most profit.

No matter which fee structure you work with, make sure you get a written estimate of what services you can expect for what price. Compare this estimate with others and select the package of services that best meets your needs at a reasonable cost.

How do you find a planner worth having?—This question is a hard one. In almost all states, absolutely anyone can call himself or herself a financial planner. No tests are required, no licensing done. But there are some terrific planners in this country. To help you find one, in the next section of this chapter you will find a complete list of specific questions to ask a planner during the initial interview. In the meantime, here are some things to remember when searching for a financial planner:

- Look for planners who are certified (CFPs). Certification does not guarantee that a person will be a wise or creative planner. It does indicate, however, that he or she has studied important subjects of the financial planning field such as wills, trusts, investments, taxes, home ownership, and life and health insurance.

Some schools give certificates in financial planning, most notably *The College for Financial Planning* in Denver (giving a Certified Financial Planner designation or CFP), *The American College* in Bryn Mawr, PA (giving the Chartered Financian Planner designation or ChFC), *The American Institute of Certified Public Accountants* offers an APFS tag, for Accredited Personal Financial Specialist. A number of colleges and universities also give financial-planning degrees. These diplomas attest that the planner has passed a number of exams, in such things as taxes,insurance, investments, and estate planning. But remember, a certificate is only a starting point. It does not say whether the planner is any good. You can get a list of names of those financial planners in your area who are certified by writing to certain professional organizations. The addresses and/or telephone numbers are given at the end of this section.

- The planner should be registered as an investment advisor. Those that are call themselves *Registered Investment Advisors*. These are people who furnish investment advice for a fee and are required to register with the Securities and Exchange Commission (SEC). This *does not* indicate that they are certified financial planners (CFPs) or have had any special training. By law, however, they are supposed to disclose their educational backgrounds and financial planning experience on the SEC Form ADV. The registration form, SEC Form ADV, is divided into two parts.

> **Part One**—Covers information used by the Securities and Exchange commission to evaluate the advisor's application. It includes detailed information about the applicant' disciplinary history, including civil or criminal actions against the applicant and disciplinary actions by federal and state regulatory agencies and self-regulatory organizations.

> **Part Two**—Includes extensive information that advisors are required to disclose to potential clients such as the method of compensation, affiliation with other financial industry activities, education, and types of service offered.

Do not do anything more than the simplest kind of business with an unregistered planner.

- Find out about the planners' professional background. He or she should have a printed handout. Avoid "planners" who are basically insurance agents or stockbrokers. Look for broader experience: maybe they worked in business, or are accountants or tax lawyers.

- Find out how long the planner has been in the business. Skip any new kids on the block, including career-switchers who have been practicing only for a couple of years. Go for 10 years of experience, at least. What kinds of clients does he or she have? Planners often specialize in doctors, entrepreneurs, entertainers, teachers, or young, upper-middle-income families. The more experience the planner has with people like you, the better.

• Recommendations of friends and colleagues could play a role as you select a financial advisor. But an investment advisor who impresses one client may be unsuitable for someone else. Be sure to select someone who has the skills and expertise to meet *your* specific needs, including being sensitive to how much risk you are willing to take with your investments.

• Do not pick a planner just because he or she gets quoted in the newspapers. The paper does not check on how good a planner is, or whether his or her ideas work out. If enough phone calls or press releases arrive at the newspaper, the reporter may eventually pick up the phone, and one quotation almost inevitably leads to more. Courting the press is one way planners advertise. It says absolutely nothing about their honesty or expertise.

• Do not pick a planner just because he or she gives investment seminars. That is a form of advertising, too. Stockbrokers and planners often arrange to teach financial planning classes at local schools. Going to these seminars makes some sense if you want to shop around before deciding what investments to purchase or which financial planner to work with. Keep in mind, however, that these seminars may also be simply an opportunity for professionals to promote their business and themselves—and they can be very personable and appear trustworthy. On a larger scale, national seminars are often given to trick people into buying a service or product. A successful planner once told his trade secrets to a magazine reporter during an interview, where he stated:

> You do not have to know as much as you think you have to know in running a seminar. All you have to know is more than your audience, and your audience usually does not know anything about your subject. You also have to remember that you are not there to educate. You are there to sell. The purpose of a seminar is twofold: one, to confuse your audience; and, two, to create dependence. As long as you are going to confuse them, do a good job of it. Then you ask for the order, so that they will come to see you afterward.

If you do attend a seminar, go with pad and pencil and a healthy dose of caution.

> • A planner should be willing to advise you on a narrow point without demanding that you take the total service. If you just want some tips on college investing, for example, the answer should be "sure." Many planners argue that, because money decisions interlock, they can not help with college savings unless they draw you a lifetime plan. But that is sheer nonsense. Narrow plans are effective, too. On specific projects, planners should work for hourly fees or flat fees per job. They might even waive the fees if you buy a product on which they earn a sales commission. If you work successfully with a planner on a narrow point, maybe you will decide to go further, if you conclude that his or her initial idea was worth following.
>
> Some people pay $500 to $5,000 for what turns out to be a risky or unsuitable plan. If you find yourself in a similar situation, do not be tempted

to keep following the plan simply because you do not want to waste the money you have invested on the planner. Instead, walk away. You will be better off losing only the money you spent up front and not all the rest of the money that might have followed.

- When searching for a financial planner, be sure that those you are considering have clean records. Call your state regulator, usually the state banking commissioner, and the Securities and Exchange Commission in Washington, D.C. (202-942-8088) to see if any of the planners have been subject to disciplinary actions. Or visit the SEC's website at **http://www.sec.gov/ index.html** to look up disciplinary actions. The *Wall Street Journal* regularly publishes the names of firms and individuals who have been disciplined as well.

The following professional designations confer some assurance of thorough training and high standards of conduct:

Who to Turn to For Financial Planning

CFP (Certified Financial Planner)—Designated by the Certified Financial Planner Board of Standards (based in Denver) to those who complete an approved course, pass a difficult 10-hour exam, meet work-experience requirements, and agree to abide by a code of ethics.

CPA/PFS (Certified Public Accountant/Personal Financial Specialist)—Designated by the American Institute of Certified Public Accountants (based in New York) to CPAs who pass an exam and have at least three years of professional work-experience in financial planning.

ChFC (Chartered Financial Consultant)—Designated by The American College (Bryn Mawr, PA) to those who complete a 10-part course of study.

Who to Turn to For Investment Analysis

CFA (Chartered Financial Analyst)—Designated by the Association for Investment Management and Research (based in Charlottesville, VA) to those who pass a rigorous three-level exam (levels of exams must be taken one year apart), each administered by the association and covering *investment principles; asset valuation;* and, *portfolio management.* Candidates must also have three years of investment-management experience.

CIC (Chartered Investment Counselor)—Designated by the Investment Counsel Association of America (based in Washington, D.C.) to those holding CFAs and currently working as investment counselors.

Who to Turn to For Investment Consulting

CIMC (Certified Investment Management Consultant)—Designated by the Institute for Investment Management Consultants (based in Washington, D.C. and Phoenix) to institute members who pass an exam and have at least three years' professional consulting financial experience.

CIMS (Certified Investment Management Specialist)—Designated by the Institute for Investment Management Consultants to associate members who pass an exam and meet financial services work-experience requirements.

Where To Turn

These professional organizations will provide you with select lists of financial planners in your area:

The National Association of Personal Financial Advisors—(NAPFA, 1130 Lake Cook Road, Suite 15, Buffalo Grove, IL, 60089, call 888-333-6659). Members charge no sales commissions. They are all fee-only planners with at least three years of experience in comprehensive financial planning. They must take 60 hours of continuing education every two years.

The American Institute of Certified Public Accountants—(AICPA Personal Financial Planning Division, 1211 Avenue of the Americas, New York, NY, 10036, call 888-999-9256). It will mail you the names of local CPAs who have taken the courses needed for the Accredited Personal Financial Specialist designation. Most APFSs charge no sales commissions on products, but some do.

Licensed Independent Network of CPA Financial Planners (LINC)—Call 800-737-2727. Lists members who are CPA/PFS fee-only planners in public accounting firms.

The International Association for Financial Planning—(IAFP Registry, Two Concourse Parkway, Suite 800, Atlanta, GA, 30328, call 800-945-4237). Most of its members charge sales commissions, in all their infinite variety. In general, the planners listed in the Registry have better qualifications than some other planners.

The Institute of Certified Financial Planners—(7600 E. Eastman Avenue, Suite 301, Denver, CO, 80231, call 800-282-7526). It gives you the names of local members, for better or for worse. These planners, too, charge sales commissions.

Remember, whatever the source—*Check 'em out!!!*

Questions to ask in a preliminary interview—After a preliminary search, the best way to finally choose a financial planner is to use the same technique that corporate America uses to find its best people—the personal interview. Like all industries, the financial sector has its share of bad apples—people who are not very knowledgeable, or are downright deceptive, and you need to do what you can to protect yourself against them. With that in mind, here are some key questions to ask in a preliminary interview to *anyone* who will be getting paid to advise you on your finances, whether he or she be a financial planner, a stockbroker, a banker, an insurance agent, or any other financial consultant. Although the list is a little lengthy, each question deals with an important consideration. Following a logical approach would dictate that you prioritize the list based on your particular needs and considerations.

- **What is your educational background, your areas of study in college, and the degrees that you have earned?**

158

- **How long have you been with your current firm; and, what is your prior experience?**

- **What financial planning designations have you earned? Have you qualified as a Certified Financial Planner (CFP), or a Chartered Financial Consultant (ChFC), or are you a member of the Registry of Financial Planning Practitioners?**—Financial planners come from a variety of backgrounds and, therefore, may hold a variety of degrees and licenses. There are no regulations in most states for the financial planning industry. However, some take specialized training in financial planning and earn credentials such as Certified Financial Planner (CFP) or Chartered Financial Consultant (ChFC). Others may hold degrees or registrations such as lawyer (JD), Certified Public Accountant (CPA), or Chartered Life Underwriter (CLU). Question financial planners carefully about their background and experience. Be certain that any planner you consider hiring has ample knowledge of taxes, insurance, estate and retirement planning issues, as well as the basics of investments and family budgeting. Be wary of individuals who promote various investment items without discussing any overall financial planning goal. They may lack the expertise to formulate one or they may be focusing solely on selling particular investments.

- **Are you a member of any professional financial planning associations?**—*The Institute of Certified Financial Planners* (ICFP), *The National Association of Personal Financial Advisors* (NAPFA), *The International Association of Financial Planning* (IAFP) are a few such organizations.

- **Are you registered with the federal Securities and Exchange Commission (SEC) or with a state agency?**—Anyone who may be giving advice on securities, use of the stock market, or the value of securities over other types of investments should be registered with the SEC or registered under state law dealing with investment advisors. Be sure to ask for the Form ADV, Parts One and Two, which will give you information about the planner's background. Do not use a planner who does not have one or will not give you a copy.

- **How long have you been offering financial planning services?**

- **How many companies do you represent?**—Someone who represents only one or two companies is probably not a financial planner, but a broker or salesperson. It will be to their advantage to see you purchase only those products offered by the companies they represent. You may want to seek an advisor who can offer you a wide range of choices to suit your needs. Remember, a fee-only planner does not represent any company.

- **What continuing education in financial planning do you pursue to keep up-to-date?**—You may want to look for a planner who enrolls in continuing education courses (or, perhaps, teaches in a business school) to keep current on tax and investment strategies. Regular members of the National Association of Personal Financial Advisors (NAPFA) and the Institute of Certified Financial Planners (ICFP), for example, are required to complete 30 hours of continuing education every year in order to maintain full membership status.

- **Will you give me the names of five clients whom I can speak with, who have been**

159

with you for at least three years?—If the planner tells you that their names are confidential, be safe and assume that he or she has no long-term clients or can not trust them to be uniformly complimentary. That is your sign to leave. When you do speak with a planner's clients, ask how much better off they are, thanks to what the planner did.

• **How many clients in my financial circumstances do you have? May I see a copy of a plan you have prepared for a client like me (with the name removed, of course)?**

• **What is the portfolio turnover rate of your clients accounts?**—Some unscrupulous brokers churn their clients accounts, buying and selling stocks and other assets simply to generate commissions for themselves.

• **Who will work on my plan—you or a junior employee of your firm? And what ongoing help will you give me to put the plan into practice?**—You will want to work consistently with someone who is completely familiar with your account. If you work with a large firm offering many financial services, ask how the firm will provide a coordinated method of referral among the various experts who advise you. If you work with an individual planner, ask if the planner will provide you with professional references.

• **Have you ever been disciplined by any of the stock exchanges, any state or Federal agency or been in an arbitration case?**—Virtually all brokerage firms make clients sign contracts that forces them to take complaints to arbitration rather than to court. This if often far less costly and time-consuming than litigation. Arbitration is also advantageous in helping to keep a firm's (or individual's) reputation intact.

• **What is your investment philosophy?**

• **How would you go about preparing my financial plan?**—Financial planners usually prepare financial plans after carefully discussing and analyzing your personal and financial history, your current situation, and your future goals. Some financial planners enter relevant financial information into a computer to generate standard financial plans. You already know my feelings about that. But if you become convinced that this type of plan may be useful, be certain your unique financial situation is taken into account. Be sure to find an advisor who will give you personalized advice for your situation. Ask if you will be given a written analysis of your financial status and the planner's written recommendations to meet your goals.

Ask the planner about the process for handling your account while you travel or, for some reason, cannot be reached. For example, if you give planners discretionary power over your account, they could buy and sell securities without your prior knowledge or approval. Discretionary authority is legal only when it is in writing. If you choose to give this power to your planner, be sure you and your planner agree in plain English exactly what action you want the planner to take. To revoke this discretionary permission, send a certified, return receipt-requested letter to the planner. Be extremely careful about handing over this power to a planner. Many complaints to regulatory agencies about planners have to do with their misuse of discretionary power. And, *always be sure the planner is bonded*. This insurance should protect you in case of fraud.

- **What is your policy on participating in sales contests and accepting prizes or bonuses from investment firms or fund managers?**—If your question draws a hostile or defensive response, consider that a warning flag. You are not being nosy or rude in raising this subject. Indeed, any good advisor should be ready and eager to give you an answer, to help assure you that he or she is not prone to conflicts of interest that could work to your detriment. With your commisssions, sales charges, or annual accounts fees, you hire this individual to act as your representative. So you have every right to inquire whether the same person takes significant compensation from some other party that has a stake in the decisions you make. Do you really want to buy a fund, a stock, or any other investment from somebody who is competing to win a free round-the-world vacation by racking up more commissions this month than anybody else in his or her firm? Think about it. While you are at it, you also might want to look at whether you compromise your own objectivity by yielding to the temptations of gifts and other incentives that are frequently offered to financial prospects for the sole purpose of luring them into doing business.

Q. Will you be periodically evaluating and updating the plan you suggest?—As previously mentioned, financial planners should develop a plan specifically tailored to your situation and needs. Some planners also will include provisions for updating your plan to adjust to changes in your life, current economic conditions, and tax laws. A financial planner should also periodically review your plan to show you the progress being made in reaching your goals. Some planners offer continuous advice and management of your investments. Ask if the prospective planner provides this type of ongoing service and what those services would cost.

Q. Will you report the overall rates of return from all my investments so I can easily monitor results as time passes?—Ask for a copy of this report for similar clients over the last five years (again, leaving the names of clients blank). Do not compare apples with oranges. Be careful not to compare stock funds to CDs or stock funds to bond funds. To assess the impact the planner's compensation on your investment results, always be sure to ask for rates of return for before and after the deduction of the planner's compensation.

Q. Ask the prospective planner, "How are you paid?"—This question is critical. A planner should hand over a schedule that discloses his or her compensation in full. Planning fees, hourly fees, the sales commissions on various products (front, middle, rear-end, and renewal commissions), continuing fees from the firms that package the financial products the planner sells, fees from the lawyers or accountants he or she refers you to, fees for managing money. Finally, ask specifically what percentage of the firm's income comes from commissions on insurance products, annuities, mutual funds, limited partnerships, stocks, bonds,and other investments. That tells you where the planner's interests lie. If the planner claims not to know where all the income comes from, he or she is either running a lousy business or having trouble with the truth, or both. Either way, you do not want to deal. You should also ask whether the firm owns an interest in any of the investments it recommends. Get a "no" answer in writing.

If you need to file a complaint—If you have a complaint against a financial planner, send a certified letter to the planner's/firm's compliance officer detailing the complaint. Also, report the problem to your state's Attorney General's Office or state Securities Commission. These offices can advise you about the next steps to take or the appropriate organization to contact to file your complaint. Depending on the product you were sold (if any), you may be referred to *The National Association of Security Dealers*, (800) 289-9999; *The Securities and Exchange Commission, Office of Consumer Affairs and Information*, 450 5ᵗʰ Street, NW, Washington, D.C., 20549 (202) 942-8088; or your state Securities Commission. You may also wish to contact *The Federal Trade Commission, Correspondence Branch*, at Washington, D.C. 20580.

Planners who have been admitted to the Registry of Financial Planning Practitioners, or who hold the designations CFP or ChFC, or are members of the National Association of Personal Financial Advisors (which represent fee-only planners) have codes that they are expected to uphold. These codes basically include honesty, avoiding misleading representations, and disclosure of any potential conflicts of interest. In addition, fee-only planners affirm that they serve as fiduciaries for their clients, which means they put their client's interest first. Should financial planners violate these standards, they could lose their association with their group and/or their designating initials.

It is up to you, of course, to decide whether you need to hire a financial planner. But if you do hire one, it is still essential for you to keep abreast of what is happening on the financial scene. No one has as much at stake as you do regarding your finances—not even your financial planner.

You may want to keep up-to-date in the field by regularly reading a variety of financial publications. Some magazines that feature money and investment information and advice include *Money Magazine, Kiplinger's Personal Finance Magazine, Consumer Reports,* and *Personal Investor. Sylvia Porter's Retirement Newsletter* and the *No-Load Investor Newsletter.* All are available by subscription or in most libraries. The following publications offer more technical information: *The Wall Street Journal, Barron's, Forbes, Fortune, Harvard Business Review, Nation's Business* and the financial pages of most metropolitan newspapers. You will find many others in bookstores, libraries, and by using the vast search capabilities of an Internet search engine.

The International Association for Financial Planning (IAFP) offers a series of free *Mastering Money* brochures on a variety of topics, including funding a college education, organizing your estate, protecting yourself against fraud, and preparing financially for marriage or having a child. To request copies call IAFP's Consumer Referral Program at 800-945-4237 or go to the web at **www.iafp.org**

Because the financial marketplace is constantly changing, no one can afford to sit back and expect a financial plan to take care of itself. By reading, talking, and attending classes on money matters, you will learn when to consider revising your financial plan and when to make new financial moves. As stated earlier in the manual, an annual review is strongly advised. In addition, changes in your personal situation, for example, marital, financial, or health, also may make a revision of your plans necessary. That holds true whether you do—or do not—hire a financial planner.

CHAPTER TWELVE

Making Mutual Funds Work For You

Trying to decide how and where to invest your retirement plan contributions may seem confusing at first. It is easy to feel overwhelmed by the thousands of investment choices available to you. Even if you have already begun investing for retirement, you may not be sure the investments you have chosen are right for your needs. This chapter is designed to help you. It deals exclusively with mutual funds. Why? Because in my opinion mutual funds have the potential to benefit the vast majority of 403(b) investors the most. Once you have finished this chapter you will understand what mutual funds are, how they work, and the many benefits they can offer you.

Do not buy individual stocks—buy mutual funds—Today there are over 8,000 mutual funds to choose from in today's marketplace—more than the total number of stocks traded on the New York Stock Exchange and the American Stock Exchange combined. Compare that figure to only about 500 mutual funds available just a decade ago. Mutual fund assets have grown from just over $100 billion in 1980 to more than $5.5 trillion today.

Mutual funds are not insured or guaranteed by any government agency, but their operations are regulated by the U.S. Securities and Exchange Commission and by state agencies. The Investment Company Act of 1940, the principal Federal law regulating mutual funds, requires funds to operate in the interest of shareholders and to take steps to safeguard their assets. Fund advisors must also provide extensive disclosure about their investment activities, risks, fees, and sales commissions. But exactly what is a mutual fund? Simply put, a mutual fund is a type of investment. You can think of it as a group of people with similar investment goals who, instead of investing on their own, put their money together—mutually.

When you invest in a mutual fund (like those usually offered in a 403(b) plan), your money is pooled together with literally hundreds of thousands of other investors with the same objective—long-term growth, for example. Mutual funds have become so popular because they offer a very simple way to invest effectively in today's increasingly complex financial marketplace. There are several reasons that have made investing in mutual funds so popular:

1. **It is easy to invest in them**— Most transactions can be completed on the phone. Often, you can make an initial investment of as little as $50.00 to $100.00.

2. **Performance**—Because mutual funds are designed for growth of capital, performance can be quite good. The average stock mutual fund's annual rate of return over the past decade, for example, is almost 12 percent.

3. **Less risk**—With mutual funds you get instant *diversification*, thereby greatly reducing investment risk. Diversification is an investment term for not putting all of your eggs in one basket. A mutual fund is diversified because the fund owns many different securities. The rationale behind diversification is that the negative performance of one security won't have as much of an impact on the fund overall since it is invested in many different securities.

4. **Flexibility**—Another benefit of mutual funds is *flexibility*: the ability to have control over your investments if your investment needs change. Unlike fixed annuities, where your money is tied up in a single investment for an extended period of time, mutual funds are designed so that you have the option to move your investments from one fund to another. Mutual funds also offer flexibility when it comes time to withdraw your savings in retirement. You can choose to annuitize to guarantee lifetime income, partial withdrawals for more flexibility in accessing your savings, or lump-sum withdrawals for access to your money immediately.

5. **Professional management**—Usually, mutual funds are managed by a fund manager, or *portfolio manager*. The fund manager searches for the best securities for the fund, given the fund's stated objective, and chooses the stocks, bonds, and money market instruments on your behalf. This means you do not need to be an investment expert or spend a lot of time researching different stocks and bonds to participate in the investment growth potential of the stock and bond markets. By entrusting your money to these professionals, you are also entrusting them with buy-sell decisions, and they do not notify you (or charge you) each time they make transactions.

6. **Less worry**—Remember, fund managers spend 100% of their work time obsessing about which investments to buy, so that you do not have to, thereby offering tremendous emotional security to the do-it-yourself investor.

<u>Example of</u>
<u>The Benefit of Diversification</u>

You invest $2,000 in a mutual fund. The fund owns many stocks and has 1% of its assets invested in ABC Manufacturing. The next day, ABC's biggest competitor makes a surprise announcement about a technological breakthrough that will render ABC's main product obsolete. The value of ABC stock drops 25%. If you had invested all you money in ABC stock, your $2,000 would be worth only $1,500. But the mutual fund, with only 1% of its assets invested in ABC, is barely affected.

Mutual Fund

Your Initial Investment Value	Value After 25% Drop in ABC Stock
$2,000	$1,995

ABC Manufacturing Stock

Your Initial Investment Value	Value After 25% Drop in ABC Stock
$2,000	$1,500

What it costs to invest—Basically, mutual funds have three types of fees or charges. All funds, regardless of the fund family, charge a management fee to cover the costs of managing the fund. This fee is calculated into a fund's share price every day (share prices are net of fees and other expenses), so you do not pay it directly. Some mutual funds have a load (front load or back load), that you pay when you invest. However, loads (sales charges) are often waived when you invest through your employer's 403(b) plan. Other mutual funds also charge a *redemption fee* that you pay when you redeem, or sell, your shares. These are usually only in effect for a short period of time (e.g., usually six months or less). They are designed to keep investors from jumping too often from one fund to another.

Fighting for 403(b) diversification—I know many of you who are reading this are saying, "But my 403(b) plan only offers annuities from which to choose. If that sounds like you—you will find the following paragraphs very rewarding—not just intellectually, but financially as well.

Many employees who qualify for 403(b) plans do not have a choice as to where to invest their 403(b) money. What a tragedy. With over 8,000 mutual funds to choose from, these people are literally stuck with an annuity that offers a sub-par return—in most cases a full 1/3 less than the average-performing mutual fund. *That is 1/3 less!* That adds up to a tremendous amount of money missed out on over the years—money that does not have to be lost.

As a matter of fact, many employees decide to pass up the 403(b) tax break rather than be forced into an annuity. They pay tax on the part of their salary that would have gone into the plan and put what is left in a no-load mutual fund. And many of them come out ahead. Their funds return enough to push their after-tax investment ahead of any pre-tax investment they would have made in a sub-par-performing annuity. Although that sounds like a wise move, you have to remember that for that strategy to work, the after-tax investment would have to have consistent above-average returns year after year, and that is a tall order.

There are employers who do offer many options—as many as 15 different investment choices—but everyone of them an annuity, with fees that are nothing more than a waste of valuable money. Another tragedy. Then why does it happen? As you may or may not know, 403(b) plans are often called *tax-sheltered annuities*. Not surprisingly, a lot of people think that something *called* an annuity has to *be* an annuity—an investment sold by insurance companies. Not so. There is another option. Back in 1973, in the midst of a terrible bear market, congress added the option of allowing tax-sheltered annuity participants to put their tax-sheltered 403(b) money directly into mutual funds.

I am not saying that you should never invest in an annuity. As a matter of fact, you will see in chapter 15 that I favor purchasing an annuity when an investor finds himself/herself in a very unique financial position, but never as a first choice. Why not an annuity as a first choice? Because annuities always come

165

with extra fees—insurance charges, commission charges, higher management fees—whose total can eat up to 3.5% or more of the account value *each and every year*. That is taking a big bite out of your retirement nest egg. And, although well-known mutual fund companies may be found wrapped *inside* the annuity, they are usually offered at double the cost (one charge for the mutual fund and one charge for the annuity wrapper), which make the two sets of fees very expensive. And the mutual funds offered are not necessarily the same as the ones they offer outside the annuity, so in essence, you usually lose more money because of sub-par performance.

Let us look at an example. Assume you start with nothing and make a contribution of $300 a month for 20 years, which earns 10%. With a no-load mutual fund you would have a total of $215,480. Because of the extra 3.5% in fees, the annuity would return only 6.5%, for a total return of only $143,890—*a full $71,590 less!!!* And remember, that is assuming the annuity would initially return the same 10% as the no-load mutual fund. In reality, annuities usually earn less. So how do you combat this seemingly hopeless situation? Well, as I see it, you have two options.

> • **The First Option**—You can mount a campaign and press for mutual fund options for your 403(b) plan. As stated in chapter 9, in 1974, Congress helped employees with their retirement plans by adding paragraph 7 to section 403(b). This later provision permits employees to contribute to mutual fund companies instead of insurance companies. But before you mount a campaign, do take a close look at the choices you presently have and the fees attached to your current 403(b). Do sales commissions shrink your contributions before any money is invested? Is there a large surrender charge—a back-end load that kicks in if you pull your money out of the annuity and switch to another investment (such as a no-load mutual fund) before the company has recovered its sales expenses? The industry average is 7% the first year, 6% the second year, and so on until it disappears after seven years. And, what about mortality and other fees? Also, look at the management fees of the funds *inside* the annuity. They are usually higher and can really affect your future returns.
>
> If you do decide to press for a mutual fund option, be prepared for some resistance. It is usually not that employers are against funds, they are simply reluctant to add to the chores of the bookkeeping/accounting/payroll department. As you are well aware, we are experiencing economic times where cutting back expenses is the order of the day, and it is the administrators who are responsible for making those cuts. And for the most part, they believe they already offer enough 403(b) plan choices. Often, they simply need enlightened. If that is the case, make it your responsibility to enlighten them. Trust me, as you will soon see, in terms of dollars and cents, it is well worth your effort.
>
> Also note that there are two different mutual fund routes: one if your 403(b) includes employer contributions (and most do not), and another if it does not. Plans that include employer contributions involve a more formal design similar to 401(k) plans, with employer-selected fund options and provisions for plan loans and hardship withdrawals. It can get a little complicated and be a little costly to the employer. But, if your employer does not kick in contributions, a simpler arrangement is available. Your employer names the fund family (or families) as an approved vendor and sends contributions to a 403(b)(7) account, which is named after the part of the law that allows direct mutual fund investment. Most such simple plans do not allow loans or hardship withdrawals, but you have more latitude in choosing among funds, and that is, ultimately, what you are after.
>
> • **The Second Option**—There is a little-known way that you might be able to get higher earnings on your retirement savings, and have more control over your money, too. This is

accomplished by contributing to your employer's plan and then transferring the accumulated savings to a 403(b)(7) custodial account that you set up with a mutual fund family. You arrange the transfers yourself.

Millions of employees with 403(b) retirement plans can transfer their accumulated savings to another investment company—such as their favorite mutual-fund or insurance company. And they can make the transfer even if they remain in the same job, and even if the investment company they choose is not on the list approved by their employer. In other words, they do not have to be stuck with sub-par investment options anymore.

Altogether, more than $100 billion of the roughly $500 billion that has accumulated in 403(b) plans could be transferred tomorrow. It is almost the same procedure as transferring an IRA. Yet few employees, financial planners, accountants, or even human-resource professionals realize this freedom exists. That is too bad because one of the biggest advantages 403(b) plans have over 401(k) plans is that employees have the capability to transfer the accumulated savings from a low-return investment (such as an annuity) to a high-return investment (such as a stock mutual fund), even without employer approval, so long as their employer has not contributed money to the plan.

In contrast, employees with 401(k) plans—and those with 403(b) plans to which their employer does contribute money—can not transfer their money anywhere until they change jobs or retire. The transfer choices are not limited to mutual funds, either. People with 403(b) money in annuities can also transfer the money to another insurance company's annuities, even if the company is not on their employer's list. The only restrictions are that the money be placed in mutual funds or annuities and that the investment company or insurer offer 403(b) transfer accounts. Most of them do.

To make a tax-free transfer of 403(b) savings, you merely contact the new investment company, which will send you a transfer form. The mutual-fund company or insurer will then contact the retirement plan sponsor used by the employer and notify them of the transfer. It is actually a simple process.

While employees can transfer the accumulated savings in eligible 403(b) plans, they are still restricted to the approved list of vendors for prospective contributions. If they want to send future contributions directly to the desired investment company, they still need to get employees together to petition the employer to add it to the employer's list.

When moving accumulated money, it is very important to consider surrender penalties. As stated earlier, most annuities offered in 403(b) plans have surrender penalties that require employees to forfeit a part of their investment if they pull their money out in the first few years. About half of these plans treat money accumulated each year as a different pot for purposes of the surrender penalty. So, money saved in 1999 might have a surrender charge of, say, 7%; money saved in 1998 might have a charge of 6%, and so on.

Surrender charges tend to be higher in variable annuities in retirement plans than in annuities sold to individuals. Still, many annuities let you withdraw some of your balance each year without a surrender penalty. Check to see whether your insurance company lets you transfer up to 10% of accumulated assets per year without surrender penalties. If you are not sure how surrender penalties affect your savings, ask the insurance company for your surrender value and make a comparison. But keep the following in mind. In most cases the money that is lost can be recouped in a year or two with a fund realizing a higher rate of return. And from that point on you come out way ahead. That benefits the long-term investor particularly.

For example, if you have $40,000 accumulated in an annuity, averaging a 4% return, that has an early-withdrawal penalty (surrender charge) of 6%, and you have 25 more years to invest. Your monthly contribution is $200. If you took the penalty and transferred the balance ($37,600) to a no-load mutual fund that averages 10% (the market average), you would make up your loss in approximately 16 months. And, at the end of the 25-year investment period, the no-load mutual fund would have returned a total of $654,050. With the annuity paying a mere 4%, you would only end up with $208,403 at the end of 25 years—*a full $445,647 less!!!* If you use the same numbers, but increase the monthly contribution to $400 a month, the no-load mutual fund returns a total of $900,715 at the end of 25 years. The annuity would return $310,173 in the same 25-year period—*a full $590,542 less* than the no-load mutual fund. *That is a half of a million dollars!!!* Is the penalty worth taking? You tell me.

To protect new contributions from surrender charges, some employees, whose investment choices are limited to annuities, park their new contributions in money-market funds, which have no surrender penalties, and then transfer the money after a year or so to a no-load mutual fund. Let us now move on to the specifics concerning mutual funds.

Shares and share price—When you purchase a mutual fund, you purchase shares. The value of one share of a mutual fund is called the *net asset value*. The number of shares you buy is determined by the share price of the fund—net asset value plus any sales charges. (When you invest in mutual funds through your retirement plan, sales charges are usually waived). For example, if a fund's share price is $10 a share, and you buy $2,500 worth, you then own 250 shares ($2,500 divided by $10).

The share price of a fund is based on the value of the underlying securities within the fund. For this reason, it is calculated every day because the value of these securities can change every day, based on what happens in the stock and bond markets and in money market instruments. To illustrate the effect of changes in share price, consider another example. In January, you invest $2,500 in a mutual fund that has a share price of $10. Your investment buys 250 shares. By March, the share price has dropped to $9 because the fund's investments in stocks and bonds within the fund have dropped in value. You still own 250 shares, but your total investment is now worth $2,250. In June, the share price rises to $11, reflecting an increase in value of the fund's investments. You still own 250 shares, but now the total value is $2,750.

How mutual funds earn money—A mutual fund investment has the potential to earn money for you in two ways. The first way is through *earnings*—the profits earned by the fund that are passed on to you. Earnings include interest from bonds, dividends from the stocks held by the fund, and capital gains (the profits earned by the fund from selling securities within the fund for more than what was paid). The second way to earn money is through share *appreciation*. Some mutual funds are designed for little or no share price fluctuation (change in price), while others can fluctuate significantly daily. As the value of the securities in a fund increases, a fund's share price increases, meaning that the value of your investment rises. If you sell your shares at a higher share price than you paid for them, you make a profit, or *capital gain*.

Keep in mind that this how you can lose money, too. As the value of the securities in a fund decreases, a fund's share price decreases, and the value of your investment decreases. If you sell your shares when the share price is lower than the price you paid, you will lose a portion of your investment, or have a *capital loss*. Note that earnings and capital gains on your 403(b) plan investments are automatically reinvested in your retirement plan account to buy additional fund shares.

Example of The Difference Between Fund Earnings and Capital Gains Fund Earnings

Fund Earnings Distributions

During the year, the fund earns money (interest or dividends and capital gains) from its stocks, bonds, and short-term investments. Suppose after fund expenses are taken out, the fund's earnings amount to $0.10 for each share of the fund. This money is distributed to the shareholders. Since you own 250 shares, $25 (.10 x 250) will be reinvested in your retirement plan account.

Your Capital Gains

Let's suppose that during the year, the fund's share price rises from $10 to $11. That price change reflects an increase in the value of the securities held by the fund. A $1 rise per share translates into a $250 increase in value for your 250 shares. If you retired now and withdrew all your shares, you would make a profit, or capital gain, of $250.

In all, you invested $2,500 and, if you had withdrawn your savings (sold your shares), you would have received a total of $2,775: your $2,500 investment, plus a $25 distribution (earnings), and a $250 capital gain. Once your savings are withdrawn, you would owe taxes on your withdrawal. Note that when you purchase shares through your 403(b) plan, you will receive two significant tax benefits

1. **Reduced taxable income**—all contributions to your retirement account are made on a pre-tax basis before federal taxes are applied. So you pay less in current income taxes.

2. **Tax-deferred growth**—all contributions and earnings accumulate tax-deferred—you do not pay taxes on the money in your account until you begin taking distributions. As stated in chapter 10, withdrawals before age 59 ½ *may* be subject to a 10% early withdrawal penalty.

Classifications of Mutual Funds—Before we discuss mutual fund types, let us talk a little about mutual fund classifications. Basically, there are two classifications:

- **Open-end mutual fund (the most common mutual fund)**—A fund that takes on new investors' money and keeps getting larger and larger. This means that there is no set limit as to how much money they will permit to be invested in the fund. At their discretion, the manager and others in authority may sometimes close the fund to new investors once they have taken in more money than they feel is manageable, but this a decision they can make anytime as they go along. At the end of each day, the manager totals up the entire value of the portfolio that constitutes this mutual fund. He/she then divides that total by how many shares are owned by the investors. This figure, whatever it comes out to, is called the *net asset value*, or *NAV*. It is what each of your shares is worth. The more shares you have, the more you make, or the more you lose—depending upon whether the fund goes up or down.

- **Closed-End Mutual Fund**—In this type of fund the number of shares that can be sold

169

to the public is decided ahead of time. Once the shares are sold, the fund is closed to new business. It will not issue new shares, the way the open-end funds will. New people can buy into a closed-end fund only if someone who owns it wants to sell it. Essentially, it is priced and traded just like a stock, so the value of its shares may not correspond exactly to the value of its holdings.

For our purposes here, we will be dealing with open-end funds only. These are the ones you usually hear people talking about, and these are the ones commonly offered in 403(b) retirement plans.

Types of Mutual Funds

While all mutual funds are similar in the way they are structured, there are several different types of mutual funds. These types of funds differ in terms of the types of asset classes they own, for example, stocks and bonds. Basically, there are three types of mutual funds—stock mutual funds, bond mutual funds, and money market mutual funds—that invest in the three asset classes:

Stock-Mutual Fund—(higher risk/higher return)—Stocks represent ownership or equity in a company. They tend to increase in value over time and have the potential to outperform other types of investments over the long term. However, stocks tend to have wilder price fluctuations than other securities.

Bond-Mutual Fund—(moderate risk/moderate return)—A bond is a type of security that pays a fixed amount of interest at a regular interval over a certain period of time. Bonds are essentially loans given to companies and government entities who promise to pay back the loan at a specified interest rate. As a bond holder, you receive that interest payment once a year. Bonds also provide income by returning the principal if it is held to maturity. Since bonds fluctuate in value based on interest rates, investors may realize a gain or loss if sold before maturity. For example, suppose you own a municipal $1,000 bond that pays 7% interest over 10 years. In this case, assuming you bought the bond at its *par value* (the face value of a bond before fluctuations in the market cause it to be sold for more or less than its original value) of $1,000 and held it for 10 years, you would receive $70 a year (7% of $1,000) for 10 years. At the end of the 10 years, you would have received $700 in interest ($70 x 10 years), and you would also get the $1,000 back.

Bonds are considered less risky investments than stocks. A bond's rating is like a person's credit rating. It gives you an idea of whether the company that issued the bond will be able to make its payments on the loan. Bond prices change when interest rates change. When interest rates are rising, bond prices tend to go down. For example, a bond that you bought at its par value of $1,000 with a 7% return is not going to be worth as much to a prospective buyer if the interest rates have risen to 9%. You would have to sell the bond at less than its par value (at a discount) to make it worth the investment when rates have gone up. Conversely, when interest rates fall, a bond that you bought at its par value of $1,000 with a 7% return is worth more when interest rates fall to 5% because it is earning better than the average return for a bond. You could sell it for more than its par value.

Short-Term Securities Mutual Fund—(lower risk/lower return)—Short-term instruments represent investments in securities with maturities of less than three years and include CDs and money market instruments. Short-term instruments pay interest and tend to fluctuate the least. However, they also tend to provide the lowest returns over the long term, often just barely keeping pace with inflation.

Every mutual fund is made up of at least one of the aforementioned types of asset classes (for example, a growth and income fund may own both stocks and bonds). And, as you may suspect, each type of fund is similar in behavior to the type of securities it owns.

170

Balancing Risk and Reward

Type of Fund	Type of Security Owned	Anticipated Share Price Fluctuation	Potential for Growth
Money Market Funds	Commercial paper; T-bills; short-term high-quality debt	None	None
Government Bond Funds	Bonds	Low to moderate	Low
Corporate Bond Funds	Bonds	Low to moderate	Low
Lifestyle (or Asset Allocation Funds)	U.S. stocks; foreign stocks; bonds; real estate stocks; money market securities	Moderate	Moderate
Balanced Funds	Stocks and bonds	Low to moderate	Moderate
Equity-Income Funds	Stocks and bonds	Low to moderate	Moderate
Growth & Income Funds	Stocks and bonds	Moderate	Moderate
Index Funds	Stocks and bonds	Moderate	Moderate
International Funds	Foreign stocks and bonds	Moderate to high	Moderate to high
Value Funds	Stocks	High	Moderate to high
Growth Funds	Stocks	High	Moderate to high
Aggressive Growth Funds	Stocks	High	High
Emerging Markets Funds	Stocks of developing countries	Very High	Very High
Sector Funds	Invests in companies in specific industries (ex.- health care)	Very High	Very High

<u>Advantages and Disadvantages of Each Type of Mutual Fund</u>

The following questions and answers will help you to better understand each type of mutual fund investment:

- **<u>What is a money market fund?</u>**—A money market fund invests in very short-term (less than 397 days), high-quality debt securities (loans) such as Treasury Bills, bank CDs, and high-grade commer-

171

cial paper (the very short-term IOUs of corporations with excellent credit ratings). Money market funds are considered very conservative investments and are appropriate for people who are investing for a short period of time or who do not want to risk losing their principal investment.

The investment holdings of money market funds are generally of exceptionally high quality. Indeed, the Securities and Exchange Commission requires that all taxable money market funds invest at least 95% of their assets in securities of the highest grade, as rated by *Moody's Investors Services* or *Standard & Poor's Corporation*. Money market funds are designed to offer investors two major benefits: stability of principal and regular income.

> **1. Stability of principal**—Every dollar you invest will be there, no matter how interest rates change. Each investment dollar is converted into a share and is managed to maintain a stable $1 share price. This is different from a stock or a bond mutual fund, in which the share price fluctuates depending on how well or how poorly the fund's investments perform.

> **2. Regular Income**—You will receive income distributions on a regular schedule. In your 403(b) retirement account any distributions you receive would be reinvested. The amount of the distributions varies and is determined in large part by current short-term interest rates, unlike CDs, which "lock in" an interest rate for a set period of time. However, unlike most CDs and bank products, money market fund yields will vary.

• **What are the advantages and disadvantages of money market funds?**—The main advantage of a money market fund is its stability of principal. Another plus is that your investment is diversified because you are lending to a wide range of corporate borrowers and to the federal government. The main disadvantage of a money market fund is that your principal does not grow. It is very vulnerable to inflation. As a matter of fact, history shows that after inflation and taxes, a money market fund investment barely grows at all over periods of ten years or more. Another disadvantage is that money market funds are not insured or guaranteed by the U.S. Government.

• **What is a government bond fund?**—Bond funds differ from money market funds in two ways in that they tend to earn higher yields (due to the longer maturity and the varying quality of their investments), and have greater volatility (due to share price fluctuations).

A government bond fund is a mutual fund that buys IOUs issued by the U.S. government and/or its agencies, state and local governments, and in some instances, foreign corporations and governments. The federal government issues three basic IOUs: 1) Treasury Bills, which mature in one year or less; 2) Treasury Notes, which mature in one to ten years; and 3) Treasury Bonds, which mature in ten years or longer. The interest on these government loans is lower than the interest on corporate bonds of similar maturities because there is virtually no risk that the federal government and its agencies will default on their loans. (Unlike corporations, the government can always raise money by increasing taxes or imposing new ones). But just because there is no default risk does not mean that government bonds or government bond funds are risk-free.

If you buy an 8% government bond and hold it to maturity, you get a fixed 8% yield for the life of the bond. But if you buy shares in a government bond fund, your interest is not fixed because a mutual fund does not hold bonds to maturity. The fund is constantly buying and selling bonds, therefore, interest earned by fund shareholders fluctuates.

The value of your principal in a government bond fund does not remain fixed, either. It rises and falls as interest rates change. If the prevailing interest rate goes up, the value of your principal—and the Net Asset Value of your fund shares—will go down. Rising interest rates always reduce the value of existing bonds. Why? Because no one will pay full price for a $1,000 bond that pays 7% if newly issued $1,000 bonds are paying 8%. The risk that your principal will shrink because of rising interest rates is called *interest rate risk*. All bonds carry this risk, including government bonds.

If you think that all of this means that the term *fixed-income fund* is somewhat misleading, you are right. In spite of what is assumed by most investors, neither interest nor principal value is fixed in a fixed-income fund. So, do not judge a bond fund's performance by yield alone. Always look at total return, which is the yield (interest) plus or minus any changes in the value of your principal as reflected in the price of your shares. As junk bond investors discovered when interest rates rose in 1989 and 1990, a bond fund can pay a very high yield but have a terrible total return. How? Investors earn high interest while their principal dwindles away.

Some government bond funds also have pre-payment risk. These are funds that buy mortgage-backed bonds from government agencies like the Government National Mortgage Association, commonly known as *Ginnie Mae*. Some mutual funds specialize in Ginnie Mae bonds. Other government agency bonds are *Freddie Macs* (issued by the Federal Home Loan Mortgage Corporation) and *Fannie Maes* (issued by the Federal National Mortgage Association). The stream of income paid by Ginnie Maes, Fannie Maes, and Freddie Macs comes from homeowners' mortgage payments. The mortgages in question are guaranteed by federal agencies, so there is no default risk. But there are other risks. Most mortgage-backed bonds have 30-year maturities, but in reality they mature much faster because homeowners prepay their mortgages when they sell their houses and move, or when they refinance because interest rates have dropped. Typically, a 30-year mortgage is repaid in seven years when the average house is sold or the mortgage is refinanced.

This makes mortgage-backed bonds particularly vulnerable to interest rate changes. Like all bonds, they lose value when interest rates rise. But they also lose value when interest rates fall significantly because millions of homeowners refinance. The homeowners pay off the mortgages backing Ginnie Maes and other mortgage-backed bonds and take out new mortgages at the prevailing lower rate. When that happens, investors in Ginnie Mae bonds get their principal back much sooner than they expected and must reinvest it at a lower interest rate. Because of this pre-payment risk, Ginnie Maes and other mortgage-backed bonds typically yield somewhat more than other government bonds chiefly to attract investors.

- **What is a corporate bond fund?**—A corporate bond fund is a mutual fund that buys the IOUs of corporations. Short-term bond funds usually buy bonds with a maturity of less than three years. Intermediate-term bond funds invest in bonds that mature in three to ten years. Long-term bond funds usually have a maturity of ten years or longer. You usually earn higher interest on corporate bond funds than on government bond funds of similar maturities because even a top-rated corporation is not as sure to repay its loans as the federal government. Although bond funds are also called fixed-income funds, the interest you receive in a bond mutual fund is not fixed at all; it fluctuates constantly as the fund buys and sells bonds. The value of your principal investment also fluctuates as interest rates move up and down.

The longer the maturity of a bond, the more value it gains if interest rates fall, and the more value it loses if interest rates rise. Because long-term bond funds are much more volatile than short or intermediate bond funds, they react more dramatically to changes in interest rates, and usually offer higher yields when purchased. Remember, your total return from any bond fund is the interest you earn (yield), plus or minus any changes in the value of your principal, as reflected in the market price of your fund shares.

- **What are the advantages and disadvantages of bond funds?**—The advantage of short to intermediate-term bond funds is that they provide a steady stream of income, while keeping your principal fairly safe. Short to intermediate-term bond funds also tend to be less volatile than stock funds, so keeping part of your 403(b) account in a bond fund can help lower the overall volatility of your portfolio.

A long-term bond fund involves more risk. It provides a relatively high stream of income and has a potentially higher total return than shorter-term bond funds. If interest rates fall, the value of long-term bonds can grow quite dramatically. The risk deals with the other side of the coin—if interest rates rise, the value of your shares could plummet.

The main disadvantage of bond funds is interest rate risk. All too often, bond fund investors do not realize that their principal will shrink if interest rates rise. They mistakenly assume that their principal will be stable in a bond fund the way it is in a money market fund. Another disadvantage of bond funds as a long-term investment is that they do not stand up well to inflation.

Because bonds can not reach for the kind of performance over time that stocks enjoy, buy only those bond funds with annual fees below 1%. Many fine ones can be had for less than 0.5%. Also, stick with no-load funds.

- **How does maturity affect risk and reward in bond funds?**—In general, the more share price fluctuation you can accept, the more potential you have for a higher yield. Usually, the highest yields are offered by funds that invest in long-term bonds and/or lower-quality bonds, and their share price tends to fluctuate the most. Funds that invest in short-term and/or higher quality bonds tend to offer lower yields, and their share price tends to fluctuate less. The chart below further illustrates these points. The money market fund type is listed strictly for comparison.

Type of Fund	Anticipated Average Maturity*	Risk and Share Price Fluctuation
Money Market Fund	90 days or less	None
Short-Term Bond Fund	3 years or less	Low
Intermediate-Term Bond Fund	3 to 10 years	Low to moderate
Long-Term Bond Fund	10 years or more	Moderate

* Average maturity refers to the amount of time remaining, on average, before a fund's bond and money market investments are due to mature or be repaid. Regardless of the average maturity of a fund, you can buy and sell shares of the fund when you choose.

- **What is an asset allocation (or lifestyle) fund?**—Asset allocation funds, or lifestyle funds as they are sometimes called, own securities from each asset class (stocks, bonds, short-term instruments, real estate stocks, etc.) thereby providing investors with greater diversification than you would get from mutual funds that you would buy separately. What makes these funds unique is that they can adjust the amount of an asset class (change the mix) held by the fund as the portfolio manager's current expectations for the economy and markets change. Often, there are different types of asset allocation funds offered in an employer's 403(b) plan—some are aggressive, primarily investing in stocks, and some are more conservative, looking for income by focusing on bonds and short-term instruments. The goal is to give you the diversification to weather virtually any market or economic environment. Because all asset allocation funds invest in stocks and bonds to some degree, their share prices will fluctuate.

- **What are the advantages and disadvantages of asset allocation (or lifestyle) funds?**—The greatest advantage of an asset allocation fund is that one fund can be used to achieve the same goals as regular growth or income funds, while making it possible to diversify among a range of security types and asset classes. A disadvantage of asset allocation funds is that you do not get to make your asset allocation decisions yourself. If you want to retain control of those decisions, you had better pass on asset allocation funds and diversify your money by investing in several different types of funds yourself.

- **What is a balanced fund?**—One of the three fund categories nicknamed *total-return funds,* the supercautious balanced fund invests in both stocks and bonds, usually in a 60% stocks, 40% bonds combination. However, the portfolio manager's freedom to decide what percentage of fund assets to invest in bonds and what percentage to invest in stocks depends on the individual fund. Over 50% of 403(b) plans offer balanced funds, making them the most common kind of equity fund.

The balanced fund is designed to provide you with both income and growth. It is a compromise, really. In a rising stock market it will not earn as high a total return as a pure stock fund; however, in a falling stock market it will not lose as much as a pure stock fund, because its income from interest and dividends will cushion the fall.

When interest rates fall, balanced funds do very well because falling interest rates benefit both bond and stock prices. But when interest rates rise, the value of both stocks and bonds is likely to fall. Therefore, a balanced fund is not the best fund to own when interest rates are rising.

If your 403(b) plan does not include any separate bond funds, you should probably put some money into a balanced fund. Otherwise you can create your own balanced portfolio.

- **What are the advantages and disadvantages of balanced funds?**—The biggest advantage of a balanced fund is that in a falling stock market, a balanced fund will not lose as much as a pure stock fund. The biggest disadvantage of a balanced fund is that in a rising stock market it will not earn as high a total return as a pure stock fund.

- **What is an equity-income fund?**—Equity-income funds invest in both stocks and bonds. The second of the three fund categories nicknamed *total-return funds,* and having similar characteristics of a balanced fund, equity-income funds try to achieve steady returns from a combination of capital gains and interest or dividends. As a result, equity-income funds behave more evenly than growth funds, dropping less in down markets but rising less in up markets. As is the case with a balanced fund, when interest rates fall, equity-income funds do very well because falling interest rates benefit both bond and stock prices. But when interest rates rise, the value of both stocks and bonds is likely to fall.

- **What are the advantages and disadvantages of equity-income funds?**—Its chief advantage is an overall smoother performance than most funds during a bumpy market ride. This, of course, benefits those investors who get stressed out when the market moves sharply. Its main disadvantage is that in a rising stock market it will not earn as high a total return as a pure stock fund.

- **What is a growth and income fund?**—The third of the three fund categories nicknamed *total-return funds,* growth and income funds invest primarily in *blue-chip stocks*—the stocks of large, well-established, very stable companies with a long history of steadily growing earnings and reliable dividends. They are considered classic middle-of-the-road funds, and are a good investment for relatively conservative investors who still want long-term growth. About 45% of all 403(b) plans include growth and income funds. These funds make for a smart choice for the investor who is just getting started in stock funds, and are good core funds to have no matter how seasoned an investor you are.

- **What are the advantages and disadvantages of growth and income funds?**—The greatest advantage of growth and income funds is that in a falling stock market, they do not lose as much as pure growth funds because the blue chips' dividends offset some of the decline in stock prices. The greatest disadvantage of growth and income funds is that in a rising stock market, they will not grow as rapidly as pure growth funds. In other words, they will lag the market.

- **What is an index fund?**—Index funds are the funds that buy all the stocks in a given market index, such as the *Standard & Poor's 500*, and thereby mimic the performance of those stocks as a whole. An index fund can be managed by a computer instead of a human being. No portfolio manager or research staff decides what an index fund will buy or sell; it simply invests in *all* the stocks or bonds that make up a particular index. For example, the *S & P 500* consists of the stocks of 500 companies: 400 industrial companies, 40 utilities, 40 finance companies, and 20 transportation companies. Other major indices include the *Dow Jones Industrial Average*, which tracks the performance of 30 blue-chip stocks; the *S & P 400*, which tracks the performance of mid-cap companies; the *Russell 2000* which tracks the performance of the stocks of 2,000 small-cap companies; and the *Shearson Lehman Brothers Government/Corporate Bond Index*, which tracks the performance of investment-grade bonds.

Those who endorse index funds like their steady if unspectacular performance, their usually low fees, and their tendency to cost you less in taxes because of their low turnover ratio (buying and selling of holdings). As a complete investor, you might consider putting your taxable money in index funds and keeping your tax-deferred 403(b) and IRAs in actively managed funds.

- **What are the advantages and disadvantages of index funds?**—The greatest advantage of an index fund is that an index fund that performs as well as the market will have a better return than most actively managed funds. Why? Because most actively managed funds underperform the market as a whole. In fact, only about 33% of actively managed funds outperform the market. Also, an index fund has lower operating expenses than an actively managed fund because index funds do not pay a portfolio manager or a big research staff. They also do not have a lot of trading expenses since they simply buy and hold one group of stocks or bonds. This means lower costs and a higher return for their shareholders.

Some actively managed funds do outperform the market, however, sometimes by a substantial margin. The greatest disadvantage of an index fund is that an index fund, which mimics the market, will *never* outperform the market, in good times or bad. A talented investment manager of an actively managed fund can minimize losses in a down market by changing its portfolio mix, and selling and buying the right assets at the right time. This can not happen with index funds.

- **What is an international fund?**—We live in an international economy. As Bob Dylan used to say, "Times they are a changing." Today the U.S. stock market represents only about one-third of the world's publicly traded stocks, as compared to a mere 20 year ago, when the U.S. stock market represented a little more than two-thirds of the world's total stock market. If you limit yourself only to U.S. stocks, you are ignoring two-thirds of the investment opportunities in the world. And some of those investment opportunities are in economies that are growing more rapidly than our own. With that in mind, it only makes sense to include international funds to your investment portfolio.

International funds invest only in non-U.S. stocks or bonds. Do not confuse them with global funds, which can invest in any country, including the United States. When you invest in an international stock fund, you are buying shares in foreign companies doing business outside the U.S. When you own shares in an international bond fund, you are lending money to foreign companies and/or governments, which most often pay a higher rate of interest than you could obtain in a domestic bond fund. If you are out to achieve big returns over the coming years, international funds deserve your consideration.

- **<u>What are the advantages and disadvantages of international funds?</u>**—The greatest advantage of international funds is that owning international stocks diversifies your total portfolio. Foreign stock markets do not move up and down in tandem with the U.S. stock market. Therefore, a good performance by international investments can help cushion your total portfolio at a time when the U.S. market is falling. One of the greatest disadvantages of international funds is the exposure to currency risk. Currency swings alone offer a volatility that you do not have to face if you stick strictly to domestic stock funds. Before the international fund can buy shares on a foreign stock exchange, its dollars must be converted into local currency, and when the fund sells shares, its investment is converted back into dollars. If the U.S. dollar falls in value compared to other currencies, your shares in an international fund can increase in value. But the currency risk works both ways. If the dollar rises in value relative to other currencies, the price of your fund shares can drop.

- **<u>What is a value fund?</u>**—Value funds buy out-of-favor and low-priced stocks with prices that do not fully reflect their real value, what we call undervalued stocks. They increase the stability of your portfolio by tilting the stock portion away from growth funds. In style, value fund managers stand in contrast with growth fund managers who look for stocks with fast-growing earnings. Note that, just like growth funds, value funds can be found among those that buy small-cap, mid-cap, large-cap, and international stocks. Something you must remember, however, is that although both are perfectly valid, the market tends to favor value funds and growth funds at different times. The problem lies in the fact that no one knows when the stock market will be responding to value and when it will be geared to growth. Therefore, it pays to own both. In a more aggressive portfolio, a sensible strategy is to try to keep about 60% of your stock fund allocation in value funds and the rest in growth funds.

- **<u>What are the advantages and disadvantages of value funds?</u>**—The greatest advantage of a value fund is that when the stock market takes a tumble, value funds normally do not fall as far as growth funds largely because a value fund tends to buy more stable dividend-paying stocks. The greatest disadvantage of a value fund is that when the bull market charges ahead, value funds do not rise as fast or as high as pure growth stocks.

- **<u>What is a growth fund?</u>**—Growth funds are a notch down in risk from aggressive growth funds. They go for stocks with fast-growing earnings, even if they feature premium prices, and normally plow earnings back into growth instead of into shareholder dividends because the main goal is not to earn current income for its investors, but to grow the value of their principal. Over the long term they, along with aggressive growth funds, get the best results. Growth funds appear in more than 40% of 403(b) plans representing about 15% of the average participant's total balance.

- **What are the advantages and disadvantages of growth funds?**—The main advantage of a growth fund is that over the long term, the companies it invests in are likely to grow at a much faster rate than inflation. That translates into forcing the real buying power of your principal to grow faster than inflation, too. As is typical of a growth fund, its biggest disadvantage is that it is very vulnerable to short-term market fluctuations. With that in mind, it is not a good investment for anyone who will need his/her money back in one or two years and might have to cash out at a time when the fund shares are lower in value.

- **What is an aggressive growth fund?**—An aggressive growth fund, sometimes called a *capital appreciation fund*, is one of the riskiest fund types of them all. They are like growth funds, only more so. They have provided the most generous returns over the past 10 years, with an average annual gain of 12.7%. Their goal is to achieve the highest possible growth of your principal. Consequently, aggressive growth funds invest in the stocks of companies that are expected to grow extremely fast. As you would expect, they also subject investors to more principal risk than other types of funds. Considered the most speculative of all the funds, they assume this high risk to get high returns. Aggressive growth funds often specialize in investing in smaller, less established companies. You need to have the stomach to ride out the occasional plunges these funds take without panicking and selling out. They will really test your nerves; however, they get the best results in the long run. If you are bothered by sharp ups and downs in the market, you need to approach these funds with caution. Do not put any more than 25% of your portfolio in these funds.

- **What are the advantages and disadvantages of aggressive growth funds?**—The biggest advantage is that in a rising stock market an aggressive growth fund will most likely outperform the average stock fund by a substantial margin. Conversely, its biggest disadvantage is that in a falling stock market, they lose more value than the average stock fund. The best aggressive growth funds are very, very good and the worst are very, very bad.

- **What is an emerging markets fund?**—As opposed to an international fund that invests primarily in the world's developed nations, an emerging markets fund is an international fund that only invests in developing countries, such as South Korea, Thailand, Malaysia, the Philippines, Indonesia, Singapore, the countries of Latin America, and the former Iron Curtain countries of Eastern Europe. The companies in these emerging markets are likely to grow much more rapidly than American companies. Some of these developing nation's economies are growing at 15% or more a year, compared to the mature U.S. economy which grows at an average of about 3% a year.

    As you start out, I suggest you stay away from emerging markets funds. But, since the stocks of developing countries are widely expected to offer the most growth potential of the next few decades, you might consider adding an emerging market fund to your portfolio mix once you get more used to market dips and as your nest egg grows.

- **What are the advantages and disadvantages of emerging markets funds?**—The greatest advantage of emerging markets funds is that the economies of the countries they invest in have the potential to grow very rapidly and create a huge demand for goods and services. Therefore, the companies that supply these goods and services have the potential to become very rich, and so do their shareholders. The greatest disadvantage of emerging markets funds is that the developing nations they invest in are very vulnerable to economic and political crises, or collapse. Therefore, any emerging markets investment is much more volatile than a domestic fund or an international fund that invests primarily in the world's developed nations.

- **What is a sector fund?**—Sector funds invest exclusively in the stocks of a single industry (like telecommunications, chemicals, or energy services) or commodity (like gold). These are among the most volatile funds of all, often landing at the top of the performance charts one year and at the bottom the very next.

- **What are the advantages and disadvantages of sector funds?**—The biggest advantage of a sector fund is that it can exhibit rocket-like growth if a specific industry really takes off. Of course, timing is critical here. The biggest disadvantage of sector funds is volatility. They will give you one of the bumpiest rides around. With a sector fund you will not get the steady advances that well-diversified funds offer. They are definitely not for the faint of heart. Do not invest any money in them that you are afraid to lose.

Loads or no-loads?—This is probably the most hotly-debated issue ever to enter the world of mutual fund investing. Should you buy load funds or no-load funds? This argument has been going on since the inception of mutual fund investing. To me, this one is a no-brainer, so I will not be giving this issue much space here. For those of you just starting out, let me explain the difference between the two types. A *load* is a sales fee you pay when investing in a mutual fund. *No-load mutual funds* are mutual funds that you buy (either through your 403(b) or personally) directly from the fund company (fund family) without any load (sales fee). *Load mutual funds*, by contrast, are those that carry a sales fee that typically run around 3% to as high as 8%. Funds that charge low loads (usually 3 percent or less) are often categorized as *no-loads*. Be sure you understand whether a no-load fund in fact charges a load.

- **Front-End Load (or front-load)**—You pay the fee when you buy shares. That fee comes directly off the top of your contribution before any of the money gets to work for you. For example, a 3% front load on a $1,000 investment would mean you are credited with buying only $970 worth of shares, with $30 subtracted as the sales charge. Load charges range as high as 8% but are more commonly in the range of 3% to 4.5%.

- **Back-End Load (sometimes called a deferred sales charge)**—You pay the fee when you sell shares. It is calculated on the total value of the shares you sell. Either your profit is cut or your loss increased. For example, a back-end load of 3% on $5,000 worth of shares is $150. That means you would receive $4,350 when you sell.

As you know, I always recommend to investors to track their investments throughout the year. When tracking your investments, you must take a close look at your *total return*—your profit when *everything* is taken into account. That is not just gains in the market and dividends from stock funds; not just gains in the market and interest in bond funds. It is the total of *all income* added up minus *all costs*—including loads.

Some people would have you believe that load funds offer greater returns and are worth the extra money. That simply is not true. They are only fooling themselves. As a matter of fact, a study done by *Morningstar Inc.*, and reported in the February 1995 issue of *Money Magazine*, came up with the eight most dependable funds in America. The eight funds beat the three and five-year increases of the benchmark *Standard & Poor's 500 index*. The result? Four were loads, and four were no-loads. When considering this, I often ask myself, "Why would anyone ever want to let a single dime of their return slip through their fingers unnecessarily?" They are literally throwing money away!" Actually, even though I hate to admit it, there are a couple of answers to that question, although the logic behind one of them is pretty weak. If you feel you must have a broker, financial planner, etc. to help you with your investment decisions, then you will probably have to go with load funds. That is what they usually handle.

Although it pains me to say this, if you are the type of person who has absolutely, positively, undeniably, unmistakably, unquestionably, no self-restraint, no self-discipline, no will power, no patience *(author takes deep breath)*, and are inclined to be so frightened by every little market drop, or so enamored by every hot fund that comes along that you will keep shifting in and out of different funds—then buy load funds. Even though I am very hesitant to say it, I would rather have you buy a load fund than shift in and out of different funds. Doing so is the surest way to lose your money. And maybe, just maybe, the hefty loads that you have committed to will be enough of a loss consideration to motivate you to stay put longer. On the other hand, if you can maintain a degree of discipline while others begin to panic, definitely buy no-load funds. The reason is simple. If no-load are just as good as loads, why pay the extra money? In chapter 7 I showed you how just an additional dollar a day can have a tremendous effect on your total return over the years. Here is another example:

No-Load Versus Load
(Beginning account balance of $0)

Fund Type	Monthly Contribution	Length of Investment	% Return	Ending Balance	Net Difference
No-Load (0%)	$800.00 ($800 - $0)	35 Years	10%	$2,719,033	+$165,861
Front-Load (6.1%)	$751.20 ($800 - $48.80)	35 Years	10%	$2,553,172	-$165,861

As you can plainly see, the front-load fund eats up a substantial part of the investment. Although it does not seem like much when viewed on a monthly basis (only $48.80), over the years it can add up to a lot of money. In this case, a net difference of *$165,861*. That is a pile of money, my friend, by anyone's standards. Why give it away? My advice? Put the load to work for you as part of your investment instead of giving it to someone else. Ultimately, it will make a real difference in your total return.

If your 403(b) plan offers a small number of investment options, your choices may be easy. Ask yourself whether you receive enough service or advice to justify a high load. Similarly, decide whether the fund's total return—especially in comparison to your other choices—makes up the difference for a high load. As stated earlier, some mutual funds that normally carry a load charge will waive the fee when the investment is for a 403(b) account. Always be sure to check before you write off a mutual fund based solely on the fact that it carries a load charge.

A Final Note

There you have it. A complete rundown on the specifics of mutual funds—what mutual funds are, how to differentiate between the different types of mutual funds, and the many benefits they can offer you. Soon, you will have to select, from the mutual fund types described in this chapter, those that will best help you achieve your goals. Lastly, you will need to narrow it down even more by selecting the *individual* mutual funds themselves. The next chapter will further help you—it deals exclusively with the concept of asset allocation. You will see how allocating your assets properly can be, when strategically teamed with prudent mutual fund purchasing, the surest route to successfully reach your retirement goals.

CHAPTER THIRTEEN

Allocating Your Assets

If you have decided that *you* are the right one to plan your retirement, you are my kind of person. Congratulations. I admire your spirit. But now it is time to get down to business. It is time to decide how to allocate (split) the money you will be putting into your 403(b). Here is where you will really be put to the test. Why? Because studies show that asset allocation accounts for a whopping 91.5% of the difference in returns among various investment portfolios. Selections of particular investments *within* asset classes accounted for only 8.5%. Asset allocation is a vital component to your retirement investment plan.

While reading this chapter, please keep in mind that, ultimately, the investment options available through your employer's 403(b) plan will be the determining factor in deciding how you allocate your retirement assets. Many 403(b) plan choices are very narrow in scope. Hopefully your 403(b) plan will provide you with an array of investments from which to choose to enable you to tailor your investment plan to your unique set of circumstances. As I have stated before, one size does not fit all. Up to this point, basically you have been asked to do three things:

1. Plug the money leaks in your budget (chapter 6).

2. Make sure you are saving enough from your income (chapter 7).

3. Set your annual savings goal (chapter 6).

If you have not accomplished all three, you are not ready to concentrate on investing. The groundwork just has not been done. On the first point, you can not maximize your savings if you are letting money leak through your budget. On the second, you can not invest properly if you do not have the money put aside to invest with. On the third, you have to know where you are heading and if you have come far enough along each year.

But let us say you are ready for the next step. Perhaps you are already an investor. Maybe you even own some stocks and mutual funds. But if you are like most people, you have not established any sense of order in your investing. Without a doubt, the temptation to invest randomly is greater than ever. There are more influences than ever trying to get you to buy stocks, bonds, mutual funds, and dozens of other kinds of investments. This bombardment with a plethora of choices does nothing more than confuse the average do-it-yourself investor. It is no wonder some investors immediately turn to a third party for help with their decisions. But you do not have to be among them. This chapter will take you far into understanding what asset allocation is and what kind of asset mix is right for you.

As stated in the last chapter, 95 percent of investors are capable of becoming a *do-it-yourself investor.* It is really not as complicated as financial experts would have you believe. The whole process revolves around a few simple considerations. To be your own planner you need to have a feel for your personal tolerance for risk; a list of investment objectives; a few simple financial products to choose from to help you meet those objectives; the right balance among your investments; realistic investment expectations with regard to return needs; and, a time frame that gives your investments time to work out. That is it!

Only you can supply the information that will determine the best investments for your needs. This chapter deals with helping you sort out that information so that you can make informed decisions concerning one of the most critical goals of successful do-it-yourself investing—achieving the proper mix or balance with your investment portfolio—what the pros call *Asset Allocation.* Fortunately, that balance does not depend upon some arcane financial formula. Instead, it depends upon you—when you will need to draw upon your savings to meet expenses and how comfortable you are with risk.

Asset allocation is simply a method of targeting or choosing investments to achieve the highest possible return consistent with your objectives and the degree of risk that you feel comfortable with. You need to evaluate those investments and the impact they will have on creating your retirement nest egg. How you apportion your money among stocks, bonds, cash, and hard assets will determine your investment return.

What you need to know about yourself—The most sensible way to invest your 403(b) account is to divide your money between investments that provide growth, investments that provide income, and investments that provide safety. You will probably need at least three different types of asset classes to do that. The crucial issue is getting the proportions right. How much of your total account should go into each type of investment? As stated above that depends on your objectives, your time horizon, your personal circumstances, your return needs, and your personal risk tolerance. Remember, only you can supply the information that will determine the best investment mix for your needs. You are the best candidate to be your financial planner because nobody else knows your goals as well as you do, has the same instinctive understanding of your risk tolerance, or has your best interests as much at heart. Let us take a closer look at those elements that will directly affect how you allocate your investment money.

Your objectives—No doubt you have been told time and again that matching your investment objectives with the funds you invest in is an important first step in your overall fund selection process. Think of it as a matter of form and content. You need to select the most appropriate objectives for your particular money building plans. Learning to form objectives will help you find the funds with the right content to fulfill them. Once you accomplish this, you will be able to invest with less stress and strain—and come out financially fit on the other end.

What is an objective? For you, an objective is a realistic, realizable end-point of a plan. It is the destination of an investment journey. For a fund, an objective is like a prospector's lantern, since a fund's objective will guide it through the maze of existing investment opportunities to those which most closely match its overall directive—be it aggressive growth of capital or conservative preservation of income.

What are your objectives? Most people answer this question with, "I want to make as much money as possible." But, unfortunately, that answer will not help you to invest more wisely and well. For one thing, everyone wants to make as much money as possible. To start with, figure out the time frame your objectives fall into—within the next 5, 10, 20, or 30 years.

Do you want to make as much money as possible over the next 30 years as you save for retirement? In that case, you will be looking at growth funds for maximum capital appreciation for the long run. Or do you want to make as much money as possible over the next six months while you are looking at houses to buy? In that case you will want to invest in a money market fund, six-month CD or six-month Treasury Bill. You still "want to make as much money as possible," (you will choose the highest yielding of these short-term alternatives) but the phrase has quite a different meaning now. You could invest the money in a growth fund, which on average has a significantly higher return than a money market, but that would not be a very suitable choice. Over this short period you will not see the fund's average return; in six months a growth fund could easily be up or down by 20%. Look at what happened from January 1, to July 31, of 1998. It is not easy closing on a house (or paying college tuition, or making any other major purchase) when you have little idea how much your savings will be worth from day to day.

So, when choosing an objective, the most important consideration is how much time you have until you are likely to need the money.

Your time horizon—This is your first consideration as you analyze your needs to determine which kinds of investment will give you the best return with the least amount of risk. Your time horizon starts when your investment portfolio is implemented and ends when you will need to take the money out. The length of time you will be invested is important because it can directly affect your ability to reduce risk. Longer time horizons allow you to take on greater risks—with a greater total return potential—because some of that risk can be reduced by investing across different market environments. If your time horizon is short, you have greater liquidity needs—the ability to withdraw at any time with reasonable certainty of value. Volatile investments such as stocks lack liquidity and require a minimum five-year time horizon; shorter maturity bonds and money market funds are the most liquid.

The longer your time horizon, the greater the risk that inflation will shrink the value of your nest egg. Remember our discussion in chapter 1? If you do not, I suggest you go back and read it again. Inflation is a killer. *Do not underestimate this danger*. If inflation averages just 3.5% a year, the cost of living will double every 20 years. That means if you plan to retire in 20 years, you will need $100,000 a year to live the way you can today on $50,000 a year. If inflation averages 5.5% a year, the cost of living will double every 13 years. With inflation at that rate, if you plan to retire in 26 years, you will need $200,000 to buy what costs $50,000 today.

That is the bad news. The good news is that the more time you have to invest, the safer it becomes for you to invest in growth assets like stocks, or stock funds, which historically have proven to be more than a match for inflation. Over a 20-year period, stocks have never had a negative return!!! When comparing the average returns of stocks, long-term bonds, and short-term securities since 1926, stocks returned an average of 11% annually; long-term bonds returned 5.6% annually; and, short-term securities returned 4.6% annually. As you can see, stocks and stock funds have a considerable edge over other investment instruments when considering long-term goals. Although in the short term, stocks are far more volatile than bonds— you can lose 20% or more in a single terrible year—in the long term, the volatility dies down. If you can wait seven years, then keep your money in stocks or stock funds. In fact, over the very long run (17 years or more), research by the Wharton School of Business shows stocks are actually *less* risky than bonds.

Time horizons tend to vary over your life cycle. Younger investors who are only accumulating savings for retirement have long time horizons. The longer your time horizon, the bigger the piece of your portfolio you should allocate to growth investments because you have no real liquidity needs except for short-term emergencies. (To help you make the right choice when selecting a portfolio mix I have included several standard asset allocation models for you to review. They follow later in this chapter).

Again, the less time you have before you reach your goal, the less you have to worry about the effect of inflation and the more you need to be concerned about short-term price fluctuations, the big drawback of stock investments. For a goal that is only five years away, such as the purchase of a house or a child's education, a more prudent allocation might be to invest as much as 50% of your portfolio in bonds and cash investments. Here, investors have greater liquidity needs. Similarly, investors who are planning to retire, and those who are in retirement and living off of their investment income, have greater liquidity needs. By the way, when you calculate your time horizon, do not make the mistake many people do by ending it on your retirement date. As discussed in chapter 1, your life will not end when you stop working at a full-time job; in fact, at that point as much as one-third of your life may still lie ahead of you. Your money will have to last all through your retirement years. This means you can not do totally without growth investments even if you are within a year or two of retiring because you have to think about the effect of inflation on your nest egg *after* you retire.

Many financial advisors offer a rough rule-of-thumb to figure out the appropriate allocation between growth and fixed-income investments for your time horizon: multiply your age by 80%. The result is the percentage of your portfolio that you should keep in bonds or bond funds. The rest should go into stocks or stock funds. Using this rule of thumb, for example, a 40-year-old man would invest 32% of his portfolio (80% x 40 = 32%) in bonds and 68% in stocks. I do not subscribe to this logic because it allows for too much bond exposure in the early years of the investor's time-line. For example, take a 35-year-old male who will be investing for his retirement nest egg for the next 25 years. The rule-of-thumb would dictate that he have 28% of his portfolio (80% x 35 = 28%) invested in bonds. That is far too much for an investor with a time horizon of at least 25 years. A more appropriate bond allocation would be 10%, or a maximum of 15% of the total portfolio. That is a difference of 13%. That 13% difference between stock and bond exposure could mean a difference, in net return, of many, many tens of thousands of dollars over the 25-year investment period. No one wants to pass up that kind of money.

Your personal circumstances—When investing, you have to adapt your investment choices to your own personal set of circumstances. Two people who are the same age, work for the same employer, and earn the same money may still have very different investment needs.

Twenty years ago, it was easier to figure out lifecycle investment needs based merely on a person's age. Financial planning books were replete with sweeping generalizations: people in their 20s were saving to buy a car, to go on a great vacation, or for the down payment on a house; people in their 30s were having children, buying a house, starting to save for college educations; people in their 40s were buying a larger house, a second car, increasing their savings for college tuitions; people in their 50s had kids in college or were adjusting to life with the kids grown and gone. Today, these generalizations do not work nearly as well. The baby boom generation has married and had children later than the previous generation did. Divorce and remarriage have changed traditional predictable lifecycle patterns. A 45-year-old who is changing diapers, shopping for day-care, and looking at the cost of pre-schools has a very different time horizon than a 45-year-old who has made the last mortgage payment and is trying to decide what to give the family's youngest child as a college graduation present. To determine how your circumstances affect your asset allocation, you need to answer the following:

- **How likely is it that you will have to use some of your retirement account to pay for a few major expenses before you retire?**

- **If there is an emergency and you have an unexpected need for money, do you have any source of available cash outside your 403(b) account?**— The answer to this question has a direct bearing on your investment allocation. If you do not have emergency money ready to go, then you might be forced to sell part of your 403(b) plan assets to cover the emergency. If those assets are down in value when they are needed, you must sell them at a loss to get the cash you need. Remember what was discussed about liquidity in chapter 6? Just to refresh your memory—a quick rule of thumb is that you should have anywhere from three to six months take-home pay as a *liquid* emergency fund (such as a money market account, for example). Having six months' take-home pay is safer, and more prudent. But do not go overboard. You do not need an emergency fund any bigger than six months of your take-home pay at the very most.

- **Do you have savings and/or investments outside your 403(b) account? If so, how are they invested? Are they allocated properly?**

- **Does your spouse invest in a retirement plan at work? If so, how is it invested?**— Once a year you should check your asset allocation by writing down all your household's investments on one piece of paper. List the retirement account investments you and your spouse have in one column; list all of your taxable accounts in another. Then divide the investments in each column into asset classes—growth, fixed-income, cash. Use a pocket calculator to add up your total holdings—retirement and non-retirement—and then figure out what percentage of the total you have in each asset class. The results will tell you how conservative or aggressive your investment portfolio really is, and show you what kind of adjustments you need to make to achieve a more appropriate mix. (See the asset allocation models in the following pages to help you choose the appropriate mix).

- **How much do you want your account to be worth when you are ready to retire?**— Chapter 1 will help guide you with this question. Remember, if you expect to incur major expenses after retirement such as college tuition, or the cost of a big wedding for one or more of your children, or if you will still owe a substantial balance on your mortgage, you will need to use the high end of the range suggested in chapter 1. Even though you will spend less on certain kinds of expenses in retirement than you do now, you will also be spending more on expenses that you do not have now. For example, you will not have expenses associated with working—such as buying and cleaning clothes to wear to work, commuting and buying lunches away from home. And hopefully, your children will be out of college and your mortgage will be paid off. But you will have increases in expenses such as travel and entertainment, at least initially. And, as discussed in chapter 4, your health care costs will undoubtedly rise during your retirement.

Your return needs—This refers to whether you need to emphasize growth or income. Most younger investors who are accumulating savings will want returns that tend to emphasize growth and higher total returns, which primarily are provided by stocks or stock funds. Retirees who depend on their investment portfolio for part of their annual income will want returns that emphasize relatively higher and consistent annual payouts, such as those from bonds and dividend-paying stocks or stock funds. Of course, many individuals may want a blending of the two - some current income, but also some growth.

Your personal risk tolerance—Risk is the level of volatility of your portfolio's value. The amount of risk you are willing to take on is your personal risk tolerance. Remember the quiz in chapter 5? Again, it is not science, but it will still give you an idea as to where you stand on risk. Being aware of your personal tolerance of risk is extremely important because investors who take on too much risk usually panic when confronted with unexpected losses and abandon their investment plans mid-stream at the worst possible time.

Every kind of investment involves risk. Not investing is also risky. Saving your money in a safe deposit box certainly will not keep it safe from the ravages of inflation. As a 403(b) participant, the biggest question you face is not *whether* or not you should take risks with your precious retirement savings. It is what *kind* of risks you should take. Most people worry about only two types of investment risk. The *first* is risk to their principal: the danger that they will lose all or part of the money that they invest. For many people, this is the most pressing concern; they feel their primary goal with retirement money is not to lose it. The *second* risk most people think about is the uncertainty of investment return. These two major concerns help explain why so many investors put all their money in such safe investments as money market funds, CDs, short-term bonds, and savings accounts, etc. The stability of these kinds of investments certainly are attractive characteristics, to a degree. But if you are more than 2 or 3 years away from retirement you are exposing your retirement money to a third risk that too many plan participants forget about—the impact of inflation.

Your primary goal, if your investment time horizon is longer than 2 or 3 years, is to grow your investment into a nest egg big enough to assure financial security for the rest of your life. That is the essence of long-term investing; however, as a long-term investor, you need to be aware of several other types of risk that can and will affect your retirement money:

Inflation Risk—We covered this topic in detail in chapter 1, but it needs to be mentioned again. This time from a slightly different perspective—as it pertains to risk. Inflation is by far the most serious danger for any long-term investor. The fact that you do not see how it erodes the value of your principal makes it all the more dangerous.

Most people think their money is safe in any investment that guarantees stability of principal, like a money market fund, because the nominal value of their account in this kind of fund is never less than the amount they originally invested. And what could be safer than an FDIC-insured bank account where your principal is stable and guaranteed by the full faith and credit of the U.S. Government? But as time wears on, that apparently stable principal is being invisibly consumed by inflation. One dollar does not buy as much today as it did five years ago, and in another 20 years, one dollar will buy substantially less than it buys today. If you are earning 4% in a liquid account and inflation is running at 4% a year, your real return after inflation is zero. Your real return after taxes is *negative*.

For a long-term goal, the last thing you want is stability of principal—if your principal does not grow, you can not possibly stay ahead of inflation. The best way to reduce inflation risk is to invest in growth assets like stocks and stock funds.

Market Risk—Market risk is the risk of losing your money in a steep market decline. This is the first risk many people think of when they think of the stock market. Everyone knows someone who has put money into a company, only to have the stock market crash two weeks later leaving that investor with totally worthless stock. Yes, it does happen. But usually not for the reason you think. Most people lose their money because they did not do their homework before making the investment.

There are two primary ways to reduce market risk. One is to diversify your investments among different kinds of assets. Hence, my reason for this chapter. The other is to ignore market ups and downs and focus on long-term results. As you will soon see in an upcoming chart, the stock market has averaged above 10% over the last 70 years. Those who invested their money, and stayed put, made money. But the most disciplined way to ignore market ups and downs, as discussed in chapter 9, is through dollar-cost averaging. By steadily investing on a regular basis, regardless of how well or badly the market is performing, you eliminate the danger of selling at the bottom.

Business Risk—This is the risk of losing your money in an investment that seemed like a sure thing, but was not. You know the story—you buy x number of shares of ABC Manufacturing and the management of that company makes a series of disastrous decisions that runs the company into the ground, along with your money. It happens all the time. The best way to reduce business risk is to, again, diversify. Invest

188

in mutual funds, for example. You automatically diversify among hundreds of different stocks and bonds, which greatly reduces the impact on your investment of any single business loss.

Interest Rate Risk—Interest rate risk is the risk that your investment will lose value because interest rates go up. It is the least understood risk you assume as a bond holder or owner of shares in a bond fund.

Remember the discussion on bonds in the last chapter? Let us review a little. Let us say you buy a $10,000 bond that pays 6% interest. A month later, you hear on the nightly news that the Federal Reserve has hiked the current interest rate. As a result, newly issued bonds with the same credit quality and maturity date as the one you own will pay 8% interest. Your $10,000 bond is now worth *less* than $10,000. Nobody is going to pay you $10,000 for a 6% bond when he/she can invest his/her $10,000 in a bond that returns 8%. So if you sell your bond, you will take a loss. And if you keep your bond, you are earning less than the prevailing interest rate.

The best way to reduce interest rate risk is to buy bonds or bond funds with shorter maturities—two to ten years for example—rather than longer-term bonds. Short- and intermediate-term bonds lose less value when interest rates rise. A 20- or 30-year bond that pays less than the prevailing interest rate loses a lot more of its value than a two-year bond that pays less than the prevailing interest rate.

Credit Risk—Credit risk is the risk that whoever borrowed your money will not make all their promised interest payments, or will not repay the principal when it falls due. This is a risk most often associated with the bond market. There are two ways to minimize credit risk. The first is to make sure you are lending to borrowers who are in good standing with the major credit rating agencies. The prospectus of a bond mutual fund tells you what credit quality bonds the portfolio manager is permitted to buy. The other way to minimize credit risk is to diversify. The credit problems of any single issuer will not have much impact on the shareholders of a mutual fund that own hundreds of bonds.

What is your risk comfort level?—Some people become more risk averse, or risk tolerant, as they get older because of an increase in the understanding of how different investments perform over different periods of time. Many investor's ideas about risk may have been based on misconceptions—thinking that stocks are always a high-risk investment or bonds are always a safe investment—or on over-simplifications that ignored essential factors like time horizon. But now you know that time horizon does have a major impact on investment risk.

Some experts think risk tolerance depends solely on your age. There is some truth here, but risk tolerance is not necessarily a function of age; a conservative investor will go through changes in asset allocation over his/her life cycle, as will an aggressive investor. For the most part, however, people become more conservative investors as they get older and closer to retirement. This shift can be appropriate. As stated before, the less time you have, the riskier it becomes to invest in stocks. But do not make the mistake of underestimating how much time you have. Remember, even after you retire, you still need growth investments like stocks to help you beat inflation. If you are 60-years-old, your real time horizon is not five years until retirement—it is a 20 to 30-year life expectancy.

Finally, your comfort level with investment risk also depends in part on your temperament. Everyone worries to a degree about their money, but some people are extremely nervous about their money and how it is affected by the stock market. To determine your comfort level, think about this—assume that in an absolute worst-case scenario, the market may temporarily lose half its value. Could you take it? (Actually, in 1931 the stock market recorded its worst hit, a loss of 37.2%). If you truly can not stand the thought of more than a 15% temporary dip in the value of your 403(b) account, invest only 30% of your total portfolio in stocks or stock funds. I must warn you, however, that you could be passing up some really incredible gains in the long run by lessening your exposure to stocks or stock funds.

A well-diversified portfolio will take a lot of the worry out of investing. The beauty of a diversified portfolio is that, to some extent, it allows you to follow your conflicting impulses. With the right asset allocation you can invest for growth, safety and income, all at the same time. I have included an asset allocation worksheet in this chapter which, when completed, will guide you to an asset allocation model appropriate for your personal set of circumstances.

One last word about risk. There is one rule about risk that never changes and that applies equally to every type of investment: the higher an investment's potential return, the greater the potential risk involved. Even if that risk is not readily apparent at first, second or even third glance, it is there. You never get a high return from a low-risk investment.

A quick way to measure an investment's relative degree of risk is to compare its yield with the prevailing rate on U.S. Treasury Bills, considered the world's safest investment. (You will find the T-Bill rate listed daily in the *Wall Street Journal* and in the business pages of most newspapers.) The higher an investment's yield above the yield for Treasuries, the riskier you can assume that investment is—no matter how it is described to you.

Asset allocation models—Many so-called experts design asset allocation models based strictly on age. They suggest one model for your 20s to early 30s; one model for your early 30s to 40s; one model for your early 40s to 50s; one model for your early 50s to 60s, etc. By now I hope you realize that those types of asset allocation models are sheer nonsense. Although age is certainly a relevant factor, deciding on which asset allocation model to follow involves many additional considerations as well.

Once you have established your investment objectives (goals), your time horizon, defined your unique personal circumstances, your return needs, and your personal tolerance for risk, *then and only then* are you prepared to select which type of asset allocation model might be right for you.

The following model portfolios illustrate some of the possible investment combinations you may want to consider. This concept of asset allocation seeks to help you minimize the impact of any one investment performing poorly, while taking into account your goals, time horizon, and level of comfort with investment risk. These portfolios are for illustrative purposes only and should not be considered investment advice per se. They are only to help illustrate the concept of diversification, given a specific investment strategy. They are examples only and are not intended to apply to your specific situation.

No matter what investment strategy you adopt, it is important that you understand your personal goals and attitude toward risk, and then invest accordingly. In addition, as your time horizon, comfort with risk, and financial circumstances change over time, you should adjust your asset mix accordingly. The asset allocation models below do not include types of investments that fall *within* each asset class. That topic will be covered later in this chapter.

Asset Allocation Models

Portfolio Type	Asset Classes		
	Stocks	Bonds	Short-Term
Aggressive Growth	85%	15%	0%
Growth	70%	25%	5%
Balanced	50%	40%	10%
Capital Preservation	20%	50%	30%
Short-Term	0%	0%	100%

The Aggressive Growth Model—This investment strategy is designed for long-term investors who seek to maximize the potential growth of their money over time and to protect it against the effects of inflation. It may be most appropriate for people who will not need access to their retirement savings for at least 10 years and who can tolerate significant short-term fluctuations in value. Because it focuses mostly on stock investments, it has the potential to grow faster than the rate of inflation over time. However, the value of the portfolio is likely to fluctuate substantially, so investors should be comfortable with this risk. In an aggressive portfolio such as this, a sensible strategy is to try to keep about 60% of your stock fund allocation in value funds and the rest in growth funds, as the market favors each at different times.

The Growth Model—This investment strategy is also designed for long-term investors who seek to increase the value of their assets over time and protect against the effects of inflation. It may be most appropriate for people who will not need access to their retirement savings for at least 7 to 10 years and who can tolerate substantial short-term fluctuations in value. Because it focuses primarily on stock investments, it has the potential to grow faster than the rate of inflation over time. However, the overall value of the portfolio is likely to fluctuate with short-term changes in the stock market. The bond portion of the portfolio is included to help moderate those ups and downs. Although not as aggressive, it is also a sensible strategy for a growth portfolio to try to keep about 60% of your stock fund allocation in value funds and the rest in growth funds.

The Balanced Model—This investment strategy is designed for investors who seek a balance between stability and growth with some protection against the effects of inflation. It may be most appropriate for people who can tolerate some short-term fluctuations in value, and who will need access to their retirement savings in about 5 to 7 years. The portions of the portfolio allocated to stock investments gives it the potential to grow somewhat faster than the rate of inflation over time, but with some fluctuation in value, especially in the short term. The bond and short-term portions of the portfolio are included to help moderate those ups and downs.

The Capital Preservation Model—This investment strategy is designed for investors whose primary objective is preservation of capital with some protection against the effects of inflation. It may be most appropriate for people who cannot tolerate substantial short-term fluctuations in value, and who will need access to their retirement savings in about 2 to 5 years. A portion of the portfolio is allocated to short-term instruments for stability and preservation of principal. The bond component gives the opportunity for somewhat higher yields than short-term investments alone, and the small portion allocated to stock investments has the potential for growth to keep pace with inflation.

The Short-Term or Current Income Model—This investment strategy is designed for investors whose primary objective is preservation of capital. Short-term instruments are the least volatile of the asset classes. A short-term portfolio may be most appropriate for people who are unwilling to risk even short-term fluctuations in value. This portfolio is allocated exclusively to short-term instruments for stability and preservation of principal with very little opportunity for price appreciation. As a result, it generally cannot be expected to protect against the effects of inflation.

Model portfolio performance—So how well have these five asset allocation models succeeded over the years? The following chart illustrates how the portfolios have performed over the last 70 years. The average annual return column shows performance through the whole period while the next four columns show gains or losses for specified periods.

191

Historical Asset Allocation Portfolios: 1926-1996

May be appropriate for investors who are . . .	Average Annual Return	Average of Down Years	Two Year Return 1973-74	Worst Annual Loss	Best Annual Gain
AGGRESSIVE GROWTH PORTFOLIO **85% Stocks - 15% Bonds** . . . very aggressive in the pursuit of longer-range goals.	10.1%	-10.9%	-30.9%	-37.2% (1931)	46.2% (1933)
GROWTH PORTFOLIO **70% Stocks - 25% Bonds** **5% Short-term instruments** . . . willing to take on more risk in an attempt to outperform more conservative investments over the long term.	9.4%	-8.8%	-24.0%	-30.9% (1931)	38.3% (1933)
BALANCED PORTFOLIO **50% Stocks - 40% Bonds** **10% Short-term instruments** . . . seeking growth combined with potentially less risk over the long term.	8.3%	-5.8%	-14.5%	-22.5% (1931)	27.8% (1933)
CAPITAL PRESERVATION PORTFOLIO **20% Stocks - 50% Bonds** **30% Short-term instruments** . . . more concerned about capital preservation than long-term growth.	6.2%	-2.4%	1.4%	-9.5% (1931)	22.0% (1982)
SHORT-TERM PORTFOLIO **100% Short-term instruments** . . . more concerned about capital preservation and/or will need this money within a short time.	3.7%	0.0%	15.5%	0.0%	14.7% (1981)

As you can see, the **Aggressive Growth Portfolio** yielded the greatest return over the 70-year period. It's no wonder that most financial experts recommend a similar asset allocation when the investor has a lengthy time horizon.

As you can see, the Aggressive Growth Portfolio yielded the greatest return over the 70-year period. It is no wonder that most financial experts recommend a similar asset allocation when the investor has a lengthy time horizon. You will notice that there is only about a 1% difference between the Aggressive Growth Portfolio and the Growth Portfolio. Do not let that little 1% fool you, my fellow investors. During a 35-year investment period, on a nominal $10,000 initial investment, that measly 1% would return *$79,310 more* for the investor using the Aggressive Growth Portfolio versus the Growth Portfolio. When compared to the Balanced Portfolio, the difference climbs to *$137,385 more!!!* It is hard to believe that a paltry 1% or 2% would make that much difference. But it does. And that is on an investment of only $10,000. Imagine what the difference grows to as you increase your principal by contributing monthly to your 403(b) account over 30-35 years!

What does all of this mean to you? An analysis of the results you obtain from completing the asset allocation worksheet that follows will give you a clearer picture as to what kinds of mutual funds to buy and where you should allocate their assets. But for now, allow me to make some obvious generalizations based on the previous chart. With a time horizon of at least 10 to 12 years, an investor should probably seek out aggressive growth investments, such as those found in an Aggressive Growth Portfolio. As the horizon gets closer, say 7 to 10 years, one might gradually ease into slightly less aggressive growth investments, such as that found in a Growth Portfolio. As the horizon gets even closer yet, say 5 to 7 years, an investor might consider being invested in a Balanced Portfolio, with roughly an equal mix of growth (stock) and of income (bond) investments. At 2 to 5 years, one might consider being more conservative with his/her investments with more exposure to short-term securities, such as that found in a Capital Preservation Portfolio.

Finally, if an investor is buying a house or sending the kids to college in less than 2 years, he/she should stick to investments he/she knows will not go down in the meantime, such as those found in a Short-Term Portfolio. In other words a money market fund, or a short-term Treasury, or CD whose maturity date closely matches (or precedes) the time when the cash is needed. Please remember, the above examples are only for you to look at as rough guides. Your own situation is unique and should be approached according to your own personal set of circumstances.

Asset allocation worksheet—The following worksheet is designed to help you plan for a specific investment goal. Should you have multiple investment goals—for short-term and long-term savings, for instance—consider completing a worksheet for *each* one. Circle your best answer to each question based on your *current* situation. Then total your points and compare your total score to the model portfolio to find which one may be most suited to your current needs. Regardless of your point score, however, if you are investing for less than two years, you may want to consider the short-term portfolio.

1. In approximately how many years do you expect to need to spend the money you are investing?

2-3 years	20
4-6 years	38
7-10 years	50
10+ years	69

2. Do you expect to withdraw more than one-third of the money in this account within seven years (for a home purchase, college tuition, or other major need)? If yes, when do you expect to withdraw from the account?

193

No	20
Within 3 year	0
4-7 years	12

3. If yes to the previous question, approximately what portion of your total investable assets—the dollar amount of the investments you currently have—will this investment represent?

Less than 25%	0
Between 25% and 50%	1
Between 50% and 75%	2
More than 75%	4

4. Which one of the following describes your expected future earnings over the next five years? (assume inflation will average 4%)

I expect my earnings increases will far outpace inflation (due to promotions, new job, etc.)	0
I expect my earnings increases to stay somewhat ahead of inflation	1
I expect my earnings to keep pace with inflation	2
I expect my earnings to decrease (retirement, part-time work, etc.)	4

5. Approximately what portion of your monthly take-home income goes toward paying off installment debt (auto loans, credit cards, etc.) other than a home mortgage?

Less than 10%	0
Between 10% and 25%	1
Between 25% and 50%	2
More than 50%	6

6. How many dependents do you have (include children you continue to support, elderly parents, etc.)?

None	0
One	1
Two-Three	2
More than Three	4

7. Do you have an emergency fund (savings of three to six months' after-tax income)?

No	8
Yes, but less than six months of after-tax income	3
Yes, I have an adequate emergency fund	0

8. If you expect to have other major expenses (such as college tuition, home down payment, home repairs, etc.), do you have a separate savings plan for these expenses?

Yes, I have a separate savings plan for these expenses	0
I do not expect to have any such expenses	1

I intend to withdraw a portion of this money for these expenses.
(Note: please answer question 2 accordingly)   3
I have no separate savings plan for these items at this time   4

9. Have you ever invested in individual bonds or bond mutual funds (aside from U.S. savings bonds)?

No, and I would be uncomfortable with the risk if I did   10
No, but I would be comfortable with the risk if I did   4
Yes, but I was uncomfortable with the risk   6
Yes, and I felt comfortable with the risk   0

10. Have you ever invested in individual stocks or stock mutual funds?

No, and I would be uncomfortable with the risk if I did   8
No, but I would be comfortable with the risk if I did   3
Yes, but I was uncomfortable with the risk   5
Yes, and I felt comfortable with the risk   0

11. Which one of the following statements describes your feelings toward choosing an investment?

I would select only investments that have a low degree of risk
associated with them (i.e., it is unlikely I will lose my original
investment)   12

I prefer to select a mix of investments, with emphasis on those
with a low degree of risk and a small portion in others that have
a higher degree of risk that may yield greater returns   9

I prefer to select a balanced mix of investments—some that have
a low degree of risk, others that have a higher degree of risk that
may yield greater returns   5

I prefer to select an aggressive mix of investments—some that
have a low degree of risk, but with emphasis on others that have
a higher degree of risk that may yield greater returns   1

I would select an investment that has only a higher degree of
risk and a greater potential for higher returns   0

12. If you could increase your chances of improving your returns by taking more risk, would you:

Be willing to take a lot more risk with *all* your money   0
Be willing to take a lot more risk with *some* of your money   2
Be willing to take a little more risk with *all* your money   6
Be willing to take a little more risk with *some* of your money   9
Be unlikely to take much more risk   12

195

Scoring Directions

A. Sum of Your Points for questions 1 & 2   _____

B. Sum of Your Points for Questions 3 - 12   _____

C. Subtract B from A = (Total Points)   _____

WHAT DOES YOUR SCORE MEAN?

Your Worksheet Score	Suggested Asset Allocation Portfolio	Why This Model Might Be Right For You
85+ points	**Aggressive Growth Portfolio** **85% Stocks - 15% Bonds**	Longer-range goals are indicated, and you may want to consider a more aggressive portfolio (100% stocks) if you can tolerate short-term price swings.
50-84 points	**Growth Portfolio** **70% Stocks - 25% Bonds** **5% Short-term instruments**	It suggests that you're willing to take on more risk in an attempt to outperform conservative investments over the long term. Consider emphasizing growth as you choose your investments
20-49 points	**Balanced Portfolio** **50% Stocks - 40% Bonds** **10% Short-term instruments**	A combination of income and capital growth is indicated. Consider spreading your investments to seek growth combined with less risk over the long run.
0-19 points	**Capital Preservation Portfolio** **20% Stocks - 50% Bonds** **30% Short-term instruments**	Capital preservation may be more important than long-term growth, so consider a conservative mixture of investments more heavily weighted toward bonds and short-term investments for your portfolio.
If you're investing for less than two years	**Short-Term Portfolio** **100% Short-term instruments**	Regardless of your point score, if you're investing for less than 2 years, short-term investments such as money market funds can provide a stable share price.

196

If your score already points you to the aggressive (85% stock/15% bond) portfolio, consider investing in a 100% stock portfolio if:

1. You are pursuing a long-term goal (such as retirement) and the sum of your planned systematic contributions over this year will exceed 15% of your current portfolio.

2. The amount that you are investing for this goal represents only the aggressive portion of your total portfolio and you already own more conservative investments such as bonds and short-term securities, that can provide a balance to the short-term fluctuations of stock.

Typically, your response to each of the twelve questions will tend to shift over time as you become more experienced and more comfortable with risk; build a more solid financial foundation; or, approach a financial goal and therefore shorten your time horizon. Because each individual's needs are different—based on his or her attitude toward risk, time frame, and financial situation—scores can vary widely from one investor to another, and even from one year to another for the same investor. For this reason, I suggest using the model portfolios only as rough guides. After all, the decision to invest more conservatively or aggressively than a model portfolio indicates is strictly a personal one. And that type of decision-making is what personal investing is all about.

Refining the mix—Two of the most common mistakes investors make are false diversification and whipsaw. If you own 8 different funds, and they are all large-cap funds, or mid-cap funds, or some other category of funds, you may think you are diversified, but you are not. This false diversification (owning several funds that invest in virtually the same things) can subject you to whipsaw (buying just before prices fall and then selling before prices recover). Here is how it happens. Let us say your money is tied up in one category of funds, and those funds lag the market average for a couple of years. You are fed up with the poor results, so you switch from those funds to another category of funds. Three years later you are fed up with that category of funds and you switch to yet another category. You are constantly chasing your tail. A sure cure for false diversification and whipsaw is to invest in several categories of funds and adjust the percentages according to results.

As previously stated, selections of particular investments *within* asset classes accounted for only 8.5% of the difference in returns of various investment portfolios. But that 8.5% means a lot. Although the specific percentage of allocation *within* an asset class is not as important as being diversified in the first place, it still ranks second in order of importance, so it needs your attention.

By now you are probably asking yourself, "What kinds of funds are available for purchase *within* a stock fund, bond fund, or short-term fund, and how do I know which ones to buy?" Again, as stated in the last chapter and at the beginning of this chapter, the answer to that question depends entirely on the investment options available to you in your 403(b) plan. Some 403(b) plans offer many mutual fund families (i.e. *Fidelity, Vanguard, Twentieth Century*, etc.), that provide many choices for their investors, and some 403(b) plans offer as little as one mutual fund family that may provide only a few choices. And, as stated in the previous chapter, some 403(b) plans offer only annuities as an investment choice.

Whatever your situation, you will find the following chart helpful. Please remember, though, that the chart is for illustrative purposes only and should not be considered investment advice per se. It was designed only to help illustrate the concept of diversification, given a specific investment strategy. The examples given are not intended to apply to your specific situation.

PORTFOLIO TYPE AND PERCENTAGES ALLOCATED WITHIN EACH ASSET CLASS					
	Aggressive Growth	Growth	Balanced	Capital Preservation	Short - Term
Stock Funds					
Large-Cap Funds	40%	35%	25%	10%	0%
Mid-Cap Funds	5%	5%	5%	0%	0%
Small-Cap Funds	25%	20%	10%	5%	0%
International Funds	15%	10%	10%	5%	0%
Totals	85%	70%	50%	20%	0%
Bond Funds					
High-Grade Bond Funds	10%	20%	30%	40%	0%
High-Yield Bond Funds	5%	5%	10%	10%	0%
Totals	15%	25%	40%	50%	0%
Short-Term					
Money Market Funds	0%	5%	10%	30%	100%
Totals	0%	5%	10%	30%	100%

Please Note: The proportions in each category would have to be adapted to the funds available in your 403(b) plan. Again, the key is not the specific percentage allocations, but diversification.

Also, you'll notice that **stock funds** categories are listed according to fund capitalization (i.e. large-cap, mid-cap, etc.), which simply indicates the size of a company in terms of dollars and cents. The specific type of stock mutual fund chosen within the portfolio (i.e. growth fund, equity-income fund, balanced fund, etc.) would be selected within each capitalization level and should be chosen with your individual preferences and goals in mind.

For example, if one's investment goal is aggressive growth, then in the Aggressive Growth Portfolio, one might choose a large-cap aggressive growth, and/or growth, and/or value mutual fund(s) that would account for 40% of the stock fund mix. One would do the same for the mid-cap (5%), small-cap (25%), and international (15%) portion of the portfolio until the 85% mix was achieved.

Rebalancing Your Portfolio

Once you select an investment mix to help meet your retirement needs, you will need to review your portfolio on a regular basis to ensure that, as the value of your investments change, you are staying on course with your strategy. As the years go by, investors often lose sight of their original asset allocation and by doing so, they could be increasing the riskiness of their portfolio. An important concept that can help you avoid this problem is known as *rebalancing your portfolio.*

While most investment professionals recommend reviewing your asset allocation at least annually, there are also unexpected events, such as a job loss or early retirement, that can trigger a portfolio checkup. In these cases, not only does the time horizon shorten, but usually an investor's risk tolerance also declines.

Obviously, you can not stay with one asset allocation mix forever. But how do you know when it's time to change from aggressive investment strategies to more conservative ones? Or vice versa? Here are some sure signs that you should go back and reevaluate your investment mix:

A material change in your life situation has altered your objectives or your time frame—Whenever your financial situation undergoes a material change, you should take a look at your original allocation to make sure that its level of risk and return still fits your goals. What is a material change? The following are just a few of the life events that could change your allocation needs:

- Marriage
- Divorce
- The Death of a spouse
- Job Loss
- Buying a House
- Selling a House
- Moving
- Inheriting a Large Sum of Money
- The Birth of a Child
- Paying College Tuition
- Retirement

You have achieved an investment goal—If you have been accumulating money for short-term goals, such as a down payment on a new car or new home, or you are nearing your long-term goals, investing in the stock market means readily subjecting your principal to the market, whether up or down, at the time you need to withdraw it. Therefore, money needed for the near term is better invested in more principal-safe products like money market funds, certificates of deposit, Treasury securities, and short-maturing bonds.

Your financial situation has changed—Chances are your earning power today is not what it was five years ago, nor is your credit card debt or discretionary income. But your investment mind-set might be. If your income is steadily increasing, for instance, it may be time to move into more aggressive investments to pursue better long-term results. On the other hand, if you are approaching retirement or taking on more debt, you may need to be more conservative.

You feel comfortable taking on more risk—If you are feeling secure about your job, have paid down your credit card debt, and saved enough money to cover any rainy day surprises that might come your way, it may be time to move out a little farther on the risk spectrum with a portion of the money you have earmarked for long-term investing. At the same time, it is important to examine whether your willingness to take on more risk is only a temporary response to the market. Studies show that an investor's willingness to be more aggressive with his or her money and current market conditions go hand-in-hand. When stocks are up, they are more willing to take risks. When stocks are down, they are less willing to take risks.

The value of your asset classes change—Also, you should consider rebalancing your investment mix when the value of an asset class changes significantly due to either a rise or fall in the market. This will allow you to maintain your original allocation based on your objectives, time horizon, personal circumstances, return needs, and risk tolerance. Rebalancing may also help you take advantage of market cycles

199

by encouraging you to sell securities that are at their peak and to buy other types of investments that may be ready to bounce back. For example, you may decide that an asset mix of 50% in stocks, 40% in bonds, and 10% in short-term instruments (a *Balanced Portfolio*) is appropriate for your situation and goals. At the end of the year, however, due to increases or decreases in your individual holdings, your portfolio may be 54% in stocks, 38% in bonds, and 8% in short-term instruments. To get back to your original allocation, you would rebalance your portfolio by selling some of your stock investments and putting the proceeds into bonds and short-term instruments.

Basic tips for all investors—Proper asset allocation requires you to continually monitor your portfolio and make the changes necessary to stay on course with your strategy. But some aspects of your investing strategy ought to stay solid and unchanging, like the following:

1. **Remember why you are investing**—Ultimately, your goal is long-term growth. The real issue is not how much money you have in your account now; it is how much money you will have years from now.

2. **Make stock funds your number one investment**—As you study the asset allocation models, you will notice that stock funds dominate the mix, and for good reason. Remember, since 1926, stocks on average have beaten the competition by a huge margin: stocks have on average returned 10.1% a year, compared with 4.8% for bonds and only 3.7% for cash securities.

A 3.7% return barely accounts for the ravages of inflation. That means that cash investments really did not return anything over nearly 70 years! Yet, believe it or not, studies show that the average U.S. household invests only about 25% of its assets in stocks or stock funds, while investing nearly 50% of its assets in fixed-income investments like bonds and bond funds. That means that the average American family is gaining only *half* as much as it could with its investments. Since asset allocation is not being done correctly—and you have to assume that in most homes it is not—Americans are getting only a fraction of what they should be getting for their investment dollar. That is not a formula for success. That is a formula for retiring old and financially insecure. What a sad commentary on the investment strategies of most Americans. What is worse is that it is totally unnecessary. Here are a couple of extra tips concerning stock funds:

- **Invest in aggressive growth and growth stock mutual funds when your primary investing goal is capital growth**—A stock mutual fund that invests primarily in common stocks with what the fund manager believes to be good growth potential is a stock growth fund, sometimes called just a growth fund. Aggressive growth stock funds use aggressive and sometimes volatile techniques in an attempt to increase profits. Considering past returns, you will normally do better using aggressive stock funds than any other type of stock fund, even if you are conservative.

- **Invest in growth and income and/or equity-income stock mutual funds for capital growth and income at the same time**—Growth and income stock funds invest in undervalued stocks in good, solid, well-established companies. The lower the price, the higher the percentage dividend yield. This approach creates a great potential for growth once the stock price begins to recover, but overall you will still do better investing in growth and aggressive growth stock funds.

3. Hang in there—What I am trying to tell you here is to stay the course instead of jumping ship. Too many people fail to make steady, sizable gains in their investments simply because they are too busy jumping into this fund and out of that one influenced by what they heard on TV or read in the newspaper. The *fund of the month* sometimes looks great by comparison when standing side-by-side to your choice of investments. Hey, it is always going to be that way. The grass is always greener. Do not worry about it. Today's hero is tomorrow's dog. Count on it. It is one of the immutable laws of investing.

Several years ago an independent study revealed that investors who purchased load funds (funds that charge a sales fee: when you buy it—a front-end load, or when you sell it—a back-end load) made as much as 10% - 20% more in a few select years than those who bought no-load funds. Does that mean that the managers of load funds are more highly talented than those managers of no-load funds. Absolutely not. The reason for the gap in performance lies in the fact that those investors who paid load charges were more inclined to stay with their investments because they did not want to throw away the load fee that they had already paid. In essence, the load charge, which is sometimes substantial, was enough of a loss consideration to motivate them to stay put. The no-load investors, on the other hand, felt more relaxed about dumping their fund(s) as market conditions changed, which consequently made other funds look more appealing. And since most investors sell when an investment is down, selling usually means losing. Think about this the next time you are tempted to sell. If you have chosen your investments well, there is rarely a reason to sell.

4. Put everything you can into your 403(b) account—This is a no-brainer. The 403(b) is by far the best place for your investments. It is a simple call. (If you need to refresh your memory as to why, review the appropriate sections in chapters 8 and 9). Simply put, the money you put into your 403(b) is not taxed, and that money is then allowed to compound untaxed until you take it out after retirement. It is a double bonus that can earn you more than double the amount earned outside the tax-deferred account. Once you reach the point where you are contributing the maximum, open an IRA, and contribute the maximum once again. Again you will enjoy the benefits of tax-free compounding.

5. Be sure to allocate all of your investment assets—Some investors make the mistake of forgetting portions of their total portfolio when figuring our asset allocation. Every last one should be included when considering asset allocation or your portfolio will be out of balance. Here is a partial list of investment assets a lot of people accidentally overlook:

- Stocks or bonds received while a child and forgotten
- Stocks or bonds received as a gift and forgotten
- Company stock held in a separate account
- Certificate(s) of deposit
- An annuity
- Rare coins or currency
- U.S. Savings bonds
- Inherited Securites
- A spouse's investments

6. Invest through mutual funds—To follow asset allocation guidelines with stocks and bonds requires the time, talent, and knowledge of markets that few individual investors possess. So do not kid yourself into thinking that you can do *everything* by yourself. You can not.

Most categories of investments—particularly international stocks and bonds and, to a lesser extent, small stocks and bonds in general—are best approached by the average 403(b) investor via mutual funds. For example, it is difficult to follow most foreign stocks easily; and the high volatility of small stocks calls for constant monitoring—something most of us do not have the time, the technology, or the knowledge to do. Instead, go for the diversification and professional management of mutual funds. Mutual funds are the do-it-yourself investor's best friend. That is why I devoted the entire last chapter to them.

7. When tracking the success of your mutual funds, look at the number of shares owned, not just the net asset value (NAV) per share—When dividends are earned for one or more stocks in your stock mutual fund, or interest is earned and reinvested in a bond fund, you will be credited with more shares since you can not take a cash distribution from a 403(b) plan. Make note of how many shares you receive when you first invest and check each subsequent statement to see if you have been issued more shares. Even if it appears you have made only 8% on your money form the price change alone, you may discover that you now have 15% more shares and have actually earned a 23% total return. To find the true value of your investment, simply multiply the number of shares shown on your last statement by the current NAV and compare to the amount of money you originally invested.

8. Ignore long-term corporate bond funds—If you are looking at mutual bond funds, forget long-term corporate bond funds—they are simply too dangerous because, as interest rates rise, principal losses wipe out annual yield and a piece of capital as well. But good yields are to be found among short-term (my favorite) and intermediate-term bonds, many of which yield more than 6% and pose little risk of loss.

9. Watch management fees—Management fees can be an even greater expense than loads if you hold a fund for a number of years. In general, try to keep the annual management fee on your stock funds, particularly large-caps and mid-caps, below 1%. Among stock funds you can make an exception for small-cap funds and international funds, which are generally more expensive to run. But have a strong reason for going above 1.3% on a small-cap and 1.5% on diversified international stock funds. As for bond funds, the rule is even stricter. With few exceptions avoid any with annual fees that exceed 0.9%. As you look around, in fact, you will find highly regarded stock and bond funds with fees under one-half or even one-quarter of 1%.

10. Be careful of funds with higher 12b-1 fees—Look for funds that have 12b-1 fees when you are purchasing mutual funds, and try to stay clear of them. Such fees allow funds to recoup their advertising and marketing costs by skimming an additional 0.6% to 1% from current shareholders (which can really add up over the long haul). Though fund companies claim that 12b-1 fees actually benefit investors by allowing funds to gather more assets and thus spread their costs over a bigger base, studies have shown that that may not be true. Load funds are where you are apt to find 12b-1 fees. Nearly nine out of ten broker-sold funds carry them, compared to only three out of ten no-load funds. There are countless top-of-the-line funds out there that do not charge a 12b-1 fee. So, why waste the money? Although you should look for those mutual funds that do not have a 12b-1 fee, purchasing one with a fee under 0.4% is considered acceptable.

11. <u>Avoid guaranteed investment contracts</u>—Many employers offer Guaranteed Investment Contracts (GICs) in their 403(b) plans. GICs are sold by insurance companies and others and guarantee a certain rate of interest for a certain period of time. They are solid as a rock, assuming that the insurance company selling them has a high rating from A.M. Best, or another insurance rating service. Then why avoid them? Chump interest. A one-year guaranteed investment contract yields around 5.5 percent, about the same as a U.S. Treasury Bill with the same maturity. And that rate is for a huge lump-sum deposit, rather than the several thousand dollars most 403(b) plan participants buy. Not only is the rate of interest for smaller deposits smaller, but there are often commission or sales charges associated with the purchase of a GIC.

As stated numerous times, people who have at least 10 years before retirement should be investing in stock mutual funds. But for those with short-term objectives, there are better investments than GICs, such as short-term bond mutual funds. Short-term bond funds have a limited downside and higher yields than GICs and offer the investor the flexibility of taking profits or getting out of the fund if it declines in value, something you can not do with a GIC.

12. <u>Remember that market declines are a chance to snap up bargains</u>—Remind yourself that as a dollar-cost-averaging investor you're buying at lower prices when the market falls.

13. <u>See the complete picture</u>—Look at how your entire portfolio is performing instead of staring at one piece of it. Remember, proper asset allocation is designed to cushion losses.

14. <u>Think in percentages, not dollars</u>—It will help keep losses in perspective.

15. <u>Do not panic when the market falls</u>—Remember that market declines are normal events. They do not last forever. Remind yourself that after the stock market lost 22.5% of its value in October 1987, it was back up 16.5% in 1988, and up another 31.7% in 1989.

If you have ice water running through your veins and are the type to really work the market, there are a couple more tips to consider. The tips that follow are for the daring who want to squeeze out every return cent they can. They are not for the faint of heart.

1. <u>Invest the bulk of your portfolio in stock mutual funds when the prime interest rate is relatively low</u>—The biggest and most consistent rise in overall stock prices generally occurs when the prime rate is lower (usually below 8-9%). Why? When interest rates are low, corporations pay less interest on the money they borrow, which increases their potential profits, which in turn helps boost stock prices. The stock market looks more attractive and demand for stocks goes up. When you have got more buyers than sellers, prices also go up. Therefore, when interest rates are low, stocks will grow and your money belongs in stock mutual funds.

2. <u>Move the bulk of your portfolio to a bond fund when the prime interest rate is high and coming down</u>—Bond mutual funds are generally the best-paying investment when the prime rate is high and coming down. During that period you will earn two profits from bonds - interest and appreciation. The appreciation can be your big profit, averaging as much as 10% to 20% in a single year. Of course, that's in addition to the interest you are also guaranteed.

3. Move the bulk of your portfolio to a money market fund when the prime interest rate begins to rise—When the prime rate is rising and reaches or moves higher than around 8-9%, move your money out of stock mutual funds and into a money market mutual fund. When the prime rate is rising, money market funds not only will give you the best return but will also be the safest investment, since periods of high interest rates are when stock prices tend to fluctuate wildly and bonds decrease in value for every jump in the prime rate. On the other hand, money market fund interest rates increase with just about every increase in the prime rate. But, without the prospect of capital appreciation that is inherent in both stocks and bonds, money market funds will not average the big returns you are looking for over longer periods of time. Therefore, think of money market funds as your safe harbor during the storm.

Study your options—As I stated earlier, once you have determined which type of asset allocation model is appropriate for you, you can begin to take a closer look at the individual fund choices that are offered within fund families (i.e., *Fidelity, Vanguard*, etc.) The chart that follows will help you decide where to look.

Sources of information on mutual funds		
If you want:	**Look at:**	**Which have:**
Specific fund information	Prospectus*; Annual and Semi-annual reports	Objectives; investment strategies; fees and expenses; holdings; performance; and benchmarks
To compare funds and fund categories	Morningstar Mutual Funds; Value Line's Mutual Fund Survey; Lipper Analytical Services, Inc.; personal finance magazines	Fund data; fund tracking; fund rankings; fund comparisons
Ongoing market information	The Wall Street Journal; Barron's CNBC; independent newsletters	General market and economic information

* A prospectus is a long legal document that reveals everything the Securities and Exchange commission believes you should know about a mutual fund before investing in it. Unfortunately, a prospectus is written by and for lawyers, which makes for extremely dull and often unintelligible reading. Usually, the most valuable information is in the first few pages. Here is what to look for:

- **Investment Objectives**—This tells you the fund's goal and the basic strategy on how the fund manager intends to reach that goal. For example, is the goal capital appreciation (growth of your principal), or current income, or safety of principal? Obviously, you want a fund with investment objectives and strategies that fit your own.

- **What types of securities will the fund invest in?**—For example, will it invest in common stocks of small-cap companies, or foreign securities? What percent of its assets will it invest in each of those securities?

- **Fees and Operating Expenses**—The most important number is the expense ratio, which shows you the fund's annual operating expenses as a percentage of its total assets. The lower this ratio, the lower the fund's expenses. This matters because expenses reduce your return. When two mutual funds have the same performance, the fund with the lower expense ratio will have the higher return. The average for a typical stock fund is 1.4%. The lower the expense ratio, the better. Once you identify the best-performing funds in the categories or groups you want, you can further narrow down your choices by seeing which ones will cost you less.

- **Performance History**—This tells you how the fund has performed over different periods of time in the past. Be sure to compare the fund's performance only with the performance of funds with similar objectives. When evaluating a fund's performance, look at its *average annual total return* over the most recent five-year period. That is more important than its total return in the most recent one-year period. You want to learn how consistent and reliable a fund is, not whether it had a single good or bad year, which may not be typical of how it usually performs. Next, if you have a choice of several funds within each asset-allocation group, say, large-cap funds, for example, focus on the ones whose total returns over five years have been in the top 20 or 25 percent of their category.

Often, a prospectus will suggest an appropriate benchmark to use in judging a fund's performance. A growth fund or a growth and income fund might use the *Standard & Poor's 500 Index* as a benchmark, for example. A small-cap stock fund might use the *Russell 2000 Index*. Also, recognize the fact that personal finance publications now make the arcane world of investing understandable and accessible to virtually anyone who reads them. If you are new to picking your own funds, scan magazines that do a good job tracking and highlighting mutual funds in every issue, such as *Mutual Funds, Smart Money, Worth*, and *Money*.

After you begin reading about mutual funds and assessing their risk, goals, and performance over three, five, ten years, you can begin to narrow the options down to a list of top choices. From your list of top choices, you can begin to make your selections. Remember, you might be limited by your employer's 403(b) plan options as to which fund family you

205

can invest through. Obviously, this will also narrow your choices as to the specific mutual funds that will be available from which to choose. One of the best resources to use when making your selections is *Morningstar*, an excellent service that rates mutual funds from one-star to the highest five-star rating. You can access Morningstar ratings and analyses of funds you are considering at the Morningstar website (see below).

Many other websites also offer on-line calculators and other advice for figuring out your retirement needs and for guiding you on how to distribute your assets. You can find them easily by doing a simple net-search with any Internet search engine (Yahoo, Infoseek, Excite, Lycos, AltaVista, HotBot, etc.), or you can examine the ones that follow that I have found to be very useful:

- *Fidelity Retirement Planner* at **www.Fidelity.com**
- *Vanguard's Retirement Planner* at **www.vanguard.com**
- *Quicken Financial Network* at **www.qfn.com**
- *FinanCenter* at **www.financenter.com**
- *Schwab* at **www.Schwab.com**
- *Morningstar* at **www.Morningstar.net**
- *Standard and Poor Ratings* at **www.ratings.standardpoor.com**

By far, my personal favorite of the above is the *Fidelity Retirement Planner* site. There you will find the *Fidelity Retirement Planning Calculator*. This site has been on-line for about 2 years now, and remains so good that it is surprising more competitors have not copied it more extensively. Without requiring that you drag out old check registers or years of past tax returns, Fidelity factors in all the major variables that will affect your retirement lifestyle: how much income you think you will need; what you can anticipate in Social Security and pension benefits; net proceeds from the sale of a home; and any income you anticipate earning from part-time work after retirement.

Inputting the required information only takes about 10 to 15 minutes—a minor invest-ment of time when compared to the valuable results you get. Once you have completed your input, the calculator produces a graph of your cumulative retirement income surplus or deficit and, in the case of the latter, tells you how much you need to adjust your annual savings to hit your target. After this reality check, you can revisit the form to tweak your assumptions as you are so inclined. Give this site a try. It is definitely A-1.

A Final Note

If you are an extremely cautious investor, as I know some of you are, begin with investing a little money in this mutual fund, a little in that one. Give it a year, see how it feels, then invest some more. It might take two or three years to deploy your money, but that does not matter. Life is long. By taking pains, you can preserve your capital and make it grow. Learning what you need to know to make your own financial decisions and choose your own mutual funds takes some dedicated effort, but is not difficult, so why pay someone else to do what you yourself can do? And the payoff is worth it: confidence that comes from knowing that the person managing your money is the person who cares about it the most—you.

I strongly encourage you to develop a general awareness of the economy and how it affects your investment's performance. Keep a running portfolio of your 403(b) funds, checking their performance regularly by turning to the fund section of the newspaper. Know how your funds are performing relative to certain meaningful benchmarks- like the *S&P 500* (for large-cap stock funds), the *S & P 400* (for mid-cap stock funds), the *Russell 2000* (for the small-cap stock funds), and *EAFE* (for international stock funds). If the performance of a particular fund or stock is steadily deteriorating over several quarters relative to similar funds or stocks (i.e., within the same industry), then it is probably time to sell and consider an alternative fund. And remember, once your plan is developed, keep it in your file and pull it out at least once a year, just to see that everything is on track, including your asset allocation mix. If your circumstances change, so will the numbers you have written down. All you have to do then is make a few adjustments and you are back in business.

CHAPTER FOURTEEN

IRAs—The Second Line of Defense

If you have gathered anything from all that you have read thus far, it is that saving as much as you possibly can for your retirement should be your number one goal. After all, you have to save it before you can spend it, right? You might also remember that statistics show that even when utilizing a 403(b) plan to its maximum (your first line of defense)—you will probably still have to save more in order to achieve your retirement goals. How? By utilizing one of the best supplemental retirement savings vehicles around—the IRA, the second line of defense in your retirement saving strategy.

Some of you might be inclined to ask, "If it is such a great retirement savings vehicle, why not utilize it first?" That is a great question, with a simple answer. The answer is that IRAs have a maximum contribution level that is far below the 403(b)—only $2,000 or 100% of compensation, whichever is less. It trails woefully behind the 403(b) in its wealth-building ability. So, while you would not want to rely on an IRA as your sole source of retirement income, it does provide an effective way to supplement your other long-term savings vehicles, such as the 403(b). Actually, an IRA complements a 403(b) plan perfectly. So, once you have contributed the maximum you can to your 403(b), you will want to consider an IRA as your next building block toward a comfortable retirement. An IRA beats a 403(b) plan only when the 403(b) offers extremely poor investment choices. Even then you have to take a comparative look at both options before you choose the IRA first.

New tax advantages for IRAs—As promised in chapter 8, here are the specifics on how IRAs can benefit the 403(b) investor. While the Taxpayer Relief Act of 1997 spelled general tax relief for millions of Americans, it offered particularly welcome news for Individual Retirement Account (IRA) investors. IRAs now provide even more attractive ways to save for tomorrow's goals—as well as more flexible ways to pay for today's expenses. Not only has the traditional *tax-deferred IRA* been enhanced, but a new *tax-free IRA* has been created. Called the *Roth IRA* after Delaware Senator William V. Roth, Jr., this new IRA offers investors an unprecedented opportunity, not just to defer taxes on earnings until they withdraw them, but to avoid them altogether. In addition to being able to choose from two types of IRAs, many Americans will also have the option of converting their existing IRA assets to the new tax-free Roth IRA. Before we examine your IRA choices in more detail, however, let us first review why it makes good sense to include any type of IRA as a supplement to your 403(b) plan portfolio.

Put the power of tax deferral to work for you—All IRAs help make it easier to maximize your retirement savings. How? By allowing any money you earn on your IRA contributions to grow free from taxes within your account until withdrawn. When your earnings are not eroded by taxes year after year, they can compound faster. Remember our discussion in chapter 6 on the power of compounding? When money is invested, it produces earnings that can then be reinvested, so that you receive earnings on your earnings in addition to the earnings on your original investment. And the longer the money is invested, the more powerful are the effects of compounding. This combined with tax-deferred investing has a magical effect on your supplemental IRA and on your entire investment portfolio. As you can see from the chart below, you can accumulate significantly more in an IRA than you would in a comparable taxable investment.

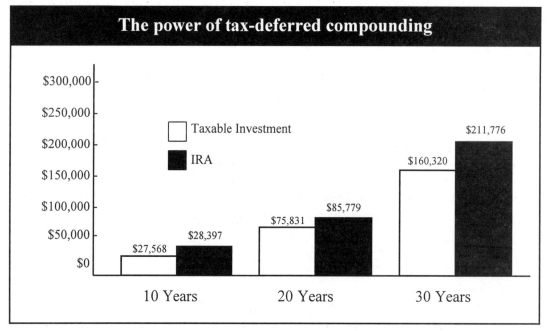

This chart assumes a hypothetical $2,000 annual investment at the beginning of each year, a 9% average annual rate of return and a 36% federal tax bracket. The IRA investments are non-deductible contributions and their earnings grow tax-deferred until withdrawn at the end of the specified period, when the earnings are taxed at the rate of 36%. Totals do not reflect that IRA distributions taken before age 59 ½ may be subject to a 10% early withdrawal penalty. The taxable investments are invested after-tax and their earnings are taxed every year and the tax liability is deducted from the balance. This hypothetical example is for illustrative purposes only and does not represent the performance of any actual security.

Understanding Your IRA Options

Recent legislation has made IRAs an even smarter choice for every retirement investor. For many Americans, the Roth IRA provides an attractive new opportunity to build assets and avoid taxes on any earnings. Even if you are not eligible to establish this new type of IRA, you will find that there are more reasons than ever to contribute to a Traditional IRA. We will now take a closer look at both of these IRA options—and how they can help you provide for your family's current and future financial needs. Earlier I status of the money you receive as distributions from your employer-sponsored retirement plan, including the 403(b). The Rollover IRA will be covered in depth in chapter 18.

Do not forget to take advantage of the Spousal IRA. If your spouse does not work outside of the home, you can also contribute up to $2,000 to his or her IRA—which may be established as either a Traditional IRA or, provided your joint AGI (adjusted gross income) is $150,000 or less, a Roth IRA. So each tax year, you and your spouse can now make combined IRA contributions of up to $4,000 per tax year provided no more than $2,000 is contributed to either of your respective IRAs.

The New Tax-free Roth IRA

The Roth IRA's entrance into the investment world is recent enough to qualify it as new. It really is a special investment vehicle. As long as your income does not exceed a certain level (see the chart on the following page), you can contribute to this attractive new type of IRA. Called the Roth IRA, this IRA offers you the opportunity to avoid taxes on your IRA earnings—*for the rest of your life!* Although you can not deduct contributions to a Roth IRA, you can benefit from its many other valuable tax advantages, such as those that follow:

Tax-free earnings and tax-free withdrawals—Like a Traditional IRA, you will not pay taxes on any earnings while they remain in a Roth IRA. Better still, *unlike* a Traditional IRA, you will not even owe any taxes or penalties on the assets you withdraw from a Roth IRA as long as:

- **Your Roth IRA has met certain five-year aging requirements**—(For Roth Contributory IRAs, the five-year aging period begins on January 1 of the year for which the first annual Roth IRA contribution is made. For Roth Conversion IRAs, the five-year aging period begins on January 1 of the year in which the conversion contribution is made).

- **You are over age 59 ½ when you withdraw the money or you are using that withdrawal to help pay for a qualified first-time home purchase**—(In addition, withdrawals due to death or disability are also tax-free and penalty-free after the five-year period). This opportunity for lifetime tax-free earnings is what makes a Roth IRA such an attractive way to build your retirement assets. In fact, depending on your circumstances, you may find that a Roth IRA could provide you with more retirement income than a Traditional IRA.

Broad eligibility requirements—What also makes a Roth IRA so attractive is that it is available to such a large majority of Americans. Anyone with compensation and is at least 18, can open a Roth IRA— as long as you meet certain income limits.

To be eligible for . . .	Your adjusted gross income (AGI) must be . . .
A full $2,000 contribution	$150,000 or less (if you file a joint tax return) $95,000 or less (if you file a single tax return)
A partial contribution (less than $2,000)	Between $150,000-160,000 (if you file a joint tax return) Between $95,000-110,000 (if you file a single tax return)

If you are eligible for a partial Roth IRA contribution, the mini-worksheet that follows can help you calculate just how much that contribution can be. To help you project how much you would have in the future if you contribute to a Roth IRA vs. a Traditional IRA, many investment companies offer a special Internet on-line tool. See the end of the previous chapter for specific company website addresses.

How can I calculate my partial contribution to a Roth IRA			
	Single Filer Example	Joint Filer Example*	Your Calculation
1. If you file a single tax return, enter $110,000. If you file a joint tax return, enter $160,000	$110,000	$160,000	$_____
2. Subtract your Adjusted Gross Income	- 98,000 = 12,000	- 155,000 = 5,000	- _____ = _____
3. To determine the amount you can contribute, divide by the appropriate factor: 7.5 - if you are a single filer; 5 - if you are a joint filer.	÷ 7.5	÷ 5	÷ _____
The Amount You Can Contribute to a Roth IRA **	= $1,600	= $1,000	= $_____

* If you are married and filing jointly, your spouse can also make a partial contribution of the same amount to his or her own Roth IRA, provided your combined contributions do not exceed your combined compensation.

** If the eligible amount is not a multiple of $10, round up to the next higher $10. If it is below $200 (and above $0), contribute $200.

If you do not qualify for a full $2,000 contribution to a Roth IRA, you can still contribute the difference to a Traditional IRA. So in essence, each tax year you can contribute to both types of IRAs—as long as your total annual IRA contributions do not exceed $2,000 or 100% of compensation, whichever is less.

Penalty-free withdrawals—Not only can a Roth IRA help you save more for retirement, it offers exceptional savings flexibility. Since Roth IRA annual contributions are after-tax and come out first when you take a distribution, you may withdraw these *contributions* anytime—tax and penalty free provided your aggregate distributions from all of your Roth Contributory IRAs do not exceed your aggregate annual Roth IRA contributions. Plus, you can withdraw both contributions and earnings at any time for the following reasons—without paying the typical 10% early-withdrawal penalty:

- **First-time home purchase**—Over your lifetime, you can withdraw up to a total of $10,000 to help you, your spouse, or any children, grandchildren, or ancestors of you or your spouse to pay for qualified first home purchase expenses. Besides being free from penalty, this withdrawal will also be free from federal income taxes, provided your Roth IRA has met the five-year aging requirements.

- **Qualified higher education expenses**—You can also take penalty-free withdrawals from your Roth IRA to help pay post-secondary education expenses for you, your spouse, or any children or grandchildren of you or your spouse. The amount you can withdraw for this purpose is limited to any tuition, fees, books, supplies, equipment, or other eligible expenses incurred at a post-secondary institution for the taxable year.

- **Other special situations**—All of the situations that previously qualified for penalty-free IRA withdrawals were also retained by the new tax law. So you can also withdraw money from your Roth IRA without penalty for the following special purposes:

  1. Major medical expenses (exceeding 7.5% of your AGI)

  2. The death or disability of the IRA account owner

  3. Distributions of certain substantially equal periodic payments

  4. Payment of health insurance premiums by certain unemployed individuals.

- **Flexible timing of distributions**—Unlike the Traditional IRA, the new Roth IRA does not require minimum distributions beginning at age 70 ½, giving you additional time to take advantage of potential tax-free earnings. In fact, you are never required to withdraw your money at any age, so you can pass your Roth IRA assets on to your beneficiaries if you wish.

213

The Enhanced Traditional IRA

While the Roth IRA is limited to those below a certain income limit, *anyone* under age 70 ½ at *any* income level can still make an annual contribution of the lesser of $2,000 or 100% of compensation (less any Roth IRA contributions) to a Traditional IRA. Better yet, since January 1, 1998, more people are able to deduct their Traditional IRA contributions! The following three benefits offer great flexibility to those who decide to utilize the Traditional IRA alone, or as an adjunct to their 403(b) plan:

1. **Expanded tax deductibility**—Whether you can deduct your contribution to a Traditional IRA still depends on two things: whether you are covered by an employer-sponsored retirement plan and your adjusted gross income. But now, both of these requirements have been liberalized.

- **No more dependence on your spouse's plan participation**—Now *your* eligibility for a tax-deductible IRA contribution may not depend on whether *your spouse* participates in a retirement plan at work. Regardless of your spouse's participation, if you are not an active participant in an employer-sponsored retirement plan, you can make a fully deductible Traditional IRA contribution of up to $2,000—as long as your joint AGI is $150,000 or less.

- **Higher income limits**—For those who *do* participate in an employer-sponsored retirement plan, the income limits used to determine whether you qualify for a deductible IRA contribution will be gradually increased over the next several years.

Don't forget
Form 8606

Remember to file IRS Form 8606 with your tax return if any part of your IRA contribution is non-deductible!

See the charts on the following page for help in determining the deductibility of your IRA contributions.

Can I deduct my 1999 Traditional IRA contribution?

Adjusted Gross Income (before IRA deduction)		Whether you participate in an employer-sponsored retirement plan*	Type of deduction you qualify for
Joint Filing	**Single filing**		
Under $51,000	Under $31,000	Yes or No	Full
$51,000-61,000	$31,000-41,000	No	Full
		Yes	Partial
$61,000-151,000	Over $41,000	No	Full
		Yes	None
$151,000-161,000	----	No**	Partial**
		Yes	None
Over $161,000	----	No**	None**
		Yes	None

How can I calculate a partial deduction for a Traditional IRA contribution?

For 1999 Tax Year	Example	Your Calculation
1. Write in $61,000 if a joint filer, $41,000 if a single filer	$61,000	$_____
2. Subtract your Adjusted Gross Income -	53,500	- _____
	= 7,500	= _____
3. Divide by 5 to determine the amount you can deduct ***	÷ 5	÷ 5
Your deduction for a Traditional IRA contribution	= $1,500	= $_____

* If you are unsure of your participation status, refer to the pension plan box on your W-2 form. If neither you nor your spouse participates in an employer-sponsored retirement plan, you can each make a fully deductible contribution of up to $2,000 provided your combined contributions do not exceed your combined compensation.

** Assumes that you spouse is an active participant in an employer-sponsored retirement plan.

*** If the deductible amount is not a multiple of $10, round up to the next highest $10. If it is below $200 (and above $0), deduct $200.

2. More flexible access to assets—IRAs have always allowed investors to withdraw assets without penalty after they reach 59 ½. And they have even allowed withdrawals before age 59 ½ to pay for certain expenses—without incurring a 10% early-withdrawal penalty. But since the beginning of 1998, both the Traditional IRA and the Roth IRA allow you to take *penalty-free* withdrawals for more purposes—as reviewed under the Roth IRA section. Again, these penalty-free opportunities include:

- Qualified first-time home purchase.

- Qualified higher education expenses.

- Major Medical expenses (exceeding 7.5% of your AGI).

- Death or Disability of the IRA account owner.

- Distributions of certain substantially equal periodic payments.

- Payment of health insurance premiums by certain unemployed individuals.

Keep in mind, though, that *any* withdrawal from a Traditional IRA may still be *subject to regular income tax.*

3. Continued advantage of tax-deferred growth—Any earnings within a Traditional IRA will continue to grow free from taxes until you withdraw them. Over time, you can still accumulate substantially more in a tax-deferred plan like an IRA than you could in a comparable taxable investment earning the same rate of return (as shown in a previous chart).

Deciding which IRA may be right for you—As you have seen, all IRAs can help you address both future and current financial needs. But how do you decide which IRA may be right for you? You can start by answering a few key questions which are highlighted in the decision chart on the next page. Then, you may want to refer to the chart on the page after that, where I have compared the key features of both the Traditional IRA and the new Roth IRA.

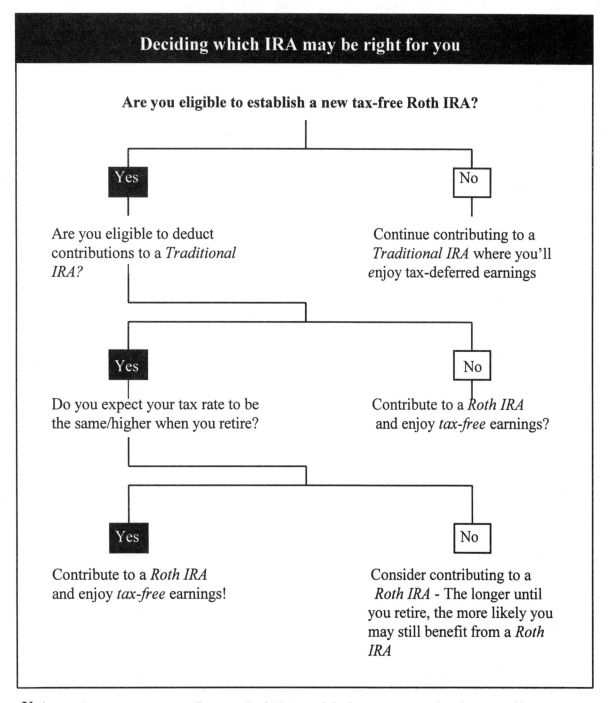

Deciding which IRA may be right for you

Are you eligible to establish a new tax-free Roth IRA?

Yes

Are you eligible to deduct contributions to a *Traditional IRA?*

No

Continue contributing to a *Traditional IRA* where you'll enjoy tax-deferred earnings

Yes

Do you expect your tax rate to be the same/higher when you retire?

No

Contribute to a *Roth IRA* and enjoy *tax-free* earnings?

Yes

Contribute to a *Roth IRA* and enjoy *tax-free* earnings!

No

Consider contributing to a *Roth IRA* - The longer until you retire, the more likely you may still benefit from a *Roth IRA*

Note: As long as you *can* contribute to a Roth IRA - and the longer you can take advantage of its tax-free earnings - the more likely you will benefit most from this attractive new option.

Comparison of the enhanced Traditional IRA and the new Roth IRA		
	Traditional IRA	**Roth IRA**
Eligibility Requirements	Under age 70 ½ with compensation, including a non-working spouse	Any age with compensation, including a non-working spouse, subject to income limits: **Single Filers:** Up to $95,000 (to qualify for a full $2,000 contribution); $95,000-$110,000 (to be eligible for a partial contribution **Joint Filers:** Up to $150,000 (to qualify for a full $2,000 contribution); $150,000-$160,000 (to be eligible for a partial contribution)
Key Tax Advantage	Tax-deferred growth	Tax-**free** growth
Tax Treatment of Withdrawals	Any earnings and deductible contributions subject to tax upon withdrawal	Contributions may be withdrawn tax-free. *Qualified distributions of earnings are tax-free* (i.e., no taxes on withdrawals if the five-year aging requirement and certain other conditions are met)
Tax-Deductible Contributions	**Yes**, subject to retirement plan participation status and AGI limits*	**No**
Maximum Annual Contribution	$2,000 per person or 100% of compensation, whichever is less (in aggregate to both a Traditional IRA and a Roth IRA) per tax year	
10% Early Withdrawal Penalty	Yes, if you are under age 59 ½ and the withdrawal is not for the reasons listed below (or in the event of the death or disability of the account owner)	
Penalty-Free Withdrawals	Yes, including higher education expenses; first home purchase; certain major medical expenses; certain long-term unemployment expenses	
Mandatory Distributions	Distributions must start at age 70 ½	No requirement to begin at any age

* For a Traditional IRA, full deductibility is available to active participants whose 1998 AGI is $50,000 or less (joint) and $30,000 or less (single); partial deductibility for up to $60,000 AGI (joint) and $40,000 AGI (single).

Whether to convert your existing IRA assets—So far, we have discussed the options you have for *contributing* to an IRA. In the next few pages, we will look at what options the new tax law provides for the IRA money you have *already* accumulated.

If you have a Traditional IRA, you now have the option of moving some or all of your existing IRA assets to a new Roth IRA—as long as your AGI is $100,000 or less. This is referred to as *converting* your existing IRA. While a conversion does require you to pay *current* taxes on the taxable assets you are moving, it then enables you to avoid *future* taxes on any subsequent IRA earnings.

How the conversion process works—If you do decide to convert your existing IRA assets to a new Roth Conversion IRA, here is how the process will work:

1. You will request a full or partial conversion distribution form you current IRA.

2. You will owe taxes on any earnings as well as any deductible or pre-tax money withdrawn. (If you converted in 1998, the taxable amount of your distribution would have been spread out over four years to help minimize the tax impact). To allow as much money as possible to grow tax free, you should pay the taxes on your IRA distribution out of your non-retirement savings. Remember, if you pay your taxes on the converted amount with your IRA assets, those IRA assets may be subject to a 10% withdrawal penalty.

3. You will then reinvest your distribution in new Roth Conversion IRA. For tax purposes, Roth IRA *conversions* and Roth IRA *contributions* must be tracked separately. So you can not convert assets to—and contribute to—the same Roth IRA. Rather, you will need to establish two separate Roth IRA accounts: one for conversions and one for ongoing annual contributions.

Even if you are *eligible* to convert, you do not *have to* convert. In fact, you can leave your existing IRA assets just where they are—and still open a new Roth IRA for ongoing annual contributions. Or if you prefer, you can convert only a portion of your IRA assets to a new Roth Conversion IRA.

Factors to Consider in Making Your Conversion Decision

1. **How long can you take advantage of tax-free growth?**—In deciding whether conversion makes sense for you, you will want to weigh the *cost* of paying taxes on your IRA distribution now with the *benefit* of enjoying tax-free growth on your Roth Conversion IRA assets from here on. And the longer you expect your assets to remain in your Roth Conversion IRA, the more you can benefit from this tax-free growth.

2. **Will your tax rate be higher or lower when you retire?**—What you expect your future tax rate to be should also play a part in your conversion decision. If you think your tax rate will be *the same or higher* when you withdraw your money than your current rate, then it may make sense to pay the tax liability now—in exchange for tax-free growth and tax-free distributions in the future. The chart that follows will help you analyze how the relationship between these two factors can impact your conversion decision. It is assumed that:

- All assets in the Traditional IRA were deductible contributions.
- The Traditional IRA is converted to a Roth IRA.
- No additional Roth IRA contributions are made after the conversion.
- Taxes are paid from non-IRA assets.
- Retirement and distributions begin at age 65.
- The IRAs are assumed to earn at least a 3% annual rate of return.

Should I consider converting my Traditional IRA to a Roth IRA?

		Expected Tax Rate at Retirement				
		15%	28%	31%	36%	39.6%
Tax Rate During My Working Years	15%	Yes	Yes	Yes	Yes	Yes
	28%	Maybe *	Yes	Yes	Yes	Yes
	31%	Maybe**	Maybe***	Yes	Yes	Yes

* Assuming a 9% annual rate of return, you should only consider choosing the Roth IRA if you are age 44 or younger.

** Assuming a 9% annual rate of return, you should only consider choosing the Roth IRA if you are age 42 or younger.

*** You should consider converting to a Roth IRA in all cases except people age 60 or older who anticipate earning 3% or less on an annual basis.

Basically, the conversion decision involves weighing the short-term tax cost with the long-term tax *advantages*—which the following chart and worksheet can help you determine.

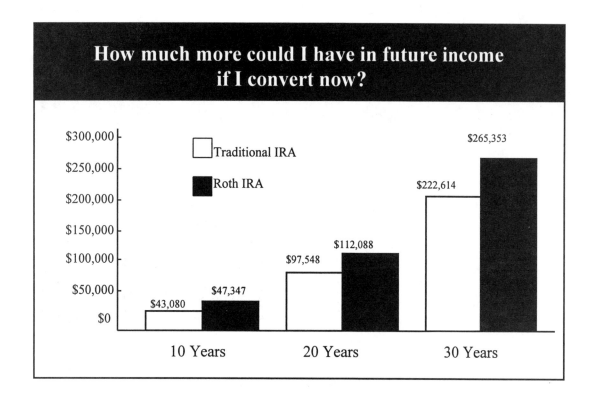

Note: This chart assumes a hypothetical Traditional IRA with a balance of $20,000 which represents deductible contributions and tax-deferred earnings, which is converted to a Roth IRA. Both IRAs assume a 9% average annual rate of return, and a 28% federal tax bracket at the time of conversion and of distribution. The value of the Traditional IRA reflects tax-deferred growth over the specified period with the entire balance taxed at distribution. Plus, because the tax due at conversion is paid from funds outside the IRA, to make a valid comparison with the Roth IRA, the Traditional IRA value also includes the value of the tax that would have been paid for the conversion (spread over 4 years) invested in a taxable investment, earning the same return; earnings are taxed every year and the tax liability is deducted from the balance. The Roth IRA value includes the full $20,000 converted value which grows and is distributed tax-free at the end of the specified period. These values also assume there were no early withdrawal penalties due upon distribution. This hypothetical example is for illustrative purposes only and does not represent the performance of any actual security.

The following worksheet will give you an idea as to how much you would have to pay in current taxes if you were to convert your entire IRA now.

		Example	Your Situation
How much would I pay in *current* taxes if I convert my entire IRA now?			
1.	Write in you current Traditional IRA assets*	$20,000	$ _____
2.	Subtract the total non-deductible contributions you've made to your Traditional IRA (as reported on your most recent IRS form 8606). **Note:** These are the contributions you've made to your Traditional IRA that you couldn't deduct on your income tax return.	- 0 -	- _____
3.	**Taxable portion of your conversion**	= 20,000	= _____
4.	Multiply line 3 by your current tax bracket (converted to a decimal).	x .28	x _____
5.	**Tax you would pay on your conversion**	= $5,600	= $ _____

* This worksheet assumes conversion of your entire Traditional IRA. If you are not converting all of your IRA assets, you must calculate your IRA basis to determine which portion of your distribution will be included in your income.

Keep in mind that the taxable portion of your Traditional IRA distribution would be included in your income over four years if you converted prior to January 1, 1999. So if your taxable income fluctuates during that period, thereby affecting your tax bracket, the amount of tax you owe may be more or less than the amount calculated here. If you find that converting all of your existing IRA assets to a Roth Conversion IRA presents too large a tax burden, consider converting just a *portion* which results in a tax payment you feel is manageable. For complete financial protection, you should consult your tax advisor to help you determine if conversion to a Roth IRA is appropriate for you.

Commonly Asked Questions

- **I already contribute to a 403(b) plan. Should I open an IRA account also?**—Maybe. You should not even consider an IRA unless you are presently contributing the maximum amount to your 403(b) plan (or 401(k) plan if it applies to you). Unless you have been contributing maximally to your 403(b) plan from the beginning, you probably will not have the amount of retirement money you will need to retire in comfort. One way to circumvent this problem is to supplement your 403(b) money with an IRA. So, *once you have contributed the maximum to your 403(b) plan*, you will want to consider an IRA as your next building block toward a comfortable retirement, but not until then.

- **How much can I contribute to an IRA?**—Each year, you may contribute up to $2,000 or 100 % of compensation (whichever is less), to a Traditional or Roth IRA, regardless of marital status. This is the *combined* annual limit for any and all IRAs you may have.

- **So which IRA should I consider?**—If you are eligible for a deductible Traditional IRA as well as a Roth IRA, a lot depends on how close you are to retirement and what tax bracket you expect to be in when you retire. As a general rule of thumb, the deductible Traditional IRA may be a better choice if you are within 10 years of retirement and you expect to be in a lower tax bracket when you do retire. Otherwise, the Roth IRA may be the better option. See the chart entitled *Deciding which IRA may be right for you* in this chapter for further information.

- **How long can I keep contributing to my IRA?**—For a Traditional IRA, you can contribute each year that you earn compensation or have earned income until the year in which you reach age 70 ½. After that age, you can no longer make contributions. However, if you invest in a Roth IRA, there are no age limits. You are not required to begin taking distributions when you reach age 70 ½, and you can continue to make contributions after age 70 ½. Because of this, the Roth IRA may carry more weight than the Traditional IRA, especially for those individuals concerned about outliving their assets during their golden years. And with life expectancies on the rise and more people retiring before normal retirement age, that is a legitimate concern to have.

- **I understand the differences between the Traditional IRA and the Roth IRA, but what about the Education IRA? How does it fit into the picture?**—The Education IRA is another new type of IRA that became effective in 1998. Actually, the name *individual retirement account* is a misnomer, because the Education IRA is not designed to help people save for retirement, but for college. The amount you contribute to an Education IRA does not count toward the $2,000 annual Traditional or Roth IRA contribution limit. (For specifics on the Education IRA see the "Education IRA" bonus gift included with your order.) For a quick side-by-side comparison of the Traditional Deductible and Nondeductible IRA and the Roth IRA, see the bonus gift "Reference Chart for 403(b)s and IRAs" included with your order.

- **What kinds of things can I invest my IRA money in?**—You can invest your IRA money in a wide range of investment vehicles, including, but not limited to mutual funds, individual stocks and bonds, CDs, zero-coupon bonds, U.S. Treasuries, etc.

- **Can I open more than one IRA?**—Yes, you can open more than one IRA; however, the aggregate amount that you may contribute to all types of IRAs (including Traditional and Roth IRAs) is $2,000 annually. If you are married, the aggregate amount that both you and your spouse can contribute is $4,000, with no more than $2,000 contributed in either of your names.

- **When can I make my IRA contributions for the year?**—For tax year 1998 you could have made your IRA contribution any time from January 1, 1998, through April 15, 1999. For tax year 1999 you may make your IRA contribution any time from January 1, 1999, through April 15, 2000. For Roth and Education IRAs you may begin making contributions on or after January 1, 1999 for tax year 1999.

- **Should I contribute to a Traditional IRA even if my contributions are not tax deductible?**—Even if you do not qualify for deducting your IRA contributions from your income tax returns, you should still consider investing in an IRA to get the benefits of tax-deferred growth, *after you have contributed the maximum to your 403(b)*. With tax-deferred growth, instead of paying taxes on your investment earnings each year, the money stays in your account, which can help your money compound faster. Also, if you wait until retirement to withdraw the money, you may be in a lower tax bracket, so your tax payments could be lower.

- **When may I begin withdrawing money from my Traditional IRA?**—You can withdraw money from your IRA anytime; but you will have to pay federal income tax on any deductible or pre-tax contributions and account earnings (interest, dividends, and/or capital gains). In addition, if you are under age 59 ½, you will incur a 10% early-withdrawal penalty unless you are in a specific situation when the penalty does not apply.

- **Would you elaborate on the specific situations that could exist in order for the 10% early-withdrawal penalty not to apply?**—There are many ways to distribute money to yourself from a Traditional IRA or 403(b) plan without triggering the 10% penalty tax that is normally levied on withdrawals before the year in which you reach age 59 ½. They are:

    The annuity exception—This exception permits you to receive penalty-free distributions from your IRA before you are 59 ½ if your withdrawals are part of a series of substantially equal payments over your life (or your life expectancy), or over the lives of you and your beneficiary (or your joint life expectancies). See chapter 10 for all the details.

    Disability—If you become disabled before you reach age 59 ½, any amounts you withdraw from your IRA to pay expenses related to your disability are not subject to the 10% additional tax. What constitutes a disability? According to the IRS, you must be unable to engage in any substantial gainful activity because of any medically determined physical or mental impairment that can be expected to result in death, or is of long (at least twelve months) and indefinite duration.

    Untimely departure—If you die before age 59 ½, the assets in your IRA can be distributed to your beneficiary or to your estate without either party owing the tax.

    Medical expenses—You do not have to pay the 10% tax on amounts you withdraw that exceed what you paid for unreimbursed medical expenses during the year of the withdrawal, minus 7.5% of your adjusted gross income during the year.

Out of a job—If you become unemployed, you will not have to pay the 10% tax on early withdrawals up to the amount of expenses for medical insurance for yourself, your spouse, and your dependents if the following conditions apply: You received unemployment compensation under any Federal or State law for 12 consecutive weeks, you make the withdrawals either during the tax year you received the unemployment compensation or in the following year, and you make the withdrawals no later than sixty days after you are re-employed. Even self-employed individuals qualify if they meet the conditions and would be eligible for unemployment compensation save for the fact they are self-employed.

- **How are withdrawals from a Traditional IRA taxed?**—Any money in your IRA that has not yet been taxed would be taxable at the time of withdrawal. This would include any deductible contributions, money you rolled into an IRA from a qualified retirement plan, or any dividends, interest, or capital gains that your account may have earned. The amount of income tax you would pay depends on your tax bracket (15, 28, 31, 36, 39.6 percent, etc.) at the time you withdraw the money. As noted in the previous question, unless you are in a specific situation, if you withdraw money before you reach age 59 ½, you may have to pay an additional 10% early-withdrawal penalty.

- **What are the tax implications if I contribute more than the annual limit?**—If you contribute more than the annual limit to an IRA, you will have until the date you file your taxes to remove the excess contribution and any associated earnings. Otherwise, a 6% penalty is applied annually to the excess portion of the contribution.

- **I understand that Traditional IRAs now offer looser restrictions on tax deductibility. What are the present income limits?**—Though almost anyone can *contribute* to an IRA, the rules to date have been very strict on who can *deduct* the amount of their contributions from their income tax returns. The new legislation relaxes the restrictions, meaning that more people can qualify for tax-deductible IRAs, making them a much more appealing investment option. In 1999, for active participants in an employer-sponsored retirement plan, the income limit that determines whether your IRA contributions are tax deductible began to rise, leveling off in 2007. See the chart that follows.

Adjusted Gross Income Limit

Tax Year	Single	Married
1998	$30,000 - $40,000	$50,000 - $60,000
1999	$31,000 - $41,000	$51,000 - $61,000
2000	$32,000 - $42,000	$52,000 - $62,000
2001	$33,000 - $43,000	$53,000 - $63,000
2002	$34,000 - $44,000	$54,000 - $64,000
2003	$40,000 - $50,000	$60,000 - $70,000
2004	$45,000 - $55,000	$65,000 - $75,000
2005	$50,000 - $60,000	$70,000 - $80,000
2006	$50,000 - $60,000	$75,000 - $85,000
2007	$50,000 - $60,000	$80,000 - $100,000

- **When did the changes to the Traditional IRA become effective?**—The changes to the Traditional IRA became effective January 1, 1998. Also on that date, the Roth IRA became available to investors.

- **After converting to a Roth IRA, I earned a higher-than-expected income which put me over the $100,000 limit. What can I do to correct this?**—If you have converted to a Roth IRA and know your AGI (Adjusted Gross Income) will exceed the $100,000 limit this year, you can reverse, or re-characterize, your conversion by transferring the assets and earnings back to a Traditional IRA without penalty. The deadline to reverse a conversion is your tax filing due date, usually April 15, plus extensions. When you are ready to reverse your conversion, call your investment company and request a copy of the Roth IRA Letter of Authorization, the only form you will need to transfer your assets from your existing Roth IRA to a Traditional IRA.

- **I converted part of my Traditional IRA to a Roth IRA and then realized the conversion will put me into the next tax bracket in 1999. I know Congress now allows reversals if one goes over the $100,000 limit, but is there any consideration for those of us who may want to reverse because of an unexpected increase in the tax bracket?**—The recently enacted IRS Restructuring and Reform Act of 1998 contains a provision you may find useful. It is specifically designed to assist individuals who erroneously convert Traditional IRAs into Roth IRAs, or otherwise wish to change the nature of any IRA contribution. It permits making a so-call *trustee-to-trustee* transfer of any IRA contribution, including a Roth conversion, to any other IRA by the due date of your tax return for the year, including extensions. This means you can simply transfer the rollover you make to the Roth back to your Traditional IRA. (You must also transfer any earnings that accrued in the Roth.) Transferred contributions are treated as if they had been made to the transferee IRA in the first place.

- **Is alimony considered compensation for IRA purposes?**—The IRS defines compensation as *wages, salaries, tips, alimony, and separate maintenance payments*. On page 5 of the latest edition of Publication 590, you will find the following statement: "All taxable alimony and separate maintenance payments you receive under a decree of divorce or separate maintenance are treated as compensation."

- **I am told that Roth IRAs can also be a valuable tool in estate planning. How?**—Roth IRAs can do a lot more than just boost your retirement income. Roths can also help with estate planning. You can use a number of the great Roth features to help you accumulate a larger retirement nest egg. Then, you can leave it largely tax-free to your heirs. (For more information on this subject, see the chapter on *Estate Planning*.)

- **Some financial experts are expressing concern that politicians could regret the loss of potential tax revenue from Roth IRA savings and change the law. Do you think this will happen?**—No, in fact, considering the existing problems facing Social Security, I look for even more measures to be taken by Congress to help individual investors more fully prepare for their future retirement.

- **What kinds of additional measures do you think need to be taken?**—Many people (myself included) feel that, although Congress has fixed some of what was wrong with the IRA program, including equalizing spousal IRAs, it left uncorrected the ultimate IRA inequity: contribution limits that are still ridiculously low. When IRAs came into being in 1974, the contribution limit was $1,500 a year. Three years later, the limit was increased to $1,750, and four years after that to $2,000. Since then, despite 18 years of inflation that has nearly halved the value of the dollar, Congress has left IRA contributions capped at a mere $2,000 a year.

Enter Senator William Roth to the rescue, again. The same man who gave us the Roth IRA, and sponsored other important IRA legislation, now wants to give Americans more responsibility, and more opportunities, to manage their retirement. The following data summarizes his proposals, which include raising the all-too-low IRA contribution limits, and also liberalizes 403(b), 401(k), and IRA rules. Senator Roth's Retirement Savings Opportunity Act of 1999 would:

1. Create a Roth 401(k), similar to the Roth IRA, enabling participants to contribute money on an after-tax basis that could then be withdrawn tax free at retirement.

2. Create a Roth 403(b) plan for non-profit group employees and government workers paralleling the Roth 401(k).

3. Raise annual contribution limits of conventional 403(b) and 403(k) plans to $15,000.

4. Set annual 403(b) and 401(k) contribution limits at $22,500 for some workers age 50 and older.

5. Raise annual IRA contribution limits from $2,000 to $5,000, to adjust for inflation since the $2,000 cap was set 18 years ago, and index the new cap for future inflation.

6. Set annual IRA contribution limits at $7,500 for workers age 50 and older.

7. Restore deductibility of contributions to Traditional IRAs for high-income taxpayers with employer-sponsored plans.

8. Raise AGI (adjusted gross income) limits for Roth IRA conversions from $100,000 in the year of the conversion to $1 million.

9. Eliminate all income limits for Roth IRA contributions.

- **I received a phone call the other day from a financial representative trying to sell me an investment opportunity that was IRS Approved. Is there such an investment?**—No. Avoid any investment touted as IRS Approved or otherwise endorsed by the IRS. This is a clear sign of deception. Those who promote legitimate investment opportunities do not pretend to have the blessing of the IRS. The IRS *does not* endorse specific tax deals.

Final Note

Everyone owning an IRA, or even thinking about IRAs, should obtain a copy of the IRS's free annual Publication 590, *Individual Retirement Arrangements*. It is often referred to as the *owner's manual* for IRAs. Call 1-800-TAX-FORM (829-3676). Another good reference is *Planning for Your Retirement,* an introductory brochure from the American Association of Retired Persons (AARP) Worker Equity Program. Write: Planning for Your Retirement, AARP, 601 E Street NW, Washington, DC 20049

CHAPTER 15

Annuities—The Third Line of Defense

The unvarnished truth is that most people reading this manual will never need to consider the annuity as an investment alternative. As mentioned in chapter 12, I recommend purchasing an annuity *only* when a certain set of circumstances exist. Toward that end, allow me to state again, *never* invest in an annuity until you have fully funded the free retirement plans available to you. The free plans being the tax-deductible and tax-deferred savings plans (other than annuities) that you are qualified to take part in, such as 403(b) plans, 401(k)s, IRAs, etc. Without question, individual and employer-sponsored plans are the best way to sock away money for your post-work years. Also, they usually give you a wider variety of investment options. But, if you are in the enviable position of owning a fully-funded 403(b) plan, and you contribute the maximum to an IRA, then you might be interested in the third line of defense in your retirement saving strategy—the annuity. According to the *Variable Annuity Research Data Service*, sales of annuities were up 12% to $98.8 billion in 1998. And total assets, fueled in part by market gains, rose an even steeper 22% to $778 billion. Of course, that is considerably less than the $5.5 trillion invested in U.S. mutual funds.

What is an annuity?—An annuity is a tax-deferred investment vehicle packaged as an insurance product. Annuities are usually sold, not bought. They are inferior to 403(b)-like plans for two main reasons. First, instead of being able to buy them with before-tax dollars, you must use after-tax dollars. Second, annuities come festooned with fees and charges, some that run as high as 9% of principal if you decide to drop out within the first 7 to 10 years of ownership. But, some people find them attractive, again for two main reasons:

> **1.** When you purchase an annuity, its earnings are tax-deferred until you begin withdrawing the money. In other words, it works the same way as a nondeductible IRA. Because you are not paying taxes along the way, you have the chance to earn gains on untaxed money, and it grows much more quickly than a taxable account does (depending, of course, on the investments you have chosen).

229

2. You can stash as much as you want in annuities. That is right, there are absolutely no limits to what you can put into an annuity. In this narrow sense, it is potentially the biggest tax shelter you could find. But, as stated above, the guaranteed payments promised in an annuity contract usually come at a high price: providers charge a variety of fees for the management and insurance of the annuity. I will cover those fees in more detail later on in the chapter.

Remember, an annuity is a retirement savings vehicle—its earnings grow tax-deferred until withdrawal; you receive a specified amount of income during retirement; you can switch between investments in your annuity tax-free; and, you can contribute as much as you want during the accumulation phase. But, given the special fees and rules associated with annuities, it makes sense to buy an annuity only under certain conditions:

- **You will not need the money for several years**—The only exception to this rule is if you are about to retire and want to put a chunk of money into an immediate annuity, which will provide you with fixed, guaranteed monthly income right away. So if you think you might need the money to pay for your child's education or a major purchase, you would probably be better off putting your money in more liquid investments such as stocks, bonds, or mutual funds.

- **You have money that is not eligible for a regular retirement plan and can invest it for a very long time.**

- **You think you will be in a lower tax bracket when you retire**—Your annuity's gains are tax-deferred, which means you will pay income tax on your withdrawals. If your tax bracket is higher *in retirement*, it might make sense to put the money in tax-efficient mutual funds instead and pay long-term capital gains of a maximum of 20% as you go, instead of ordinary income tax on gains which can be as high as 39.6% for federal tax alone.

- **You are a very aggressive investor**—If you switch money among your funds so often that you never get to take advantage of long-term capital gains rates anyway, then an annuity can give you a tax-sheltered environment. Just be sure to choose an annuity that has a good selection of subaccounts, though, because moving among subaccounts is easy, but moving from one annuity to another can involve red tape.

An annuity has two phases: the accumulation phase and the distribution phase. The *accumulation phase* is the time period between the date you first contribute to an annuity and the date you begin taking payouts from it. As stated above, during the accumulation phase, you can contribute as much as you want and the earnings in the annuity grow tax-deferred. During the *distribution phase*, also called the *payout phase,* you start receiving your money, either by taking a lump-sum or by receiving a monthly check.

An annuity consists of an insurance wrapper and a subaccount. The subaccount is simply the annuity's underlying investment—typically a mutual fund. The *insurance wrapper,* whose extra fees diminish the compounding benefits of an annuity, is the more complicated part of the annuity. It defines the terms of the annuity, such as: whether it is fixed or variable; whether it is a certain or life term annuity; whether it is deferred or immediate; and, the annuity's death benefit. Let us take a closer look at each.

Fixed or Variable?—There are two broad types of annuities: fixed and variable. A *fixed annuity*, the more conservative choice, provides a set return backed by an insurance company, much as a bank provides a stated rate of return on a savings account. Although the rate of return varies somewhat, depending on prevailing interest rates, the return is more stable than the variable annuity's. Fixed annuities look more attractive when inflation is higher. Seven percent seems to be the magic number. When interest rates top 7% on fixed annuities, investors look at them favorably. A *variable annuity* invests in stocks, bonds, or money market funds, depending upon the type of subaccount you choose. It get its name from the fact that your return on the account is variable, not fixed. That is, you will receive various returns over the life of the account. This is in contrast to the fixed annuity which guarantees a fixed rate of return for the life of the account.

Usually, you select the subaccount based on the level of risk and return you want in your annuity, just as you would when purchasing a mutual fund. For example, a company might offer as many as 20 subaccounts, ranging from conservative money market funds, to equity-income funds, to growth funds, or to the riskier aggressive growth funds. As you would expect, the more conservative subaccounts invest in money market and bonds, and the more aggressive invest in stocks. Of course, the amount of return depends on the actual return of the subaccount investment.

Certain or Life?—If the payout phase of an annuity is for *life*, it pays the owner during his or her entire lifetime. The payments cease when he or she dies. If an annuity's payout is *certain*, it pays the owner for a specified period, and if the owner dies before the period ends, then a beneficiary receives the payments until the certain term ends. In other words, if the annuity owner has a certain term of 10 years for an annuity but receives only 5 years of payments before dying, then the owner's beneficiary will receive payments for another 5 years, and then the payments would cease.

An annuity can also be a combination of life and certain terms. For example, you can purchase an annuity for *life*, but with a *certain* period of ten years. If you live longer than the ten-year period, the annuity continues to pay throughout your lifetime, and at your death, the payments cease. If you die before the certain term expires, your beneficiary will receive payments until the certain term ends.

Deferred or Immediate?—You can purchase a deferred annuity, which means you intend to wait a while and let the annuity earn money before withdrawing from it. An immediate annuity, which begins paying you immediately is used primarily by older investors who want an immediate and continuing stream of income. You can also convert your annuity from a deferred to an immediate annuity. Most of the current hoopla centers on the deferred-variable annuity.

Death Benefits—Depending on how you have set up the beneficiaries to your annuity, your heirs may receive money from your annuity when you die. Here are some examples:

> **Deferred Annuity**—If the owner dies while the annuity is still in the accumulation phase— the phase before the payout phase, the owner's heirs will receive whatever amount has accumulated in the annuity. The heirs will need to pay income taxes on the amount, not to mention mention estate taxes if the entire estate amounts to more than $650,000. In other words, if you contributed $80,000 to an annuity, and it has grown to $190,000, your heirs would receive the $190,000 as taxable income if you died before the payout phase began. In some cases, the insurance company may guarantee to pay your beneficiary the principal amount of your investment if it is greater than the account's current value—a real boon if the market drops before you do. But be prepared to pay extra for that guarantee.

231

Certain Annuity—As noted before, if you purchase a certain annuity, and the payout phase has begun, and you die during the certain period, your beneficiary will receive payment until the end of the certain period.

Fees—Annuity providers charge a variety of fees, which have gone down significantly in recent years. Here is a summary of the types of fees your annuity may charge. (Remember, each plan is different, so you need to compare annuities' fees carefully when making your choice). Here is a hint about annuity fee quotations: they are often quoted as basis points instead of percentage points. So a fee of .55% is referred to as "55 basis points."

Insurance Fees—These fees, also known as mortality fees, are similar to premiums for term life insurance. You pay a certain percentage of your annuity's value to the annuity provider *each year* in exchange for some type of guaranteed payment. This is a fee that ranges from 0.5% to 1.75% a year. The annuity industry average is about 1.4% a year. Insurance companies defend this fee on the grounds that it covers the cost of providing an insurance benefit, but as often as not, half or more of the insurance charge goes instead to sales staff commissions, other marketing costs, or just profit.

Management Fees—These fees, also referred to as *fund operating expenses,* run around 0.75% to more than 1%. The industry average is about 0.8% per year. They are expressed as a percent of the net assets. They are identical to management fees charged by mutual fund companies. You pay the annuity provider for the management of the subaccount. But you must take into consideration that when you add this fee to the others, the total annual charge can exceed 2%-3%, which is considered outrageous in a mutual fund.

Maintenance Fees—These fees are usually $25 to $40 a year for keeping your account's records in order and keeping you informed.

Commission Fees—If the annuity is purchased through a broker, you will undoubtedly pay a hefty commission. This expense must be taken into account when comparing the annuity to other investment options.

Surrender Charges—Most annuities charge a substantial penalty if you cash in on your annuity too soon. For example, an annuity might charge a 7% to 9% surrender charge that decreases by one point each year for seven to nine years (depending on the charge), which means that if the initial surrender charge was 7% and you cashed in after one year, you would pay a 6% surrender charge; after 2 years, you would pay 5%, after 3 years, 4%, and so on.

Compare annuities to mutual funds—Recently, companies have begun offering annuities with lower fees and better value. This has made their number one benefit—tax-deferred earnings—more attractive. However, before rushing out and purchasing one, you need to carefully consider what is, for some, a better option: a taxable mutual fund. Remember, I am operating on the assumption that you are considering an annuity because you have already fully funded your 403(b, and subsequent to that, your IRA. In comparing annuities to mutual funds, there are three main considerations:

- How long will you hold the account?
- Will you need early access to the funds?
- Are you planning to pass the money along to your heirs?

The Earnings Race—Variable annuities typically charge anywhere from 0.8% to 3% for the combination of a managed "subaccount"— basically a mutual fund—and an insurance envelope. The envelope allows your earnings to grow tax-free until withdrawal. Some insurance even promises minimum annual returns. The trouble is that this insurance comes at a price. A typical U.S. stock mutual fund will charge less than a 1% management fee. A mutual fund stock index fund will charge around only 0.4%. The added annuity fees lower your returns. Moreover, when you withdraw money from an annuity, it will be taxed as ordinary income. Withdrawals from a mutual fund, on the other hand, will primarily be taxed as capital gains. For many, the difference is significant. Someone paying 20 percent on long-term capital gains could readily end up paying 40% in combined federal and state income taxes on ordinary income. That is quite a difference—and a costly one at that!

In the end, it comes down to a foot race. Given your investment horizon and income tax rate, which will earn you more money? Given enough time, the annuity will always win. The benefit of tax-deferred earnings will overcome the burden of higher fees and taxes, but it would probably take 20 years or more. Statistics show that if $25,000 were invested in a variable annuity and an identical mutual fund, both earning 10% a year, it would take 25 years—in one typical case—before the after-tax redemption value of the annuity surpassed that of the mutual fund. That is a long time to wait for an investment vehicle that is already the third choice in the lineup.

Annuities Are For Life—If you are looking for a place to park your money, but you think you might eventually need the earnings to pay for a new home, an extended vacation, or anything else, find a good mutual fund. With an annuity, you will have to pay taxes on your earnings plus a 10% tax on any withdrawals of earnings made before 59 ½. And do not forget those hefty surrender fees if you take your money out too soon.

Annuities Are No Way to Plan for Your Heirs—Annuities are long-term investments, but you should plan on withdrawing all the money before you die. If you die with money left in your annuity, your beneficiary will have to pay state and federal taxes on any gains you made (taxed as ordinary income) during your annuity's contract life. On the other hand, with a mutual fund, the cost basis is stepped-up at death, meaning your heirs will avoid having to pay taxes on the gains. Both annuities and mutual funds are subject to estate taxes on anything over the maximum that can be passed on tax-free to children and heirs, which is $650,000 in 1999.

Finding an annuity—If you decide that an annuity is right for you, it is time to do some comparison shopping. As you are considering various annuity providers, keep the following tips and questions in mind:

> **Comparison shop at least four or five annuities**—Competition has become very stiff among the insurance companies, mutual funds families, and securities firms selling annuities—so much that variable annuities sales alone are expected to be $150 - $200 billion by the end of the year. For detailed performance figures on most variable annuities, order *Morningstar's Variable Annuities/Life Performance Report* by calling 1-800-735-0700, or by visiting their website at **www.morningstar.com**. Their reports list almost all annuities

presently on the market.

Check annuity features—Fixed or variable, life or certain, deferred or immediate, etc. Be sure to choose an annuity with investment features you really like. Some large mutual fund companies offer a no-load annuity. These annuities have no surrender charges and low insurance company charges. Since an insurance agent or broker usually guides you through a standard annuity contract, a luxury you do not get when you buy a no-load, you might consider the services of a fee-only planner to perform the service for you with a selection of no-load funds. The planner might not only explain, but screen out less desirable annuities. It would be worth the one-time fee a fee-only planner would charge.

Watch fees and expenses—Make sure you know what you are paying for. Find out what the insurance fee (often called the *mortality fee*) is. Also, find out what the management fees for the various subaccounts are. Other expenses to investigate include the surrender charge and, if you decide to buy through a broker, the commission which he or she receives for helping you make the purchase and manage the account in the future.

Ask about the number of funds—The more flexibility you have in selecting how you want to allocate your investments, the better. If only three or four subaccounts are offered, that may not suit your needs, especially if you are making a sizable commitment of, say, $60,000 or more. Ten or more choices might be more to your liking.

Make sure the subaccounts offered match your investment style—If you are looking for a balanced account, for example, you should look for annuities with subaccounts that have exemplary performance records in that particular class of subaccounts.

Check the quality of the funds—Who is the manager? What is his/her track record? Ask these and a number of other appropriate questions that you can select from the list that appears near the end of chapter 11.

Beware of clones—These are the subaccounts that are related to well-known mutual funds. Even if the subaccount has the same name and manager as the famous fund, the returns can be quite different. Look at performance and compare.

How difficult is it to transfer among funds?—Is this inexpensive and simple to do. Will it be easy to modify your annuity at a later date?

How reliable is the annuity provider?—Who stands behind the payment of the annuity?

Points to Remember

- **Contribute the maximum amounts to your other retirement plan options first**—Do not even consider an annuity until you know you will be able to make maximum contributions to all other tax-advantaged retirement plan options available to you (i.e. a 403(b) plan and an IRA).

- **The longer, the better**—Think about accumulating earnings in a low-cost annuity for a period of *at least* 8 years if you intend to cash out in a lump-sum withdrawal; longer if the annuity carries higher costs. You will need that much time to compensate for the taxes you will pay on the large lump sum. This period of accumulation can be shortened considerably if you plan on withdrawing your money as income over a number of years.

- **Look for low-cost annuities**—Remember, the higher the expenses, the longer you have to hold your annuity to reach the break-even point.

- **Look for flexibility**—Seek out annuities with a wide range of investment options to take advantage of changes in various sectors of the market.

- **Be aggressive**—If you have some time to work with, explore more aggressive investments when selecting an annuity's subaccounts, with emphasis on stocks and stock funds for their long-term growth possibilities. Capital appreciation is the only way to go because you want the account to grow at a faster rate than the expenses required to have the account. If your timeline is shorter, maybe you should consider a taxable investment instead.

- **Withdraw gradually**—If you can, withdraw your money gradually when you retire. The longer your money is in the annuity, the more you may benefit.

Take the following short quiz to help you decide if you should consider buying an annuity:

1. Are you contributing the maximum amount to a tax-deferred qualified retirement plan like a 403(b), then subsequent to that, an IRA? **YES   NO**

2. Do you want to use this money before age 59 ½? **YES   NO**

3. Are you looking for additional tax-deferred investment opportunities? **YES   NO**

4. Are you nearing retirement age and looking for a product that would pay you a guaranteed income for life? **YES   NO**

If you answered "no" to question #1, do not even think about purchasing an annuity. Fully fund the "free" retirement plans available to you first.

If you answered "yes" to both question #1 and #2, forget the annuity. Remember, with an annuity, you will have to pay taxes on your earnings plus a 10% tax on any withdrawals of earnings made before 59 ½. Also, remember there are hefty surrender charges if you take your money out too soon.

If you answered "yes" to question #1, and "no" to question #2, then "yes" to either question #3 or #4, you are a probable candidate for an annuity. Even so, it might be of benefit to you to talk the matter over with your tax consultant.

Questions and Answers

- **I am currently contributing to a 403(b) plan and I am looking for another investment vehicle. What about annuities?**—Before you invest in an annuity, be sure you are contributing the maximum to your 403(b) plan. Once you reach the 403(b) plan contribution limit, work up to contributing the maximum to an IRA, even if it is nondeductible. Why? Because with the 403(b) you are investing pre-tax money that is tax-sheltered. And at the very least, with the IRA, regardless as to which one you choose, you get tremendous tax advantages. Then, if your retirement is still a decade or more off, and you have a good lifestyle, and some extra money that you are looking to invest to supplement your retirement savings, you can consider an annuity, which is contributed to with after-tax money. Even then you need to ask yourself if you are starting at an age young enough to make the tax deferral pay. Older investors should probably buy mutual funds instead of annuities, unless they will turn the payout into an income for life.

• **I am told that there are disadvantages to owning an annuity. If that is true, then why would anyone want to purchase one?**—If you carefully analyze your retirement income needs, taking into account both a long life-expectancy and inflation, you may find that your first two lines of defense—your 403(b) plan and your IRA—will leave you short of your retirement goals. If so, than a variable annuity may be an effective way to build additional assets for your retirement on a long-term, tax-deferred basis. But take advantage of your free options first.

• **I have read that annuities are less attractive after passage of the Taxpayer Relief Act of 1997. Should I sell mine?**—No. Once you purchase an annuity, it is hard to justify getting out because of the costs involved. One of the biggest mistakes investors make is to jump in and out of investments, incurring big fees and commissions. Tax deferral does not yield benefits until you hold the annuity for around 10 years or more. And keep in mind, many of them carry heavy back-end fees that apply only when you sell them. The passage of the Taxpayer Relief Act does put more emphasis on what tax bracket you will be in when you withdraw your money from an annuity. Remember, all money withdrawn from an annuity is taxed as ordinary income. For someone in the top bracket of 39.6% who stays there after retirement, this means a *19.6%* spread over the current capital gains rate. That is a tremendous tax difference.

• **When is a good time to cash in my annuity?**—Generally speaking, you should not cash it in when you retire. Instead, take the money over several years to keep the tax shelter running longer. This improves its return, when compared with a mutual fund. You need to be aware of the fact that the annuity might not pull ahead of the break-even point until you are in late old age.

• **What does break-even point mean with regard to annuities?**—Break-even point refers to the holding period—the number of years during the accumulation phase it takes for a variable annuity's tax-deferred compounding to offset its higher costs and taxes, and its value begins to exceed that of a taxable investment with the same rate of return like, say, a mutual fund. One recent study indicated that an increase in annual annuity expenses of just one-quarter of 1% increased the break-even point by five years for investors in the 28% tax bracket, and three years for investors in the 39.6% bracket. It benefits you to pay close attention to annuity expenses. Also, because the new tax rules have lowered the capital gains rate from 28% to 20% for securities held longer than 18 months in taxable accounts, most annuities have to be held significantly longer to make up that 8% difference. This means that you should consider holding a variable annuity for *at least* 8-10 years to make it a worthwhile investment.

• **From what I have read, most annuities are purchased by older Americans. Is this true?**—The average age of annuity buyers is 52-years-old. But, it is not the age that is significant here, it is whether there is a *need* for an annuity. And, it just so happens that those investors, who reach that stage in their lives where an annuity becomes the next logical investment choice, happen to be about a decade away from full retirement. But purchasing an annuity at age 52 still gives you 33 years of tax-deferred compounding since you do not have to make your first withdrawal from most annuities until age 85.

- **Are bonds a good investment choice where annuities are concerned?**—The more of your money you put into bonds, the less likely it is that an annuity will benefit you. To take an extreme example, say that you are fully invested in short-term bonds at 6%. It would take a low-cost annuity more than 20 years to outperform a mutual fund. A high-cost annuity could take more than 30 years. You need big gains to overcome the annuity's price.

- **What can I do if I purchase an annuity then change my mind?**—All annuities offer a grace period, a few days where you can re-think your commitment. If you do not feel comfortable with your decision after a few days, by law you are allowed to exit the program without a penalty.

- **How can I find out how reliable an annuity provider is?**—Annuities are contracts with life insurance companies. That means you need to find a company with a very strong credit rating to make sure you get your future payments. You will want a company with a rating of *AA* or better. All insurance companies are rated by *A.M. Best* (908-439-2200), *Standard and Poor's* (212-208-8000), *Duff and Phelps* (312-263-2610), and *Moody's* (212-553-0377).. Any company should be glad to furnish you with its rating. If it does not, walk away. One other note: do not overlook mutual fund companies as a source of variable annuities. Some of them have set up insurance companies specifically to offer annuities.

- **Is there anything available on the market to help me decide if an annuity is right for me?**— Yes. Most companies that sell annuities will provide tools to help you analyze whether you could benefit from an annuity. One that I favor is *Fidelity's Annuity Match*. It is a simple, straightforward worksheet that takes into consideration your accumulation time frame, payout plans, and annuity expenses, and offers options based on your individual situation. You can access it at Fidelity's website at **www.fidelity.com**, or call a Fidelity annuity specialist at 1-800-544-4702.

CHAPTER 16

Liquid After-Tax Investments

As stated in Chapter 6, there is one concept that many investors forget to address when planning their retirement strategies. That is the concept of liquidity. They are so eager to make money on their investments that they overlook this most necessary component of total portfolio fitness. One should always be concerned with adequate liquidity. By liquidity, of course, I mean cash on hand or that is easily accessible—such as money invested in stocks, bonds, money market funds, CDs, etc.—that can be quickly drawn upon in an emergency.

How much should you have in a liquid account? Well, a quick rule of thumb is that you should have anywhere from three to six months' take-home pay as a liquid emergency fund. Having three months' take-home pay is acceptable, but having six months' take-home pay is safer, and in my opinion, more prudent for the average investor. Of course a more accurate—and a more time-consuming approach is to match possible emergency needs with readily available resources. The difference between these two is your liquidity need. If you need to refresh your memory, go back and review Chapter 6. It is very important to the complete investor.

I know what some of you are probably saying to yourselves right now. "I do not need a liquid investment. I will just borrow from my 403(b) if I have an emergency." You need to really think about that one. There are many sins when it comes to investing for retirement. Not putting the maximum amount you are able to put away in your 403(b) is one of the biggest. Putting a lot of money in low-yielding investments is another. But the biggest sin of all, when it comes to investing for retirement, is borrowing from your nest egg. Believe it or not, people borrow from their 403(b) plan to finance cars, boats, homes and other items. And these are not even emergency situations. There is only one word for this kind of behavior—foolish. I apologize if that statement offends anyone, but the whole point of separating your money into different pots—one for current expenses, one for your children's education, one for retirement, etc. is to give yourself the discipline to stick with a plan for the long haul. The operative word here is discipline.

Although I covered this topic more fully in Chapter 10, let me just state now that when you borrow from your 403(b) plan, you are literally mortgaging your future. I know, you would rather enjoy yourself now and worry about the consequences when you are 70. But even in the best of times, that would be foolhardy given the state of Social Security and Medicare, both of which are likely to run out of money in the not-too-distant future.

Not only that, even if you borrow from your account and plan to repay it all back within a month with no deduction at all for interest, you would be foolish. Why? Because that portion of money is not invested in wealth-building securities, which is critical to long-term performance. Most gains in the stock market occur in short periods of time. The problem is that no one ever knows when those gains will occur. What if the market goes up 10% during the month that you borrow from your 403(b)? Unlikely? Look at the monthly gains from the end of 1998 through the first few months of 1999. Compounded over time, losing that amount of growth would literally cost you tens of thousands of dollars over the long term.

In essence, borrowing on your 403(b) plan could be incredibly risky. Yet about 23% of people enrolled in 403(b) plans have a loan outstanding against their account. They face an enormous downside—possibly not being able to repay the money and, consequently, having nothing in the pot when they retire. How tragic! Try not to make that mistake.

Worthwhile liquid investments—Well then, since borrowing from your retirement plan is out, then what kind(s) of investment(s) should you consider when addressing the concept of liquidity? First of all, let me state that I am not going to recommend one specific investment type for your liquid account. I would need to make an in-depth analysis of your financial situation before I could do that. And, of course, that can not be done here. But I can give you some options to consider. It is up to you to choose what is most appropriate for your situation.

With that in mind, let us run through the list of potential candidates for the job. The list is not prioritized since each investor could have a special need for one particular investment type over another. Once again, one size does not fit all. Also, take note that the following list by no means includes all other investment types available to investors. I have only included those that, in my opinion, fit the concept of liquidity. Finally, keep in mind that my objective in this section is not to offer in-depth instruction on each investment type listed. It is simply to make you aware of the variety of alternatives and how they could possibly suit your liquidity needs. Therefore, as far as explanations are concerned, I will only introduce each of them, with the hope that you will more fully investigate any that seem to fit your individual style and objectives.

Stocks—To meet their short-term cash requirements corporations usually borrow from banks. But when corporations need long-term financing, they may sell ownership interests in the company (stocks) to the public, or borrow from the public by selling bonds. Stocks exist to enable companies in need of long-term financing to sell pieces of the business as stocks (equity securities) in exchange for cash. This is the principal method that big business uses to raise capital other than by issuing bonds. When the stocks of these corporations are owned by the public at large they are said to be publicly held. These publicly held shares can be traded (sold) to other investors in the stock market and are, in this case, known to be liquid, or readily converted to cash.

Purchasing individual stocks and bonds is a sure way to achieve liquidity in your investment portfolio, as well as growth (the stock market has returned an annual average of 10.1% to its investors over the last 70 years). Shares of stocks are traded daily in the stock market. Some advisors would caution you to stay away from stocks if you may need the money for a large purchase in the very near future, thereby reducing the risk of forced selling if the market drops. Ordinarily, when discussing your entire portfolio, that is pretty sound advice. But our strategy in this chapter is to concentrate only on a small portion of your total portfolio, that which would be used strictly for emergency needs. And let us be realistic. When an emergency strikes and you need the money yesterday, the last thing you are going to be worried about is whether your liquid fund has lost a few cents on the day's trading.

Investing in the stock market is considerably different than simply earning interest from deposits in savings institutions. The stock market poses a much greater risk, mostly because one needs to be very selective when investing in the market. Poor selection means poor results. And to be selective you need to be very knowledgeable. You must understand the dynamics of stock-market investing before attempting to test its waters. If you are not that familiar with the stock market, or if you have never invested, you would be wise to read at least one in-depth book on how the stock market operates before you even consider risking your money. There are hundreds of excellent books that have been written on the subject and can be found in any library or bookstore. As a matter of fact, almost all the financial websites on the Internet have a recommended reading section that is geared toward the individual investor. All you have to do is make a selection.

Just make sure that before you attempt investing in the stock market you become familiar with the terminology associated with the stock market; become familiar with the mechanics of stock and bond purchases; learn how to read stock quotation tables; recognize tax strategies for different investment objectives; and become aware of how brokerage fees affect your potential profits. If all of this sounds a little too intimidating, you might be interested in a very similar, but safer alternative for your liquid investment-mutual funds.

Mutual Funds—Because the stock market is so complicated, and the risk of losing money is so great for the non-professional investor, many investors turn to the logical alternative—mutual funds. With mutual funds you can purchase stocks (stock funds), bonds (bond funds), and short-term securities (money-market funds). Chapter 12 gives you everything you need to know about mutual funds in order to make prudent investments so I will not add much to the subject here. Just remember the advantages that mutual funds offer. They pool and diversify investor money to give the small investor the same diversification as the large investor, but with a fraction of the risk. There is continuous supervision of your investment by professional management at reasonable cost.

Most mutual funds have high liquidity. You can cash-in almost immediately, by mailing in a request, or even quicker, by making a phone call and requesting a redemption of your shares. Another point to keep in mind with regard to mutual funds is that their shares are acceptable collateral for a bank loan. If you do not want to sell your shares and risk losing out during a market growth spurt, you could simply borrow funds against them—a good strategy to consider. As stated in Chapter 12, mutual fund returns vary according to the type of fund you invest in. It is not uncommon to achieve an average annual growth rate of 10% or more when invested primarily in stock mutual funds.

Bonds—Unlike stocks, in which you purchase part of a company and become, in essence, part-owner, a bond is a loan you give to a company or government. You become a lender rather than an owner. This means that the company or government you lend money to has a pledge to repay the full amount of the bond including interest. This makes bonds a more stable investment vehicle than stocks, although some bonds are more stable than other bonds. Investors generally purchase bonds for their relatively safe, stable income. The issuer must pay the bondholder a fixed amount of interest periodically, and to repay the principal value of the bond on a specific maturity date.

Bonds are considered fixed-income securities (that is, they offer a steady rate of interest income), and are sometimes called *debt obligations* (since they represent a loan to the bond issuer). Bonds are priced differently from stocks, and the vast majority are traded OTC (over-the-counter). The bond market is even bigger than the stock market. Bonds are attractive to investors for two primary reasons:

1. Income—Bonds generally provide higher and steadier income than cash reserve investments such as money market funds or bank passbook accounts. Accordingly, many investors, particularly retired individuals, use bonds as the cornerstone of their investment portfolios. Unlike money market funds and passbook accounts, however, bonds will fluctuate in value as interest rates change. The current nationwide interest rate on bank loans governs the price of any bond, old or new. As with stocks, bonds on the open market are worth only what others will pay for them—more or less than par. For example, if you hold a 10-year bond paying 12% interest, and interest rates in the U.S. for bonds of similar risk rise to 14%, your $1,000 bond will drop in price to $896. Conversely, the price of your $1,000, 10-year bond will rise to $1,123 if interest rates for new money fall to 10%. This peculiarity arises from the fact that the dollar amount of interest paid on the bond is fixed when it is issued and never changes. Since the bond generates a fixed stream of income, bond buyers will bid up prices as this fixed income becomes an attractive return when compared to other interest-paying alternatives. Conversely, prices will fall as this fixed income becomes less attractive.

2. Diversity—Bonds have investment characteristics that are quite different from those of common stocks. Though sometimes volatile, bonds are often considered less risky than stocks and can serve to balance a portfolio of stocks or stock mutual funds. Here are some terms you should know when considering bond purchases.

- **Par Value**—The face value of the bond (typically $1,000) before fluctuations in the market cause it to be sold for more or less than its par value.

- **Coupon Rate**—The stated interest rate on the bond.

- **Maturity Date**—The date at which the face value and final interest payment of a fixed income security (for example, bond or note) is due and payable by the debt issuer.

- **Premium**—A bond is said to sell at a premium when the market price is greater than the par value (face value).

- **Discount**—A bond is said to sell at a discount when the market price of the bond is less than par value (face value).

Let us look at the various types of bonds, as well as their risks and rewards. There are three principal types of bonds—Corporate bonds, Municipal bonds, and U.S. Government bonds and securities. All have a high level of liquidity and are excellent collateral for loans.

Corporate Bonds—Business corporations issue IOUs called corporate bonds and notes. A corporate bond or note is simply the firm's IOU issued for a specified number of years. It is an interest bearing certificate of indebtedness. Corporations such as public utilities, railroads, and industrial firms regularly issue bonds to raise capital to finance plant expansion and new equipment. The bonds are issued by corporations in various maturities—from short-term (maturing between 1 and 5 years), to intermediate-term (maturing between 5 and 15 years), to long-term (maturing in more than 15 years).

They take the form of either *debentures*, which are backed by the general credit of the corporation, or *asset-backed* bonds (sometimes called *mortgage bonds*), which are backed by specific corporate assets like property or equipment. These bonds are usually fully-taxable, top-rated bonds that are nearly free of risk or default and have a higher yield than government bonds. Most bonds issued today are registered —that is, the name and address of the buyer are registered with the company. When the interest is due—usually every six months—the company mails a check to the bondholder.

Since the investor purchasing a bond is, unlike a stockholder, a creditor he/she has a legal claim to the company's assets prior to that of the stockholder. The bondholder's claim (interest) must be paid before stockholders can receive dividends. For this reason, a corporate bond is viewed as being less risky than the common stock of a corporation. Consequently, the returns from owning corporate bonds are lower, on average, than from a common stock investment. Corporate bonds generally have returned more, however, than government bonds of equal maturity. In the past, when the prime-interest rate was high and beginning to come down, high-quality corporate bonds and notes have paid out interest rates as high as 8% to 9.5%. At present, the average rate of return is 6.5%. High-yield bonds (i.e., *junk* bonds) pay higher interest, but have been known to lose up to 30% of their value overnight. Junk bonds are very risky, to say the least.

Tax-Exempt Municipal Bonds—At present, the average rate of return on municipal bonds is 4.2%, making them particularly attractive to those in high income brackets; these IOU bonds are issued by states, cities, towns, counties, and their agencies (port authorities, water districts, etc.). These bonds (usually referred to as *munis* or *tax-exempts*) are sold in denominations from $1,000 to $5,000, and are free of federal tax and often from state and local tax in their state of issuance. It should be noted, however, that there is a municipal issue subject to federal tax (see below). Like corporate issues, municipal bonds are categorized by the form of collateral used to back them and to raise their revenue. They are:

> **General Obligation Bonds**—Nicknamed GO bonds, they represent the largest group of municipal issues. Paid back by general revenues—secured by the government's tax revenue and its ability to impose new taxes—these bonds are only slightly less secure than similar government issues. By law, the government is required to levy taxes in order to pay its bondholders.

> **Revenue Bonds**—Used in the development of toll roads, bridges, tunnels, airports, etc., or any revenue-producing projects, these bonds are paid off by the revenue generated from the specific development. They typically offer a higher rate of interest than GO bonds, as payment is more narrowly backed.

> **Industrial Development Bonds**—These specific bonds are issued by state and local governments to fund the construction of new industrial parks or plants, or any development that might attract businesses and increase leasing revenue for the state. The financial strength of the private businesses involved in the project generally determines the quality of the bond. Most of these bonds are now taxable under the Tax Reform Act of 1986.

> **Redevelopment Agency Bonds**—Used for the construction of commercial projects, these bonds are secured by part of the property taxes levied on the development.

> **Airport Bonds**—One type of airport bond is used toward, and secured by, general opera-

tions and usage. Another riskier bond is tied specifically to facilities leased by individual airlines and is secured by the leasing contract itself.

Since newspapers and financial journals do not carry complete information on municipal bonds, current prices, and trading data, investors must turn to specific bond publications to track these issues. The bible of bond issuance, pricing, and trading is the annual publication *Moody's Municipal and Government Manual.* Organized by state, city, town, and political subdivision, the compendium lists all bond issues and offers information critical to bond buyers, from state tax revenues and census figures to statistics on attendance at local schools. Updates are published in a semi-weekly newsletter that lists new and changed issues as well as call notices.

Tax Equivalent Yield—Today, individuals hold over $41 billion dollars in municipal bonds (buying more than 1 million bonds annually). Since most municipal bonds are tax-exempt, a 6% non-taxable yield may be the equivalent to a percent anywhere from 7.06% to 9.93%, depending on your federal income tax bracket. The following table shows the Tax Equivalent Yield. Simply, this table helps you calculate what you would have to earn on a taxable investment to net the same rate of return as the tax-deferred or tax-free investment. For instance, let us say you are in the 28% tax bracket and are comparing two different investment alternatives. One is a corporate bond yielding 9.5%. The other is a tax-exempt municipal bond yielding 8%. Use the table to tell you what you will need to earn in a taxable investment to achieve the same annual growth. Find both the 28% tax rate and the 8% interest rate. You'll see that they intersect at 11.11%. This means you would need to find a taxable investment paying 11.11% to achieve the same growth rate, after paying taxes, as the tax-deferred or tax-free investment of 8%.

Tax-deferred Interest Rate	A Federal Tax Rate of:				
	15%	28%	31%	36%	39.6%
	What a taxable investment must earn during accumulation:				
2.5%	2.94	3.47	3.62	3.91	4.14
3.0%	3.53	4.17	4.35	4.69	4.97
3.5%	4.12	4.86	5.07	5.47	5.79
4.0%	4.70	5.56	5.80	6.25	6.62
4.5%	5.29	6.25	6.52	7.03	7.45
5.0%	5.88	6.94	7.25	7.81	8.28
5.5%	6.47	7.64	7.97	8.59	9.11
6.0%	7.06	8.33	8.70	9.38	9.93
6.5%	7.65	9.03	9.42	10.16	10.76
7.0%	8.24	9.72	10.14	10.94	11.59
7.5%	8.82	10.42	10.87	11.72	12.42
8.0%	9.41	11.11	11.59	12.50	13.25
8.5%	10.00	11.81	12.32	13.28	14.07

Where applicable, add the appropriate state income tax to the federal tax rate.

If you would like to do the calculations yourself, here is the formula:

Equivalent Taxable Yield	**Example**
tax-deferred rate (1 - your tax rate)	8.0 (tax-deferred rate) divided by (1 - 28%) = 8.0 divided by .72 = 11.11% (the taxable equivalent you need)

All interest rates referenced are for illustrative purposes
only and do not necessarily reflect current rates.

All interest income from tax-exempt municipal bonds is exempt from all federal and state income taxes. Also, because they are purchased (traded) through brokers or banks, you can sell them at the current market price any time prior to maturity. This gives them a high liquidity listing. Municipal bonds do, however, have lower interest rates than comparably-rated corporate bonds and U.S. government securities.

U.S. Government Bonds and Securities—U.S. Government Securities are considered the most creditworthy and safest of all debt instruments because they are backed by the full faith and credit of the U.S. government. But because of the near absence of default risk they offer lower interest rates than do corporate issues. These government IOUs—bonds, notes, and bills—differ from each other in terms of yield, denomination, and maturity. They are divided into two classes: marketable government securities—treasury bonds, treasury notes, treasury bills, agency bills; and, non-marketable government securities—E and H Series government bonds. Since we are most concerned about the level of liquidity in this chapter, I will cover only those government securities classified as marketable and can be traded in a secondary market. Government issues are actively traded on the over-the-counter market after their initial sale to large investors through an auction conducted by the Treasury. They are also exempt from state and local income taxes.

U.S. Treasury Bonds (T-Bonds)—Also known as the *long bond*, these *long-term* IOU bonds are issued intermittently, according to government needs, in denominations of at least $1,000. Like T-Notes they come in denominations of $1,000, $5,000, $10,000, $100,000, and $1,000,000 and are popular with traders and institutional investors. You can purchase new bonds through the Federal Reserve Bank and its branches. (If purchased directly from the Federal Reserve Bank or branches, there is no sales charge). Upcoming sales of the bonds are usually reported in the financial news. The Treasury usually announces new bonds about two weeks before final payment must be made. Buyers must act quickly since the bonds are sold at auction.

U.S. Treasury bonds usually mature in ten years or longer (up to 30 years) from the date of issue. Interest on these bonds is paid semi-annually. Coupons attached to the bond are clipped out and turned in for interest payments. Treasury bonds can also be purchased from the Bureau of Government Financial Operations, in Washington, D.C., 20222, through a broker, or through your local bank.

Liquidity is high for U.S. Treasury bonds since there is an active market through brokers and banks. The price of particular Treasury bonds are quoted daily in the financial news. Since these bonds are marketable, their prices fluctuate with supply and demand—similar to stocks and bonds. They are highly sensitive to interest-rate movements. At present, their average rate of return on a 30-year bond is 5.3%.

U.S. Treasury Notes (T-Notes)—U.S. Treasury notes (T-notes) are *intermediate-term* notes that are

245

sold in series maturing from one to ten years, in minimum denominations of $1,000, up to $1,000,000. Most notes are sold in $5,000 denominations. T-notes yield a steady stream of interest. You will always receive the stated interest rate on the note; however, since the price of a note will fluctuate with supply and demand, your real yield will fluctuate also. Treasury notes can be purchased from a broker or from your local bank. Since there is an active market through brokers and banks, the liquidity level is high for U.S. Treasury notes. The average rate of return on a 10-year U.S. Treasury note is 4.8%.

U.S. Treasury Bills (T-Bills)—These short-term IOU bills are sold at weekly auctions. Large institutional buyers have money to lend to the government. Insurance companies, savings and loans, and banks bid against each other, and the government sells its IOUs to that buyer who will charge the least amount of interest. Small buyers submit bids and usually accept the average interest determined by the big buyers. U.S. Treasury bills have the shortest maturation of all government securities: 91, 182, or 364 days. The minimum face value investment is $10,000, though the bills come in $5,000 multiples over $10,000. Interest is calculated as a discount from the face of the bill. No interest is paid to you. Rather, your return is the difference between the purchase price and the par value. For example, say a $10,000 Treasury bill costs you $9,400. When you cash it in at maturity, you get the full $10,000. Your return on this investment would be 8.5%—$800 divided by $9,400. Since there is an active market through brokers and banks, the liquidity level is high for U.S. Treasury bills, just as it is for U.S. Treasury bonds and notes. The average rate of return for a 6-month U.S. Treasury bill is 4.3%.

Agency Bonds and Securities—Federal government agencies, such as the Government National Mortgage Association, known as *Ginnie Mae*, the Farmers Home Administration, known as *FHA*, the Federal Home Loan Mortgage Corporation, commonly known as *Freddie Mac*, the Federal National Mortgage Association, known as *Fannie Maes*, the Export-Import Bank, the Tennessee Valley Authority, the U.S. Postal Service, and the Federal Intermediate Credit Bank (FICB) frequently finance their debts by issuing IOUs of their own. The federal government does not back all these issues, however it does authorize the above-mentioned agencies to issue debentures and notes to finance their operations. Rates and sales procedures differ widely from the other government investments. You may purchase these securities through banks or brokers (at a stated sales charge) who act as dealers for the various agencies. Price and current yields are published in the financial section of your newspaper. The average rate of return for U.S. Agency bonds and securities is 5.65% at present. As a group, these securities offer a higher rate of interest than direct U.S. Treasury obligations, even though the majority are backed by the full faith and credit of the U.S. government. Certain issues are also exempt from state and local taxes. Liquidity is high since there is an active market through brokers and banks.

· · · · · · ·

Remember, government securities are backed by the U.S. Treasury or the issuing governmental agency. Because of this, they are probably the safest investments anyone can make. Yields are usually higher than from banks and savings and loan associations, particularly during periods of "tight" money (when loan money has a high interest price tag on it). And since interest on these issues is usually exempt from local and state income taxes, you earn a yield which is, in effect, even higher. One negative to consider is that interest paid on these securities is simple annual interest. It is not compounded daily.

Finally, almost all bonds carry a letter-coded rating to indicate their relative credit quality. They are rated for quality based on: *rate of income, degree of risk,* and *cost*. The bonds are rated by key business-analyst firms such as *Moody's and Standard and Poor*. The following quality ratings were compiled by the *Moody's Investors Service*:

AAA—Judged to be the best quality, carrying the smallest degree of investment risk. U.S. Government and Agency Securities have AAA ratings.

AA—Judged to be of high quality by all standards. Together with the AAA group, they are known as *high-grade* bonds.

A—Possess many favorable investment attributes and are considered as *high, medium-grade* obligations.

BAA—Considered *medium-grade* obligations (i.e., they are neither highly protected nor poorly secured).

BA—Judged to have speculative elements (i.e., their future cannot be considered well-assured).

B—Generally lack characteristics of a desirable investment.

CAA—Poor standing; may be in default.

NR—Not Rated.

Money Market Funds—Although money market funds are included under the mutual funds umbrella, because of their unique structure I felt they should be discussed separately. Although this topic was covered in Chapter 12, I felt I should cover it briefly again, to maintain the continuity of our discussion on liquidity.

Money market funds are one of the most widely held types of mutual fund. Sold on a no-load basis, money market funds, or money funds as they are sometimes called, invest in short-term securities of credit-worthy corporations, bank obligations, debt instruments of the Federal government, and other highly liquid, low-risk securities. There are taxable and tax-free money market funds. In the taxable category there are three principal types: General Purpose Money Market Funds; U.S. Government Money Market Funds; and, Treasury Money Market Funds. There are two principal types of tax-free funds: National Municipal Money Market Funds; and Single-State Municipal Funds.

The investment holdings of money market funds are generally of exceptionally high quality. In fact, the Securities and Exchange Commission requires that all taxable money market funds invest at least 95% of their assets in securities of the highest grade, as rated by *Moody's Investors Services* or *Standard & Poor's Corporation.* So, the high quality of a money market fund's holdings also helps provide relative safety and stability.

Money market funds seek to maintain a stable net asset value (or share price) of $1.00, while providing a current level of income. You should keep in mind that while all money market funds expect to maintain a steady net asset value of $1.00 per share, there is no assurance that they will be able to do so. In addition, money market funds have a degree of credit risk. An investment in a money market is neither insured nor guaranteed by the U.S. government. Bank money market accounts, on the other hand, are guaranteed by the Federal Deposit Insurance Corporation or other government agency.

Money market funds purchase short-term securities ranging in maturity from one day to one year. However, the average maturity of a money market fund's holdings in total may not exceed 90 days. Because of this very short maturity, a money market fund's exposure to interest rate risk (that is, share price

247

fluctuations) is effectively eliminated.

The protection of principal is the primary appeal of money market funds, but along with safety, money market funds offer several other advantages. The biggest advantage, at least as far as our concerns go, is its level of liquidity—most money market mutual funds offer free checkwriting privileges, so your money is readily available to you when you need it. Typically, there is a minimum amount for checks—$250 to $500 is average. In addition, you may call the fund's sponsor and sell shares at any time, making them a perfect choice for emergency situations. The proceeds of the sale can be sent directly to your home in the form of a check or wired to your bank account. These funds also offer investors current income in the form of monthly dividends. Money fund yields are tied directly to short-term interest rates—meaning that yields and rates rise and fall in unison. Current yields range from just over 4% to nearly 5% on taxable money market funds, and about 2.5% to 3% on municipal bond money market funds.

The primary risk to a money market fund holder is inflation. Over the past 30 years, the return of U.S. Treasury bills (the virtual equivalent of returns earned by taxable money funds) has averaged 6.8% per year (its current average is 4.3%). Inflation, meanwhile, has averaged about 5.3% over the past 30 years (the current average is 1.6%). So over the last 30 years an investor's real return—after adjusting for inflation—would amount to only 1.5% (current real return would be 2.7%).

Insured Money Market Accounts (IMMA)—These highly liquid accounts combine competitive money market interest rates with the accessibility and convenience of a checking account. The IMMA is a tiered account with the interest determined by the balance in the account—the higher the balance, the greater the earnings. Interest is computed daily and credited monthly. With the IMMA, your account is easily accessed through teller transactions or by writing checks. Most accounts offer an optional ATM card, which gives you 24-hour cash access nationwide. You receive a monthly statement of your account activity and may have your Social Security, pension, or payroll check automatically deposited into your account. Insured money market accounts are guaranteed by the Federal Deposit Insurance Corporation or other government agencies and, at present, the national average rate of return for an insured money market account is 2.7%.

Certificates of Deposit—A Certificate of Deposit (CD) is a contract with a financial institution that pays a contractual rate of interest over a specified period of time (term). The term of a CD is usually 30 (the least), 60, or 90 days; 6 months; 1 year; 5 years; but can go as high as 10, 15 and 20 years (the most). Usually, the longer the term, the higher the rate of interest available. For example, at present, the average rate of interest on a 30-day CD is 4.26%. On a 3-month CD the rate is 4.61%. On a 6-month CD the current average rate of interest is 4.87%. On a 1-yr. Jumbo CD (a CD with a minimum deposit of $100,000, the average rate of return is 5.41%. And on a 20-year Jumbo CD the average rate of return at present is 6.41%.

When searching for the best rate, be prepared to do some hunting. Sometimes the best deals can be found at small institutions that do not have large branch networks or do not offer a full-range of banking services. Do check, however, to make certain that the institution carries federal insurance on deposits of as much as $100,000 per depositor. Also, when inquiring about CDs, ask whether they are Callable, or Callable-Multi-Step CDs. Callable CDs pay interest to the depositor at the contractual rate of interest over the life of the CD. In all cases, the CDs have a period of time during which they are non-callable. This means the issuing institution cannot cut short the CD and give back the deposit. At the end of the non-callable period, usually one or two years from the issue date, they may be called or redeemed for the full amount of the original deposit. There is no simple way to predict when a call will occur. However, when interest rates decline, the probability of a fixed-rate deposit being called increases significantly. Conversely, when interest rates rise, it is usually much less certain that such a deposit will be called by the issuer. Only the issuer and not the depositor may call a CD. If it is not called, it will continue to pay interest until the next call date. Issuers normally announce the exercise of their call privilege in advance.

Callable, Multi-Step CDs are CDs whose interest rates increase or decrease over their life on a predetermined schedule. There are two types of Callable-Multi-Step CDs: *Step-Up Bonus Rate* and *Step-Down Bonus Rate.* Step-Up Bonus Rate CDs' interest rate increases over the life of the CD to a high, or bonus, ending rate of interest. Step-Down Bonus Rate CDs' interest rate decreases from a high, or bonus, beginning rate to lower rates over the life of the CD. In all cases, Callable, Multi-Step CDs have a period of time which they are non-callable. At the end of the non-callable period, usually one or two years from the issue date, they may be called or redeemed for the amount of the original deposit. If they are not called (cut short), the issuer must pay the new interest rate for the next non-call period. The CDs are usually callable on each subsequent interest payment date. Like a fixed-rate Callable CD, it is difficult to project when a CD might be called. Business sense would dictate that if interest rates rise, a Step-Up CD will less likely be called. And conversely, when interest rates fall, Step-Down CDs will less likely be called. As is the case with Callable CDs, only the issuer and not the depositor may call a CD. Issuers normally announce the exercise of their call privilege in advance.

One of the best ways to get CDs is to go through a brokerage firm. There is no commission and, while you will not get the highest rates in the land, average yields on broker CDs generally beat those at most banks and savings and loans. The minimum deposit typically required for broker CDs is $1,000. Banks and savings and loans that offer the best CD rates have minimums that can be as low as $100.

Since the minimum term for a CD is 30 days, you may not want to lock your money up if you feel you might need it during that time period. However, the financial institution must give you your deposit back when you ask for it. Even if you want to withdraw your money out of a CD before it matures, you generally can do so if you are willing to pay a penalty. Before purchasing a CD, be certain you understand the penalties associated with early withdrawal. Read the find print. Also, watch out for "special deals" that banks, etc., will advertise periodically in which CDs will be offered at two or three percentage points above the average of other financial institutions. Make sure you fully understand the conditions and unique features of such offers, because some of them are really off the wall.

Finally, considering the early-withdrawal penalty associated with the CD you may be wondering why I have it listed as a worthwhile liquid investment. The answer is simply because CDs can be used as collateral to borrow against (at a nominal rate of interest) in case you need money quickly. This gives the CD a high level of liquidity.

Credit Union Accounts—An employee's credit union is a voluntary, non-profit organization of depositors (called shareholders), and borrowers from the profession. The credit union provides employees with a convenient means of saving and borrowing. Basically, employees pool their money for the benefit of each other. Credit union accounts enjoy a high liquidity level. Savings are available upon demand, and loans are much easier to arrange than at banks and at savings and loan associations.

About 50% of all types of credit unions have federal charters. The rest are state chartered. Share accounts are insured with the National Credit Union Association Share Insurance Fund (providing the credit union meets certain financial standards). Therefore, credit unions enjoy an enviable reputation for safety.

Employees may establish a payroll deduction plan, which is a convenient way to save, although the passbook accounts they offer are not the best hedge against inflation. Shareholders receive dividends which, in actual terms, is interest. The dividend rate that credit unions pay is only slightly higher than those paid by banks and savings and loan associations—currently, the national average for credit unions is 3.5%. And some unions only credit interest quarterly, which means making a withdrawal before the quarter's end could result in lost interest for that quarter.

Passbook Savings Accounts—Offered by banks and savings and loan associations, a passbook savings account is a standard savings account where interest is compounded daily and is credited quarterly on the last day of March, June, September, and December of each year. Many banks require a minimum balance in their passbook savings accounts, and will not pay interest to these accounts during the time the balance is less than the minimum (the national average is $300). Also, a monthly service charge is levied if the account balance drops below the stated minimum. Deposits and withdrawals can be made in any amount at any time, which makes the passbook savings account very liquid. Usually, automatic periodic transfers from a checking account to a passbook savings account can be arranged. At present, passbook savings account returns offer the lowest yields in the nation, averaging around 2.0%. On the plus side, the account can usually be used as collateral by a customer, such as when borrowing money for an emergency.

Collectibles—If you are a collector of gold and silver coins, art, precious stones, antiques, or old coins and stamps, you may have accumulated enough in liquid assets in the process to help out in an emergency situation. As an expert in your field, you are probably already aware of how much your collection is worth. Just be sure you are willing to part with some, or all, of it before you tag it as your sole defense in an emergency situation. And remember, it is very difficult, if not impossible, to get a quick, fair price for a collectible when you desperately need to sell an item and the potential buyer(s) are aware of that fact.

Comparing types—What follows is an Interest-Rate Comparison Chart for the current national averages of the fifteen liquid investment types highlighted in this chapter, as of the date of this publication. Although a changing market would modify these individual rates dramatically, this chart still provides you with an opportunity to see how one type of investment usually compares to another from the perspective of investment return.

Interest Rate Comparison Chart	
The 15 Liquid Investment Types	Yield Percentage
Individual Stocks	10.1%[1]
Stock Mutual Funds	10.1%
Individual Bonds	4.8%[2]
Bond Mutual Funds	4.8%
Corporate Bonds	6.2% - 6.8%
U.S. Government Agency Bonds	5.5% - 5.8%
U.S. Treasury Bonds	5.2% - 5.5%[3]
U.S. Treasury Notes	4.6% - 5.0%[4]
Money Market Mutual Funds	4.3% - 4.9%[5]
U.S. Treasury Bills	4.2% - 4.5%[6]
Municipal Bonds	4.1% - 4.3%[7]
Certificates of Deposit	4.2% - 4.5%[8]
Credit Union Savings Accounts	3.3% - 3.7%
Money Market Accounts	2.5% - 2.9%
Bank Passbook Savings Accounts	1.8% - 2.1%

[1]Historical average from 1926-1996. [2]Historical average from 1926-1996. [3]30-yr. bonds. [4]10-yr. notes. [5]Taxable funds; tax-exempt funds average 2.5%-3%. [6]6-month bills. [7]10-yr. tax-exempt GO bonds. [8]30-day rate.

Finally, I want to address a common concern with regard to liquid accounts. Many people fear losing out on valuable growth when invested in a liquid fund, considering that statistics show that, since 1926, bonds and cash securities have only returned 4.8% and 3.7%, respectively. And a 3.7% return barely accounts for the ravages of inflation. Growth is a valid concern, but you must remember that with a liquid account your primary goal is to be, well, liquid—having cash or cash equivalents that you can use right away in case of an emergency. I am not suggesting that the growth issue should not be addressed, it is just that with this very narrow strategy, it should not be a primary concern. With that in mind, I will conclude by stating that if growth is still a nagging issue with you when dealing with the concept of liquidity, then you should keep one fact uppermost in you mind—on average, since 1926, stocks have beaten the competition by a huge margin—returning a 10.1% average over the 70-year period. And remember, if the idea of investing in the stock market is enough to give you chest pains, there is always the alternative, the do-it-yourself investor's best friend—mutual funds (stock funds, bond funds, and money market funds).

CHAPTER SEVENTEEN

Countdown to Retirement

During most of your working life, it is natural to think of retirement as a final goal. But, when you begin to approach the age at which you can finally retire, you will start to realize that retirement is really the beginning of a new phase of your life. A phase that could last 20 to 30 years. Hopefully, your retirement goals are both time—and dollar-specific. But no matter how carefully you have been planning your retirement finances through the years, once you get within 4 or 5 years of retirement you should stop and review some of the factors that could make or break your retirement. The quality of your daily life during your retirement will depend in large part on several far-reaching decisions you must make when you are still 4 or 5 years out.

Some of these decisions, like the payment method you select for taking distributions from your 403(b) plan and other retirement accounts, are irrevocable. Other choices will have a greater effect on your finances than you may now realize. For example, where you choose to live in retirement will determine your cost of living and, by extension, your investment allocation in retirement because your ability to live comfortably will depend on whether your nest egg earns enough money to meet your expenses. In addition, your life insurance needs will probably change. The point is that you will not be able to make informed choices at retirement unless you have taken the time to study the pros and cons of the many options that will be available to you on your official retirement date.

When you are about 5 years away—When your retirement date is about 5 years away, there are some important issues you should be thinking about. Be sure to consider the following very carefully:

1. **Refigure how much you will need**—Go back and complete another "cash flow" and "retirement savings worksheet." This is crucial. This exercise will tell you just how wide you are of the mark. If it turns out, after completing the worksheets again, that you are seriously short of the total capital you will need to accumulate before you retire, then you still have some time to do something about it, including postponing your retirement for a little while.

2. **Adjust your plan to meet with reality**—If you do have a shortfall, and it is major, you

have some real decisions to make with concern to current investments. If you have been consistently following a plan, you had better find out what went wrong with it and make some changes. More likely, though, you will find yourself short by a manageable amount that you might be able to make up over the next five years. In this case you have a couple of options. They include:

- **Accelerate your 403(b) contributions**—Do this to the fullest extent if you have not done so already.

- **Open and contribute the maximum to an IRA**—Even if your contribution is not tax-deductible.

- **Increase other savings**—If you have not been saving all your raises, then start. If your kids are through college, and your house is paid off, you are probably spending more and more money on things you can really do without— things like longer vacations, a more expensive wardrobe, a more expensive car (or two), more frequent trips to expensive restaurants, etc. You know where the fat is. Trim it. Then invest all of it.

- **Check your life insurance**—The important issue here is that your greatest need for life insurance may have passed, yet you may be paying high premiums that are being at least partly wasted. Ask yourself a few questions. Are your children grown and out of the home? If you were to die, would your spouse and other dependents be financially secure without the proceeds of your insurance? If so, then you are overinsured. Cut the insurance and invest the savings. You may still want to carry some coverage, but it probably will not have to be as much as when you were still building your wealth and your family was in a vulnerable financial state. Never cancel or change a policy without checking with your doctor and having a thorough physical. If there is a medical reason, you may want to keep insurance you otherwise would not have needed.

- **Invest more aggressively**—This could be a little risky when you are so close to retirement, but if you have not followed an "aggressive-growth", or at least a growth portfolio model over the years and you find yourself short of the mark, then your investments are probably invested in securities that have been too conservative. However, if you do decide to invest more aggressively because you have fallen behind, then I would suggest that, at this stage of the game, you consider hiring a professional to help bail you out. Since time is limited, it is too easy to turn a bad situation into a much worse one if your catch-up investing is done without the utmost care. If you do decide to hire a professional planner, hiring a highly recommended fee-only planner is probably your best bet. A commission planner may be far too tempted simply to dump your poor-performing investments in favor of ones that will bring him/her commissions. And the temptation to sell you financial products you simply do not need—like costly life insurance, annuities, long-term-care insurance, etc., might be equally irresistible.

3. Pay off your mortgage—If you have not already paid off your house (or second house), then consider making extra payments against any outstanding balance on your mortgage. Eliminating the mortgage by the time you reach retirement is one sure way to lower your future cost of living.

4. Pay off your credit card(s)—Make a major effort to pay off any large, outstanding balances on your credit cards. Most people do not realize what a good investment this is. Paying off credit card debt is an excellent way to increase your disposable income. If your credit card debt costs 18%, for example, paying it off has the same effect on your income stream as putting your money into a no-risk investment that pays an 18% after-tax return!

5. Review your asset allocation—Even if you are on target with your investments, you should reassess your asset allocation to see if you are well-positioned to meet any major expenses that you expect to coincide with your retirement. You want to be able to cover these expenses without having to sell shares in a stock or bond fund whose value might be temporarily depressed, forcing you to take a loss. This may be a good time to increase your allocation to a less volatile part of your portfolio. Also, you should take some time to check your overall asset allocation splits. You would be amazed at how far an investment strategy can drift off its original course. Here is what you should do:

- Put together all of your investments, those inside your 403(b), IRA, annuities, Keoghs, savings plans, and any bank and brokerage accounts you have. Leave nothing out.

- Go back to your basic allocations and see how your current allocations differ from your original plan.

- Make any necessary adjustments by adding to, or subtracting from, those asset classes that have grown out of balance with your original allocations.

- Do not forget to do this every year from now on.

6. Decide where you will live—As pointed out earlier, deciding where you will live in retirement will have a huge impact on your cost of living and how you will allocate your assets to meet those costs. Although most people stay in the home they have lived in during their work lives, more and more people are looking into retiring to a different part of the country where living expenses could be much higher. Actually, many retirees decide to purchase a second home in a favorite vacation spot. While this is the most expensive way to go, many retirees do it with an eye to eventually giving up the homestead and making the second home their full-time retirement home. Whatever your decision, it will involve considerable variations in costs. You should work these costs out as closely as you can, far in advance, so that you will know what you can and cannot afford when the day of retirement comes.

7. Check your health insurance options—Will your employer continue to insure you after you retire? Probably not. But many employers will allow their retirees to purchase

255

health insurance coverage at the employer's group rate until they become eligible for Medicare. Find out what your situation will be before retirement creeps up on you.

8. Meet with your benefits people—Now is the time to get an assessment on the size of your pension. It is important that you know these numbers early so you can calculate your retirement finances in a more and more detailed way as you get closer to retirement. It is a mistake to wait until near the very end to talk to your benefits department, because there are almost certainly topics you don't know enough about that will substantially affect your retirement finances.

9. Check your spouse's benefits too— Now is the time to find out if your spouse's post-retirement benefits are going to be a lot better than yours. If so, you may want to enroll in your spouse's plan before you retire so that you will be able to share in those additional benefits after you both are retired.

10. Check with Social Security—If you follow my suggestion in chapter 2, by the time you reach retirement age you will have received an official estimate of your future benefits about every 5 years. But, since now is the right time to review everything it would be wise to make that call again and get a completely up-to-date projection of your Social Security benefit. Call toll-free (800) 772-1213, or contact their website at **www.ssa.gov**, and request Form SSA-7004-PC. This form will give you estimates for Social Security retirement, and for disability and survivor benefits as well.

11. Run through a series of "what-if" scenarios—In order to plan for the unexpected, it pays to do a little exercise called *what-if planning*. For example, what if you move to your dream spot to live only to discover that you miss home so much you wish you would have never moved in the first place. (Answer: try renting there first). What if your spouse dies soon after retirement? What if you decide to forego the traveling you planned to do in order to help pay for your grandchildren's college education? What if you actually hate not working? The whole purpose of this type of exercise is to help develop an intelligent plan to work with if different elements work their way into your original plan.

When you are about 6 months away—The final day is almost here. But before it comes there are a few things you will need to review carefully and deliberately. It has taken what seems like an eternity to get here, so make sure it was worth the wait. Here are some last minute issues that demand your attention:

1. Go back and complete yet another retirement savings worksheet—It is time to total up all of the saving and investing you have done over the years and compute a final figure which will show how close you are to your goal. The figures you entered on your worksheet before were just rough estimates. Now they will be more accurate than ever. If your asset allocations have been commensurate with your investment objectives, then you should be very close to your goal.

2. Take out a reverse-mortgage—If you find yourself short of the mark with your retirement money, you can implement a strategy that will supply you with income to take the place of that missing cash. It is called a *reverse-mortgage*. A reverse mortgage is basically a home equity loan. Generally, to qualify for a reverse-mortgage, one of the spouses must be at least 62, and the mortgage must be paid off. It can be a lifesaver for retirees who see that they are short of money, or who find themselves running out of money too soon.

Here is how it works: you take out a loan at a certain rate. In return you receive a monthly check for a specified amount, say $800. Depending on the terms of the mortgage, you will receive that monthly check for as long as you live in your home, or for a specified number of years. With a reverse-mortgage you are actually giving yourself a second pension which is tied to the value of your house. It is kind of a reversal of the standard mortgage. Instead of you sending the bank a monthly check, they send one to you. In return for your monthly check, you give the lender part or all of the value of your home including a percentage of the price appreciation that occurs during the term of the mortgage. The money you receive is tax-free because it's considered a loan, not income. And it will not affect your eligibility for Social Security and other federal programs. At the term's end, or when you move or die, the loan must be repaid to the lender, usually by selling your home.

As already stated, in essence, you gradually sell the equity in your home to the bank. But do not worry—you are not going to have to eventually find another place to live. You can avoid that danger by taking out a *tenure* reverse-mortgage. This type of reverse-mortgage supplies you with monthly checks for the rest of your life. The alternative, the *term* reverse-mortgage, runs for a set time, usually no more than 25 years. After that time, the bank sells the house. Of course, with the term reverse-mortgage, the older you are, the more you get in your checks.

Reverse-mortgages are not for everyone, and some types can be downright dangerous. Before you make a decision about reverse-mortgages, contact the National Center for Home Equity Conversion (NCHEC), an independent, non-profit organization that educates consumers about reverse-mortgages. For more information, visit the NCHEC's website at **www.reverse.org**.

3. Talk to your benefits personnel again—Not only do you want to notify them of your planned retirement date, you will want to go over a number of complicated issues related to your actual retirement. For instance, you will want the final numbers on your pension, an explanation on what benefits you may lose, which ones will be cut back, and which ones, if any, will stay in place. You should also arrange a second meeting to handle the questions that you will undoubtedly have from the first "final" meeting.

4. Arrange to get covered—As indicated earlier, you will need to arrange health insurance if your employer will not allow you to stay on the group plan at your expense. Since Medicare will not be available to you until you are 65, you may be responsible for the entire bill for your health care coverage until then. Of course, you will know what your options will be at this point. It is up to you to get the necessary coverage in time to make a smooth transition from your employer's plan. Your group life insurance will likely end when you retire, also. Although you may not need any life insurance coverage at all at this point, you may want to keep some in case of a medical emergency. See *check your life insurance* under the previous section *adjust your plan to meet with reality* in this chapter).

5. Decide how to receive your retirement income—Will it be a lump sum or an annuity? Your choice between the two will be contingent upon your strengths and weaknesses as a money manager. Since most of the entire next chapter is devoted to helping you make that choice, I will not spend any more time on it here.

6. Re-allocate your assets—Experts agree that investors should begin to weigh their options about re-allocating their retirement income generally about six months prior to retirement. I will also cover this strategy in detail in the following chapter.

7. Arrange for a home-equity line of credit—Hopefully, by now you have paid off all, or at least most, of your personal debt. That is bound to make you feel good about your financial situation. But keep something in mind. Emergencies may still arise, and you may need to borrow money. And even though your credit record is probably exemplary, lenders may be a lot less eager to let you borrow for that emergency once you are retired and your income has shrunk substantially. To overcome that potential problem, simply set up a home-equity line of credit while you are still working. You can draw on it any time you want and take out as much as you want without having to go through the standard credit routine. And remember, not only is the interest far lower than that on credit cards, it is also fully deductible.

8. Make a decision about Social Security—You should apply for Social Security benefits several months before you want the checks to start. Give yourself enough lead time to get things moving so that you will not miss any checks. As stated in chapter 2, the longer you wait to draw on Social Security, the more money you will receive in each check. Most experts say that statistically, you are better off waiting until you can collect 100% of your benefit. It is true that if you start at 62, you will collect benefits for a few extra years. But by the time you are in your mid-70s, you will have collected about the same total amount, whether you started at 62, 65, or 66. And, thereafter, you will collect more if you are eligible for 100% of your benefit. That could mean a substantial amount of money, because today the average Social Security recipient lives well into his or her 80s. On the other hand, if drawing Social Security when you first become eligible allows you to continue to leave your retirement money grow untouched for a longer time, it might be to your advantage to do so.

If you and your spouse are both eligible for Social Security benefits, you should calculate every possibility before deciding on what makes the most sense. Check your telephone book for the Social Security agency's local office and call and make an appointment. They will be more than willing to help you with these calculations.

9. Start looking for a job—I know, I know. No, I am not crazy. I realize that *most* of you have worked your whole life to get to the point where you no longer *have* to work. But not everyone will enjoy having leisurely days off with nothing pressing to do. Not everyone will be satisfied with traveling, gardening, or hitting the links. If that is what you want, congratulations. It is yours. But some people actually *want* to keep busy by working. Many retirees still want to work, but do not want to have to keep the same rigid schedule they had to keep for so many years. A part-time job, where the worker can choose his/her hours, is just what a lot of retirees want and look forward to. The point is, if you are interested in looking for part-time work to help round out your time, you should start looking about six months before you are due to retire. Give yourself some time to find that job.

Remember though, if you are receiving Social Security and you decide to work part-time, your part-time earnings could affect your benefits. You can continue to work and still get all of your Social Security benefits as long your earnings are under certain limits. These limits increase each year as average wages increase. In 1999, the earnings limits are $9,600 for people under age 65 and $15,500 for people age 65 through 69. Earnings in or after the month you reach age 70 will not affect your Social Security benefits. If your earnings go over the limit, some or all of your benefits will be withheld. Here is how it works:

- **If you are under age 65**—Social Security will deduct $1 in benefits for each $2 you earn above $9,600.

- **If you are age 65 through 69**—Social Security will deduct $1 in benefits for each $3 you earn above $15,500.

At the beginning of each year, anyone under age 70 who expects to exceed the earnings limit should report that fact to Social Security. Estimate how much you are likely to earn. Your monthly check will be adjusted accordingly. The following year, at tax time, you will have to report your earnings to Social Security as well as to the IRS. You can send in Form SSA-777 (available from any Social Security office) or a letter with a copy of your tax return or W-2.

If you retire and start collecting Social Security and then decide to start working again, you have the option of temporarily halting your Social Security benefits. You can resume them again later, with a recalculated retirement age that might entitle you to collect an even bigger amount.

CHAPTER 18

Reaping the Rewards—How to Handle
the Biggest Wad You Will Ever Own

Finally, it is here, my friend, what you have worked your whole life for—retirement. If you have followed a plan that was carefully laid out and implemented from start to finish, you probably have an account that contains a pile of cash that is big enough to choke the largest of horses. But, as mentioned in the previous chapter, you still have some real planning to do in order to hold on to all of that money. There is a relative of yours who has been waiting patiently for a very long time to get a large chunk of that cash. His name is Uncle Sam. Somehow you have to extract your money in a way that puts most of the money in your pocket and the least in his.

Uncle Sam is a very picky uncle. Withdraw money before you turn 59 ½, and he wants an extra 10% on top of your regular taxes. Take out too much in a year, and he will slap you with a 15% excise tax. Take out too little after age 70 ½, and you are hit with a 50% penalty. And if you die with too much money in your accounts, he will burn your heirs with a 15% penalty on the so-called excess accumulation, on top of the income taxes they have to pay. (The entire next chapter is devoted to help you with the last concern).

No, the extraction of your retirement money is not a simple process. There are many considerations worth reviewing. Fortunately, buried deep within the voluminous U.S. tax code are a few strategic ways to help ease the burden of your decision-making. But before we cover these strategies I would like to emphasize a very important point. When extracting your retirement money you must negotiate some absurdly complicated tax rules, and many of the decisions you face are irreversible once made. Make a mistake and you are stuck with it for the rest of your life. With that in mind, be warned: just as you would not attempt to scale Mount Everest without a knowledgeable guide, you should not try to develop a retirement savings withdrawal strategy without some experienced help. If ever there is a time when it pays to get professional help with your finances, this is it. If you want to pick your own mutual funds or fill out your own tax return, fine. But trying to pick a retirement withdrawal strategy without the help of a trained professional is like trying to perform brain surgery on yourself. Do not do it.

The information that follows is not intended to take the place of professional counsel. My sole intent is to provide a broad overview of the topic, so that you can be better prepared to meet with professional advisors.

Withdrawal Options—Remember, when cashing in on your retirement your primary purpose is to convert your retirement money into a stream of income that will cover your living expenses in retirement and last as long as you do. But before you pull that money out there are two absolutely essential questions that you will need to answer:

1. Should I take a lump sum, an annuity, an installment (if permitted), or leave it where it is?

2. If I take a lump sum, should I pay tax on it right away at a favorable rate, or roll my money over into an IRA?

As promised in chapter 10, we will take a closer look at each option. Remember, options vary from one investment company to another, and from one plan to another.

Leaving It Where It Is—You could leave some, or all, of the money in your 403(b) plan if the company permits but you must have a minimum balance in your account to do this. This choice makes sense if you like the investments available in the plan and the plan rules permit withdrawals that are frequent enough to meet to your needs. Also, leaving your money where it is has no immediate tax consequences, and you can always roll the money into an IRA at a later date (see *Rolling it Over* which follows in this chapter). Remember though, the federal government will allow you to put off paying taxes on this money only for so long.

Taking Installments—Some companies will pay you a specific monthly amount over a ten-or-fifteen year period. You pay taxes on the money only as it is distributed. If you die before collecting all of your money, your heirs receive any balance remaining in your account.

Installment plans have their own built-in drawbacks, however, including possible restrictions on how you can invest your money and whether you can change your mind once the installments start. Even if the plan allows you to direct your own investments, you will still be stuck with your 403(b)'s investment menu. Also, if you take an installment payment from your plan and do not withdraw the remaining lump in the same calendar year, you have forever blown the chance to use *tax averaging* to lower your tax bill should you later need to get at your money all at once. (Tax averaging is explained in this chapter).

There are other inherent risks as well when choosing installments as an option: If you elect annual installments of less than 10 years, 20% of each distribution is automatically withheld; plan assets are no longer eligible to be rolled over to an IRA or transferred to a new employer's plan; the value of your fixed installment payments will be eroded by inflation; and, you may outlive your money.

Annuitizing Your Retirement Money—Here is something to think about. You receive a huge chunk of cash that must finance the rest of your—and maybe your spouse's—life, and you alone are responsible for investing it all. If the very mention of this frightens you, you might be better off choosing an annuity instead of a lump-sum distribution. Even if you know a fair amount about personal finance and have been a reasonably successful investor over the years, being out there on your own is different when you do not have your regular job to fall back on. And if the responsibility of managing all of your retirement money makes you feel a little nervous now, imagine how you will feel after you are retired and have less to occupy your mind. You will probably worry even more. How will you feel when the stock market is misbehaving?

A few sleepless nights, now, might well turn into months of sleepless nights. You might also want to consider how meticulous you will be, as you get on in years, in tending your portfolio. In short, the best thing about an annuity is peace of mind. Period.

Some companies give you the option of taking a 403(b) payout in the form of a lifetime annuity. If your company does not offer to annuitize your 403(b), do not worry. There is nothing to prevent you from taking a lump-sum payout and buying a contract yourself. To do that, simply roll over your 403(b) money into an *immediate* annuity).

To annuitize, the company will typically purchase an annuity contract from an insurance company with the money in your 403(b). The annuity then pays a monthly benefit for your lifetime alone or, if you choose a joint-and-survivor annuity, for your lifetime and your spouse's. The chief attraction of an annuity is peace of mind. You do not have to worry about managing your money in your waning years. Your money will never give out before you do because even if you live well past your life expectancy, the insurer is obliged to keep cutting checks until you die.

The contract offering the most generous monthly checks is known as a *single-life* annuity. It may make sense to choose this option if your spouse has a pension of his or her own. The size of the check is determined by the sum your are annuitizing, the level of interest rates when you start the annuity, and your life expectancy. The law, however, requires companies to give married participants a *joint-and-survivor* annuity, unless the spouse waives his or her right to it in writing. If you choose a joint-and-survivor annuity, you will receive a smaller monthly benefit, typically 10% to 15% smaller than from an annuity covering you alone, but it is guaranteed to last for two lifetimes—yours and your spouse's.

The advantage of an annuity is that it provides a guaranteed lifetime benefit. The disadvantage is that, because it is a fixed benefit, its purchasing power will be steadily eroded by inflation each year. When you take into consideration the fact that a 4% annual rise in consumer prices would halve the purchasing power of a fixed annuity check in about 18 years, you might consider investing some of your money in an annuity, and investing the balance for growth. Of course, if you took the money in a lump sum and invested it intelligently you should be able to make your money grow fast enough to keep you ahead of inflation. That is where the unquestioned charm of the lump-sum comes in. The lump-sum option is covered in more detail in the discussion that soon follows.

It should be noted that the people who sell insurance often urge retirees who are trying to choose between a single life and a joint-and-survivor annuity to take the larger, single life benefit and use the extra income it provides to buy a life insurance policy on the retiree. They explain that when the retiree dies, the survivor can use the life insurance policy proceeds to buy another annuity to replace the terminated pension income. That scenario is called *pension maximization*, or *pension max*. Unfortunately, pension max typically does not allow for the taxes you will owe on the extra life income or for future interest rate changes that unexpectedly may increase the cost of the insurance policy down the road, maybe forcing you to drop it and leave your spouse unprotected. People who buy into the pension max strategy very often wind up with less income than if they had stuck with a joint-and-survivor benefit.

If you are trying to decide which is better for you—a joint-and-survivor annuity or a single-life annuity plus a life insurance policy—you owe it to yourself and to your spouse to get a reliable *after-tax* comparison between these two options from a tax professional who has no vested financial interest in your decision.

Taking It All In A Lump Sum—If you do not need the money right away and you can meet your needs with money from other sources, including investments in taxable accounts or income from a part-time job, your best move is to leave your tax-deferred savings untouched as long as possible. Why? Any distribution you take from such retirement plans will be taxed as ordinary income, whereas money from other parts of your portfolio may include relatively lightly taxed capital gains or even nontaxable returns of capital. By taking money from those sources, you are using funds that are taxed at lower rates. Equally important, waiting to tap your tax-deferred accounts allows your nest egg to keep building without being taxed. Over time, there is no better way to help your money grow. To be considered a lump-sum distribution for tax purposes, the following must apply:

- The money must come from an IRS-qualified plan, such as a 403(b), etc.

- It must be payable due to separation from service, death, disability, or after you have reached 59 ½.

- You must receive the entire amount in your account within one tax year.

There are a couple of ways to handle a lump-sum distribution, each with its own tax ramifications. Here is a short overview of the alternatives:

Take all of your money and pay the taxes—This may be an option to consider if the lump-sum is small or if you have a pressing need for the money to pay unexpected bills, tuition, a mortgage, etc. The fact that real wages have been waning in buying power for a couple of decades does not make it any easier to resist the temptation to take the money and run. Actually, more often than not, retirees succumb to the temptation to take a lump-sum distribution in cash instead of rolling it over. In 1996, almost 60% of retiring employees opted to receive their funds directly.

The first problem you have to deal with if you withdraw your 403(b) balance all at once is sneaking that pile of cash past Uncle Sam without losing most of it. The reality is that you will lose a large chunk of that money immediately to taxes. And in most cases, we are talking about a lot of money. It is not uncommon for 403(b) accounts to grow to $500,000 to $1,000,000 or more in a 25- to 30-year work life. That is a large pile of jing by anyone's standards. And, you lose the benefit of tax deferral unless you reinvest the money in a tax-favored investment such as a tax-exempt mutual fund or a tax-deferred annuity, which means any future earnings on the remaining balance, if invested, will be taxed as they are earned.

In 1996 Congress voted to suspend the limit on how much you can take out of your account, penalty-free, until the end of the decade, however, it will be revived January 1, 2000. Previously you got hit with a 15% excise tax on every dollar you withdrew above the limit, which this year would have been $160,000, or $800,000 if you emptied the balance.

Tax Averaging—Under current tax law, you may get a special break when the lump sum comes from a 403(b) or a rollover IRA (you can not average when you pull money out of a Traditional IRA)—you can often lower the applicable tax rate by using a calculation called tax averaging. The government gives you a tax break by allowing you to figure your tax as if you had received your lump-sum over a 5 or 10-year period. Although you still must pay the total tax liability in the first year (see note), your tax savings could be substantial. Generally, the larger your lump-sum distribution, the less you save in taxes.

To be eligible, you must have participated in the *qualified* plan for a minimum of five years before the year of distribution; you must have reached age 59 ½; you must apply tax averaging to your entire distribution and to all other lump-sum distributions received in the same tax year; and, you must not have used averaging before (unless it was prior to 1986)—this is a one-time only election.

A common misconception with 5 or 10-year averaging is that the tax on a distribution can be paid over a 5 or 10-year period. This is incorrect. The total tax must be paid in the year you get the payout. Tax averaging simply allows you to figure your tax *as if* you had received your lump-sum over a 5- or 10-year period. Spreading out the amount in this fashion drops you into lower brackets than you otherwise would have to face. Consult your tax advisor for an explanation of how 5- or 10-year averaging may be beneficial to you. Here is how it works:

- If you were born before January 1, 1936 you may use either a 5 or 10-year averaging formula. If you participated in the plan before 1974, some portion of your distribution may qualify for a flat 20% capital gains tax rate. If you use 5-year forward averaging you are taxed at today's rates. With the 10-year option, you will have to pay 1986 tax rates, which are significantly higher. Therefore, if you are pulling out more than $400,000 in a single pop, 5-year averaging is preferable. If the withdrawal is smaller, the 10-year strategy is probably a better choice.

- If you were born after December 31, 1935, and are at least 59 ½, you are currently eligible for 5-year averaging. Pre-1974 capital gains treatment is not available to you. The chart that follows illustrates how tax averaging can save you tax money.

Size of Lump-SumDistribution	Tax Liability on a Lump-Sum Distribution Under These Tax Options		
	Take 5-Year Averaging	**Take 10-Year Averaging**	**Do Nothing - Pay Ordinary Income Tax**
$100,000	$ 15,000	$ 14,470	$ 27,304
$200,000	$ 41,215	$ 36,920	$ 62,554
$300,000	$ 69,950	$ 66,330	$101,254
$400,000	$100,950	$102,600	$140,854
$500,000	$131,950	$143,680	$170,554

Assumptions—The taxpayer is married, files jointly with spouse, and has taxable income of $25,000 in addition to the retirement distribution.

Five-year lump-sum averaging will not be available for distributions beginning after December 31, 1999, but 10-year averaging and pre-1974 capital gains treatment will continue to be available to persons who turned 50 prior to January 1, 1986. There are many rules and restrictions on tax averaging. If you think you qualify for either 5 or 10-year averaging, you may want to ask your tax advisor to get IRS Form 4972, which can be used to compute your tax both ways to see which tax option would be most advantageous to you.

Having the opportunity to take your money out in a lump-sum and pay a substantially lower tax on it than you would normally owe is a big advantage. However there is one glaring disadvantage—after you have taken the lump-sum distribution, your money is no longer in a tax-deferred retirement account. That means that the only way to avoid tax on any future earnings is to invest it in tax-exempt instruments which traditionally pay a much lower return than stocks and most bonds.

Before discussing IRA rollovers, there are two special (and very rare) IRS averaging breaks that you should be aware of. The first one, known as the *minimum-distribution allowance*, is nothing short of amazing. If your lump-sum is less than $70,000, part of it is tax-free. Half of the first $20,000 is exempt. Above that amount, the tax-free element phases out. At $30,000, $8,000 is tax-free; at $40,000, it is

$6,000; at $50,000, it is $4,000; at $60,000, it is $2,000; and at $70,000 or more, the exemption is zero. The second averaging break I briefly mentioned earlier. If you were born before January 1, 1986, and earned some of your retirement benefits before 1974, then part of your distribution can be treated as a capital gain, with a favorable 20% tax rate. Compare that to current income tax rates of up to 39.6%. Be sure to check it out.

Rolling It Over—One of the most important terms people receiving lump-sums can learn is *rollover.* A rollover permits you to postpone paying any tax on your lump-sum until you withdraw it. It is a lump-sum distribution which is transferred or rolled over from one employer's qualified retirement plan to another plan or to a *rollover IRA* (sometimes called a conduit IRA) within 60 days. Qualified retirement plans include 403(b)s, 401(k)s, and Pension and Profit sharing Plans. An IRA, or any portion of an IRA, can also be rolled over into another IRA within the 60-day limit. A rollover IRA is not subject to the $2,000 restriction, and you can put your money into one, two, or more IRAs, if you like.

There is a very important difference between a rollover IRA and a regular IRA: a rollover IRA contains only money that originally came from a 403(b) plan, a 401(k) plan, or other qualified pension plan. Remember, if you roll your money over into an IRA, be sure to establish a special *conduit IRA.* It makes record keeping easier and if you do not mingle the funds from your lump-sum distribution with any other funds, you may have the option of one day transferring those funds to another employer's plan if ever you want/need to.

Instead of a Traditional IRA, many people want to consider a Roth IRA as their rollover vehicle. While the government does not allow you to convert assets from a qualified retirement plan directly to a Roth IRA, you can rollover an eligible distribution to a Traditional IRA and then convert that IRA to a Roth IRA.

A rollover is a way to keep your retirement money doing what it was meant to do—working and growing to help provide you with a financially comfortable retirement, while putting off taxes until you need to make withdrawals. By "rolling over" qualified distributions, you can defer paying federal income tax on the distribution. Plus any income, dividends or capital gains earned on the distribution can continue to accumulate tax-deferred. Rollovers let retirement money keep its tax-deferred status until withdrawals begin.

The Direct Rollover—Once you decide to roll your distribution over, you must then decide whether the rollover will be a *direct rollover* (also known as a *trustee-to-trustee transfer*) or an indirect rollover. A direct rollover is the direct sponsor-to-sponsor (or trustee to trustee) transfer of a qualified distribution from your employer's qualified retirement plan to your IRA or new employer's retirement plan (if you are simply changing jobs). *You do not touch the money.* You let the two employers or the two financial institutions transfer the money for you. Let us say you want to transfer your 403(b) or IRA funds from one mutual fund family to a new fund with a different family. Call up the new family and let the new fund contact your old family and handle the transfer.

According to the IRS, a direct rollover may be accomplished by any reasonable means of direct payment, including a wire transfer or the mailing of a check to the eligible retirement plan. If the payment is made by wire transfer, the wire transfer must be directed only to the trustee of the eligible retirement plan. If payment is made by check, the check must be negotiable only by the trustee of the eligible retirement plan and should be addressed as follows: "(Name of the trustee) as trustee of (name of eligible retirement plan)." For example, if the name of the IRA is *IRA of John Doe* and the name of the trustee is *ABC Investments*, the payee line of the check should read "ABC Investments as trustee of IRA of John Doe." If the plan is not an IRA, the payee line of the check need not identify the trustee by name and may read "Trustee of the 403(b) plan for benefit of John Doe."

When you make a direct rollover, no money is withheld for taxes and you do not have to remember to write a check to reinvest it. (Remember, only a Traditional IRA can be used for rollover contributions from employer plans. A Roth IRA is not eligible to receive rollover contribution from employer plans). Here is something else to remember. If you do not request a direct rollover, the company is required by law to withhold 20% of the amount distributed for federal taxes. You must roll over the remaining 80% within 60 days or else it becomes subject to tax and may be subject to a 10% early distribution penalty. In addition, you must replace from your own money the 20% withheld by the company and roll it over to an IRA within the same 60 days. If you do not roll it over within this time, it is also subject to tax and may be subject to a 10% early distribution penalty as well. For example, if you have a $300,000 lump-sum distribution, the amount you receive will only be $240,000 ($300,000 less the 20% withholding of $60,000, which will be sent to the IRS). Thus, you will only have $240,000 to rollover. If you do not happen to have $60,000 lying around and you do not come up with it and put it into the IRA, then that $60,000 will be considered a taxable distribution, even though part of it may be refunded to you when you file your tax return. And, if you received your distribution before you are 59 ½, it probably will be subject to a 10% early distribution penalty as well.

To avoid tax hassles and lost investment returns on the withheld amount, *always* have the institutions transfer your money. Never take possession of retirement money that is intended for a rollover or transfer.

The Indirect Rollover—If you do request your employer or investment company to issue a check directly to you from your retirement account, and you plan to roll it over to another plan or IRA, it is considered an *indirect rollover*. In this situation, you have 60 days to roll over the assets if you want to preserve the tax status of the account. However, your employer or investment company is required by law to withhold 20% of the amount paid to you as prepayment of federal income tax (you may recoup the 20% withholding when you file a credit on your income taxes for that year). If you want to roll over the entire amount of your distribution, you can make up the difference using money from your other savings. Because a direct rollover is more convenient and there is no danger of missing the IRA deadline, most investors prefer this option.

Questions and Answers

- **What exactly is a Rollover IRA?**—The Rollover IRA is a type of Individual Retirement Account designed for people who are leaving a job or retiring and receiving money accumulated in an employer-sponsored retirement plan. Eligible distributions from such plans may be rolled over directly into a rollover IRA. A direct rollover, allows you to avoid the mandatory 20% withholding for federal income tax, to avoid possible penalties for early withdrawal, and to continue deferring income tax. IRA rollovers permit you to postpone paying any tax on your lump-sum distribution until you withdraw it. A Rollover IRA can be invested in mutual funds, stocks, bonds, or other securities, including CDs and treasuries. This flexibility makes opening a Rollover IRA a good opportunity to rebalance your retirement portfolio, by rolling your savings into instruments not traditionally offered by employer plans.

- **How is a Rollover IRA different from a Rollover Annuity?**—The main differences are the investment choices they offer and their cost. You can fund a Rollover IRA with almost any type of investment—from CDs and mutual funds to stocks and bonds. With a Rollover Annuity, the investment choices depend on which type of annuity you select. A fixed annuity offers you a guaranteed, fixed rate of return. A variable annuity allows you to allocate assets in variable investment options. (For more on annuities see chapter 15). A Rollover Variable Annuity also may cost more than a Rollover IRA. That is because you are paying for the two additional benefits most annuities offer: a guaranteed death benefit and a guaranteed income for life, which are subject to the claims paying ability of the issuing insurance company.

- **How do Rollover IRAs help me avoid paying taxes on my lump-sum distribution?**—Rolling over your eligible distribution directly to a Rollover IRA allows you to avoid a possible 10% early withdrawal penalty, mandatory 20% withholding for federal income taxes, and to postpone paying taxes on the amount rolled over until it is withdrawn from your IRA. It also lets your eligible rollover assets continue to accumulate any earnings on a tax-deferred basis. If you want to avoid the 20% mandatory withholding for federal income taxes at the time of distribution from your employer's plan make sure that you directly roll over your eligible distribution into a Rollover IRA or other eligible retirement plan. Also, Rollover IRA funds should be held separately from your Traditional IRA assets or you will forfeit the ability to invest your Rollover IRA in another employer-sponsored plan in the future if you so desire.

- **If I do decide to do a rollover do I have to roll over my entire distribution?**—No. If you do not want to roll over your total distribution, you can take part of it yourself and pay regular income tax on it (plus the 10% early withdrawal penalty if you are under 59 ½). But if you make such a split, you can not use tax averaging.

- **Will the IRS charge me a penalty if I change investments within my investment company?**—You will not be hit with a penalty if you shift funds from one investment vehicle to another within the same institution as long as you never withdraw the money yourself. In other words, if you maintain an IRA or a 403(b) at a financial institution or investment company that offers a number of investment vehicles, you may shift funds from one vehicle to another within that institution as many times as the financial institution or investment company permits, without penalty.

- **Can I move an existing IRA to another institution?**—Yes. There are two methods:

   1. **Direct (trustee-to-trustee) Transfer**—By completing an IRA transfer form for your present trustee, in addition to an application to the new trustee, you can authorize the new trustee to transfer your IRA from the other trustee to the new one.

   2. **Sixty-day Rollover**—You can withdraw your IRA from your present trustee and reinvest it in a new one. You must complete the rollover within 60 days of receiving the withdrawal to avoid income taxes and, if you are under age 59 ½, the 10% IRS early-withdrawal penalty. Only one rollover is allowed per IRA in a 365-day period. The 365-day rule applies separately to each IRA. You can avoid this whole problem by using a trustee-to-trustee transfer, in which you instruct your IRA trustee to forward your funds to another IRA trustee. In this way, you never have touched the money, therefore, the 365-day rule does not apply.

- **Can I just reinvest the check my investment company sends me?**—Yes, you can. But remember, if your investment company makes the check payable to you, 20% of your eligible retirement plan distribution will be withheld for federal income taxes. The only way to avoid this withholding is to have your current investment company make your distribution check payable to the financial institution you've chosen as custodian for your new rollover plan. Either you or your current investment company should then send this check directly to the new financial institution.

- **I already received a check made payable to me—and 20% was withheld. If I reinvest my**

money now, can I get that 20% back?—Yes, but first you will have to replace the 20% that was withheld with your own savings. Then you will have to reinvest that 20% along with the 80% you already received—all within 60 days of receiving the distribution. If you do, you can receive credit for the 20% that was withheld toward your income tax liability when you file your tax return. However, if you do not have the cash to make up for the 20% withheld, the IRS will consider that 20% as a distribution, making it subject to taxes and a possible 10% early withdrawal penalty.

- **Can I roll over all the money in my retirement plan account to a Rollover IRA, or is there a limit?**—You can roll over all the contributions made to your plan that have not yet been taxed—referred to as pre-tax contributions. You can also roll over all the earnings on those contributions. If you made contributions to your plan with income that had already been taxed—referred to as after-tax contributions—you will need to put that money in a separate non-retirement investment account. You can not roll over after-tax contributions, although the earnings on such contributions may be rolled over. In addition, minimum required distributions and distributions of certain substantially equal periodic payments are not eligible to be rolled over to an IRA. For tax purposes, the government needs to track which money you have paid taxes on and which money you have not. To determine how much of your contributions and earnings were "pre-tax" versus after-tax, review the statements you received, and/or ask your current investment company for assistance.

- **What should I do with my after-tax contributions?**—While you can not directly roll over these contributions into a Rollover IRA, you can still invest them in a non-retirement account so they can continue to earn more money for your retirement. For example, you can invest any after-tax contributions into a variety of mutual funds. To keep this money growing tax-deferred, you may want to consider a fixed or variable annuity. (see chapter 15).

- **What if I need my retirement money to pay expenses?**—Your best bet may still be to roll your retirement plan money into a Rollover IRA. If you do need money to pay expenses later, you can always withdraw just what you need—when you need it. And there is no automatic 20% withholding on withdrawals from a Rollover IRA. Remember, however, that the withdrawal from the IRA is subject to ordinary income tax and may be subject to a 10% early withdrawal penalty. There may be some situations, however, which would cause the distribution to be eligible for special tax treatment. Ask your tax advisor about income averaging.

- **Can I add more money to my Rollover IRA later?**—Yes, you can add additional money to your Rollover IRA—as long as this money is also an eligible distribution from another qualified retirement plan. For example, a lump-sum distribution from a company pension plan can be added to a Rollover IRA that was set up for a distribution from a 403(b) or 401(k) plan. However, if Rollover and Traditional IRA funds are combined in the same account, you will forfeit the right to rollover your Rollover IRA into another employer-sponsored plan in the future if ever you so desire. In addition, if 403(b) and 401(k) assets are commingled in a Rollover IRA, you will not be allowed to rollover those assets to either a 403(b) or 401(k) in the future.

- **I might be changing jobs soon. What are my options for the money in my account?**—One of the reasons why 403(b)s have become so popular is that they are portable. Generally speaking, you can take your retirement assets from job to job (with some exceptions). If you decide to change jobs, you generally have three options for your money:

1. If you have more than $5,000 invested in your account you can usually leave your money in your current retirement plan account generally until age 70 ½. (Consult your plan for your specific options.)

2. You can also directly roll your eligible money over to another retirement plan or to an IRA. The Rollover IRA (also known as a *conduit IRA*) is designed to give you a way to move eligible retirement money directly from your former employer's plan to an IRA and then into another employer's plan. Just be sure to do a direct rollover.

3. Your third option would be to take a full or partial withdrawal payable to you (instead of rolling it over). This option has many tax implications. For any portion that you do not directly roll over (by having the check made payable to your IRA or next employer's plan), 20% will be withheld for prepayment of your federal income tax. In come cases, if you are under age 59 ½ there may be a 10% early withdrawal penalty as well.

Remember, you can only move pre-tax contributions and investment earnings to a Rollover IRA or a new employer's plan. Any after-tax contributions can not be rolled over, but can be moved to a taxable non-retirement account, or to an annuity. If you are planning to move rollover money to another employer's plan, do not make additional contributions to the account.

 • **If I roll my retirement plan assets over, when does the 60-day time period begin?**—It depends on whether you are making a direct rollover or you actually receive the money. If it is a direct rollover, the 60-day rule does not apply because distribution and rollover are considered to be simultaneous. However, if you receive the money (an indirect rollover), the 60-day period begins on the date the distribution is received. The IRS has held that if a distribution is received in more than one payment, for purposes of the 60-day rollover period you are deemed to have received all distributions on the day the last payment is received.

 • **What if there is a delay in receiving the proceeds of a direct rollover—can other money be used to set up a new account?**—Generally, this would not be a problem since the 60-day rule does not apply. However, the administrator of the plan will only be liable if you provide adequate information and it fails to make a rollover. The administrator is not required to verify independently the accuracy of information, as long as it is not clearly erroneous. To avoid liability, the plan administrator must have been furnished with the name of the IRA or qualified plan to receive the distribution; a representation that the recipient plan is an IRA, a tax-sheltered annuity, or a qualified plan; and any information necessary to permit the plan administrator to accomplish the direct rollover (i.e., the name and address of the recipient trustee).

 • **How do I manage my IRA Rollover account?**—Your Rollover IRA, along with your other assets, should be managed using a diversified portfolio in a manner suitable for your investment objectives, in accordance with your age, time horizon, return needs, personal risk tolerance, etc. (see chapter 13).

Choosing between an IRA rollover and lump-sum taxation depends on how much and how soon the retirement funds will be needed. If you expect to withdraw your retirement funds gradually over your retirement years, your overall financial position will be enhanced by making an IRA rollover. Why? Because letting your money grow tax-deferred for a few more years usually turns out to be more valuable than the tax savings you get from averaging. However, if you will need significant amounts within a few years of retirement to start a business, build yourself a retirement dream house, etc., you generally will benefit by taking the lump-sum distribution and use the 5-year or 10-year tax averaging strategy. But, the only way to know for sure what will work best in your unique situation is to hire a financial advisor to create a retirement scenario and run the numbers for you.

- **How To Keep From Outliving Your Money**—There was a time that when a person retired, conventional wisdom dictated that they make sure most of their assets were safely parked in income-producing investments. After all, with a limited time horizon, who could afford to ride the equity rollercoaster and risk an extended market downturn? But, as mentioned in chapter 1, people are living longer than ever today. The number of people aged 100 or over has doubled every decade since 1950. In fact, the over-85 age group has lately been the fastest-growing age group in the United States. As the joint life expectancy table for last survivors shows (see below), a couple, now both aged 65, can expect that at least one partner will live another 25 years. A couple, both 75, can plan on one of them living another 17 years. A 65-year-old man today has a 35% chance of living to celebrate his 90th birthday. If he is married to a 65-year-old woman, there is a 28% chance that one of them will be blowing out at least 95 candles.

Joint Life and Last Survivor Expectancy (Current Life Expectancy of the Survivor)						
Your Spouse's Age	**Your Age**					
	55	**60**	**65**	**70**	**75**	**80**
55	34	32	31	30	29	29
60	32	30	**28**	26	25	25
65	31	28	25	23	22	21
70	30	26	23	21	19	18
75	29	25	22	19	17	15
80	29	25	21	18	15	13

Example: If you are 65 and your spouse is 60, the average life expectancy of the last to die is 28 more years.

Demographers are projecting that more than a million baby-boomers will make it past 100. That is good news as long as you have enough retirement money to enjoy those twilight years. Without proper funding, however, those years can make for sheer agony. So how do you avoid outliving your money? Well, first of all, as mentioned in the last chapter, you must stop thinking of retirement as the end point of your investing career. Think of it as the beginning of a new phase that figures to last 20, 25, or even 30 years or more. Over that length of time inflation will be eating away at the real value of your portfolio and the income it produces. To stay ahead of inflation you will have to continue to think like a growth investor. That means that some of the investment strategies you might have thought you could forget still apply. To keep from outliving your money you should:

Continue to save in earnest—If your retirement funds are to keep growing, you can not spend all the income your portfolio produces. You must put some if it back into your investments as a hedge against inflation. For example, if inflation is running at 3% a year and your investments return 9%, you will have to reinvest a third of your return just to stay even after inflation. This is especially important to remember if you annuitize. Since most of your investment return will arrive in the mail each month, you must figure out what you need to spend and reinvest the rest, so that in a few years you can supplement your income with another source to meet the extra need created by inflation.

Spend less—You may recall from Chapter 1 that I stated that most financial experts say that you will need about 80% of your pre-retirement income to maintain your current lifestyle during retirement. You may also recall that I stated that people are living longer these days, and therefore, a more prudent estimate would range anywhere from 100% to 120% of your pre-retirement pay. If you followed the 80% recommendation then you just might find yourself with less money than you need. If so, keep track on where your money is going for a few months and determine where you might be able to trim your expenses. You may have to cut back on what are often lavish travel and entertainment expenses so that your money will stretch farther.

Be careful what you give away—A lot of retirees are more generous than wise when it comes to their retirement money. They shoot themselves in the foot by giving their children down payments for homes, setting up accounts to finance college for their grandchildren, etc., with money that they can ill afford to give away. The problem is that these generous people do not realize that they will need the money they give away for their long careers as retirees. Am I advocating a just say no policy for elderly parents and grandparents to follow? Certainly not. I am simply suggesting that the only time retirees can afford to be generous with their retirement money is when a careful analysis of their financial situation identifies a significant amount of money or hard assets that can be safely earmarked for their charitable endeavors.

Keep investing for growth—Even in retirement you will have to invest your money as skillfully and almost as aggressively as you did before retirement. Make no mistake about it, you will still need the high returns that only the stock market can provide. To counteract the ravages of inflation, you should always have some money in stocks. If you can increase your real, after-inflation return by 3 or 4 percent you can make your money last an extra couple of decades, or even longer. Investing for growth is especially vital to those in the early stages of retirement. You have to think of yourself as a growth investor because you have to be prepared to keep your income rising for a matter of 10 to 20 years or more. Not only will you need the higher returns that you get from the stock market, but you will still have the time to ride out any market downturns.

Even when you get deeper into retirement, when safety of principal becomes a more important goal than future growth, you should not abandon stocks entirely. Stocks should still account for around 20% of your holdings. More on this later on in the chapter when I discuss investing in retirement.

Take your minimum required distributions—Just when you thought you were too old to have to play by anyone else's rules, along comes the government with another one. Between age 59 ½ and 70 ½ you can take money from your tax-deferred accounts without penalty, as long as you do not take too much. But whether you need the money or not, you *have* to start taking a *minimum required distribution (MRD)* from your 403(b), 401(k), IRA, or other tax-deferred retirement plan (excluding the Roth IRA, for which MRDs are not required) by April 1 of the year after you turn 70 ½. No tax deferral lasts forever. Eventually, Uncle Sam wants his cut. By the way, a rollover from your 403(b) account to an IRA is not a taxable distribution.

You will be happy to know the government has softened its stance a little with concern to MRDs. The IRS ruled that beginning January 1, 1997, if you are still employed when you turn 70 ½, you are allowed to wait until April 1 of the year following the year in which you retire before beginning distributions from your plan. (Please note that your plan may require you to take distributions earlier than this). However, for assets in another plan, like an IRA, minimum required distributions must begin no later than April 1 of the year following the year in which you turn age 70 ½, even if you are still an active employee of another organization.

MRDs are based on your account balance and your life expectancy. You must calculate your MRD for each of your retirement accounts (403(b), IRAs, Rollover IRAs, etc.) at all financial institutions. You do not have to withdraw the MRD from each account, however, it is the *total* withdrawal that must meet the MRD requirement. (Remember, Roth IRAs are excluded).

Unless stated otherwise, you must take a minimum required distribution from your account at least once a year. The government established minimum distributions to ensure that you actually use your 403(b) account balance for *retirement* and not, for instance, to pass onto your heirs. Therefore you can not withdraw your MRD and roll it into another tax-deferred account, like an IRA.

If you do not start taking money out of your account at age 70 ½, the IRS hits you with a 50% excise tax on the difference between what you withdrew from your account and what you should have withdrawn from your account. And you will owe that excise tax annually until you have made the appropriate withdrawal. In other words, if you should have taken $16,000 from your retirement account and you did not, you will owe the IRS $8,000 a year until you take out that $16,000. Of course, when you do take it out, you will owe income taxes on it. Remember, the 20% withholding I talked about earlier in the chapter does not apply to your MRD.

Again, the important date to remember is April 1 of the year following the one in which you turn 70 ½. By then you *must* begin withdrawals. That is also when you must make two irrevocable decisions: You must select a method to calculate your minimum required distribution (considering single vs joint life expectancy); and, you must name a beneficiary. The selection between single and joint life expectancy is an easy one. The joint life expectancy option reduces the minimum distribution required, thus giving you more flexibility with your required minimum distributions. You can always take out more than the minimum. The tricky part is choosing the method of withdrawal. Let us look at the three methods for computing distributions:

• **The Term-Certain Method**—To figure out how much you need to withdraw using this approach, look up your life expectancy, or the joint life expectancy of you and your beneficiary, in IRS Publication No. 590. Unless the beneficiary is your spouse, the IRS limits the age difference between beneficiaries to 10 years for computing a joint life expectancy—meaning you can not stretch out the withdrawals by naming your five-year-old grandson as beneficiary. Next, divide the total value of all your tax-deferred accounts by your life expectancy, or the combined life expectancy of you and your spouse or other beneficiary.

With this method, your retirement money will be depleted at the end of your life expectancy period. For example, say you are 70 years-old, have a single life expectancy of 16 years, and have an account of $600,000. Using the single life expectancy of 16 years, you would have to pull out 1/16 of the money in your plan, or $37,500. The next year, you would have to take out 1/15, and so on down the line until you turn 86 and clean out the balance.

If someone has a serious illness and it is clear that their life expectancy is less than the actuarial tables, then they almost always would be well-advised to look at the term-certain method. That allows the money to stay in the account after the person dies, so the heirs benefit from tax-deferral.

- **The Recalculation Method**—Unless you state differently, most institutions will assume that you have elected the recalculation method, which will be applied by default, even if you later decide it is not the best method for you. This is one of the few places where the statistical odds are actually stacked in your favor. Each year the life expectancy of you and your beneficiary is recalculated. The older you get, the longer you are expected to live. For example, at age 75, the IRS assumes you will live to 87 ½, more than a year and a half longer than they thought you would live when you were 70. Therefore, retirement money should last longer because your minimum distributions will be lower. In other words, the recalculation method provides a withdrawal stream that can not be outlived.

So if longevity runs in your family, you may want to use the recalculation method to make sure you do not run out of cash too soon. Here is how it works: each year you recalculate the minimum withdrawal, based on your new life expectancy. At 71, for example, the IRS expects you to live for another 15.3 years, so you divide your balance by 15.3 to come up with the amount you have to take out. A year later, your life expectancy will have dropped only nine months, meaning you divide the balance by 14.6. Each year your minimum distributions will be lower. The good new is that the IRS life expectancy tables go to age 115. The bad news? Seriously, if you have got the good health to live to be 115, and you have still got money in your tax-deferred accounts, how could there be any bad news?

The recalculation method tends to be the better option for people whose net worths are under $600,000; it slows down the rate of outflow because life expectancy rises for every year you live. With the recalculation method comes a fatal flaw, which may greatly harm the tax-deferred compounding potential for the next generation of beneficiaries. The flaw occurs when the primary beneficiary used for recalculation purposes pre-deceases the participant. In this case, the account will end with the passing of the participant, with all funds paid out and taxed by the year after the participant passes. The negative implications for the next generation of beneficiaries is they lose the ability to extend the tax-deferred compounding benefit of the account. This is a huge opportunity cost to pay. But you can avoid the problem by selecting the hybrid option.

- **The Hybrid Method**—With this variation, professional advisors will often recommend the older person (assumed to be the owner of the account for this discussion), select the recalculation method, and the younger person (assumed to be the spousal beneficiary for this discussion), select the term-certain method. The minimum distribution will be greater than pure recalculation, but less than the fixed option. The big benefit is if the beneficiary pre-deceases the owner-participant, the account will not be forced to distribute all the assets by the year following the passing of the owner-participant. The account may live for the fixed term after the owner-participant passes. The potential tax benefits from the extended tax-deferred compounding for your beneficiaries are huge. Although it is more complicated, it provides greater flexibility for estate planning and extending life expectancy.

Allowable Distribution Methods

Designated Beneficiary

Account Owner	Spouse	Other than Spouse
Term Certain	Term Certain	Term Certain
Term Certain	Recalculation	Term Certain
Recalculation	Recalculation	Term Certain
Recalculation	Term Certain	Term Certain

To set up the hybrid withdrawal method, you must notify your plan sponsor that you plan on using it. You will also need specific instructions to help you calculate the mandatory distribution percentage using the this method.

As discussed earlier, there are stiff penalties for not taking the minimum distribution. But some people have just the opposite problem. If you are among the fortunate few who will retire wealthy, you should be aware that under current tax law, if distributions from all of your qualified retirement plans are greater than $160,000 in a single calendar year, an excise tax (sometimes referred to as the *success tax*) of 15% will be levied on the amount over $160,000. Lump-sum distributions from qualified plans may be subject to the excise tax when they are greater than $800,000. This has prompted some experts to question the wisdom of putting as much money as possible into tax-deferred accounts. But studies show that the benefits outweigh the penalty. Remember, as stated earlier in the chapter, this excise tax has been suspended until January 1, 2000, at which time it will be reinstated.

Draw on principal carefully—Most investors incorrectly assume that once in retirement the earnings from their nest egg will be more than enough to carry them all the way through to the end. After all, everyone knows that touching your principal in retirement is taboo, right? Not any more. That may have made sense many years ago when it was less risky to invest entirely in bonds and spend all of the income they produced. But things are a little different today.

As stated many times before, today's retiree should have substantial holdings in growth stocks which, consequently, do not yield much in the way of dividends or interest payments. Therefore, to make ends meet you will have to sell some of them off (draw down your principal). But do not worry. As long as your investments continue to grow and stay ahead of inflation it really does not matter where your money comes from, just that it lasts. As long as you spend only what you need and reinvest the rest, it should not matter whether the money you spend comes from capital appreciation (growth of your securities) or income (dividends, interest, etc.). All that really matters is whether there is enough money in your account to buy the quality of life you want for as long as you want.

Realistically, most middle-class retirees will have to use most of their principal if they manage to live well into their nineties. If you are surprised at this you still have not totally absorbed the lesson of inflation. Remember the *million dollar* example in chapter 1? It sounds like more money than you could ever dream of amassing right now, but over time, with average inflation, that million dollars will provide an average couple with a retirement income of only $31,476 *in today's dollars*. After taxes, that could be just under $25,000

Because your retirement money has to last as long as you do, you must take care not to draw down your principal too fast. If you withdraw from your nest egg at the same annual rate at which it's growing (after inflation), it will stay the same size. Or, as shown in the following chart, you can gradually reduce the amount to zero by withdrawing at more than the growth rate.

Using What You Earn

The money you start with	Amount you can withdraw monthly for the number of years below, reducing your nest egg to zero [1].			
	10 years	15 years	20 years	30 years
$ 50,000	$ 580	$ 448	$ 386	$ 332
$100,000	$1,160	$ 896	$ 772	$ 668
$150,000	$1,740	$1,340	$1,160	$ 999
$200,000	$2,320	$1,790	$1,550	$1,330
$250,000	$2,900	$2,240	$1,930	$1,660
$300,000	$3,480	$2,690	$2,320	$1,990
$350,000	$4,060	$3,138	$2,706	$2,322

[1] Based on a rate of return at 7% interest, compounded monthly

For another example, we will use the conventional rule-of-thumb for retirement account withdrawal. Here you draw out 5% of your capital in your first year of retirement, then each year increase your subsequent annual withdrawals by the amount of inflation. For example, if your nest egg is $600,000, in the first year of your retirement you would draw down 5%, or $30,000. Assuming a 4% inflation rate, in the second year you could draw down $31,200 ($30,000 x 4% = $1,200; $30,000 + $1,200 = $31,200), the third year $32,448 ($31,200 x 4% = $1,248; $31,200 + $1,248 = $32,448), and so on. Here is how it looks:

Second Year		**Third Year**	
$ 30,000	First year's withdrawal	$ 31,200	Second year's withdrawal
x 4%	Rate of inflation	x 4%	Rate of inflation
$ 1,200	Inflation adjustment	$ 1,248	Inflation adjustment
+30,000	First year's withdrawal	+31,200	Second year's withdrawal
$ 31,200	Second year's withdrawal	$ 32,448	Third year's withdrawal

276

The chart below illustrates how long your money will last when you tap into your retirement nest egg using the above strategy. Here is how it works: Look in the far left-hand column to find the percentage of your nest egg you want to withdraw every year. Let us assume you go with the conventional rule-of-thumb and choose 5%. Next, look at the numbers across the top if the chart until you find the average annual return you expect the rest of your nest egg will earn. Let us assume 7%. Then run your finger down from 7% until you reach the same line you were on in step number one. You will come to the number 29. This is the number of years your money will last if you withdraw 5% of your nest egg the first year after you retire, increase your withdrawal annually to keep up with a 4% yearly inflation rate, and continue to earn a 7% annual return on your investments.

TAPPING YOUR NEST EGG IN RETIREMENT
NUMBER OF YEARS YOUR MONEY WILL LAST

% of capital withdrawn yearly	Interest rate earned on savings, assuming 4% annual inflation										
	4%	5%	6%	7%	8%	9%	10%	11%	12%	13%	14%
2	50	68	151	--	--	--	--	--	--	--	--
3	33	40	52	96	--	--	--	--	--	--	--
4	25	28	34	42	69	--	--	--	--	--	--
5	20	22	25	29	36	53	--	--	--	--	--
6	17	18	20	22	25	31	43	--	--	--	--
7	14	15	16	18	20	23	27	35	--	--	--
8	13	13	14	15	16	18	20	24	30	65	--
9	11	12	12	13	14	15	17	19	21	26	40
10	10	10	11	12	12	13	14	15	17	19	23
11	9	9	10	10	11	11	12	13	14	16	17
12	8	9	9	9	10	10	11	11	12	13	14
13	8	8	8	9	9	9	10	10	11	11	12
14	7	7	8	8	8	8	9	9	10	10	11
15	7	7	7	7	8	8	8	8	9	9	10

Obviously, this rule-of-thumb will not work unless your investments are outpacing inflation over the long haul, constantly replenishing your nest egg. (That is the primary reason why having a portion of your portfolio in growth stocks is so vitally important). How long your money lasts depends on your average rate of return versus the average inflation rate. If the $600,000 nest egg earns an average 7% annual return, as illustrated above, you can increase your withdrawal amounts by the 4% annual inflation rate every year, and your money will last 29 years. But the situation changes dramatically if you draw down your capital too fast. If you take out $72,000, or 12% of that $600,000 nest egg in the first year of retirement, and then each year increase your annual distributions by the same 4% inflation factor, and earn the same 7% average annual return on investments, you will run out of money in just 9 years. As you can see it pays to spend down your principal with the utmost control. Otherwise, that lengthy retirement you've always dreamed of may just turn out to be a financial nightmare.

Investing In Retirement—Making decisions about how to access your retirement money also requires some thought about asset allocation. It is here where many investors can sell themselves short. As mentioned earlier, investors often fail to recognize how two key elements—longevity and inflation—should factor into decisions about how to allocate funds. Not doing so can mean underestimating long-term financial requirements.

A byproduct of the increase in life expectancy is more freedom—and necessity—for retired investors to take an aggressive approach to their investing. Today's retirees are nearly obligated to emphasize stock funds in their portfolio. Given the pervasiveness of inflation, an overemphasis on current income virtually dooms the retiree to a steadily declining standard of living. Twenty to twenty-five years is a long time to get along every month on the same size interest checks from bond and money funds.

Studies show that the number one problem with retirees is that they are too conservative with their investment style. As they age, retirees collecting fixed pensions with no cost of living allowance are likely to face higher expenses such as health care costs, and their income steams should account for that possibility. Consequently, they should have some part of their portfolio in something that is going to combat inflation, namely growth stocks. But that is tough for people to do because the natural instinct is to be more conservative as they age.

Although the retiree's time horizon (life expectancy) is an important factor in determining a strategic asset allocation mix, the retiree's tolerance for risk has to be addressed also. Many retired people simply do not have the necessary risk tolerance to put 70%-80% of their assets in equities. In that case they need to follow an asset allocation mix that is more conservative. The chart that follows is designed to guide the retiree in making asset allocation decisions. You will notice that there are three portfolio types:

    1. A **capital preservation portfolio**—for retirees who have a 3-5 year time horizon and/or have a lower risk tolerance.

    2. A **moderate growth portfolio**—for retirees who have a 6-10 year time horizon and/or are willing to take on a moderate amount of risk.

    3. A **growth portfolio**—for retirees who have 11 years or more to invest and are willing to take on a substantial amount of risk.

Remember, the asset allocations presented are for illustrative purposes only. The final decision on an asset allocation model is yours, based on your individual situation, needs, goals, and tolerance for risk. However, if you will be withdrawing close to 100% of your assets within the next two years, you should consider keeping *all* your money in short-term investments.

A good guideline to follow when considering asset allocation as a retiree is to be as aggressive as your risk tolerance will allow you to be. Remember, statistics show that the average annual returns for stocks and stock funds over longer holding periods have always been positive. Losses have been virtually nonexistent when stocks were held 15 years or more.

Asset Allocation in Retirement

Portfolio Type	Asset Mix	This Mix Might Be Right For You if . . .
Growth	70% Stocks 25% Bonds 5% Short-term	Your tolerance for risk is fairly high and you are willing to take on more risk in an attempt to outperform conservative investments over the long term.
Moderate Growth	50% Stocks 40% Bonds 10% short-term	Your tolerance for risk is more moderate and you need a combination of current income and capital growth. Consider spreading your investments to seek growth combined with less risk over the long term.
Capital Preservation	20% Stocks 50% Bonds 30% Short-term	Your tolerance for risk is low and you are looking for a more conservative mixture of investments that are more heavily weighted toward bonds and short-term investments that will provide current income, while an investment in stocks can provide an element of growth to help protect your assets from inflation.

Because your choice of an asset allocation model is based on current circumstances, you should review your investment strategy at least once a year or when any of your personal factors change.

Summary

It is probably apparent by now that taking distributions from your retirement savings is not quite as simple as you might first think. There are a number of critical decisions to be made as you approach and enter into your retirement, each of which impacts

1. The level of income you will receive.

2. The taxability of this income.

3. How long the income will last.

These decisions should be given serious consideration *well before* your actual retirement begins. While the regulations that govern retirement plans are complicated, there is no reason that your transition into retirement should be anything other than a rewarding experience, provided that you follow basic tested guidelines. That involves, first and foremost, planning ahead and considering carefully how you will handle all of your retirement plan distributions, including any monies you expect to receive over the years from other sources. You also need to explore your options thoroughly before you move or draw on your capital assets, and be wary of the tax traps that may snare the unsuspecting investor. Please remember, if you are ever in doubt along the way about how to proceed, do not hesitate to seek help from a qualified tax advisor or financial planner. Remember also that each decision you face should be made in the context of your overall financial situation. Nowhere is it written that you must take an all or nothing approach to your retirement. For instance, it may make sense to arrange for part of your retirement assets to be paid out as an annuity or systematic installment that you cannot outlive, and to invest the remainder in a diversified portfolio of mutual funds that can provide income and capital growth to keep pace with inflation.

Indeed, just as mutual funds are an ideal investment vehicle for building your retirement savings, they are also an ideal vehicle for managing your accumulated assets during your retirement. The flexibility, diversification, and range of investments available from mutual funds enable you to easily adjust the mix of your retirement assets to meet your changing objectives. Most mutual fund organizations also offer convenient services for distributing your retirement assets. For example, a systematic withdrawal plan allows you to receive regular monthly distributions from your mutual fund. And many fund sponsors will calculate your minimum required distribution for you, so you can be certain of complying with the IRS guidelines.

Finally, if there is money left in your retirement accounts after you die, you will want it to go to your heirs and not the IRS. Without careful planning, the combination of income, estate, excise and penalty taxes can easily devour more than 80% of the balance. The next chapter was written to help you prevent that from happening.

CHAPTER NINETEEN

Estate Planning—Protecting Your Heirs

A manual on retirement planning just would not be complete without including a chapter addressing the importance of proper estate planning. The following contains references to many complex issues that have legal, accounting, and tax implications. However, this information is not intended as legal, accounting, or tax advice. I have painted with a very broad brush, so a great deal of simplification and omission of details is inevitable. My sole intent is to provide a broad overview of the topics presented, so the reader can be more knowledgeable in exploring options, and better prepared to meet with professional advisors. To cover each topic in strict detail is beyond the scope and purpose of this manual.

Are you married? Do you have children? Do you own a home or other valuable assets? If you answered "yes" to any of these questions, you probably need an estate plan. "What," you say, "is an estate plan?" In short, it is the blueprint of your assets and your family's financial future after you are gone. It determines who will care for your children, who will inherit your assets and in what amounts, who will disburse your assets, and to some extent, how much your estate may owe in federal income taxes and administrative costs. And, if you own a business, an estate plan spells out who will inherit the business and who will run it. Ask yourself if you . . .

1. **a.** Want a say in who receives your assets after you are gone?

   b. Think it is okay for state law to determine who inherits your assets—even if mean Uncle Ed, whom you have not spoken to in years, inherits the house?

2. **a.** Want your children or grandchildren to receive their share of assets when they are mature enough to handle the responsibility—and not all at once?

   b. Would have no problem if state law provided that your 18-year-old would get that $50,000 you managed to save for college . . . today?

281

3. **a.** Want someone you know to handle the distribution of your assets? (Preferably some one who agrees with you that the family heirlooms stay in the family.)

   b. Think a court-appointed administrator would be fair, even though he or she would not be aware of your preferences or consider the sentimental value of your prized possessions?

4. **a.** Think it is important to maximize the amount of money you provide to your beneficiaries, and minimize court costs and taxes?

   b. Figure your estate is big enough to handle those extra administrative costs and taxes, and still leave enough for your heirs?

5. **a.** Want to select the appropriate guardian for your child?

   b. Are sure the court will appoint a responsible guardian (Oh no! Not mean Uncle Ed again!)

6. **a.** Want your part-time business to continue after your death.

   b. Are not concerned about any devaluation and family hardships that might result fro a forced sale of your part-time business to pay unexpected costs, including possible taxes and fees.

If you selected any "a" answers, you should consider creating an estate plan.

Six Reasons to Plan Your Estate

With a Plan:	Without a Plan:
1. You decide who receives a share of your assets.	1. State laws determine who inherits your assets - they could pass to an estranged relative.
2. You decide how and when your beneficiaries will receive their inheritance.	2. The terms and timing are set by law. Your children could be left unfettered control of a sizable estate.
3. You decide who will manage your estate (executor, trustees, etc.).	3. The court appoints administrators - administrators whose ideas may not be compatible with your own.
4. You can reduce estate taxes & administrative expenses.	4. Costs are usually greater, due to required administrative expenses and unnecessary taxes.
5. You select a guardian for your children.	5. The court appoints a guardian for your child(ren).
6. You can provide for the orderly continuance or sale of a family business.	6. An untimely forced sale of your business may cause financial loss and family hardships.

Tools For Developing Your Plan—The following is a list of tools designed to help you develop your estate tax plan:

Wills—Everyone Should Have One—If you think wills are only for the rich, think again. A will is an essential part of any estate plan. It is the primary document for transferring wealth upon your death. Simply put, a will is a piece of paper that says who gets what when you die. When you are dealing with a will, you are dealing with the courts, because a will is a legal document. If you die *intestate* (without a will), state law controls the disposition of your property. Without a will, settling most estates is more troublesome and more costly. While we can not cover all of the critical elements of an effective will, there are three major provisions your will should include to ensure that your financial wishes are carried out. It should:

- Appoint a guardian for your children.

- Create trusts to accomplish certain goals.

- Name an executor, your personal representative after your death.

A Guardian for Your Children	Creation of Trusts	Naming an Executor
The will should name a guardian for minor children in case both you and your spouse die. Selecting a guardian to care for your children deserves a lot of thought. Name someone whose ideas on rearing children are similar to yours, and be sure the person you select is willing to accept the responsibility.	All a will can do is direct the disposition of your estate. To accomplish other goals, such as funding a child's education, distribute assets to your heirs, providing for the discharge of any and all estate taxes and settlement expenses, or providing for an elderly parent, you must include instructions for the creation of trusts.	An executor is your personal representative after your death. The executor has several major responsibilities, including: • Administering the estate and distributing assets to your beneficiaries. • Making certain tax decisions. • Paying any debts or expenses of your estate. • Ensuring that all life insurance benefits are received. • Ensuring that all retirement plan benefits are received. • Filing the necessary tax returns and paying the appropriate federal and state taxes.

Executors—What They Do, How to Choose One—You should appoint an executor, the individual who will have the most impact in ensuring your wishes are carried out. As mentioned above, the executor is responsible for:

- Administering the estate and distributing the assets to your beneficiaries.

- Ensuring that all life insurance and retirement plan benefits payable to your estate are received.

- Filing the necessary tax returns and paying the appropriate federal and state income taxes.

- Making sure that all other necessary tax returns are filed and taxes and expenses are paid.

A trustee performs many of the same responsibilities as the executor, but instead of administering the entire estate, a trustee is designated to administer and distribute the assets from a particular trust you may create.

<u>Keys to Selecting an Executor</u>—

- Weigh the advantages of naming an individual as executor (more familiar with family and less costly) against the advantages of naming a corporate executor or trustee (specialists in handling estates and trusts, no emotional bias, more availability). See the chart that follows.

- If you select an individual, make sure that person is willing to serve as your executor, and that he or she fully understands the responsibilities. Consider paying a fee for the services. The job is not easy. Not everyone will want to accept the responsibility.

- Make sure your executor or trustee does not have a conflict of interest. For example, someone who owns part of your business may have different goals than your family members. The person or entity you select should know you and have no biases with respect to your estate.

<u>Selecting Your Executors and Trustees</u>

Corporate Executor/Trustee Advantages	Individual Executor/Trustee Advantages
- Specialist in handling estates/trusts - No emotional bias - Impartial - usually free of conflicts of interest with the beneficiary - Never moves or goes on vacation - Never dies or gets sick	- More familiar with the family - Administrative fees may be lower
Disadvantages	**Disadvantages**
- Usually has little familiarity with the family - Administrative fees may be higher	- Probably not experienced in handling estates or trusts - May have an emotional bias - May not be impartial - Could have schedule conflicts - Could be incapacitated at times

284

Trusts—Types, Features and Benefits

What is a Trust?—While your will directs how your assets will be distributed, a trust can be established to achieve specific financial goals. A trust is the holding of property and the equitable management of that property by one person (a trustee) for another person (a beneficiary). If you transfer property to a trust, you would be considered a grantor. Reasons to create a trust include:

- You can transfer valuable assets out of your estate, while controlling how the trust property is invested and distributed to your beneficiaries long after your death.

- You can designate a trustee who is more capable of providing financial management of the property than your beneficiaries.

- You can decide whether to distribute your assets immediately upon death, or over the beneficiary's lifetime. Without a trust, all funds would have to be distributed at the age of majority (usually between 18 and 21 under state law). And if you have kids, you can structure payments to encourage them to earn additional income.

- You can provide life insurance for your kids without adding to your taxable estate. By naming the trust as the owner of the life insurance policy, the proceeds may be excluded from your estate.

Types of Trusts—Revocable vs. Irrevocable Trusts—With a *revocable trust*, the grantor (the individual who transferred property to the trust) retains the right to all trust income, an unlimited right to withdraw property from the trust and a right to terminate the trust if he or she chooses. Because the grantor maintains these rights, he or she is taxed on the trust income; no gift has been made for gift tax purposes, and the property will still be included in the grantor's estate for estate tax purposes. With an *irrevocable trust,* the grantor may choose not to retain certain rights and powers to ensure that the trust income is not taxable to the grantor, and that the property may be removed from the grantor's taxable estate. Transfers to irrevocable trusts will still be considered gifts of future interest, and so will not qualify for the annual gift tax exclusion unless special provisions are made.

Living Trusts: A Sure-Fire Way to Avoid Probate—A *living trust* or *in vitro* trust is a trust that is created and funded during the grantor's lifetime, not as the result of a provision in a will. It can carry out your wishes for distribution of your property after death in the same way as a will. So why have both? On the following page are some reasons why you might want to create a living trust in addition to your will.

285

Probate can be time consuming ... slow ... costly!

For these reasons, avoiding probate usually should be one of the main goals of your estate plan. Here's how you can do it:

A self-declaration, or living, trust is a legal document that resembles a will. It contains your instructions for the management of assets should you become disabled, as well as the directions for the distribution of assets upon your death.

After the trust is created, the title on your assets is changed from your name to the name of the trust. During your lifetime, assuming no disability, you control the trust assets. The trust does not have to file a tax return or pay taxes. You act as your own trustee, thus eliminating any professional fees. You dispose of the assets as you please, retaining the same degree of control that you had before creating the trust.

Assets in living trust do not go through probate!

One advantage in using a trust is that, to the extent that these are assets in the trust, at death, those assets are not subject to the probate process. Therefore, if all of your assets are in a living trust when you die, your estate completely avoids probate. Assets are transferred sooner to family members at a lower administrative cost. Also, you assets are not exposed to public record as they are if they go through probate. In addition to keeping your affairs private, a living trust makes it more difficult for anyone to challenge the disposition of your estate.

Finally, a living trust provides a perfect vehicle for managing assets in the event of your disability. A will carries no such benefit: wills function only in the event of death.

Remember one thing: Only those assets titled in the trust's name avoid probate. Upon the creation of the trust, make sure that you change the title of your assets.

Even if you place your assets in a living trust, it is a good idea to draft a "pour-over" will. This document gives instructions for the disposition of assets not put in the will.

If you are considering a living trust, keep in mind that creating a living trust can involve higher costs than creating a will, and funding a living trust can be time consuming.

Life Insurance and Estate Planning—Life insurance can be an important part of your estate plan. It can provide:

- For the equitable distribution of assets to your heirs.

- Ready funds to pay estate taxes and settlement costs without the delay and costs of probate.

- A significant death benefit for your beneficiaries cost effectively.

- Favorable tax treatment of death benefits.

Estate Taxes—You think your federal income tax rate is high? Try out a marginal estate tax rate as high as 55%. Add to that the administrative costs of settling some estates, and more than half of what you worked for during your life can disappear when you die. Careful estate planning is your best protection against losing those assets you want to give to your beneficiaries. Do you need to worry about estate taxes? The answer depends on how much your estate is worth. In 1998, the law allowed each taxpayer an Applicable Exclusion Amount of $625,000. This means that those who died in 1998 could have transferred up to $625,000 of property during their life, at their death or a combination of both without paying gift or estate taxes. Those whose taxable estates exceeded $625,000 in 1998 would have been subject to marginal tax rates ranging from 37% up to 55% (See chart below).

Estate Tax Rates for 1998

Taxable Estate 1998	Tax (assumes maximum credit)	Marginal Tax Rate
$625,000	$ 0	37%
$750,000	$46,250	39%
$1,000,000	$143,750	41%
$1,250,000	$246,250	43%
$1,500,000	$353,750	45%
$2,000,000	$578,750	49%
$2,500,000	$823,750	53%
$3,000,000	$1,088,750	55%

The applicable credit amount of $202,050 (the tax on the first $625,000) has been built into this table. The benefits of the graduated estate and gift tax rates and credit are phased out for transfers of over $10 million. Annual lifetime gifts which exceed the annual exclusion (generally $10,000 per donee per year) will also reduce the estate owner's credit.

The Applicable Exclusion Amount increases over the next several years until it reaches $1 million in 2006. The chart below shows the scheduled increases in the Applicable Exclusion Amount, and the marginal estate tax rate as it increase.

Year of Transfer	Applicable Exclusion Amount after Martial and Other Deductions	Marginal Tax Rate
1998	$625,000	37%
1999	$650,000	37%
2000	$675,000	37%
2001	$675,000	37%
2002	$700,000	37%
2003	$700,000	37%
2004	$850,000	39%
2005	$950,000	39%
2006 on	$1,000,000	41%

But do not worry, there are ways to protect yourself against taxes.

Basic Estate Strategies—Are your life savings at risk? The answer depends on how much your estate is worth at the time of your death. The Applicable Exclusion Amount in an estate is exempt from federal estate taxes. So your goal should be to find a way to keep the estimated value of your taxable estate from going higher, while still ensuring that you and your heirs enjoy access to your assets when they are needed and wanted. Generally, your estate must pay taxes for every dollar it is valued over the Applicable Exclusion Amount. And the more valuable your estate, the higher the estate tax rate you will pay. Fortunately, there are several ways to reduce your estate tax exposure, while still providing for your heirs after you're gone. Here is a sampling of some basic estate tax savings ideas you can take advantage of:

The Unlimited Marital Deduction—Federal estate tax law provides an unlimited marital deduction—one of the most powerful estate planning tools available. If you distribute assets to your surviving spouse, the spouse receives them estate and gift tax free (if your spouse is a U.S. citizen). If property passes outright to your spouse through a will, trust or operation of law, it should qualify for the unlimited marital deduction at your death. But, it will be included in the taxable estate of your spouse unless it is spent or gifted during the survivor's lifetime, or unless the surviving spouse remarries and the unlimited marital deduction allows the estate to pass to his or her surviving spouse.

Marital Trusts—What if you do not want to give your assets directly to your spouse? You may use a Marital Trust (sometimes referred to as *Trust A in an A-B Plan*) to hold assets for the benefit of your spouse, and still qualify for the marital deduction. A Marital Trust pays all of its income to the surviving spouse.

This is a requirement. The spouse may also be entitled to certain amounts of principal upon request. You may even provide the trustee with discretion to make distributions to the surviving spouse as the trustee feels appropriate. There is one other requirement that the Marital Trust must meet. It must be included in the surviving spouse's gross estate when that spouse dies. If the estate of the surviving spouse, including those assets, is large enough, it may be subject to estate taxes. Estate tax is deferred at the time of the first spouse's death, not avoided.

QTIP Protection—One special type of marital trust is the QTIP Trust. The QTIP (Qualified Terminable Interest Property) Trust allows an individual to provide a surviving spouse with income from the trust for the spouse's lifetime. However, unlike other marital trusts, once the surviving spouse dies, the remaining trust assets are passed to those beneficiaries named in the first spouse's will. Thus, an individual may provide financial support for a surviving spouse, but retain control of, or direct, the trust assets after the surviving spouse's death. Upon the death of the surviving spouse, the entire value of the QTIP trust is included in the surviving spouse's gross estate and may be subject to estate taxes.

Credit Shelter Trusts—A Credit Shelter Trust (also referred to as a *Family Trust, By-Pass Trust,* or *Trust B in an A-B plan*) is a valuable tool which helps married couples avoid paying unnecessary estate taxes. It does this by ensuring that the Applicable Exclusion Amounts of both spouses are fully utilized. Here is how it works. At death, an individual leaves an amount equal to the Applicable Exclusion Amount to a Credit Shelter Trust. In 1998, this was equal to $625,000, and will increase over the next several years until it reaches $1,000,000 by 2000. The exclusion amount is applied to this transfer and it is, thus, exempt from federal estate taxes. The trust can be used to provide the surviving spouse with income for life and principal payments if needed to maintain lifestyle. When the surviving spouse dies, the entire value of the trust, including appreciation, is passed to the heirs of the original spouse, tax free. Upon death, the Applicable Exclusion Amount of the surviving spouse is applied to value of his or her estate independent of the assets in the trust. Thus, the maximum tax savings is achieved by ensuring that the Applicable Exclusion Amounts of both spouses are fully utilized.

The Annual Gift Tax Exclusion—The annual gift tax exclusion is a great way to reduce your estate taxes while keeping your assets within your family. Each individual can gift as much as $10,000 per person per year without tax consequences. A married couple can give away $20,000 per person, per year. Beginning in 1999, the gift tax annual exclusion was indexed for inflation and rounded down to the next lowest multiple of $1,000. By making annual gifts to children or grandchildren, or to a trust in their name, you can potentially reduce your future exposure to estate taxes in two ways:

- You eliminate assets from your estate.

- You eliminate the possibility that these assets will appreciate as part of your taxable estate.

Not sure you want to gift thousands of dollars into the hands of minors? You can gift to a child through the *Uniform Gifts to Minors Act*, known in some states as the *Uniform Transfers to Minors Act*. Under this act, the minor is considered to be the owner of gifted property from the outset, but it is held, managed and distributed by a custodian. When the minor reaches the age of majority as set by law (18 - 21 depending on the state), the property passes to the beneficiary outright. Trusts can be used in a similar way to provide gifts without giving underage children control of valuable assets. Talk to your estate planning professional to find out about these arrangements.

Beware of the Combined Gift-Estate Tax Exclusion—The estate and gift tax system is unified, meaning taxable gifts are subject to the same progressive tax rate schedule as taxable estates. Therefore, taxable gifts valued up to the Applicable Exclusion Amount (discussed above) create no gift tax, and estates valued up to the Applicable Exclusion Amount create no estate tax. *Beware: these are combined transactions.* For example, if an individual died in 1998 after making $200,000 of taxable gifts during life, only $425,000 could have been excluded from estate taxes at death ($625,000 - $200,000 = $425,000). The Applicable Exclusion Amount is first applied to lifetime gifts, then to transfers at death.

Why You May Want to Start Gifting Today?—Even with the unified gift tax system, you may want to start gifting today to potentially reduce your future exposure to estate taxes. By gifting sooner, you remove the assets and future appreciation and income from your estate.

Giving Appreciating Assets—Gifts do not have to be in cash. Any asset qualifies. In fact, you will save the most in estate taxes by giving assets with the highest probability of future appreciation. For example, Gina gave her daughter a municipal bond worth $10,000. During the next five years the bond generated $700 of income annually, but did not appreciate in value. After five years, Gina had passed $13,500 of assets that otherwise would have been includable in her estate.

Suppose Gina gave her daughter $10,000 in stock. If the stock generated no dividends during the next five years but doubled in value, as you can see in the following chart, Gina would have given her daughter $20,000 of assets and taken them out of her estate.

	Municipal Bond	Appreciating Stock
Value of gift	$10,000	$10,000
Income and appreciation (5 years)	+ 3,500	+10,000
Total excluded from estate tax	$13,500	$20,000

Note: By giving an appreciating asset, Gina takes an extra $6,500 out of her estate.

Charitable Giving—If you share your estate with charity, it will usually reduce your estate tax bill. Direct bequests to charity are generally fully deductible for estate tax purposes. Therefore, if you leave your entire estate to charity, you should not owe estate taxes.

The Role of Life Insurance—Life insurance may be an important tool in creating a successful estate plan for the following reasons:

- **It can help maintain your heirs' lifestyles in the event of your death**—The lost earning power resulting from your death can have a devastating effect on your family's lifestyle. Life insurance can help ease that burden by providing a sum of cash to your heirs which can be invested and drawn upon as needed.

- **Insurance is sometimes the best solution for liquidity problem**—Estates are often cash poor if they are comprised primarily of assets such as closely held business interests, real estate or collectibles. Your heirs may need a sizable amount of cash to pay the administrative and tax liabilities on your estate. And the assets in your estate may be difficult to sell or, for personal reasons, you may not want them sold. Life insurance can help preserve your estate by providing your heirs with the help they need to pay the estate taxes, administrative costs and funeral expenses relating to your death.

- **Insurance can be an excellent vehicle for equalizing distribution of your estate among heirs**—For example, a child that is active in your business can inherit the $1 million of stock, while your other child can inherit $1 million of insurance proceeds.

Keep Life Insurance Proceeds from Adding to Your Estate Tax—If you own a life insurance policy at your death, the proceeds are included in your taxable estate. Ownership is usually determined by who has the right to name the beneficiaries of the policy proceeds. The way around this problem? Do not own the policies when you die. One way is to create an *Irrevocable Life Insurance Trust (ILIT)*. Most effective for estates with values higher than the Applicable Exclusion Amount, an ILIT is also called a *wealth preservation trust* because it helps preserve an estate's value. Here is how: The grantor makes tax-free gifts to the trust using the $10,000 annual gift exclusion ($20,000 if married and the spouse consents). The trust ultimately uses the cash to pay premiums on a life insurance policy which it has purchased. The trust owns the life insurance policy and is the beneficiary, and the insured is usually the grantor and/or the grantor's spouse. In turn, the grantor's spouse and children can be the beneficiaries of the trust, so that when the insured dies, the death benefit is paid to the ILIT and the proceeds can be available for the benefit of the spouse and children.

The life insurance proceeds from the policy in the trust should not be taxed in the insured's estate, and if under certain conditions the proceeds remain in the trust, they will not be included in the estate of the surviving spouse. The insurance proceeds are also not subject to income tax. Be sure to get legal, accounting and tax advice before setting up an ILIT. A properly structured trust could save you 55 percent in estate taxes on any insurance proceeds.

When should you update your Plan?—Many investors wonder how often they should update their estate plan. To help guide you, just ask yourself if since you first structured your estate plan:

- Have the tax laws changed?

- Have you married or divorced? Have you had children or grandchildren?

- Have you gotten a promotion or a raise? Has your net worth changed?

291

- Have you moved to a different state? (different states have different rules governing estates).

- Have any special circumstances occurred? For example, do you have a child with special needs, or has your spouse's ability to earn a living changed due to a disability?

If you answered "yes" to any of the above, you should probably update your estate plan to reflect these important events. It could make all the difference in ensuring your affairs are carried out in an orderly fashion that coincides with your wishes.

Questions and Answers

- **My colleague tells me that upon my death my 403(b) assets might not pass to my daughter, who I have designated as the sole beneficiary in my will. How can that be?**—It depends on who is the designated beneficiary of your 403(b) account. Retirement accounts by law must be held in an individual's name, and the sponsoring company is required by law to honor those beneficiary designations stated in the account. Even though retirement plans are considered part of your estate, for tax-planning purposes they are uniquely titled, and therefore are not covered by your will. If there is a discrepancy between that beneficiary and the designated beneficiary in the will, the beneficiary designation of the retirement account wins out. That us the primary reason why it is important that *all* beneficiary designations are up-to-date. Additionally, keep in mind that life events like marriage, divorce, children, grandchildren, illness, etc., could trigger changes in your estate planning. But if you do not keep up with those changes in your retirement plan, you may end up leaving the bulk of your estate to someone you have not even spoken to in years.

- **What happens if I fail to name a beneficiary on my retirement account assets?**—Too many people do leave that part of the investment application form completely blank, assuming that they will get around to it later on. But without a designated beneficiary, you lose control of those assets to the fund company's, or the trustee's, default mechanism. In most cases this means that the retirement account money gets dropped into your estate in a lump sum, and can trigger both income taxes and estate taxes. As a consequence, this could leave you heirs with very little money. Also, unlike most assets in an estate, 403(b) and Traditional Deductible IRA assets are subject to double taxation—income and inheritance taxes. If the retirement plan has not been properly structured, your beneficiaries could end up collecting only around 20% of the retirement assets once Uncle Sam takes his cut.

- **What happens if I fail to name a second beneficiary and my first beneficiary dies before I do?**—That is even more common than not naming a primary beneficiary. But, under this circumstance, the results are the same—the account assets are subject to the fund company's distribution policies.

- **Would it be wise to name my estate as the beneficiary of my 403(b) account?**—No. In most cases, this means a quick liquidation of the 403(b), triggering both income taxes and, potentially, estate taxes.

- **What other considerations should I keep in mind with regard to estate planning and my 403(b)?**—Three things come to mind:

1. Be sure that if your intent is to name minor children as the beneficiaries to your 403(b) if you and your spouse die, don't name them directly. If you name your children directly, and you and your spouse die, the state controls the money, even if under your will you have set up a trust for those children. They will not see that money until they reach the age of majority, which is 18 or 21, depending on the state. Instead, make sure the trust itself is named as the beneficiary.

2. Deals with designating multiple beneficiaries. Simply leaving assets to be divided equally among your children does not take into account the distinct possibility that one of your children may die before you. In this case, the assets would be divided among the surviving children, when, instead, you may have wanted a portion of the deceased child's money to go to his/her grandchildren.

3. There is the *account distribution choice* concern. This can be one of most expensive mistakes the owner of a retirement plan can make. When the holder reaches 70 ½, he/she is required to start taking minimum distributions. At that time, the holder can choose a distribution plan based on his/her life-expectancy alone, called the *term-certain method*; choose a distribution plan based on both the holder and his/her spouse's joint life-expectancy and recalculates life-expectancy each year, called the *recalculation method*; or choose a distribution plan that combines the first two, called the *hybrid method*. With the hybrid method, the owner of the account usually selects the recalculation method, and the beneficiary selects the term-certain method. Although it is more complicated, it provides greater flexibility for estate planning and extending life expectancy.

- **Much has been written about the importance of the Roth IRA as an estate planning tool. Is it as good as it sounds?**—The Roth IRA can be a very effective estate planning tool, indeed. But there is a common misconception that may minimize the Roth IRA's value in this area. The misconception is that the Roth IRA will pass to your beneficiaries 100% tax free. That simply is not true. The truth is, while the earnings are free from income tax, the estate must still pay estate taxes. For estate planning purposes, it is especially important to fully understand the tax ramifications of each type of IRA, particularly the Roth IRA. Therefore, you should consult your tax professional before making any final decisions.

Note

The material presented contained references to concepts in estate planning that have legal, accounting and tax implications. It was not intended as legal, accounting or tax advice. I strongly urge you to consult your own attorney and/or accountant, and/or tax professional for advice regarding your particular situation.

CHAPTER TWENTY

Your Next Steps

Now that you have completed the manual, you are ready to implement a strategy and begin investing your money, or possibly make changes to an existing strategy. To help you put your strategy into action, I have provided a checklist of items, along with its chapter reference, that you should review to help you reach your retirement savings goal. Start saving for retirement as soon as possible!!!

- Plug the money leaks in your budget by completing a *Personal Balance Sheet* and a *Cash Flow Statement*. (chapter 6)

- Free up as much money as you can for investing by employing the *Cost-Cutting/Saving Strategies* found in this manual. (chapter 7)

- Complete a *Retirement Savings Worksheet*. This will help you develop a retirement goal and an annual savings target to meet that goal. (chapter 6)

- Determine your personal tolerance for risk. (chapter 5)

- Determine your bottom-line liquidity needs. (chapters 6 and 16)

- Take precautions to protect your present and future assets. (chapter 4)

- Identify a pre-retirement investment strategy with which you are comfortable. Select an asset allocation model that best matches your personality and retirement goals. (chapter 13)

- Select specific funds that match your asset allocation model by studying publications and companies that analyze, track, and rate investment products, such as no-load mutual funds, etc. (chapter 13)

- Employ dollar-cost averaging. Set up a regular program to save money for retirement and stick with it. Start by saving *at least* 10% of your income. Remember, pay yourself first! (Chapter 9)

- If your employer does not have a 403(b) plan, suggest that they start one. (Chapters 9 and 12)

- If your employer does sponsor a 403(b) plan, determine your MEA and *contribute the maximum allowed*. If you can not contribute the maximum, contribute what you can and slowly work up to the maximum. (Chapter 9)

- Once you contribute the maximum allowed to your 403(b) plan, open an IRA and make the maximum annual IRA contribution. Whether your contributions are tax-deductible or not, next to a 403(b) plan, an IRA is still one of the best ways to save for retirement. (Chapter 14)

- If you are leaving your job and receive an eligible rollover distribution from your 403(b) plan, consider rolling it over directly into a Rollover IRA or other eligible retirement plan. (Chapter 18)

- Consider an annuity to put away additional money on a tax-deferred basis after you maximize your 403(b) plan and IRA. (Chapter 15)

- If you have any self-employed income or own a small business, make the maximum allowable contribution to a Keogh or SEP-IRA. (Chapter 8)

- Make sure your retirement assets continue to be allocated (diversified) appropriately. Review your investment strategy carefully at least once a year. (Chapter 13)

- Increase the amount you are saving each year to account for the effects of inflation. (Chapter 1)

- Choose a withdrawal option to handle your qualified retirement plan(s) distribution(s). (Chapter 18)

- Follow strategies designed to help you avoid outliving your retirement money. (Chapter 18)

- Choose an asset allocation strategy to be followed in retirement that will carry you through the life of your retirement. (Chapter 18)

- Be sure to correctly name your 403(b), IRA, and annuity beneficiaries and structure the payouts. (Chapter 19)

- Congratulate yourself for having the confidence to do-it-yourself.

Some Pearls of Wisdom—If followed, the preceding statements will serve you well when investing for your retirement. Yes, you have already read some of them, but they are so very important.

- Think long-term. You will sleep better.

- Know yourself—create financial goals and figure out how much risk you are comfortable with.

- Do not invest a dime in something you do not understand.

- Do not base investment choices on the recommendations of co-workers. A recent survey shows that a full 20% of investors base their investment decisions on the advice of co-workers and friends! You should not do the same. One size does not fit all.

- Do not try to time the market. Those who do usually end up with far less than those who do not.

- Only use a financial planner if you feel you must, and then only for a narrow question or two.

- Keep a watchful eye on expenses, such as commissions, management fees, etc.,—they eat into your return.

- Do not make investment selections without taking into account what else you own. Look at your whole portfolio, including your spouse's retirement plan.

- Do not make the mistake of allocating assets based on the total number of available options (for example, if your employer offers 10 funds, you put 10% in each). That entails no more thought than cutting an apple pie into eight slices—and that is your future!

- Reduce risk by allocating investments in different asset classes (stock funds, bond funds, and cash funds).
- Diversify *within* asset classes (for example, owning mutual stock funds of small *and* large companies).
- Do not choose the safest investment, without understanding that *all* investments involve risk.

- Do not assume that the most aggressive investment will automatically produce the greatest return.

- Reinvest all dividends and interest of long-term investments.

- Think for yourself, even if you have a bevy of advisors.

- Keep adequate records.

- Engage in watchful waiting—keep track of your investments and economic/financial news, but do not be swayed by short-term moves regarding your long-term investments.

You now have within your grasp the information necessary to develop and implement your own strategy for retirement investing. All you need now is the fortitude to move forward.

You can do it! Good luck!

Glossary of Investing Terms

A

AAA—Highest rating given by bond rating agencies—highly unlikely to default.

Actuarial Evaluation—A life-expectancy calculation by a professional actuary.

Adjusted Gross Income (AGI)—Total personal income for the tax year minus allowable adjustments, such as unreimbursed business expenses, contributions to a traditional IRA, and alimony payments. It is the income used to calculate federal income tax. It is also referred to as AGI.

ADR(American Depositary Receipt)—A way U.S. investors can invest in foreign companies without buying shares in overseas markets. Receipts for shares of foreign companies are in U.S. banks for U.S. shareholders and entitle the ADR purchaser to all dividends and capital gains.

Agency Bonds—Bonds issued by U.S. government-related agencies, such as Fannie Mae and Freddie Mac. These bonds are very safe and backed by assets, such as home mortgages. They pay slightly more interest than U.S. Treasury bonds.

Aggressive Investment—A volatile, difficult-to-predict investment that is subject to rapid gain or loss. This type of investment seeks maximum growth by investing in companies whose earnings are expected to grow significantly, and is generally appropriate for long-term holdings (10 or more years), and for investors willing to accept fluctuations in the value of their investments. Usually, the companies pay little or no dividends.

Alternative Minimum Tax—A parallel tax system devised to ensure that at least a minimum amount of tax is paid by high-income individuals and corporations.

American Stock Exchange (ASE or AMEX)—One of the three major stock exchanges in the United States.

Amortization—A method of paying off debt in which a borrower pays off a portion of the interest and principal periodically. Amortization numbers are found on balance sheets.

Amounts Previously Excludable—Used in computing the available maximum exclusion allowance. Generally they consist of all employee contributions to a 403(b) plan that were either excludable from gross income or in excess of the limit in prior taxable years. They also include prior contributions to a qualified plan of the employer.

Annuity—An investment product offered by insurance companies, which usually guarantees a fixed or variable rate of interest for a period of time. These investments can be quite safe, depending on the insurance company's financial stability; however, they tend to provide low-yields investments.

Appreciation—An increase in the value of an asset such as a stock, bond, commodity or real estate.

Ask—The lowest price at which someone is willing to sell a security.

Assets—Cash, stocks, bonds, mutual funds, real estate or anything else with value.

Asset Allocation—The mix of assets in an investor's portfolio (e.g., cash equivalents, stocks and bonds). The proper balance of assets depends on the expected return and risk of each asset class as well as the investor's risk tolerance, age, and goals.

Asset class—Typically refers to securities that have similar features. For example, stocks and bonds are the two main classes. They may be subdivided into other classes like mortgages, common stock, and preferred stock. Asset classes are used in the process of asset allocation to control the risk and return characteristics of a portfolio. In the long run, with a diversified portfolio, over 90 percent of your returns as an investor are determined by the class of assets you decide to hold. The remaining percentage of your return depends on which specific stock, bond or mutual fund you buy and when you buy it.

Averages—There are several averages that are used to measure the performance of the stock market or a certain type of stock. An average is the average price for a collection of stocks that are typical examples of the market they represent. Some examples of averages are the Dow Jones Industrial Average, the Russell 2000 Average, and the S & P 500 average.

Average Annual Return—on average, how much the investment gains in value each year. Make sure that the average annual return of the investments you are looking into include gains from dividends, interest and distributions, not just gains in the price of the asset.

Average Annual Total Return—Often called the internal rate of return (IRR), the average annual total return is a percentage equal to the interest rate on a bank account that would give you the same total return on your investment. It takes into account money earned by the investment (interest, dividends, capital gains distributions) as well as changes in share price. Since it is an annual rate, it acts like a bank interest rate that compounds annually. Also called the return on investment (ROI) or total return on investments.

Average Maturity—The lifetime of a bond, concluding when the final payment of that obligation is due.

B

Back-End Load—A fee to sell shares in a mutual fund. The fee is usually a percentage of the total amount withdrawn and often decreases the longer a shareholder remains in a fund. (A front-end load is a fee to buy shares in a mutual fund. No-load mutual funds charge investors nothing to buy or sell shares in the fund.)

Balanced Fund—A kind of mutual fund that typically buys a mixture of bonds, preferred stock, and common stock to achieve the highest return with the lowest risk. It blends long-term growth from stocks with income from dividends.

Balance Sheet—An official financial statement that includes a company's assets (things it owns, such as cash, capital equipment, and investments) and liabilities (things it owes such as accounts payable and long-term debt). To determine a company's net worth, you subtract its liabilities from its assets. You can use a company's balance sheet to determine its financial health.

Bear Market—A bear market is one that is declining; that is, stock prices are falling, and so is the amount of money that companies have to spend on growth. This is the opposite of a bull market, which is growing.

Before-Tax Earned Income—Income earned from your employment before you pay your taxes. It includes salaries, commissions, wages, tips, self employment income, etc. — basically, what you get from working. It does not include income from your savings and investments (which is called unearned income).

Beta Coefficient—A measure of a stock's volatility relative to the stock market overall. The beta coefficient of the S&P 500 is 1. Any stock that is more volatile than the market as a whole has a beta value higher than 1. If the beta coefficient is less than 1, the portfolio or asset is considered to be less risky than the market. Conservative investors tend to invest in stocks with low beta coefficients, whereas investors willing to take more risk tend to invest in high-beta stocks.

Bid—In a stock market, the bid is the price that a potential buyer is willing to pay for a security. The ask (or asked price) is the lowest price the seller will accept for the security. The difference between the two prices is known as the spread.

Bill—Bond maturing in less than one year (generally refers to the government's Treasury Bills)

Blended-Average Annual Return—The average annual return is based on the combined performance of all transactions for the stock or mutual fund for the history of the portfolio.

Blue-Chip Fund—A type of mutual fund that invests in blue chip stocks (a type of growth fund).

Blue-Chip Stocks—Stocks of seasoned companies that have paid regular dividends in both good and bad years. Investments in blue-chip stocks are relatively conservative and have relatively low risk. Some examples of blue-chip stocks are the 30 securities used to calculate the Dow Jones Industrial Average.

Bond—A type of security that pays a fixed amount of interest at a regular interval over a certain period of time. Bonds are essentially loans given to companies and government entities who promise to pay back the loan at a specified interest rate. As a bond holder, you receive that interest payment once a year.

Bond Maturity—The lifetime of a bond, concluding when the final payment of that obligation is due.

Bond-Oriented Mutual Funds—A type of mutual fund that invests primarily in bonds. Investments in bond-oriented mutual funds are relatively conservative and have a lower risk than investments in stocks.

Book Value—The book value of a company is the difference between the company's total assets and its intangible assets, such as good will, patents, and so forth. The book value does not include current liabilities either. The book value is the net asset value available for payment of a particular item.

Broker—A broker is someone who handles the transferring of a security from a seller to a buyer. Brokers must be licensed by the Securities and Exchange Commission (SEC).

Brokerage—A brokerage is a business that employs brokers to enact transactions between securities sellers and buyers. There are three types of brokerages: full-service brokerages, discount brokerages, and deep-discount brokerages.

Bull Market—A market in which prices are moving upward. This is the opposite of a bear market, in which prices are declining.

Buy—Purchase of a security.

Buying On Margin—Buying on margin means that the investor borrows money from a broker to buy a security. Investors usually do this when they are confident that the price of a security will go up.

Buy to Close—You close a short option position when you buy it back.

Buy to Open—You open a long position when you buy an option.

Bypass Trusts—Simply put, for estate planning purposes, you can exclude assets from someone's estate by putting the assets into a trust. For example, to keep assets out of your spouse's estate after you die, you can put the assets in a trust such that the spouse gets the income from the trust, but upon the spouse's death, the body of the trust goes to the children. In essence, the spouse's estate has been "bypassed." For large estates, this can reduce estate taxes significantly.

C

Calendar Year—A 12-month period beginning January 1 and ending December 31.

Call Option—Gives its buyer the right to buy or sell 100 shares of the underlying security at a fixed price before a specified expiration date. Call buyers hope the price of the stock will rise. Call sellers hope the price will stay the same or go down.

Capital Appreciation (or loss)—An increase (or decrease) in the price of securities you own.

Capital Gain for Mutual Funds—Arises when an investment is sold at a higher price than originally paid. In a mutual fund, capital gains are created when the fund buys and sells underlying securities at a premium over purchase price. These gains are then distributed to unitholders at least annually. Unitholders can also earn capital gains by redeeming their fund shares at higher prices than they originally paid.

Capital Gain—The difference between an asset's purchase price and selling price. (The difference is called a capital gain only if it is a positive amount.)

Cash Flow Statement (Personal)—A statement measuring the money going into and coming out of the household. If a household has negative cash flow, this means the household must borrow money to keep going. If a household has positive cash flow, this means the household has extra money to spend on discretionary items such as investments, vacations, etc.

Cash Investment—A very short-term loan to a borrower with a very high credit rating. Examples of cash investments are bank certificates of deposit (CDs), Treasury Bills (T-Bills), and money market funds. A cash investment typically offers investors great principal stability, but little long-term growth.

Cash-Value Life Insurance—This combines basic insurance protection with tax-deferred investing. A portion of your annual premium pays for insurance, while the rest goes into the policy's investment or cash-value account. Your investment earnings accumulate free of taxes until you withdraw them, but it often takes 10 years or more for the tax-deferral benefits to overcome the drag of the commissions charged by insurers.

Certificate Of Deposit (CD)—A CD is an FDIC-insured investment offered by financial institutions that guarantees a specified rate of return for a specified term. Maturities range from overnight to many years. It is generally considered a conservative investment.

Closed-End Mutual Fund—A mutual fund that has a set number of shares available to investors. You buy and sell closed-end mutual funds on the open market, unlike open-end mutual funds, which you buy and sell through the mutual fund company (or a broker). The supply and demand for a closed-end mutual fund determines its price, not its net asset value.

Common Stock—Securities that represent an ownership interest in a corporation.

Compounding—The computation of interest paid using the principal plus the previously earned interest which is reinvested.

Commercial Paper—Short-term debt obligations maturing in 2 to 270 days, issued by banks and corporations.

Combined Weighted Expected Return—The sum of the average annual return of each asset in the portfolio multiplied by its weighting in the portfolio. For example, an investor who had $2 invested in bonds yielding 7 percent, $3 invested in a growth fund which experienced a gain of 10 percent a year and $1 invested in a money market fund yielding 4 percent a year could expect a combined weighted expected return of 8 percent a year.

Contrarian Investing—A method of investing which involves ignoring market trends and buying neglected and depressed stocks of well-managed companies. Contrarians select the opposite of what most people are investing in at a given time by looking for healthy companies in unpopular industries or overlooked firms. A contrarian adviser tends to buy stocks with low price-earnings ratios (P/Es). Some mutual funds use contrarian investing.

Convertible Bond—Under certain conditions, it may be exchanged for other securities of the issuing organization, usually stock.

Corporate Bond—Debt obligations issued by corporations as an alternative to offering equity ownership by issuing stock. Like most municipal bonds and Treasuries, most corporate bonds pay semi-annual interest and promise to return their principal when they mature. Maturities range from 1 to 30 years. Corporate bonds are generally traded on major exchanges, and have a face/par value of $1,000. Interest earned is fully taxable.

Correction—A relatively short-lived drop in market prices. It is called a correction because professionals consider it a return to appropriate values.

Coupon Rate—The stated interest rate on the bond.

Current Ratio—A company's current assets divided by its current liabilities. From this ratio, you can determine whether a company could pay off its debts with its current assets if it needed to. A ratio greater than 1 is better than a ratio below 1. For example, a ratio of 1.45 to 1.0 indicates that the company has $1.45 to cover each $1.00 of its current debt. Ranking competitors in an industry by their current ratios is an accepted method for judging their relative financial strength.

Current Yield—The annual interest on a bond divided by the current market price.

Custodial Account—A type of funding vehicle under which assets are held by a bank or other person approved by the Commissioner and invested in regulated investment company stock (mutual funds) as required by IRC 403(b)(7).

D

Day (Only) Order—An order condition that causes your order to be canceled at the end of the current day's trading if the specified limits can not be met.

Debit Card—A type of card that gives you electronic access to your money. Although it looks like a credit card, it is more like using cash or a check to pay for your purchases. Funds are immediately withdrawn from your bank account—there is no float on your money. You may not get the same protection from problem products or stolen cards that you get with a credit card. Debit cards are usually easier to obtain than credit cards and more commonly accepted than checks.

Deferred Gain—The gain in the value of an investment (either in interest, dividends or both) that is not taxed until a later date (for example, when you sell a home and reinvest the proceeds in a new home).

Defined Benefit Plan (aka Pension)—A company retirement plan in which you expect to receive a fixed amount on a regular basis from your employer based on salary history and years of service.

Debenture—a bond which is not backed or secured by collateral.

Default—The bond issuer's failure to pay the interest or principal that has come due on its bonds.

Defined Contribution Plan—A company retirement plan such as a 401(k) or 403(b), in which the employee elects to defer salary into the plan and directs the investments of that deferral.

Direct Rollover—An eligible rollover distribution from a 403(b) plan that is paid directly from the plan to an IRA or another 403(b) plan.

Discount—A bond is said to sell at a discount when the market price of the bond is less than par value (face value).

Distribution—For mutual funds, the distribution is the amount paid out to investors. Capital gain distribution refers to the profits the fund makes selling its investments. Income distribution refers to the money the fund earns when its investments grow in value. The money that is withdrawn from a 403(b) plan without penalty, when done after the investor reaches at least age 59 ½, is also known as a distribution.

Diversification—Spreading investment dollars among different kinds of securities, asset classes and time horizons to balance ones portfolio and reduce risk.

Dividend—A dividend is an amount of money or stock that a corporation pays to its shareholders quarterly. Typically, only larger companies pay dividends; smaller companies need to invest their own profits to grow. Some investors interested in producing income invest in dividend-producing securities; growth-oriented investors often also buy dividend-producing securities to round out their portfolio.

Dividend Amount—Value of last quarterly cash dividend or the number of shares an investor receives for each share owned in a stock dividend.

Dividend Reinvestment Plan (DRIP)—A DRIP allows a shareholder's dividends to be reinvested automatically in more shares of a company's stock rather than receiving a check. Many large companies offer DRIPs.

Dividend Yield—Dividend yield is the annual percentage of return paid to a stockholder by a company. Dividend yield is the result of dividing the amount of dividends per share by the stock's current market price. For example, if a stock's current price is $40, and the company pays a $5.00 dividend per share per year, then the dividend yield is 12.5 percent (5/40 = 0.125, which equals 12.5 percent). Several popular investing strategies are based on stocks' dividend yield.

Dollar Cost Averaging—A technique for reducing risk in an investment portfolio. The investor buys a fixed dollar amount of securities at regular time intervals (usually monthly, for example) so that he/she can buy more shares when the price is low and fewer shares when the price is high, resulting in an average cost between high and low.

Dow Jones Industrial Average (DJIA)—An index of 30 large industrial stocks (blue chips), considered leaders in the market. Though often cited by analysts and the media, this index is far less representative of the market as a whole than the broader indices, such as the S&P 500, the Russell 2000, and the Wilshire 5000.

E

Earned Income—Income from your employment before you pay your taxes. It does not include income from your savings and investments.

Earnings—A corporation's profits. An earnings report is a statement a company issues to shareholders and to the public declaring its current profits on either a quarterly or annual basis.

Earnings Limits—Limits, based on income, governing who may qualify for a program. Many tax credits and special savings plans, such as IRAs, have earnings limits.

Earnings Per Share (EPS)—The net income (or earnings) of a company for the past 12 months divided by the current number of shares. For example, if a company has $1 million in net income and 2 million outstanding shares, then its earnings per share is $.50. Many investors consider this an important fundamental to consider when deciding whether to buy or sell a stock.

Earnings Per Share Date—Date of the last earnings announcement.

Earnings-Price Ratio (EPR)—A corporation's earnings per share divided by its current stock price. It is used to compare the attractiveness of stocks, bonds, and money market instruments. It is also known as the earnings yield.

Education IRA—Beginning in 1998, couples with an adjusted gross income of $150,000 or less ($95,000 for singles) can contribute up to $500 per year for children (up to age 18) to an Education IRA. The Education IRA is a trust or custodial account established to help pay the higher-education expenses of your child, grandchild or other designated beneficiary. Like the Roth IRA, this account is funded with after-tax (nondeductible) contributions, but the earnings accumulate tax free, and the amounts in the IRA may be withdrawn free of tax to pay for college

Elective Contributions—Contributions that arise because of an employee's election between current compensation or deferral under the plan.

305

Elective Deferrals—Elective contributions by a participant made to a qualified 403(b) plan, except they do not include contributions made pursuant to one-time irrevocable elections at initial eligibility to participate in the plan nor contributions made as a condition of employment. They are subject to the IRC limit of $10,000.

Electronic Funds Transfer—Transferring funds between accounts and firms electronically.

Eligible Rollover Distribution—Any distribution from a 403(b) plan made to an employee of all or a portion of the balance to his credit, not including required minimum distributions, periodic distributions and distributions not otherwise includible in gross income.

Emerging Market Stocks—Stocks issued by companies in developing countries, such as Chile, Thailand and Mexico.

Emergency Fund—Most financial planners recommend that you keep enough money in a readily accessible fund to cover 3-6 months of living expenses should an emergency arise and your sources of earned income be cut off or reduced. An emergency fund is usually kept in savings accounts, very short term CDs, or money market or fixed income mutual funds that allow check writing on the account.

Emerging Growth Fund—A type of mutual fund that invests in stocks of young, growing companies.

Employee Stock Ownership Plan (ESOP)—A qualified retirement plan designed to give you an ownership stake in the company. Companies contribute shares of stock without requiring you to invest your own money.

Employee Stock Purchase Plan (ESPP)—A plan established by a company that permits employees to buy company stock, usually at a discount. If the stock price goes up, employees can sell their stock for instant wealth. Stock options generally come in two flavors: non-qualified stock options (NCOs) and incentive stock options (ISOs). NCOs are most commonly offered to non-executive employees, whereas ISOs are generally given to execs. In both cases, employers offer employees the right to buy a certain number of shares in the company at a fixed price and over a fixed term.

Employer Contribution (to tax-deferred savings)—Some employers add to your qualified plan contributions, often as an incentive for you to save for your own retirement. The employer might match your contribution, or a portion of it.

Equity—Ownership. When you own part of something, you have equity in it. So, for example, when you own 5,000 shares of Company XYZ's stock, that is your equity in the corporation. In other words, you and other shareholders own a piece of the corporation. In the case of real estate, your home equity equals your down payment plus any principal you've paid on your mortgage.

Estate—All the assets you possess at the time of your death. These include securities, real estate, physical possessions, and cash. Your estate is distributed to your heirs according to the provisions of your will.

Estate Planning—Planning to insure that your assets pass to those that you want to have them in an orderly and efficient manner. When you die, Uncle Sam wants to make sure that he gets his share of what you own—your estate. The rules are complex, and penalties for honest mistakes can be severe. You can avoid problems by drawing up a will, setting up

306

trusts, and planning ahead to avoid unnecessary taxes.

Executor—An Executor is named in a will as the personal representative of the person making the will and as Executor they are charged with the duty of carrying out the intent of the will.

Excess Contributions—They are contributions to a custodial account in excess of the normal limit.

Excess Deferrals—Elective deferrals that are in excess of the limit.

Ex-Dividend Date—Date a split or dividend is reflected in the price of the security (if you buy a stock on the ex-dividend date, you are not entitled to the dividend); for splits, this is the trading day after the distribution is made.

Expense Ratio—The percentage of total investment that shareholders pay annually for mutual fund management fees and operating expenses. Common stock funds tend to have higher expense ratios than bond funds; likewise smaller funds have higher ratios than larger funds. International funds and precious metal funds have higher ratios than domestic funds. Fixed income and index funds tend to have very low expense ratios, but the lowest expense ratios are usually charged by funds aimed at institutional investors.

F

Face Value—The displayed value on a bond also called principal or par value.

Fannie Mae (FNMA)—Federal National Mortgage Association, a public company whose debt is implicitly backed by the U.S. government. Fannie Mae sells bonds which are secured by home mortgages. They are quite safe bonds.

Federal Estate Tax Bracket—If your gross estate is less than $600,000, you generally will have no estate tax problems. Also, if you leave everything to a spouse, there will be no immediate estate tax problems. However, when the second spouse dies and the estate is more than $600,000, there can be very serious estate tax consequences. Estate taxes start at around 35% and can go as high as 55%!!

Fiduciary—One is legally required to act in the best interest and trust of a beneficiary or minor.

52-week High—The highest price at which a security has traded within the previous 52 weeks.

52-week Low—The lowest price at which a security has traded within the previous 52 weeks.

Fill or Kill (FOK)—An order condition that cancels a security order if it cannot be filled immediately in its entirety.

Fiscal Year End (FYE)—FYE is the end of an accounting period that covers 12 consecutive months, which does not necessarily correspond to a calendar year. At the end of the fiscal year, the books are closed and profit or loss is calculated.

Fixed Income Securities—Another term for bonds. Debt securities or IOUs for borrowed money. They obligate the borrower to pay the owner interest during the term of the loan and to return the principal or face value, when the loan matures. A variety of institutions issue debt obligations including the U.S. government, state and local governments, publicly held companies, banks, and savings and loans.

401(k)—A popular retirement plan adopted by many employers which allows either employer or employee—or both—to contribute. Money put into these accounts is tax-exempt until retirement.

403(b)—Similar to a 401(k) only used more in universities and non-profit institutions.

457—Retirement plan specifically designed for those who work for governmental agencies.

Front-End Load—A front-end load is a fee to purchase shares in a mutual fund. (A back-end load is a fee to sell shares in a mutual fund. No-load mutual funds charge investors nothing to buy or sell shares in the fund.)

Funding Vehicle—Refers to the type of investment arrangement for the assets of a 403(b) plan.

G

Ginnie Mae (GNMA)—A government agency which guarantees payment of mortgage-backed securities representing a pooling of residential mortgages.

Global fund—An international mutual fund that invests in securities from around the world, including the United States. See also International fund.

Good Until Canceled (GTC)—An order condition which will remain open until it is filled or until you cancel it or for 60 days (whichever is first), if it is not filled immediately due to conditions placed on the order.

Government Bond—A bond sold by the U.S. government.

Growth and Income Fund—A mutual fund that seeks both capital appreciation and current income by investing in dividend-paying and growth stocks for capital appreciation and bonds for current income. A growth and income fund combines long-term capital gains with steady income. Invest in growth and income funds if you find growth funds too risky or if you depend on income produced by your assets.

Growth Fund—A growth fund is a mutual fund that invests in growth stocks. Investors who want high capital appreciation tend to invest in growth stocks, which are more conservative than income funds. Growth stocks are usually purchased as a long-term holding, with the expectation that they will appreciate in price per share (and perhaps pay dividends) in the future.

Growth Stock—Stocks of younger or smaller companies, have relatively high risk and represent relatively aggressive investments. Usually, they have grown significantly in the past 3 to 5 years and are expected to continue growing for the next few years. Dividends, if any, are small and erratic, mostly because growing companies prefer to reinvest earnings in development efforts rather than set aside a percentage for shareholders. Growth stocks are usually purchased as a long-term holding, with the expectation that they will pay dividends (as well as appreciate in price per share) in the future, thus providing income at a later time.

Guaranteed Income Contract (GIC)—An insurance company contract investment that promises to pay a fixed rate of interest and to return the investor's principal after a specified term, usually one to five years. GICs are generally considered low-risk investments but long-term bonds, stocks and other investments generally have a greater return.

H

Health Maintenance Organization (HMO)—A type of health care plan that offers patients a low deductible and little or no copayments for visits to approved physicians and hospitals. Pure HMOs require members to use doctors and hospitals that belong to that HMO network.

High—The highest execution price of a trade that day, or on the last trading day.

High Risk—Compared to other assets over a specific time frame, the risk of losing the money you invested is relatively high (but implicitly acceptable) given the return.

Home Equity Loan—Also called an equity loan or a second mortgage. A home equity loan is a line of credit secured by your home. When you use this credit line to buy something, the financial institution giving you the line of credit places a second mortgage loan on your home until the debt is paid off, after which the credit line may again be used to buy something else. The interest rate on such loans is usually lower than on standard second mortgages or credit cards. Most interest on home equity loans is tax deductible. Like any mortgage, if a home equity loan is not paid off, your home may be sold to satisfy the debt.

House Call—The amount of money an investor needs to deposit to their brokerage account to meet the broker's minimum maintenance level in a margin account.

I

Immediate or Cancel—An order condition that requires all or part of an order to be executed immediately. The part of the order that cannot be executed immediately is canceled.

Includible Compensation—Generally all salary, bonuses and other wages from the employer includible in gross income for the employee's most recent one-year period of service ending with or within the taxable year excluding amounts contributed on the employee's behalf to a 403(b) or qualified plan.

Income Fund—An income mutual fund invests in securities that provide its investors with current income. Typically, these funds invest in different types of bonds or possibly utility stocks that provide high dividends. You are taxed for the income fund's distributions in the year that you receive them (unless you hold the income fund in a tax-deferred account such as an IRA or Keogh).

Income Stocks—Stocks of stable companies, having relatively low to moderate risk and representing relatively conservative investments. If you want to invest for both growth and current income, buy income stocks because of their potential for regular dividend payments. Income stocks tend to be in stable service industries, such as communications and utilities, and can offer both higher-than-average dividend payments and the possibility of capital appreciation.

Index Fund—An index fund is a mutual fund that invests in all the stocks upon which an index is based. For example, an index fund based on the S& P 500 invests in all the stocks included in the S & P 500 index. By investing in every stock in the index, the index fund performance closely mirrors the performance of the index itself.

309

Indexing—Investing for market returns by purchasing shares in an index fund.

Inflation—Inflation is a rise in the price of commodities and services. For example, $1.00 buys less today than it did a decade ago because of inflation. Inflation occurs when spending increases and supplies decrease. Moderate inflation is an expected result of economic growth.

Inflation Rate—The rate at which prices are rising. The higher the rate, the faster the value of your money erodes.

Initial Public Offering—Also known as IPO. When a company goes public, it offers shares on the market for the first time in an initial public offering.

Interest—Money a borrower pays to a lender. When you get interest on a bond, for example, you are lending money to a company at a fixed rate of interest.

Intermediate-Term—Generally viewed as 2-5 years and refers to the length of time until maturity of an investment (e.g., bond).

International Bonds—Bonds issued by foreign companies and governments. These investments generally resemble U.S. government bonds except there is the added risk of currency fluctuations.

International Fund—A mutual fund that invests only in stocks of companies based outside the USA. See also Global fund. These investments involve greater risks than U.S. investments.

International Stocks—Stocks issued by companies in foreign, usually industrialized, countries, such as France and Japan.

Investment Income—This is income from investments rather than from work. It includes interest, dividends, capital gains distributions, capital gains (and losses) on sales, etc.

Investment Portfolio—This is the collection of assets that you have that are not used for everyday living expenses or short-term expenditures (those to be made in less than 1 year). Retirement accounts such as 403(b)s, 401(k)s, IRAs, SEPs, etc. should be included. An investment portfolio may contain Certificates of Deposits, money market accounts, savings accounts, mutual funds, individual stocks and bonds, annuities, real estate (other than your personal residences), collectibles, precious metals, futures and commodities, etc.

IRA—An Individual Retirement Account in which some or all of the contribution may be deductible from current taxes, depending on the individual's adjusted gross income and coverage by an employer sponsored retirement plan. The invested money grows tax deferred until retirement. Usually referred to as a Traditional IRA.

IRA Rollovers—Many employees receive distributions from 403(b)s or other retirement plans when they retire. If you take the cash, the investment company is required to withhold 20% of the amount for federal income taxes and you will have to pay income tax on the proceeds. An alternative is to open a Rollover IRA (or other qualified plan that accepts rollovers). By doing this (and if you do not need the money right away), you avoid the 20% withholding and the income tax. Your money will continue to earn tax-deferred in the Rollover IRA.

IRC—Internal Revenue Code.

Irrevocable Living Trust—An irreversible legal plan to transfer funds from the donor to

310

the beneficiary, generally offering tax advantages.

J

Junk Bonds—These low-rated, high-yield securities are issued by companies without much earnings or sales records, with weak or unknown credit strength, or with limited track records of sales and growth. These bonds are rated below investment-grade by bond rating companies. They are often issued for use in takeovers and buyouts. Junk bonds are considered very risky.

K

Keogh—A Keogh plan is a tax-deferred savings plan for individuals who are either self-employed or self-employed partners. The account can be set up as a Profit-Sharing Keogh, a Money Purchase Keogh, or a Paired Keogh.

L

Large-Cap Stocks—Large company stocks (also called large-cap stocks) are stocks of companies with a total market value (or market capitalization) of around $1.5 billion or more, such as those that make up the Standard & Poor's 500 Index of stocks. These are established, successful companies that are more likely than smaller companies to pay dividends. These stocks are considered more stable than stocks of smaller companies.

Last Split Date—The last date on which the shares of a security were increased or decreased by splitting.

Last Trade—The price at which the last trade was executed; after market close, this is the closing price.

Last Trade Date and Time—The date and time the security was last traded.

Liabilities—Money you owe (usually due to an obligation that has already occurred).

Liquidity—The ability to convert assets quickly into cash.

Liquid Investment—An investment that can be easily converted to cash.

Liquid Net Worth—Your net worth is the total of all of your assets (stocks, bonds, bank accounts, home equity, real estate, personal property, business receivables, notes receivable, etc.) minus the total of your liabilities (outstanding loans owed, credit card balances, taxes payable, bills payable, etc.) Unfortunately, many of these assets will not be readily accessible if cash is needed in a hurry; therefore, we will use only your liquid net worth in determining your financial health. Liquid net worth only includes assets that can readily be turned into cash without a major loss in value; therefore, do not include real estate or business equity, personal property and automobiles, expected inheritances, or funds already earmarked for other purposes.

Liquid Reserve—Personal savings that can be accessed immediately.

Limit Order—An order instructing a broker to execute an order at a specific price or better. Buy orders are executed at or below limit price. Sell orders are executed at or above limit price.

311

Limitation Year—The 12-month period used for applying the contribution limit. It is usually the calendar year, unless the participant elects otherwise or is in control of the employer.

Living Trust—A Living Trust is a legal entity set up to hold assets. Assets are transferred to the trust, owned by the trust, but remain under the control of the Trustors, who can be you and your spouse. With a Living Trust, you can avoid lengthy and costly court probate of an estate, and with proper planning, you can lower estate taxes. The person or persons who create the Living Trust are called Trustors.

Living Will—This preserves your voice in medical decisions if you are unable to speak for yourself as a result of medical incapacitation. This is used to express your desires rregarding do not resuscitate orders, being kept on life support devices, etc.

Load—A load is a sales fee you pay when investing in a mutual fund. A front-end load means you pay the fee when you buy shares. A back-end load means you pay the fee when you sell shares.

Low—The lowest execution price of a trade that day, or on the last trading day.

Long—Investing long means buying and owning a security.

Long-term—5 years or more (generally refers to the length of time until the maturity of an investment such as a bond).

Low Risk—Compared to other assets over a specific time frame, the risk of losing the money you invested is relatively low but implicitly acceptable given the return.

Lump-Sum Distribution—A single payment of all your retirement money from an account, usually given when you leave a company or when you retire. Prior to retirement, lump-sum distributions are usually rolled over into another retirement plan or into an IRA. There may be tax consequences when you take a lump-sum distribution. You should consult a financial professional to discuss the taxes that may apply to any action you take with a lump-sum distribution.

M

Management Fee—The fee a mutual fund pays to its investment advisors. This fee is expressed as a percentage of fund assets, and is paid by the mutual fund's shareholders.

Margin—Using eligible securities to back a margin loan through a broker-dealer.

Marginal Rate—The tax rate you pay on your last dollar of income.

Margin Balance—The net open balance in your margin account. If negative, this is the amount owed to the brokerage firm. If positive, the balance is available to earn interest.

Market Capitalization—This term refers to the dollar value of a company, or to put it another way, the amount of money someone would pay to buy the company today. Market capitalization is the total number of a company's shares multiplied by the current price per share. For example, if a company has 10 million shares, and the current price per share is $20, then the company's market capitalization is $200 million ($20 x 10 million). When investors refer to small-cap, mid-cap, or large-cap stocks, they are referring to the amount of the stocks' market capitalization: Large cap: over $1.5 billion in market capitalization; Mid cap: Between $200 million and $1.5 billion; Small cap: Between $50 million and $200 million.

Market Indicators—A variety of indices that give an indication of the overall direction and strength of the market.

Market Order—Order which instructs a broker to execute an order as quickly as possible at the best price available. During market hours, this means orders for widely traded securities will usually execute at or close to the current quotation. Buy orders will execute at or close to the ask price and Sell orders will execute at or close to the bid price. If a market order is entered when the market is closed, the order will usually execute at or close to the opening price the next trading day. To prevent entering an order at the market price, one of the following price conditions must be selected: Stop, Limit or Stop Limit.

Market Price—The price or last reported price at which a security is currently trading. Also called market value.

Matching Contributions—Any employer contributions made to a defined contribution plan or a 403(b) plan on behalf of an employee on account of the employee's elective deferrals or employee contributions.

Maturity Date—Date at which the face value and final interest payment of a fixed income security (for example, bond or note) is due and payable by the debt issuer. For bonds, maturity can range from one day to 30 years or more.

Maximum Exclusion Allowance—The amount that may contributed on a pre-tax basis to a 403(b) plan satisfying the requirements of IRC 403(b). Note that it may not be possible to contribute the full exclusion allowance tax free.

Medium-Cap Stocks—Stock issued by medium-sized companies, such as those that comprise the Standard & Poor's Midcap Index of stock. Mid-cap companies generally have market capitalizations between $200 million and $1.5 billion.

Medium-Term—Generally viewed as 2-5 years and refers to the length of time until maturity of an investment (e.g., bond).

Micro-Cap Stock—A micro-cap stock is from a company with market capitalization of less than $50 million.

Mid-Cap Stock—A mid-cap stock is from a company with between $200 million and $1.5 billion in market capitalization.

Minimum Required Distribution (MRD)—The minimum dollar amount that you must withdraw each year from your 403(b) account. This minimum distribution is based on your account balance and your life expectancy.

Money Market—This is a market for short-term debt instruments such as certificates of deposit, commercial paper, banker's acceptances, Treasury bills, and discount notes of the Federal Home Loan Bank and the Federal National Mortgage Association, among others. Elements of the money market have two things in common: safety and liquidity.

Money Market Fund—A money market fund is a mutual fund that invests only in money market investments. Most money market funds allow limited check writing and keep your principal constant but vary the interest rate. Although fund managers seek to maintain a $1 share price, there is no assurance that the fund will maintain that level. Some money market funds are FDIC insured.

Mortgage-Backed Bonds—Bonds that derive their income from a pool of mortgages.

Moving Average—In security charts, the moving average is a curve that averages price fluctuations over 50-day or 200-day intervals. Each point on a 50-day (or 200-day) moving average curve is calculated by averaging the closing prices from the previous 50 (or 200) days of trading. The moving average is a way to compare long-term price trends with recent price changes. When these lines cross, it indicates a change away from trend.

Municipal Bond—Debt issued by states and local governments; public purpose bonds are exempt from federal, and in some cases, state and city taxes. There are several kinds of bonds (also called "munis"), such as General Obligation (repaid from the issuer's general revenue, and backed by the full faith and credit of issuer) and Revenue (repaid from and backed by the revenue from a specific project, such as sewer systems). Some investors in bonds or bond funds may be subject to the Alternative Minimum Tax.

Mutual Fund—A mutual fund is a group of securities owned by a group of investors. It is managed by investment professionals who make buy and sell decisions for the group in a variety of securities, such as stocks, bonds, and money market instruments. Investors choose to purchase shares in mutual funds for a couple of reasons: they can diversify their holdings more easily with a smaller amount of money (because the mutual fund has the money to buy shares in many different types of securities); and they can rely on investment professionals to make trading decisions for them. Most open-end mutual funds stand ready to buy back (redeem) its shares at their current net asset value, which depends on the total market value of the fund's investment portfolio at the time of redemption. Most open-end mutual funds continuously offer new shares to investors.

N

NASDAQ—National Association of Securities Dealer Automated Quotations system, designed to facilitate over-the-counter stock trading.

Net Asset Value (NAV)—The value of one share of a mutual fund. For a no-load fund, this is also the offering price. The value of a mutual fund share is calculated only once each day after market close. The net asset value comes from dividing the value of all the fund's holdings by the number of shares in the fund. This net value does not include any sales charges or other fees.

Net Change—The amount and direction of a security's price change since its previous close.

Net Earnings Per Share (Net EPS)—The net earnings per share is a company's latest yearly earnings divided by the number of shares outstanding at that time.

No-Load Mutual Fund—A no-load mutual fund is a fund that has no sales fees to purchase or sell shares of the fund. (A front-end load is a fee to purchase shares; a back-end load is a fee to sell shares.)

Nominal Rate—Also known as nominal yield. The percentage of annual interest which would be earned from a fixed income investment (for example, bonds) if the security was purchased at par value; actual rate of return is usually different.

Non-elective Contributions—Contributions that are not elective contributions.

Non-matching Contributions—Non-salary reduction contributions which are not matching contributions.

Non-salary Reduction Contributions—Non-salary reduction contributions are contributions that are not salary reduction contributions. They include both matching and non-matching employer contributions.

Note—Intermediate-term debt obligations maturing in 1 to 10 years.

O

Odd Lot—Less than the normal unit of trading, which generally means less than 100 shares of stock.

Open—The price at which a security opened for trading on a given day.

Open-end Fund—A mutual fund with no limit to the number of shares that can be issued. These shares are purchased directly from the fund company itself, or through a brokerage firm.

Option—A contract that permits the owner (depending on the type of option held) to purchase or sell a security at a specific strike price until a specified expiration date. An option to purchase a security is a call. An option to sell a security is a put. The price of the option itself is the premium.

P

Par Value—This term refers to the face value of a bond (typically $1,000) before fluctuations in the market cause it to be sold for more or less than its par value.

Pay date—The date the shares from a split or dividend are sent to the shareholders.

P/E Ratio—The P/E ratio, or price-earnings ratio, is the ratio of a company's stock price to its earnings per share. To figure out the price-earnings ratio, you divide the stock's price per share by its earnings per share for a 12-month period. For example, if a stock is selling for $30 a share and is earning $3 a share, its P/E ratio is 10 (30/3). Some investors choose stocks with relatively low P/E ratios because they believe the low ratio indicates that the stock is undervalued.

Pension—A retirement plan which defines the specific benefit (pension) an employee receives at retirement, based on salary history and years of service.

Penny Stocks—Stock typically selling for less than $1.00 per share.

Points—This is the same as percent. Two points equals 2%.

Portfolio—A collective noun for investments. A portfolio is all securities, cash and real estate owned by a person.

Position—Security holdings in an account or portfolio.

Preferred Stock—Preferred Stock has a fixed dividend, has preference over common stock when paying dividends and liquidating assets, and generally carries no voting rights.

Premium—A bond is said to sell at a premium when the market price is greater than the par value (face value).

Price—The cost for a security. For mutual funds, price is the net asset value (NAV). For mutual funds with a load, the price including the load is the Public Offering Price (POP).

Prime Rate—The interest rate that banks charge their best, most credit-worthy customers.

Principal—The amount of money that is financed, borrowed, or invested.

Principal Risk—The risk of losing the money you invested due to default, bankruptcy or some other calamity that the company or government experienced which prevents them from paying you back.

Probate—Probate is a court process used to transfer property from a decedent to his/her named heirs in an estate. The purpose of probate is to establish clear title to property before it passes to heirs. Before title passes all claims to the property must be settled.

Profit Sharing—This is an employer-sponsored tax-deferred retirement plan that allows employees to share in company profits. The employer makes contributions in profitable years to individual employee accounts. The account grows tax-deferred until the employee retires or leaves the company.

Prospectus—Legal document describing the objective, terms, risks, and expenses of investing in a registered security. Mutual funds may be sold only by prospectus.

Put Option—Gives the buyer the right to sell a number of shares of stock at a price until the option's expiration date. Put buyers hope the price of the stock will fall. Puts may also be purchased to protect an investment in case the price of the stock goes down.

Q

Qualified Retirement Plans—These are plans that have been approved by the IRS for tax-favorable treatment (full deduction in year of contribution, tax-deferred earnings). This includes, 403(b)s, 401(k)s, SEPs, IRAs, Keoghs, SIMPLEs, defined-benefit pension plans, defined-contribution pension plans, etc. Each plan has a different limit on the amount that you can contribute.

Quick Ratio—The quick ratio is a measure of a company's ability to meet its financial obligations with its more liquid assets. To determine the quick ratio, you divide the company's cash, accounts receivable and marketable securities by its current liabilities. In general, a healthy company should have a quick ratio of at least 1 to 1.

R

Realized and Unrealized Gains—A gain is realized when an investment is sold after increasing in value. An investment that has increased in value, but has not yet been sold, has an unrealized gain, sometimes called a paper gain.

Real Estate Investment Trust (REIT)—This is a trust that holds real estate or mortgages. REITs issue shares that trade on stock exchanges like shares of common stock. There are three types of REITs: mortgage REITs that invest primarily in real estate debt (such as mortgages); equity REITs that primarily own real estate; and hybrid REITs that are a combination of the two. Equity REITs raise money and invest it in various real estate endeavors, such as shopping centers, apartments, industrial buildings, or combinations of different types of property. They are highly liquid, pay quarterly dividends (cash flow passed on from the properties), and are not highly correlated with stock.

Real Return—The return on your money after inflation is taken into account. Inflation normally lowers nominal, or unadjusted returns.

Required Beginning Date—The date at which distributions of a minimum amount must commence.

Repurchase Agreement (Repo)—A contract in which the seller of securities agrees to buy them back at a specified time at a predetermined price. Repos may be contracted for as short a period as overnight.

Retirement Income Account—Generally, a defined contribution program specifically for a church or a related organization maintaining a 403(b) plan. In rare instances, a retirement income account may be a defined benefit plan.

Retirement Plan Distribution—A withdrawal of funds from a retirement plan.

Return on Investment (ROI)—The dollar amount of your investment earnings divided by the dollar amount of your investment, expressed as a percentage. For example, an investment of $1,000 earning $100 equals a 10% return on that investment: 100 (earnings) divided by 1,000 (investment) =.10 (or 10%).

Rights—Rights allow existing shareholders of a corporation to subscribe to shares of a new issue of common stock before that stock is offered to the public. A right usually has a life of 2 to 4 weeks, is transferable, and entitles the holder to buy the new common stock below the Public Offering Price. Rights are often granted to protect existing shareholders from the effects of dilution.

Risk—There are many types of risks in investing. For example, principal risk is the risk you take that you might lose your initial investment. Investment risk, also known as volatility, is the price swings that your investments experience during the period when you own them. Market risk is the inherent risk of just putting money into the market and cannot be diversified away. Interest rate risk is the risk that your investment will change in value with the fluctuation of interest rates.

Risk-Adjusted Performance—Risk-adjusted performance is a method of evaluating and comparing mutual funds that's used by many business magazines and investment newsletters, as well as services like Value Line and Morningstar. It takes the performance of the fund and factors in the risk level (or volatility) of the stocks and bonds in which the fund is invested. Thus you can better compare funds within categories.

Risk/Return Factor—The relationship between an investment's growth potential and its exposure to loss.

Rollover IRA—A tax-free transfer of assets from one qualified retirement plan to another. See IRA Rollover.

Roth IRA—A type of individual retirement savings account created by changes made to tax law in 1997. Unlike a traditional IRA, contributions to a Roth IRA aren't tax-deductible. However, there is no tax on withdrawals made after the taxpayer reaches 59½. The maximum yearly contribution is $2,000 per spouse. The contribution allowed depends on adjusted gross income (AGI). In order to qualify for a full contribution, a married couple filing jointly must have an AGI less than $150,000 and an individual must make less than

317

$95,000. However, a married couple filing jointly still qualifies for a reduced contribution if their income is between $150,000 and $160,000. An individual still qualifies for a reduced contribution if his or her income is between $95,000 and $110,000. Self-employed people are not eligible for a Roth IRA. If you are self-employed, you can establish a Simplified Employee Pension (SEP) for yourself.

Russell 2000—The Russell 2000 is a market index considered to represent the market of small cap stocks. If you invested in small cap stocks, you might compare the performance of your stocks to the Russell 2000 index to see how they are faring.

Round Lot—Exactly 100 shares of stock. Ten round lots equal 1000 shares.

Rule 12b-1 fee—One type of ongoing fee that is taken out of mutual fund assets has come to be known as the rule 12b-1 fee. It most often is used to pay commissions to brokers and other salespersons, and occasionally to pay for advertising and other costs of promoting the fund to investors. It usually is between 0.25% and 1.00% of assets annually.

S

Salary Reduction Agreement—The agreement between the employer and employee under which salary reduction contributions are made.

Salary Reduction Contributions—Contributions made by an employer as a result of an agreement with the employee to take a reduction in salary or forego an increase in salary, bonuses or other wages. See also elective deferrals.

Savings Incentive Match Plan for Employees (SIMPLE-IRA)—A retirement plan that may be funded by both employee elective deferrals and employer contributions. Employer contributions are required.

Securities and Exchange Commission (SEC)—A federal agency that regulates federal securities laws, including the trading of public company securities, the firms that handle these transactions, and most professionals who provide investment advice.

Security Type—The type of security such as stock, bond or mutual fund.

Sell—To sell a security you own.

Sell Short—Selling a stock not owned in the hope that the price will go down. The seller must indicate that the sale is a short sale when the order is entered. This is used for stock only, and can only be done in a margin account. If available, the stock may be borrowed from a brokerage firm for delivery to the buyer and must be bought back at a future date. The firm reserves the right to call the security back at any time. Short sales require the equity be deposited in a margin account to ensure that the stock can be repurchased even if the price goes up.

Sell to Close—A long option position is closed when it is sold.

Sell to Open—A short position is opened when an option is sold.

Share—A unit of ownership in a corporation or a mutual fund.

Share averaging—A risk reduction technique for investing in equities. Shares are accumulated over a period of time by buying a set number of shares at fixed intervals of time regardless of price.

Short Cover—Buying back stock originally borrowed from the broker in a short sell transaction, in order to return it to the broker.

Short Position—A stock that has been borrowed from the broker. The value of short positions is simply the sum of each short position multiplied by the current price.

Short Sell—Selling stock borrowed from a broker.

Short-term—6 months to two years.

SIMPLE IRA—A SIMPLE IRA, or Savings Incentive Match Plan for Employees, is a tax-deferred retirement plan provided by sole proprietors or small businesses of fewer than 100 employees who do not contribute to any other retirement plan. Contributions are made by both the employee and the employer. In a SIMPLE IRA, contributions and the investment earnings grow tax-deferred until withdrawal—usually at retirement—at which time they are taxed as ordinary income.

Simplified Employee Pension IRA (SEP-IRA)—A retirement plan for self-employed people, owners of small companies, or any individual with any self-employed income—even if part-time—which allows them to defer taxes on investments intended for retirement with tax-deductible contributions.

Small-Cap Stock—A small-cap stock is one issued by a company with between $50 million and $200 million in market capitalization. Investment advisors sometimes recommend that investors interested in long-term growth invest in small-cap stocks because they often they have the greatest potential for growth that beats the market indexes. However, these stocks tend to be relatively more volatile than stocks of larger companies and are less likely to pay dividends. Some small company stocks may be highly speculative, with volatile or no earnings.

S & P 500—Also known as the Standard & Poor's 500. This is a large cap market index of 500 widely held stocks that are considered to represent the market as a whole. When investors refer to their portfolio or mutual fund beating the S&P, they mean that their investments are earning a better return than the S&P 500 index.

Special Conditions—Special conditions may be applied to an order, such as All or None (AON) or Do Not Reduce (DNR).

Spousal IRA—If your spouse does not work for pay, the IRS allows you to contribute $2,000 to a Spousal IRA (above your regular IRA contributions of up to $2,000 per year). The total contribution between two spouses can be up to $4,000.

Stock—Equity or ownership in a publicly traded corporation. Common stocks are the voting shares of a corporation; dividend payments vary. Preferred stocks pay dividends at a specified rate, and take precedence over common stocks in dividend payments.

Stock Dividends—A dividend paid in stock rather than cash.

Stock Split—An increase or decrease in the total number of a company's shares you own. For example, a two-for-one stock split will double the number of shares in your portfolio.

Stop Order—An order that becomes a market order once the security has traded through the designated stop price. Buy stops are entered above the current ask price. If the price moves to or above the stop price, the order becomes a market order and will be executed at the current market price. This price may be higher or lower than the stop price. Sell stops are entered below the current market price. If the price moves to or below the stop price, the order becomes a market order and will be executed at the current market price.

Stop Limit Order—An order which becomes a limit order once the security trades at the designed stop price. A stop limit order instructs a broker to buy or sell at a specific price or better, but only after a given stop price has been reached or passed. It is a combination of a stop order and a limit order.

Strips—Zero coupon Treasuries issued by the U.S. at a discount from face value. Interest is paid as a lump sum at maturity.

Surrender Charges—Fees for terminating a CD, insurance or annuity contract before it matures.

Switch/Swap—This type of order is used only for mutual funds to move money from one mutual fund to another. If this type of order is placed over the phone, it would be called a swap or an exchange. How and when this order is executed varies with the time of day entered and the specific fund involved. As a rule, the sell will be executed on day and the buy order the next.

Symbol—The symbol used to designate a security for trading.

T

Taxable Equivalent Yield—The return a taxable investment must earn to provide the same after-tax return as a tax-free investment.

Tax Deferred—This refers to investments whose earnings are taxed, but at a later date. For example, you pay no taxes on amounts put into a Traditional IRA, or on the accumulated earnings—until you take them out, at which time they are subject to income tax. Tax deferral can be good if you anticipate being in a lower tax bracket at the time of withdrawal, such as retirement.

Tax-Deferred Annuity—An investment that postpones (but does not eliminate) taxes on earnings until you dip into the savings, usually for retirement. A fixed annuity pays a set amount at regular intervals. Payouts from variable annuities change, because they depend on the success of the investments that make up the annuity. You usually have no restrictions on how much you can save, but you can not dip into the savings until you are 59-1/2 years old (or else you face significant taxes, tax penalties, and penalties from the company issuing the annuity).

Tax-Exempt—A category of investments that refers to tax-exempt securities, such as Federal, state and local bonds. The IRS and state taxing authorities usually don't tax interest earned on these investments.

Tax Free—This term refers to investments whose earnings are never taxed. For example, municipal bond fund dividends are never taxed at the federal level. However, you may still have to pay capital gains taxes if you sell them at a profit!

1099—Reports interest (1099-INT) and dividends (1099-DIV) paid. It is sent to the IRS and to the taxpayer. 1099-OID statements report Original Issue Discount securities.

Term Life Insurance—Usually the least expensive form of life insurance, term life insurance covers you for a fixed period (term) of time that you select. People you name as beneficiaries collect a death benefit if you die while covered. Unlike whole, universal, and variable life insurance, term insurance does not build up any savings for you. In this respect, it is pure insurance.

Time Conditions—The following time limits may be applied to Stop, Limit, or Stop Limit orders: Day Only; Good Until Canceled; Fill or Kill; Immediate or Cancel.

Time Horizon—How long you wait until you sell or need to sell your investment(s).

Total Net Worth—Your total net worth is the total of all of your assets (stocks, bonds, bank accounts, home equity, real estate, personal property, business receivables, notes receivable, etc.) minus the total of your liabilities (outstanding loans owed, credit card balances, taxes payable, bills payable, etc.)

Total Return—The change in price of your investment plus any interest or dividends earned.

Trade—To trade shares of stock (or mutual fund shares) is to buy or sell them.

Treasury Bills (T-bills)—A short-term government security, sold through the Federal Reserve Bank by competitive bidding at weekly and monthly auctions, in denominations from $10,000 to $1 million, in $1,000 increments. T-Bills mature anywhere from 3 months to a year, are sold at a discount, and return to their full face value at maturity. The interest earned is the difference between the face value of the bill and the purchase price. T-bills are the most widely used of all government debt securities and are a primary instrument of Federal Reserve monetary policy. U.S. Treasury securities, including Treasury Notes and Treasury Bonds, are considered conservative investments. Treasury bills are backed by the full faith and credit of the U.S. government.

Treasury Note—A mid-term debt security of the U.S. Government, with maturities ranging from two to ten years that pay a fixed rate of interest every six months and returns its face value at maturity. Minimum denomination is $5,000 plus $1,000 increments for a two to three-year maturity, or $1,000 plus $1,000 for a four to ten-year maturity.

Treasury Security—Debt obligations of the U.S. Government that are issued through the Department of the Treasury. Since they are backed by the full faith and credit of the U. S. Government, they are considered virtually free from risk of default. For individual investors, the income of Treasuries is exempt from state and local taxes.

Trust Account—A legal plan by which the trustor places assets in trust for a beneficiary.

Trustee—A Trustee is an individual (or individuals) who handle the administration of a Trust Account.

Turnover Ratio—Rate at which a portfolio (e.g., a mutual fund) trades its holdings. The percentage of a mutual fund's holdings that was replaced during a one-year period. A fund's turnover ratio tells you how aggressively the portfolio manager buys and sells investments. You can find this information in the prospectus.

U

Unit Investment Trust (UIT)—A portfolio of securities that are purchased and held in trust. Units in the trust are then sold to investors who receive a share of interest payments and a share of the principal, as the securities in the portfolio mature or are called.

Universal Life Insurance—Like whole life insurance, universal life insurance provides coverage for your entire life and builds up savings over time. People you name as beneficiaries collect a death benefit if you die while covered. Unlike whole life, you can use the interest from your accumulated savings to help pay your premiums, which are flexible.

U.S. Agency—A government-related organization like Fannie Mae and Freddie Mac that issues securities such as bonds.

U.S. Treasury Bills—Short-term debt issued by the U.S. Treasury. T-Bills are considered a very safe investment since they are backed by the full faith and credit of the U.S. government.

V

Value Investor—In Wall Street slang, a value investor is an investor who looks for stocks selling for less than they are really worth. By contrast, a growth investor looks for stocks of companies whose earnings are growing rapidly.

Variable Annuity—A Variable Annuity is a contract by insurance companies that you buy (and you can add to). Variable Annuities offer fixed income or mutual fund choices, plus an option to receive guaranteed income for life.

Variable Life Insurance—Like whole life insurance, variable life insurance provides coverage for your entire life and builds up savings over time. People you name as beneficiaries collect a death benefit if you die while covered. Unlike whole and universal life insurance, you can invest your savings in one of several mutual funds, which often are managed by the insurance company.

Vested Amount—The participant's allocable portion in the 403(b) plan that is nonforfeitable. It is the amount to which the exclusion allowance applies.

Vested—The percentage of ownership in a retirement plan's assets.

Volatility—How rapidly the price of a security (stock, bond, mutual fund, comodity, etc.) rises or falls within a short period of time. A measure of an equity fund's volatility relative to the overall market is called its beta coefficient: For example, if the S&P 500 Index of stocks is set at 1, a stock, mutual fund, etc. with a beta of 1.3 means that it is 30 percent more volatile than the S&P 500 Index.

Volume—The daily number of shares traded in a security.

W

Warrants—A type of security usually issued together with a bond or preferred stock that allows the holder to buy a proportionate amount of common stock at a fixed price (usually above the market price at the time of issuance) for a period of years or to perpetuity. Warrants are transferable and trade on the major exchanges. They are also known as Subscription Warrants.

W-2—The statement that employers issue to employees and the Social Security Administration, which reports the employees' taxable wages and the taxes withheld by the employer.

W-4—A form issued by the IRS that allows an employer to determine how much federal income tax to withhold from an employee's wages. An employee fills out Form W-4 when he or she is hired.

Whole Life Insurance—Also called ordinary life insurance or straight life insurance, whole life insurance provides coverage for your entire life. People you name as beneficiaries collect a guaranteed death benefit if you die while covered. Unlike term insurance, whole life insurance uses part of your level premium payments to build up cash value over time. Whole life may pay dividends, which can be taken in cash, used to reduce your premium or left in your account

Will—A will is a legal document that specifies how assets in your name only will be distributed after your death and outlines guardianship of minor children. Without one, the state in which you live will determine how the assets will be distributed. This is known as dying intestate. A will is absolutely critical for someone with children.

Y

Years of Service—Used in computing the Maximum Exclusion Allowance, it includes all years of service with the employer ending with or within the taxable year.

Yield—In general, it is the return on an investment. It is the income from interest or dividends received from an investment vehicle. When talking about stocks or mutual funds, it is the percentage rate of return, also called dividend yield. For instance, if a share's price is $1 and the company pays a dividend of $0.05 a year, its dividend yield is 5%. When referring to a bond, it is the percentage return you will receive if you keep it until it matures. It's a ratio of how much interest you get from the bond divided by how much you paid for the bond.

Z

Zero Coupon Bond—Zeros are securities that do not pay interest during their terms but are sold at a discount from their face value. A zero coupon bond generally increases in value as it approaches maturity, and the return comes solely from its appreciation. The dollar amount difference between the purchase price and the maturity value represents the yield or accretion value. Maturities range from 1 to 30 years.